Israel !

Citizenship and Management in Public Administration

To our wives, Shlomit and Ruth

Citizenship and Management in Public Administration

Integrating Behavioral Theories and Managerial Thinking

Edited by

Eran Vigoda-Gadot
Senior Lecturer of Organizational Behavior and Public Administration, University of Haifa, Israel

Aaron Cohen
Associate Professor of Organizational Behavior and Public Administration, University of Haifa, Israel

Edward Elgar
Cheltenham, UK • Northampton, MA, USA

© Eran Vigoda-Gadot and Aaron Cohen 2004

Published by
Edward Elgar Publishing Limited
Glensanda House
Montpellier Parade
Cheltenham
Glos GL50 1UA
UK

Edward Elgar Publishing, Inc.
136 West Street
Suite 202
Northampton
Massachusetts 01060
USA

A catalogue record for this book
is available from the British Library

Library of Congress Cataloguing in Publication Data
Citizenship and management in public administration : integrating behavioral theories and managerial thinking / edited by Eran Vigoda-Gadot and Aaron Cohen.
    p. cm.
  Includes bibliographical references.
  1. Citizenship. 2. Organizational behavior. 3. Public administration. 4. Civil service. I. Vigoda-Gadot, Eran, 1966– II. Cohen, Aaron, 1952–
  JF801.C569 2004
  351—dc22

2004043320

ISBN 1 84376 498 9

Printed and bound in Great Britain by MPG Books Ltd, Bodmin, Cornwall

Contents

List of Contributors   *viii*
List of Figures   *x*
List of Tables   *xi*
Preface   *xiii*

PART ONE
THEORETICAL AND CONCEPTUAL FRAMEWORK OF
CITIZENSHIP AND WORK IN PUBLIC ADMINISTRATION

Foreword   3

1. Citizenship Behavior and the New Managerialism: A Theoretical
   Framework and Challenge for Governance
   Eran Vigoda-Gadot and Robert T. Golembiewski   7

2. From Responsiveness to Collaboration: Governance, Citizens
   and the Next Generation of Public Administration
   Eran Vigoda-Gadot   27

PART TWO
CITIZENSHIP INVOLVEMENT AND THE WORKPLACE

Foreword   57

3. An Empirical Assessment of the Relationship Between General
   Citizenship and Work Outcomes
   Aaron Cohen and Eran Vigoda-Gadot   61

4. The Growth Value of Good Citizenship: An Examination of the
   Relationship Between Civic Behavior and Orientations and Work
   Outcomes
   Aaron Cohen and Eran Vigoda-Gadot   83

5. Politics and the Workplace: An Empirical Examination of the
   Relationship Between Political Behavior and Work Outcomes
   Aaron Cohen and Eran Vigoda-Gadot   103

PART THREE
ORGANIZATIONAL CITIZENSHIP BEHAVIORS IN PUBLIC
DOMAINS

Foreword   121

6. Do Good Citizens make Good Organizational Citizens? An
   Empirical Examination of the Relationship Between Good
   Citizenship and Organizational Citizenship Behavior in Israel
   Aaron Cohen and Eran Vigoda-Gadot   125

7. Internal Politics in Public Administration Systems: An Empirical
   Examination of its Relationship with Job Congruence,
   Organizational Citizenship Behavior and In-role Performance
   Eran Vigoda-Gadot   151

8. Work Congruence and Excellence in Human Resource
   Management: Empirical Evidence from the Israeli Non-Profit
   Sector
   Eran Vigoda-Gadot and Aaron Cohen   179

PART FOUR
DILEMMAS AND NEW DIRECTIONS IN THE STUDY OF
CITIZENSHIP AND MODERN BUREAUCRACIES

Foreword   203

9. Are You Being Served? The Responsiveness of Public
   Administration to Citizens' Demands: An Empirical
   Examination in Israel
   Eran Vigoda-Gadot   207

10. The Role of Public Sector Image and Personal Characteristics in
Determining Tendency to Work in the Public Sector
Aaron Cohen, Yair Zalmanovitch, and Hani Davidesko 235

11. Administrative Agents of Democracy? An Empirical
Examination of the Relationship Between Public Sector
Performance and Citizenship Involvement
Eran Vigoda-Gadot 261

Conclusions 293

Index 305

Contributors

Eran Vigoda-Gadot

Senior lecturer of Organizational Behavior and Public Administration at the School of Political Sciences, University of Haifa, Israel. He is the head of the Masters program of Local Government Administration (MLGA) and member of several projects and consulting committees working closely with public institutions and local municipalities in Israel and in Europe. His research focuses on the relationship between citizens and governments, management in public administration systems, citizenship behavior inside and outside organizations, Organizational Politics (OP), and behavior and performance in the public sector. Vigoda-Gadot is the author and co-author of more than 40 articles and book chapters, author/editor of five books, and has many other scholarly presentations and working papers. Received his Ph.D. from the University of Haifa in 1998 and spent time as a visiting scholar in several universities in Britain, Canada, and the United States.

Aaron Cohen

Associate Professor of Organizational Behavior and Public Administration at the School of Political Sciences, University of Haifa, Israel. He is the head of the Masters program of Public Administration for Executives. His research focuses on organizational commitment and organizational citizenship behavior. Aaron Cohen is the author and co-author of more than 50 articles and book chapters, as well as many other scholarly presentations and working papers. He is the author of *Multiple Commitments in the Workplace* (2003). Received his Ph.D. from the Technion - Israeli Institution of Technology (1989) and spent time as a visiting scholar in several universities in Canada and Australia.

Robert T. Golembiewski

Distinguished Research Professor (Emeritus) at the Department of Political Science, School of Public and International Affairs, University of Georgia, USA where he is part of the Public Administration program. Bob Golembiewski is an internationally-active consultant in planned change, and he is the only academic who has won all of the major research prizes in management: the Irwin in business, Waldo Award in PA, the NASPAA Award in public policy, two McGregor awards for excellence in the application of the behavioral sciences, and the ODI Prize for global programs in planned change. He has made over 1000 contributions to various literatures; and has authored/edited over 75 books. Received his Ph.D. from the University of Yale (1958). He is a leading authority in the fields of organizational development, management, and public administration.

Yair Zalmanovitch

Senior lecturer of Public Policy at the School of Political Sciences, the University of Haifa, Israel. He is the head of the Masters committee at the department and his research focuses on the health systems and public policy in various other state agencies. Yair Zalmanovitch is the author and co-author of many articles and book chapters and has various other scholarly presentations and working papers. Received his Ph.D. from the Hebrew University in 1990 and spent time as a visiting scholar in Canada.

Hani Davidesko

Graduate student of Organizational Behavior and Public Administration at the University of Haifa.

Figures

1.1   Multi-dimensions of citizenship behavior and its effect on public service systems   19

2.1   An evolutionary continuum of PA–citizen interaction   35

2.2   Collaboration among social players: an insight into the next generation   41

3.1   Direct model (1a)   67

3.2   Mediated model (1b)   68

6.1   The research models   135

8.1   A general relationship between work congruence and work performance   186

8.2   A suggested specific model for the relationship between work congruence (POF and ME) and work performance   194

11.1   Five alternative models of the relationship between PA performance and citizenship involvement   276

Tables

3.1	Descriptive statistics and intercorrelations for the study variables	75
3.2	Goodness-of-fit summary	76
4.1	Descriptive statistics and intercorrelations among research variables	90
4.2	Multiple regression analyses (standardized coefficients) of civic behavior variables on work outcomes	92
4.3	Interaction findings (standardized coefficients)	94
5.1	Means, standard deviation, Cronbach's alpha, Pearson's r correlations for the variables	111
5.2	Multiple Hierarchic Regression Analyses (Standardized Coefficients) between independent variables set and dependent variables set	112
6.1	Descriptive statistics and intercorrelations for the study variables	138
6.2	Goodness-of-fit summary	140
6.3	Structural coefficients and squared multiple correlations for OCB altruism and OCB compliance	142
7.1	Descriptive statistics and intercorrelations for the study variables	165

7.2   Confirmatory factor analysis for employees' performances (20 items of OCB and in-role behavior)   166

7.3   Goodness-of-fit summary for the research models   168

8.1   Descriptive statistics and reliabilities of the research variables   190

8.2   Pearson's r correlations among the research variables   191

8.3   Regression summary for Study 1 (Public Sector): The effect of POF and ME on work outcomes (standardized coefficients)   192

8.4   Regression summary for Study 2 (Third Sector): The effect of ME on work outcomes (standardized coefficients)   193

9.1   Descriptive statistics, reliabilities and intercorrelations among research variables   220

9.2   Findings of multiple hierarchical regression analysis (standardized coefficients) for the effect of independent variables on PA's responsiveness   222

10.1   Basic statistics and correlation matrix   250

10.2   Regression analysis (standardized coefficients) predicting three forms of public sector image and tendency to work in the public sector from the independent variables   252

10.3   Hierarchical regression analysis (standardized coefficients) predicting tendency to work in the public sector by the independent variables controlling for public sector image   254

11.1   Descriptive statistics and intercorrelations for the study variables   279

11.2   Goodness-of-fit summary for the research models   282

11.3   Explained variance (R^2) for the dependent variables in the research models   283

Preface

Citizenship is a political concept that has special meaning for organizations in general and for bureaucracies and public administration in particular. In the organizational context citizenship behavior and orientations generally describe an extra effort exhibited by individuals for the sake of other fellow-workers or for the organization as a whole. It means doing more and better for the organizational community, becoming involved in various activities that promote the collective wealth, prosperity and success of the organization, its members, its clients and its other stakeholders.

This book was written in an attempt to extend our knowledge on the nature and meaning of citizenship in modern public worksites. We try to provide an interdisciplinary work oriented toward the integration of various independent domains in the social sciences. The book suggests an interdisciplinary journey into several studies dealing with the relationship between two separate but close worlds: citizenship orientations and citizenship behavior as reflected in political science theory on one hand and organizational sciences, work studies, management and public administration on the other.

In fact, the relationship amongst these disciplines has fascinated and preoccupied us for almost a decade. During recent years we have conducted an intensive effort to explore new theoretical avenues and provide empirical evidence that will demonstrate what we call a 'missing link' in the study of political science, sociology, management and public administration. Can the concepts of citizenship behavior and other political-oriented behaviors be brought together and exported effectively into the world of work and management? What may be the benefit of such a transition? Which theories are more relevant and what is their potential merit for managers and administrative personnel, especially in the public sector? These were only a few questions that sparked our original interest and yielded, within a period of only a few years, a substantial wealth of knowledge about the meaning of citizenship behavior in the context of work and public sector organizations. The prime goal of this book is to offer a theoretical and empirical platform for better understanding of the relationship among citizenship and modern worksites. The book will probe some of the main questions in this linkage and thus try to point toward new interdisciplinary developments for the future.

One may first ask what made this area so worthy of our scholarly attention and effort? What may be the net benefit of relating the political idea of citizenship and other developments in public organizations? And how may this linkage advance our knowledge of both organizations and citizenship/ political orientations in our modern societies? These are important questions that need to be addressed before we dive into theoretical arguments and empirical data. In our view, such a discussion must be conducted on two parallel but supplementary tracks. First, we believe that the concepts of citizenship and citizenship behavior add substantially to our understanding of various managerial and organizational behaviors. Throughout the book we will argue that citizenship has many faces and that one of its interesting yet least studied aspects can be found in the organizational context. Furthermore, an elaboration on citizenship orientations in the organizational context also advances knowledge in other disciplines such as political science, sociology, and psychology. The conceptual spillover from one discipline to another has reciprocal advantages for all social sciences, as will be demonstrated in the following chapters. We see this mutual process as a prime effect that pulls together some remote but necessary pieces of the biggest puzzle of human conduct.

Taking a somewhat different argument we will also argue that citizenship behavior in the managerial and administrative realm is important for having a relationship with various aspects of organizational success. As management theory is concerned, a consensus exists on the need to develop better explanations about performance, effectiveness and productivity that may take organizations the 'extra mile' toward success. For many years the intra-organizational dynamics dominated this discussion, but with time it became clear that other, more extra-organizational provinces, also needed to be explored and considered. This statement is especially important for public sector organizations that are the focus of this book. The public sector, more than private business firms, is seeking better ways to improve its services and overcome its endemic illnesses of low motivation and widespread political obstacles. Hence, the concept of citizenship and especially 'good citizenship behaviors' in organizations is fundamental for better management in this sector. Such behavior patterns describe the extra effort exhibited by individuals for the sake of other fellow-workers or for the organization as a whole, and thus for citizens as well. While they may turn out to be useful for every organization, their relative impact on public sector agencies is potentially much higher.

Naturally, political science theory provides much insight into the meaning of good citizenship in our states, cities, communities and worksites. We propose this book with the vision and anticipation that organizations need to become familiar with these theories and concepts in order to find better ways to improve, revitalize and renew themselves. Such developments will undoubtedly lead to higher levels of organizational performance, and in the public sector they also imply better services to the people and improved quality of life. Since citizenship behavior is closely tied to political involvement, 'voice' and participation in one's environmental dynamics become the secret weapons underlying actions and reactions. Understanding the role that this concept plays is necessary for every manager, be it in the private or public sector. Unfortunately, so far management theory has not provided satisfactory answers as to changes in organizational performance. It is our expectation that a better exploration of the linkage between citizenship, politics, and the workplace may put some of the previous explanations of organizational success and failure in a different context which is more pragmatic, interdisciplinary oriented, and innovative.

It is easier to explain how our interest in the relationship between citizenship, politics and work has evolved from the original presentation of the idea of 'Organizational Citizenship Behavior' (OCB) in 1980. The seminal book by Dennis Organ (1988) titled *Organizational Citizenship Behavior: The Good Soldier Syndrome* actually followed several earlier articles on this theme (that is, Bateman and Organ, 1983; Smith, Organ and Near, 1983) but it was this book that paved the way for a growing number of studies on this topic in the next years. For the first time studies made an explicit link between the values of good citizenship and organizational outputs. Following this work other studies made an effort to explain the meaning of the 'good soldier syndrome' in organizations and the implication of its understanding for productivity, performance, effectiveness and efficiency of individuals and groups. The 1980s and 1990s saw a sharp rise in the number of conceptual and empirical works that focused on the extra effort exerted by some individuals and groups in the workplace, thus making some organizations better performing than others. All of these studies have reframed the meaning of active citizenry involvement and contribution, to make it a valuable tool in the hands of managers and theoreticians alike.

With the passage of time we became aware of the fact that the term 'citizenship' is meaningful and applicable to various sectors, cultures and behaviors at work. The bridge between citizenship and politics on one hand, and management and administration on the other has widened and matured. We have realized that the meaning and characteristics of citizenship in the workplace have a reciprocal effect on the mother disciplines of these concepts as well. That is, the theory of political participation, community involvement, and voluntarism is also enriched by organizational theories that examine the managerial context of such behaviors and attitudes. For example, the spillover theory has emerged as a good explanation of the transformation of attitudes and behaviors from one arena (the national and communal) to another (the organizational one). Moreover, work/non-work theories have provided additional explanations about the linkage between general citizenship and politics, and organizational prospects of these activities. These ideas were used to explain how citizenship involvement and political participation in one sphere is manifest in another sphere and turns out to be a useful tool for either political or organizational socialization.

Factors such as sectors and cultures have also become meaningful. Since political science theory has long argued that political behavior and citizenship orientations take different shape in various sectors and cultures, we probed these changes in the organizational context. Our Israeli based analyses have provided us with an additional unconventional perspective on the meaning of citizenship behavior at non-American worksites. Since political behavior is a major component of citizenship behavior, especially as perceived by political scientists and political sociologists, we have found it useful to link, integrate and join together the existing research on citizenship from a political point of view and management in administrative work. We further realized that these areas needed to be considered in depth if one seeks full coverage of the potential interactions between citizenship and the public administration arena.

TARGET READERS

Following these developments we decided to put together some of the more important outcomes of our research in one comprehensive book that can be of use for various readers coming from a range of disciplines. Our hope is to spark an interest in and a discussion about citizenship and bureaucracies as a field that is largely understudied and underdeveloped, but is simultaneously under continuous development and exploration. Thus, the book includes extensive readings taken from multiple scientific perspectives.

First it may prove essential reading for managers and administrators in both private and public organizations. These managers face multiple variations of organizational citizenship involvement by employees and frequently seek a better understanding of its nature. They also look for practical ways to encourage such activities. Nonetheless, while the book may be basically oriented toward pure managerial theory, it will be of great value for scholars and practitioners from other disciplines as well. For example, we believe that many political scientists and governmental officers may find it useful to see how theories of political activity are manifested in the world of public management. Sociologists may discover that the concepts of community, communitarianism and voluntarism are usable in management theory and that citizenship behavior has implications for one's quality of life through the general spillover of good values from one arena (work) to other life domains (family, community and states). Moreover, scholars and experts who are interested in public administration may find that most of our empirical data is based on the non-profit sector, of which 'pure public agencies' are the majority. Some studies even compare profit and not-for profit organizations as a means of determining the implications of sectors as well. Our work, perhaps for the first time, pulls together a considerable number of studies on the important role of good citizenship in governmental agencies. Beyond the specific contribution to the core disciplines as mentioned above, we hope to enrich knowledge about citizenship and participatory politics, as well as their relationship with other sub-disciplines of the social sciences such as organizational behavior, labor studies and occupational psychology. Thus, many students from these fields are amongst the potential readers of this book as well.

THE FRAMEWORK OF THE BOOK

The book consists of four separate parts with parallel development on several tracks. Part 1 serves as an introductory chapter. It presents several theoretical chapters that together define the core terminology used hereafter and explains the rationale behind the other works. This is the basic section on which the other chapters are built. Part 2 specifically deals with the meaning of citizenship involvement and its implications for organizations. Consequently, Part 3 describes the relevancy of organizational citizenship behavior as a dominant construct in the study of performance in organizations. Finally, Part 4 questions some of the recent studies on citizenship and work. It deals with important topics such as (1) the question of the citizen's role in shaping administrative performance and culture, (2) public administration image in the eyes of citizens and their willingness to work in public services, and (3) citizens' intentions to participate in public service.

Part 1 provides a theoretical overview of some core concepts such as citizenship, political behavior, participation and active involvement as defined in political science and managerial literature. This introductory part proposes the theoretical arguments on which the other parts build both theory and implications. Two key works are included here. First, in a chapter entitled 'Citizenship behavior and the new managerialism: A theoretical framework and challenge for governance' by Vigoda-Gadot and Golembiewski we elaborate on the contribution of the term 'citizenship' to organizational theory. This chapter develops an integrative understanding of the relationship between citizenship behavior in and around organizations and administrative thinking. The chapter emphasizes the idea of New Public Management (NPM) and analyses the meaning of citizenship for public sector organizations that have been going through major NPM reforms in the recent years. It is argued that the current theory of NPM underestimates the economic, symbolic and educational contribution of many voluntary actions, generally termed citizenship behavior, to public organizations as well as to modern society. Relying on this argument the chapter develops a multi-dimensional model of citizenship behavior that can be applied in the public sector. The model deals with Micro-citizenship, Midi-citizenship, Macro-citizenship, and Meta-citizenship. Citizenship is thus promoted as a vital construct for the formation of the new managerial spirit, and at the same time as a major future challenge for governance. Finally, the chapter elaborates on several responsibilities for social players in fostering values of voluntarism and spontaneous involvement. These can promote a healthier public service, a more efficient bureaucracy, and a richer life in prosperous modern communities.

The second chapter in this part is Vigoda-Gadot's theoretical discussion of the potential contribution by citizens to our modern states and communities. The most prominent contribution identified here is the enhancement of collaborative actions among governments, administration bodies, and 'good citizens'. Thus, this article is titled 'From responsiveness to collaboration: Governance, citizens, and the next generation of public administration'. It suggests that the evolution of the New Public Management (NPM) movement has increased the pressure on state bureaucracies to become more responsive to citizens as clients. This trend is perceived as an important advance in contemporary public administration, which finds itself struggling in an ultra-dynamic marketplace arena. However, together with such a welcome change in theory building and in practical culture reconstruction it is argued that modern societies still confront a growth in citizens' passivity. Putting it another way, citizens tend to favor the easy chair of the customer over the sweat and turmoil of participatory involvement. The essay has two primary goals. The first is to establish a theoretically and empirically grounded criticism of the current state of new managerialism, which obscures the significance of citizen action and participation by overstressing the (important) idea of responsiveness. Second, the chapter proposes some guidelines for the future development of the discipline culminating in enhanced collaboration and partnership among governance and public administration agencies (G&PA), citizens, and other social players such as the media, academia, and the private and third sector. The chapter concludes that despite citizens' being formal 'owners' of the state, ownership will remain merely symbolic for the G&PA–citizens relationship in a representative democracy. The alternative interaction type of movement between responsiveness and collaboration is thus more realistic for the years ahead.

Part 2 discusses the meaning of citizenship and the value of citizenship involvement as related to the workplace. This part is based on three works, each one elaborating on a different perspective of citizenship involvement in organizations. First is an attempt to analyse the linkage between individuals' citizenry orientations and performance in the workplace. This essay, entitled 'An empirical assessment of the relationship between general citizenship and work outcomes' by Cohen and Vigoda-Gadot examines the relationship between general citizenship (for example, political participation, community involvement, general altruism, and disillusionment with government) and two work outcomes (perceived performance and turnover intentions). Two alternative models were proposed in order to test whether the effect of citizenship behavior and orientations was direct or mediated by participation in decision making. The respondents in this survey were 268 nursing personnel from public health organizations in Israel. Path analysis using LISREL VIII showed that the direct model best fit the data. This model supports the notion that the resources acquired by involvement in the civic setting can contribute to the work setting. The findings also showed the complexity of the relationship between community involvement and work outcomes. This variable has a negative relationship with perceived performance but a positive one with participation in decision making. The chapter concludes with several implications for the continuing examination of general citizenship in its relationship to behavior at work.

Second is another piece by Cohen and Vigoda-Gadot called 'The growth value of good citizenship: an examination of the relationship between civic behavior and orientations and work outcomes'. In this chapter the authors examine the relationship between civic behavior (general altruism, civic participation, political efficacy, and disillusionment with government) and several work outcomes such as perceived performance, turnover intentions, and organizational commitment. The first finding was a relationship between civic behavior and these variables. In addition, general altruism and disillusionment with government had a significant relationship with the outcome variables, definable as modest but meaningful. Civic behavior variables did not explain a large portion of the variance of work outcomes but this relationship held beyond the effect of the control variables. The chapter offers several conclusions and recommendations for further examination of the relationship between civic behavior and work outcomes.

Finally, Cohen and Vigoda-Gadot's 'Politics and the workplace: an empirical examination of the relationship between political behavior and work outcomes' tries to put together some conceptions with dual meanings in political science and public management thinking. The goal of this research was to test the effect of political behavior on work outcomes such as actual performance as measured by supervisors' evaluation, and job satisfaction, organizational commitment, and participation in decisions in the workplace. The respondents in this survey were 200 administrative and medical personnel from one of the major public health organizations in Israel. Supervisors in each of the clinics provided the data on the performance of the employees. The findings showed in general that political behavior was related to performance and attitudes in the work setting. The relationship can be defined as modest but consistent. It is modest because the political behavior variables did not explain a large portion of the variance in the four work outcomes. It is consistent because all work outcomes were related to one or more of the political behavior variables, and this relationship holds beyond the effect of the control variables. The findings also showed that the relationship between political behavior and performance and organizational commitment is stronger for females than for males. The chapter ends with several conclusions and recommendations for the continuing examination of the relationship between political behavior and work outcomes in private as well as public worksites.

Part 3 is dedicated to a core concept in the field of citizenship and work, namely 'Organizational Citizenship Behavior'. We have decided to include three works in this part. First is another joint work by Cohen and Vigoda-Gadot asking, 'Do good citizens make good organizational citizens?'. This empirical examination of the relationship between general citizenship and organizational citizenship behavior portrays a theoretical linkage between variants of general citizenship behavior (for example, political participation, community involvement, general altruism, and faith in citizen involvement) and OCB. The potential contribution of such a relationship to public administration agencies and to society is also developed. Respondents were 200 employees and their supervisors from one of the major public health organizations in Israel. Path analysis using LISREL VIII supports the notion that contextual work attitudes mediate the effect of general citizenship on OCB. The prime implication is that the organization constitutes an important factor in determining whether general citizenship behavior will be transformed in the organization.

Second is another look at Organizational Citizenship Behavior, this time taking an intra-organizational and intra-political view. This chapter by Vigoda-Gadot is an empirical examination of political behavior in public sector organizations and its relationship with OCB and additional in-role performances. It suggests that employees' perception of organizational politics mediates the relationship between job congruence (for example, person–organization fit and level of met expectations (ME)), and employees' performances (for example, OCB and in-role performance). Israeli public personnel provided data on T1, and supervisors completed an assessment of employees' OCB and in-role performance on T2, six months later. Path analysis using LISREL VIII was implemented to evaluate two alternative models, direct and indirect. Findings of the study show that the indirect model fits the data better than the direct model, and therefore supports a mediating effect of perceptions of organizational politics scale (POPS) on the relationship between job congruence and employees' performances. Structural coefficients among the research variables support the theory on the effect of job congruence and POPS on OCB and in-role behavior. The findings contribute both to the understanding of antecedents of POPS as well as to the exploration of some of its consequences. The chapter concludes with several implications and suggestions for further inquiry into politics in public administration systems.

Third is Vigoda-Gadot and Cohen's examination of 'Work congruence and excellence in human resource management'. Here again, empirical data of two samples (n1=244, n2=155) from the Israeli non-profit sector is used to test a variety of hypotheses on the effect of person–organization fit and met expectations on the performance of employees from the non-profit sector. Data of the first sample were collected from employees of a public sector organization. Findings from it generally revealed that job satisfaction and organizational commitment were higher in employees who better fit the organizational sphere and in those who better fulfilled their expectations. These employees' intentions of voice, in-role performance, and organizational citizenship behavior also increased as a result of higher met expectations. Job neglect, intentions of exit, and perceptions of organizational politics increased in employees with a lower level of met expectations, while strong perceptions of organizational politics were related to lower levels of person–organization fit. Data for the second sample were collected from employees of a third sector organization. Findings from this sample provided additional support for the centrality of the role of ME in determining work outcomes. Our main conclusion is that expectations exert a notable effect on work outcomes of employees in the non-profit sector. Moreover, person–organization fit has a secondary effect, perhaps via its relationship with met expectations. Several theoretical and practical implications of these results are noted, especially for non-profit systems, which embody a unique organizational culture substantially different from the private sector.

Finally, Part 4 discusses dilemmas and future trends in the study of citizenship and work in modern bureaucracies. This part is based on three chapters. First is 'Are you being served? The responsiveness of public administration to citizens' demands: An empirical examination in Israel' by

Eran Vigoda-Gadot. The chapter suggests that research in public administration is preoccupied with questions of efficiency and effectiveness that are aimed at improving public sector performance. According to the new public management approach, addressing this major challenge must rely upon a comprehensive understanding of citizens'/clients' perceptions of public sector operation and the extent to which public organizations are aware of public needs. This chapter suggests a theoretical grounding and empirical examination of the relationship between citizens' demands and public administrations' responsiveness. Participants in the study were 281 residents of a large Israeli city who reported their feelings, attitudes and perceptions of local government activities in a variety of fields. Results indicate that perceptions of public administrations' responsiveness are affected by both policy and cultural factors (for example, business or social orientation of the public authority, entrepreneurship and initiation of changes, ethics, organizational politics) and by the quality of the human resource system and of public servants (for example, quality of leadership and management, quality of employees, general stress when contacting public officials). Implications of the study are discussed in light of the ongoing debate regarding the need for a more responsive and efficient new public management and the difficulties it faces in western societies.

Second is a chapter by Cohen, Zalmanovitch and Davidesko dealing with 'The role of public sector image and personal characteristics in determining tendency to work in the public sector'. The authors suggest that very little research has examined the tendency to work in the public sector. This study of Israeli students in their last year before graduation examined three research questions on this issue. First, what are the determinants of the public sector image in the eyes of citizens; second, what are the determinants of citizens' tendency to work in the public sector; and third, do the determinants of the tendency to work in the public sector relate to it directly, or indirectly through the mediating effect of the public sector image. The research model consisted of three groups of independent variables: demographic variables, background and experience variables, and personal–psychological variables. Questionnaires were distributed by mail to 1640 students: 660 usable questionnaires were returned, a response rate of 40%. The findings showed that the tendency to work in the public sector and the public sector image were related, and that the image of the public sector mediated the relationship between the proposed determinants and the tendency to work in the public sector. The findings showed that the issues examined here offer a promising and challenging future research area.

Finally, Vigoda-Gadot's examination of the relationship between administration actions and citizenship values is presented in 'Administrative agents of democracy? An empirical examination of the relationship between public sector performance and citizenship involvement'. This study examined the relationship between public sector performance (PSP) and several aspects of citizenship involvement as perceived by 260 households in a large Israeli city. Participants reported their perceptions of local municipality operation (for example, human quality of public servants, initiation and creativity, morality and ethical standards), resultant organizational performance (for example, satisfaction with operation and satisfaction with services), as well as two types of citizenry values: faith in citizenship involvement and active citizenship involvement. Five alternative models were suggested to test the relationship. Path analysis of latent variables was used to test the models. A structural equation modeling (SEM) using LISREL VIII showed the superiority of one model, in which (1) perceptions of public service operation positively affected performance and faith in citizenship involvement and (2) active citizenship involvement was positively affected by faith in citizenship involvement, and, simultaneously, was negatively affected by PSP. The implications of these results are discussed, especially regarding the paradoxical effect of public sector performance on active citizenship involvement.

SUMMARY

All in all we have reason to believe that the chapters presented here are of merit to many disciplines and that they may serve as a link between theories in political science, sociology, psychology and management. Today, many social scientists share a common view about the great potential of interdisciplinary studies. This view has recently received much attention in public sector studies (that is, Vigoda, 2002). Such ideas rely on the assumption that our knowledge of social nature is limited and will remain so as long as conceptual separation, segregation and isolation endure and dominate the scientific reality. Bringing together knowledge and experience that represents the best research from close but different fields of study has long been recognized as a complex mission, but one with significant merit to the modern sciences. This book adopts a comprehensive interdisciplinary approach to address an important issue in the social sciences that is still not fully understood or satisfactorily covered in the literature. The meaning of citizenship for organization and bureaucracies is thus perceived as a promising field of future study. We believe that, while there is still much work to be done, our book is definitely a step forward and a bridge toward a better understanding of the meaning of citizenship and participatory politics in organizations, especially those of the public sector.

REFERENCES

Batemen, T.S. and Organ, D.W. (1983), 'Job satisfaction and the good soldier: The relationship between affect and employee citizenship', *Academy of Management Journal, 26*, 587–95.

Organ, D. (1988), *Organizational Citizenship Behavior: The Good Soldier Syndrome,* Lexington, MA: Lexington Books.

Smith, C.A., Organ, D.W., and Near, J.P. (1983), 'Organizational citizenship behavior: Its nature and antecedents', *Journal of Applied Psychology, 68*, 653–63.

Vigoda, E. (2002), *Public Administration: An Interdisciplinary Critical Analysis,* New York: Marcel Dekker.

PART ONE

Theoretical and Conceptual Framework of
Citizenship and Work in Public Administration

Foreword

Why should we study the meaning and interrelations of citizenship and work in public organizations and in the bureaucratic landscape? What are the theoretical and conceptual foundations of such integration and how useful is it for a better understanding of our modern administrative systems, governance, and life quality in democratic cultures? The first part of this book is dedicated to shedding more light on these two major questions and to building a solid rationale for the linkage between the topic of citizenship and the administrative state. The works that are included here provide some support for the belief that citizenship and bureaucracy influence one another, a belief that contributes to both the theory and practice of management and public administration. As a starting point we have decided to elaborate on the meaning and implications of core concepts, namely *citizenship* and *bureaucracy*. Following this short discussion is a more analytical set of arguments about the links that can and should be made between them.

Defining the meaning, boundaries and implications of the term *citizenship* is a complex task. Citizenship has multiple meanings in the judicial, statutory, national, psychological and social senses of the word. It frequently denotes an official state of the individual in a national environment, where he/she also holds a variety of rights and duties, privileges and obligations, liberties and responsibilities. The roots of the term 'citizenship' date back to antiquity and appear in various cultural contexts. Conventional wisdom argues that citizenship was first recognized by the ancient Greeks who also introduced the concepts of 'civic virtue', 'good citizenship', and 'civic duties'. For example, Aristotle argued that citizenship was born in Greece's city-states, small enough to give their members the chance to 'know one another's character' (Aristotle, 1948:1326b). He identified as citizens 'all who share in the civic life of ruling and being ruled in turn' (p.1283b), but emphasized the importance of and participation by which citizens could influence their leaders and the governance process, thereby affecting their environment as well as their day-to-day life. Centuries later, Machiavelli used the term 'civic virtue' to describe the obligations a citizen has toward his/her state and community. These obligations should be acquired through education, religion, and a healthy fear of the consequences of the dereliction of civic duty (Oliver and Heater, 1994:14). Machiavelli pointed out the coercive role of the state in shaping citizens' obedience. However, he ignored altruistic and voluntary behavior adopted by citizens of their own free will and aimed at improving the welfare and prosperity of the state or community.

Later variations also reflected this central core of ideas. In the seventeenth century, Hobbes promoted the idea that people and governments should have a kind of mutual agreement, later known as a social contract. This contract asks for people's obedience and loyalty to the government in return for the government's commitment to provide the people with certain basic 'natural' rights. It advocates bi-directional transactions of human resources promoting the mutual interests of citizens, states and society. Similarly, Montesquieu in 'The Spirit of the Laws' argued that unlike other forms of government, a state based upon popular participation depends on the civic virtue of its good citizens for its stability. Rousseau emphasized the importance of citizens' freedom, political participation, and a 'general will' which calls for an altruistic contribution to the governing and administrative process made solely with the thought of advancing the common interest. The liberal tradition of citizenship expanded with American independence and the French revolution in the late eighteenth century. Subsequently, democratic values were embraced in many other European countries during the nineteenth century. They emphasized the contribution that the citizens' voluntary political action made to the creation of the common good and a prosperous society.

In comparison to citizenship, *bureaucracy* represents what seems to be a whole different set of values and principles. While citizenship is based mainly on a balanced view of the rights and duties of an individual, bureaucracy is basically uninterested in the individual as such and emphasizes the power of administrative institutions, which frequently has quite a negative image. This negative image stands in sharp contrast to the favorable image of (good) citizenship behavior. As suggested by Goodsell (1983) in 'The Case for Bureaucracy', we all tend to hate bureaucrats and bureaucracy. Bureaucracy is attacked in the press, in popular magazines, and in best sellers. It is denounced by the political right and left. It is assaulted by molders of culture and professors of academia. It is castigated by economists, sociologists, policy analysts, political scientists, organizational theorists and social psychologists. In addition, it is charged with a wide array of crimes, which we have grouped under failure to perform; abuse of political power; and the repression of employees, citizens as clients, and other individuals. These failures bring in their wake a cynical attitude toward bureaucracy that is commonplace and widespread. The difficulties modern states have found in serving the public's needs have turned bureaucracies into an icon of red-tape, ineffectiveness, ineptitude and heavy-handedness. However, like citizenship, bureaucracy also reflects two main domains in our lives. It represents our social institutions and the formal mechanisms of the administrative state (Richardson, 1997). For some scholars in the political sciences and in public administration bureaucracy is the most essential instrument of a modern nation. It is the tool through which the state discharges its obligations to serve and govern its people. Bureaucracy means the power to govern by state officials, by public professionals, and by experts in policy implementation. Despite its popular, negative image, bureaucracy is necessary in our lives. It becomes even more essential as time goes on and citizens' needs and demands increase.

Thus, we suggest that there is a clear theoretical linkage between citizenship and bureaucracy in modern democracies. Citizens are an essential part of the bureaucratic state and play an increasing role in modern democracies. By applying 'citizenship behavior' in various areas and at various levels, citizens can influence the actions and decisions of bureaucrats and bureaucracy. For sociologists like Max Weber (1958) and Talcott Parsons (1982) bureaucracy is merely a social institution whose function is to serve the people. Notwithstanding, the world we live in has changed rapidly in the second half of the twentieth century. Western democracies have made remarkable progress in terms of managing the state. Perhaps the most impressive milestone is that people in democratic nations become more and more involved in community action through individual enterprises or via third-sector organizations. In recent decades the third sector has become a grass-roots platform of citizenry action that is operated by the people and for the people, above and beyond the governmental umbrella. Some would even say that these actions are in opposition to the impotency of bureaucracy. However, more conventional wisdom implies that modern welfare states cannot and should not take responsibilities away from the people in order to make their lives better. Citizens themselves should bear some of the direct social burden. Consequently, citizenship behavior is recognized today as an essential tool for the effective functioning of every social institution. The 'good soldier syndrome', as presented by Organ (1988) and which will be discussed more extensively in Part 3, reflects a powerful civic virtue that is widely encouraged inside and outside all organizations. There is no doubt that its actual and potential impact on public organizations is immense.

REFERENCES

Aristotle (1948), *Politics,* translated by E. Barker, Oxford: Clarendon.

Goodsell, C.T. (1983), *The Case for Bureaucracy: A Public Administration Polemic*, Chatham, NJ: Chatham House Publishers.

Oliver, D. and Heater, D. (1994), *The Foundation of Citizenship*, London: Harvester Wheatsheaf.

Organ, D.W. (1988), *Organizational Citizenship Behavior: The Good Soldier Syndrome*, Lexington, MA: Lexington Books.

Parsons, T. (ed.) (1982), *Talcott Parsons on Institutions and Social Evolution: Selected Writings*, Chicago: University Press of Chicago.

Richardson, W.D. (1997), *Democracy, Bureaucracy, and Charter: Founding Thought*, Lawrence, KS: University Press of Kansas.

Weber, M. (1958), *The Protestant Ethic and the Spirit of Capitalism*, New York: Scribner.

1. Citizenship Behavior and the New Managerialism: A Theoretical Framework and Challenge for Governance[1]

Eran Vigoda-Gadot and Robert T. Golembiewski

INTRODUCTION

At first glance, citizenship behavior and new public management (NPM) may seem an odd couple. Citizenship in modern society draws its substance from ideas such as political participation, community involvement and communitarianism, social justice, humanitarianism, voluntarism, and shared responsibilities of individuals (Box, 1998; Fredrickson, 1997). By contrast, the NPM approach, which has become so important in contemporary public administration, centers on different forces and mechanisms: competition and business operation, effectiveness and efficiency of public organizations, and quality of services (Bozeman, 1993; Lynn, 1998; Perry and Kraemer, 1983; Pollitt, 1988). This essay attempts to explain, however, why and how these two important streams in management thinking can and should be related.

Citizenship behavior is a powerful construct of human activity that deserves more attention in the study of public administration and management. Beyond the basic constructs of obedience and loyalty, constructive citizenship behavior in modern societies encompasses active participation, involvement and voluntary actions of the people in managing their lives. Nonetheless, this idea has so far received scarce consideration in NPM thinking. Until the 1980s, only a few attempts had been made to develop a comprehensive analysis of citizenship behavior that could be related to general management science, and especially to images of public administration theory and action. Studies concerned with exploring the citizenship–management connection took a relatively narrow perspective. One line of research focused on citizens' involvement, participation and empowerment in the national and local environments (for example, Pateman, 1970; Barber, 1984). More recent studies fostered the notion that voluntarism and spontaneous actions of individuals are useful tools for governments in their efforts to overcome budgetary difficulties, advance stability, and promote effectiveness in public arenas (Box, 1998, 1999; Brudney, 1990; Fredrickson, 1997; Rimmerman, 1997). Other studies, mainly in management and organizational psychology, emphasized a valuable self-derived contribution by employees that can lead to better efficacy and success inside the workplace. Prosocial/altruistic behaviors (for example, Brief and Motowidlo, 1986) and organizational citizenship behavior (OCB; for example, Morrison, 1996; Organ, 1988; Smith, Organ, and Near, 1983) were mentioned as necessary for the creation of a healthy organizational atmosphere, and particularly for promoting service quality and general outcomes of public organizations (Podsakoff and MacKenzie, 1997). In addition, a budding interdisciplinary approach elaborated on the possibility that higher levels of citizens' involvement on the state or community level are related to more involvement in the job and to enhanced organizational democracy that improves organizational outcomes (Peterson, 1990; Putnam, 1993; Sobel, 1993). Organizational democracy and participatory climate were found as good predictors of employees' performance in private and public systems, and thus received increased attention in recent years (Cohen and Vigoda, 1999; 2000; Cotton et al., 1988). All the above studies pointed to the added value of citizenship behavior, in its many forms and settings, to management in general and to public organizations in particular. Regretfully, these efforts have not matured into a broader perspective on the overall relationships between characteristics of citizenship behavior and new trends in modern managerialism. Knowledge about different aspects of the citizenship–management connection have not been combined in an effective way that could lead to better understanding of both fields. Hence, the advantages of such mutual enrichment have been overlooked and left as 'unfinished business'.

Reviewing theoretical and empirical studies on NPM, citizenship behavior and potential interrelationships between them, the present study elaborates on several questions: What is so important about the relationship between multi-dimensional citizenship and new managerialism, especially in the public sector? What are the variants of citizenship behavior in and around organizations that can be used to enhance public management goals? On what theoretical grounding can we assume that citizenship behavior and NPM are in fact related? Who should be involved in fostering citizens' involvement and participation that may promote what we define as 'a spirit of new managerialism', and what duties and responsibilities should each participant carry? Answers to these questions may contribute to a development of more responsive public administration and healthier democratic societies. Our theoretical discussion also leads to a model for understanding the territory. It suggests that planned strategic cooperation and a genuine partnership among players in the political, administrative and social arenas are crucial and possible. In our view it is a prime managerial challenge for the future.

CITIZENSHIP AND NEW PUBLIC MANAGEMENT: A CRITIQUE

This essay criticizes new public management for not doing enough to usher in the idea of citizenship behavior through the main entrance of modern managerial halls. Unlike traditional public management approaches the NPM movement focuses on citizens as sophisticated clients in complex environments. Relying heavily on private sector management, citizens of modern democracies are perceived more and more as clients with multiple alternatives for consuming high-level services. Public authorities must treat the public well, not only because of their presumed administrative responsibility for quality in action but also because of their obligation to democratic rules, to accountability demands, transparency criteria, and sometimes even because of their fear of losing clients in an increasingly competitive business-like arena. Hence NPM opposes the more classical approach to governance and public administration that used to see citizens as simple constituents or voters. However, NPM creates a different obstacle to productive citizenship behavior that must be recognized and isolated. We argue that NPM encourages passivity among the citizenry whereby citizens acquire a power of *exit* (which indeed was virtually unavailable in the past) but at the same time discourages use of the original power of *voice* by citizens who may have much to contribute to their communities.

To better explain our arguments and criticism on the current status of NPM we focus on two major groups of players that are involved in governmental and administrative processes in democracies. Each of these has a special function and a unique set of duties. One group comprises rulers and public administrators who are responsible for the proper management of large organizations and bureaucratic agencies. The second is the public, the 'citizens', and mainly authentic citizen-leaders who agree to be managed by 'others' and must develop and sustain the appropriate control, involvement, and participation in the administrative process. Hobbes argued that these groups are tightly bound in a kind of mutual agreement. According to Hobbes, the people and their government have a *hidden social contract*, which calls for the people's obedience and loyalty to the government in return for government's commitment to provide for some of their basic 'natural' rights. In its elementary configuration, this contract advocates bi-directional transactions of human resources promoting the mutual interests of citizens, states and society.

While recent developments in the study of NPM focused on the responsibilities of the first group (rulers and administrators), they paid much less attention to the second (citizens). NPM favors a massive socialization of business management practices in the public sector to provide rulers with better tools for policy implementation (for example, Lynn, 1998; Pollitt, 1988). The only problem is that these orientations and practices have, thus far, simply not been integrated with another key construct of healthy democratic systems. That construct is the active role of the public, its participation and involvement in running its own life more effectively, and the responsibility of administrators to encourage such a blessed public contribution. This underestimation of active and constructive citizenship behavior is a weakness in contemporary NPM theory.

For example, Box (1998:73–7) suggests that NPM takes a very clear and unfavorable approach to active citizenship involvement in the administrative process. According to Box there are three types of citizens classified along a continuum of desire to affect the public policy process: (1) 'freeriders' are considered consumers of public services who receive public goods for free and let others do the work of citizenship; (2) 'activists' in contrast, are deeply involved in public life and in citizenship actions for the community; and, (3) 'watchdogs', in the middle of the continuum, are involved only in key issues of relevance to themselves personally. Practically and theoretically NPM mostly encourages the 'freeriders' and perhaps some of the 'watchdogs'. It does not, however, elaborate on the significance of 'activists'. So far, NPM has not emphasized the need for better reciprocal linkage between rulers and citizens. At most it has concentrated only on one direction of flow of influence, from rulers to citizens. In many respects this position does not adequately consider the positive effect of citizens' action on (new) public systems.

Why and how has such a tendency occurred? Several answers can be identified within the evolutionary development of modern public administration. During the 1960s and 1970s a growing number of observers perceived public administration as an old and declining discipline that no longer could provide the public with satisfactory answers to its needs and demands. The contract between rulers and citizens, once a fundamental principle of democratic societies, seemed to have lost its glory. Governments and governors in Europe and in America became unpopular in the eyes of many citizens as well as elites (Rainey, 1990:157), and public administration seemed to have no adequate answers for problems in education, transportation, employment, crime, natural resources and other salient social issues. All these evinced a declining image of public administration. Theoreticians and practitioners were left with epidemic social dilemmas waiting for new solutions.

In the search for alternative answers, business management theory was proposed as a source for new and invigorating ideas (Bozeman, 1993). It was suggested that *public management*, rather than public administration, could manifest a new understanding of how to run governments more efficiently, how to improve their relationships with citizens as clients, and thereby to surmount some of society's pandemic ills. This process of 'liberalization' in public administration, which is recognized today as 'New Public Management', was elegantly defined by Garson and Overman (1983:278) as 'an interdisciplinary study of the generic aspects of administration...a blend of the planning, organizing, and controlling functions of management with the management of human, financial, physical, information and political resources'. Focusing on different resources that may contribute to better performance of public organizations, NPM has emphasized strategies successfully applied in private-sector firms. Drawing on the business sector's experience, scholars expressed a more 'demanding' attitude to dynamics, activities, and productivity of public organizations (for example, Thomas, 1999). Demands for more consideration of proper managerial tools and principles were directed mainly at policy makers and public administrators. The public sector was urged to treat citizens as clients, and to provide competitive as well as high-quality services. Indeed, these were appropriate goals for a public service, which prior to the 1980s paid scant attention to the economy of bureaucracies.

Today, despite the popularity in America and Europe of the theme of running government like a business, it also carries an unexpected difficulty. NPM has taken the lead in the study and practice of public systems, highlighting the main direction of flow of responsibilities: the commitment and obligation of public institutions to citizens as passive clients. Conversely, however, the idealized relationship between citizens and governments has been described more in terms of a *uni-directional treaty* rather than the *bi-directional relationship* consistent with representative democracy. Administrators are encouraged to assume greater responsibility toward citizens while citizens' participation and involvement in the administrative process is perceived by politicians and by public servants as problematic. As King, Feltey and Susel (1998) argued, 'although many public administrators view close relationships with citizens as both necessary and desirable most of them do not actively seek public involvement. If they do seek it, they do not use public input in making administrative decisions . . . (and) believe that greater citizen participation increases inefficiency, delays, and red tape'.

Hence, NPM tends to overlook the importance of self-derived, spontaneous, and voluntary actions that are both vital and economic for prosperous societies (Etzioni, 1994; 1995) as well as successful organizations (Katz and Kahn, 1966). Ironically, this behavior has enjoyed considerable attention in the business management literature, which served as a role model for NPM but has never been properly utilized in its original form. For example, since the early 1980s many studies of organizational behavior elaborated the importance of pro-social and extra-role activities later known as 'Organizational Citizenship Behavior' (OCB). Organ (1988) defined this behavior as the 'good soldier syndrome', and other scholars sought to relate it to a broader concept of citizenship on the national and community levels. A progressive definition of citizenship behavior refers to voluntary actions inside and outside the workplace that can be beneficial for private or public organizations (for example, Graham, 1991; Organ, 1988; Van Dyne, Graham and Dienesch, 1994). Still, many issues have been overlooked in NPM literature, including engaging the public in administrative processes, encouraging citizens to take an active part in managing local governance, OCB and spontaneous involvement of public employees inside the workplace, and the general promotion of citizenship and altruistic behavior at all social levels.

Consequently, NPM traditionally does not elaborate on the advantages of citizenship behavior within or around the public system. Most of the writing in the field focuses on simplistic business-like orientations; these are necessary and important, but they fail to effectively cultivate the many dimensions of human enterprise. The conventional perspective of NPM calls for a massive implementation of business standards in the public sector by strategies of privatization, outsourcing, PIs (Performance Indicators), and orientation to quality service. It does call for improved communication channels with citizens, but only as passive clients (Pollitt, 1988). It also views rulers and administrators as the major agents of managerial change. In this view, public administration adopts a 'patronage' position toward citizens who are left with only minor responsibilities, such as becoming 'good customers' or 'sensible clients'. It does not, however, encourage more voluntary active effort and participation by citizens in the administrative process.

An advance across ground broken by Fredrickson (1997) in *The Spirit of Public Administration* suggests that a revitalized spirit of *new* public administration is necessary. In line with this idea we further argue that a balanced reciprocal relationship between citizens and rulers may lead to the creation of '*a spirit of new managerialism*'. This spirit is relevant to the twenty-first century and may flourish only in a soil rich in mutual contributions by different parties. There is a need to develop the theory of the advantages of multi-dimensional citizenship behavior and to elaborate on its contribution to modern societies via NPM. Our argument is that citizenship behavior is vital for any public system and administrative bureaucracy in quest of effectiveness, efficiency, fairness, social justice and overall healthy growth and development. Citizenship behavior, whatever form it takes, carries significant values for the environment.

A more comprehensive inclusion of citizenship behavior in the study of new managerialism is also in line with the contemporary business management approach because of the relatively low costs of voluntary action (Brudney, 1990; Brudney and Duncombe, 1992). From an economics viewpoint, the NPM approach does not take advantage of its most powerful, valuable and inexpensive resources: good will, civic virtue, spontaneous initiatives and innovation by individuals. Even in its own business-oriented terminology, contemporary NPM theory is limited and incomplete. It needs a much more sound understanding of how to relate citizenship behavior with the management of public systems. In the following sections we try to portray this multi-dimensionality of citizenship behavior and to prepare the ground for a model of integration between citizenship and NPM. Such a discussion is vital to better understand how to incorporate manifold voluntary enterprises in modern public management.

DIMENSIONALITY OF CITIZENSHIP BEHAVIOR

Foundations and Settings

Previous research has pointed to three core elements of general citizenship behavior: obedience of the people to social rules, loyalty to social institutions, and participation in social life (Marshall, 1950). While obedience and loyalty naturally belong to a worldwide definition of citizenship, the essence of citizenship behavior is *participation*. Participation concerns active involvement of citizens in three main settings: governance (a *national* arena), local lives (a *communal arena)*, and the workplace (an *organizational* arena*).

The National and Communal Arenas

Montesquieu in *The Spirit of the Laws* argued that a state based upon popular participation, as distinct from other forms of government (for example, those based on obedience or loyalty), depends for its stability on the civic virtue of its good citizens. Rousseau emphasized the importance of citizens' freedom, political participation, and a 'general will', which calls for contribution to the governing and administrative process without gaining any personal advantages, only the common interest. Active citizens assist in safeguarding and supporting sound governance (for example, by holding or electing others to executive positions) and in adjudicating violations (for example, by serving on juries). They also participate (directly or through representatives) in changing laws in response to new needs and in evolving an understanding of the common interest. Consequently, citizenship behavior includes devoting time and effort to the responsibilities of governance and administration, keeping well informed, sharing information and ideas with others, engaging in discussions about controversial issues, voting in whatever manner is provided under the law, and encouraging others to do likewise (Graham, 1991; Putnam, 1993; Van Dyne et al., 1994).

Community involvement and participation in local administrative processes constitute another unique aspect of participatory citizenship. Communal citizenship represents more informal participation than national activity (Sobel, 1993). Some people may decline to participate in citizenship behavior at the national level through disinclination or indifference. They may prefer a closer, perhaps more personal domain such as the community. While much research has been conducted to uncover the mechanisms of individual voluntary action at the national level (for example, Almond and Verba, 1963; Milbrath, 1965; Verba and Nie, 1972) recent studies have emphasized the importance of citizenship participation and voluntary action at the communal level (Barber, 1984; Etzioni, 1994; 1995; Hurd, 1989; King and Stivers, 1998; Putnam, 1993). For example, Barber (1984:303) argued that 'political participation in common action is more easily achieved at the neighborhood level, where there are a variety of opportunities for engagement' and Hurd (1989) noted that 'the need to foster responsible citizenship is obvious. Freedom can only flourish within a community where shared values, common loyalties and mutual obligations provide a framework of order and self-discipline, otherwise, liberty can quickly degenerate into narrow self-interest and license'. King and Stivers (1998:195-6) argued that 'active citizenship is different from voting, paying taxes, or using government services in active citizenship citizens rule and are ruled in turn'. Putnam (1993) concluded that communities with higher levels of voluntarism and civic engagement become better places to live, characterized by more trust in government, better government performance, and positive relations between citizens and the state.

The Organizational Arena

Beyond the national and communal spheres active citizenship participation also has an organizational aspect. Studies in organizational behavior have long argued that more participation in the workplace, high job involvement, and opportunities to use an effective voice may lead to high job satisfaction, low turnover and absenteeism, and better performances of organizations (Keller, 1997; Lum et al., 1998). Other studies found that public organizations that promote values of employees' empowerment and participation in decision making are more likely to enhance communication throughout units, increase commitment to stakeholders, and improve productivity as well as quality of services (Berman, 1995; Young, Worchel and Woehr, 1998). Hence, an analysis of citizenship behavior in modern societies entails a broader conceptual discussion, applicable not only to nations, states and communities but also to organizations, bureaucracies and public agencies. In a rapidly changing environment, organizations and the workplace have an important task. Organizations' productivity leads to significant improvement in quality of life. Citizens' demands and needs grow faster and reach farther than ever before. The expansion of welfare services provided by the state to its citizens, directly or by proxy, must cohere with such demands and satisfy more people more frequently and more extensively. In practice, organizational change in these agencies only partly follows the rapid transformation of the environment and it needs better support of quasi-public and non-public organizations (the 'third sector'). Therefore, the idea that self-derived citizenship activity should be related to management and organizational sciences, as well as to public administration operation, has attracted growing attention in recent decades (Katz and Kahn, 1966; Organ, 1988).

Two basic patterns of relationship between citizenship behavior and the organizational arena should be mentioned in this regard. (1) Enhanced involvement of citizens in the administrative process (for example, becoming members or supporters of public or third sector agencies) generates commitment to a healthy public service, proper understanding of what is right and what is wrong in managing public organizations, and education toward constructive participatory democracy. (2) Improved intra-organizational citizenship behavior by public employees improves performance by public and third-sector agencies. The advantages of self-inspired contributions of employees reach far beyond the merits of formal authority and bureaucratic mechanisms. Recently, Rimmerman (1997:19) suggested that increased participation by citizens in workplace decision making processes is important if people are to recognize their roles and responsibilities as citizens within the larger community. This idea is consistent with an earlier work of Pateman (1970), who argued that through participation in decision making (on the state, community, and organization levels) the individual learns to be a public as well as a private citizen.

We thus suggest that participation in multiple settings such as the national or communal arena, as well as participation inside organizations, should be borne in mind when NPM strategies are developed. The involvement in and contribution of citizens to the state, community, workplace and society in general are valuable. Citizens' involvement has the advantage of being the lowest-cost input in the administrative process. Participation also enhances individuals' commitment to their environment and approval of public administration's legitimacy. Also, the increase in political participation carries improvement of political stability and accountability of the public sector (King and Stivers, 1998). Stability and accountability create proper responsiveness and effectiveness of services to the people.

Levels of Analysis

Citizens' participation is manifested in two major ways: personal initiatives and organized action. McKevitt (1998:42) suggests that participation and active citizenship are frequently portrayed as an individual quality, but at the same time they have strong overtones of collective responsibility. Box (1998:71-4) also emphasizes the centrality and current trends in individualism and collectivism, especially in communities. Like McKevitt, Box identifies a struggle for 'a point of balance' between individualism and collectivism that largely influences the nature of citizenship in America. The tension between the individualistic and the collectivist ideas of citizenship is real, and disagreement exists over its boundaries. Following this, we identify two levels of active citizenship behavior that are discussed in the psychological, sociological, managerial and administrative literature: (1) *Individual:* altruism and voluntarism of persons in the national, communal and organizational settings; (2) *Collective:* organized or semi-organized citizenship behavior as represented by interest groups, volunteers' associations, volunteers' programs, not-for-profit organizations, and the 'third sector'. Together, these levels comprise the citizenship behavior hierarchy of modern societies.

The Individual Level

Individual citizenship behavior refers to the very basic construct of personal actions and reactions taken by individual citizens. These are spontaneous actions of unorganized persons who render altruistic actions aimed at enhancing the prosperity and development of their environment. Citizens may show compassion for other citizens, contribute time, money and other resources to help the incapable, and provide assistance for others whenever the situation requires it without seeking any personal advantage or compensation (for example, Conover, Crewe and Searing, 1993; Monroe, 1994; Piliavin and Charng, 1990). Moreover, inside public organizations citizens–employees may exert additional effort to help fellow employees in fulfilling their duties and in serving the public without seeking any personal rewards. General management literature has defined these enterprises as Organizational Citizenship Behavior (OCB), which reflects an informal contribution that participants can choose to make or withhold without regard to sanctions or formal incentives. As noted in previous studies (for example, Organ, 1988; Organ and Konovsky, 1989; Podsakof and MacKenzie, 1997) many of these contributions, aggregated over time and persons, considerably enhance organizational efficiency and effectiveness. Further studies concluded that working under multiple pressures, public organizations should better understand the relationship among citizenship behavior inside and outside the workplace, management, and organizational outcomes (Cohen and Vigoda, 1999; 2000; Graham, 1991). Encouragement of citizenship behavior in and around public agencies may contribute to these organizations' productivity, competence and success, hence to society in general.

The Collective Level

This level of citizenship behavior comprises semi-organized and fully organized actions initiated by groups of individuals. Usually, citizenship behavior at this level emerges when a group shares mutual interests and all members are willing to be actively involved in collective voluntary endeavors. The group's ambition is high and there is recognition that it will be almost impossible to achieve and secure most of the joint goals as individuals. Among these groups one finds neighborhood associations, ad hoc groups that seek limited ecological goals, volunteer programs inside organizations, and even altruistic support groups offering help to those in need from others who experienced similar needs (for example, quitting smoking, avoiding drugs or alcohol, supporting families in distress, etc.). Previous research has demonstrated that the emergence, growth, and decline of voluntary groups can be explained by human capital variables, emergence of leadership, socioeconomic status, and competition with other groups (Janoski and Wilson, 1995; McPherson and Rotolo, 1996). It was also found that membership in voluntary groups increased forms of political expression and participation (Michael, 1981), and membership in volunteer programs in the public sector had economic merit for public organizations as well as symbolic effects of citizen participation (Brudney, 1990; Brudney and Duncombe, 1992).

Apart from the semi-organized citizenship actions the collective level of analysis also includes highly organized and fully institutional collective endeavors. The most obvious representative of this sub-category is the organized not-for-profit sector, which has grown rapidly in recent decades. Collective institutional citizenship derives from ambitious interests of large groups that have undergone a relatively complicated process of institutionalization and formalization. Management and public administration sciences have devoted considerable attention to this field (Brinton, 1994; Coble, 1999; O'Connell, 1989; Smith and Lipsky, 1993). In many ways, these organizations (also known as non-profit or voluntary organizations) represent increased public involvement aimed at providing services in which the state is unable or unwilling to play a significant role. This 'third sector' is distinct from the traditional public and private sectors (Gidron and Kramer, 1992). In recent years voluntary organizations and the third sector constituted about 10 percent of the economic size of all governmental activities in the US (O'Connell, 1989) and their relative size continues to grow. Such figures may indicate that citizens of modern societies have more needs/demands and that they are disappointed with governments' operation and inability to provide satisfactory welfare services. Hence, it seems that today, more than ever before, citizens are willing to engage in collective voluntary actions (both semi-organized and fully organized) to support their needs (King, Feltey and Susel, 1998).

A Multi-Dimensional Model of Citizenship Behavior and Public Administration

The complex construct of modern citizenship behavior and its limited employment in NPM theory calls for a revised conceptual framework that can unite this 'odd couple'. This framework should advocate the co-existence of as well as mutual solidarity between the public as represented by citizens on the one hand, and the administration as reflected in NPM on the other. Figure 1.1 presents a suggested model of multi-dimensional citizenship behavior and its effect on public service systems as stemming from the NPM approach. Based on the settings of citizenry action (communal and national versus organizational) and on the levels of analysis (individual versus collective action), we distinguish four types of citizenship behavior: Micro-citizenship (MC1), Midi-citizenship (MC2), Macro-citizenship (MC3), and Meta-citizenship (MC4). Each type is then related to the relevant construct of managerial operation and outcomes. Together they are intended to provide a synthesis of the fields.

Setting Level	Organizational	Communal and National
Individual	**MC1** Micro-citizenship ↓ Employees' Performance	**MC3** Macro-citizenship ↓ Personal Welfare
Collective	**MC2** Midi-citizenship ↓ Organizational Performance	**MC4** Meta-citizenship ↓ Social Welfare

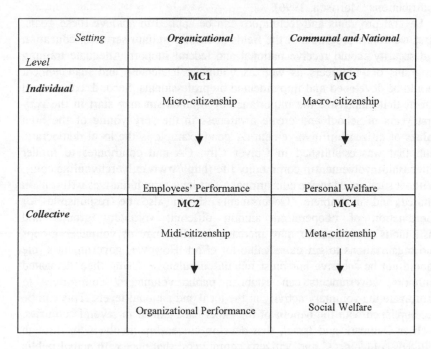

Figure 1.1 Multi-dimensions of citizenship behavior and its effect on public service systems

Micro-citizenship

Micro-citizenship (MC1) is the very basic image of citizenship actions as taken by individuals in the limited sphere of the workplace. Employees may present high levels of participation in workplace activities and greater willingness to support others even when not asked or ordered. These employees may be defined as good organizational citizens (Organ, 1988). They differ from other individuals who show lower levels of citizenship behavior or withhold such positive behaviors entirely. Some of these employees may even engage in organizational misbehaviors, such as stealing organizational property or sabotaging the work itself (Vardi and Wiener, 1996). Micro-citizenship of individuals inside the workplace has been shown to have a direct and significant impact on employees' performance (Vigoda, 2000a). Findings suggest that organizations benefit from using measures of OCB as an integral part of their routine performance evaluation strategy because of the valuable information they provide on employees' informal contributions (Morrison, 1996).

Several programs and techniques can be applied to achieve these goals. First, volunteer programs in the fields of health, welfare services, education and security should receive national and federal support. Adequate training programs of volunteers as well as volunteer leadership and management should be developed and implemented by professionals. Second, educational efforts that emphasize the importance of voluntarism may start in the very first years of school and create awareness in the very young of the high values of citizenship involvement. A good example is the local democratic club that was established in Culver City, CA and contributes to higher citizenshipinvolvementin community life (http://www.culvercityonline.com). Without such an extensive educational effort long-term initiatives will remain limited and incomplete. Governments should also be responsible for coordination of cooperation among different voluntary groups and institutions. Coordination may increase the efficiency of volunteer groups and organizations to get more value for effort. However, government's role should not be coercive but must remain consultative. Using their delegated authority, governments can establish public volunteers' committees to coordinate the voluntary activity at the local and national levels. This can be accomplished with the benefit of the experience gained in several countries, such as Denmark and Israel, that develop citizenship involvement through 'citizens conferences' and 'citizens committees' that deal with actual public interests and try to influence decisions on issues that are not fully addressed by governments (for example, see http://www.zippori.org.il/English/index.html). Governments will maintain their advisory position, providing the citizens with sufficient conditions and experience to work out their spontaneous ideas.

Citizens and citizens' leaders, for their part, have several roles in the process of generating the new spirit of managerialism: (1) The most elementary role is taking an active part in running their own lives and encouraging others to do likewise. As proposed above, this can be accomplished on the individual or collective level. Participating in neighborhood associations or voluntary groups, active involvement in parents' committees at schools, donating money, time or effort for the development of community services, and encouraging others to take part in such activities are all valuable and important missions; (2) All citizens should exhibit constructive criticism of the public system to provide feedback for politicians and public servants, thereby increasing their responsiveness and sense of responsibility, furthermore; (3) Citizens and citizens' leaders should serve as socialization agents of voluntary actions. The educational mission of citizens is to avoid passivity and to contribute to motivation for involvement by future generations. This is how better understanding of shared responsibilities in social life can be promoted.

SUMMARY AND CONCLUSIONS

Fredrickson (1997) suggests that the spirit of public administration must develop a theory of the public that goes beyond interest-group pluralism, beyond public choice theory or representative democracy, and beyond a customer-service orientation, to a refined and expanded idea of citizenship. In accordance with this, our essay has advanced a new perspective of modern citizenship that may be a starting point for the spirit of *new* public administration.

According to Marshall (1990), the center of the administrative art and science is the citizen being served. But should it be a uni-directional flow of services, or a bi-directional one that involves self-responsibility and active involvement of citizens? Marshall argues that there is a definite need for enhanced citizenship in the administrative process. The good citizen is interested in, active in, and responsible for his/her place in society. Box (1998) attempts to 'bring public administration back to democracy by drawing on new roles for practitioners and citizens in the governance of their own communities' (1998:xi). He challenges the idea, drawn from the private marketplace, that local residents are only *consumers* of public services, people who should be treated like customers as the NPM literature continuously argues. Instead, Box suggests that individuals are returning to their earlier role as *(good) citizens*, people who are the owners of the community and take responsibility for its governance (p. 3).

In line with these ideas we developed a multi-dimensional perspective of citizenship behavior that does not necessarily contradict but indeed blends well with the trends of new managerialism and NPM. Our perspective elaborated on (1) settings of citizenship (national/communal and organizational); (2) levels of analysis (individual and collective), and; (3) integration of these dimensions with NPM ideas to create a 'spirit of new managerialism'. This spirit may be defined as a mutual power of MC1, MC2, MC3 and MC4. It asks that governments take strategic steps to promote citizenship values at all levels, and that citizens actively participate in spontaneous initiatives and in the process of social building. Public administration structure and culture must become more flexible and responsive to citizens' needs (Vigoda, 2000b). To achieve this goal it should become active and entrepreneurial in the initiation of partnerships between public servants and citizens. The focus of NPM should adjust more vigorously to include transformation of 'good will' to 'effective operations'.

In contrast with 'old' managerialism, the new spirit of public management must call for multivariate citizenry action. Public administration, through its professional cadre, should initiate this process and learn its lessons. Investment in spontaneous behavior is low-cost and economic compared with other reform efforts, so it should receive higher priority on the NPM agenda that calls for improved performance of public agencies.

Furthermore, an encouragement of the mini-citizenship pattern may lead to improvement in all other patterns (midi-, micro-, and meta-citizenship). Organizational behavior theory and general management literature can provide additional guidelines as to the nature of this phenomenon and its recommended application in the public sector (Podsakoff and MacKenzie, 1997). Citizenship behavior should be an integral part of NPM as well as of any other new reform in the public sector. Similarly, much can be learned from research on communitarianism, organizational citizenship behavior, volunteer groups and programs, the third sector, and various other aspects of individuals' altruistic behavior. As suggested by Kramer (1999) and King and Stivers (1998), building relationships among citizens, administrators and politicians is a long-term and continuous project. For truly democratic government, administrators and citizens must engage each other directly on a regular basis in full-throated public dialogue, neither side holding back anything important. Democratic public administration involves active citizenship and active administration that uses discretionary authority to foster collaborative work with citizens. In sum, this chapter proposed that there is something unique about NPM compared with other managerial practices that makes citizenship behavior especially important to incorporate. Thus, the challenge for governance and new managerialism is a more comprehensive application of this valuable knowledge in public administration strategies. Accordingly, this chapter has suggested an insight into a wider effective use of the concept of *citizenship* in the study of new managerialism.

NOTE

1. Based on Vigoda and Golembiewski (2001), 'Citizenship behavior and the spirit of new managerialism: A theoretical framework and challenge for governance', *American Review of Public Administration*, **31** (3) 273–95. Copyrights with permission from Sage Publishing.

REFERENCES

Almond, G.A. and Verba, S. (1963), *The Civic Culture: Political Attitudes and Democracy in Five Nations: An Analytic Study,* Boston: Little Brown.

Barber, B. (1984), *Strong Democracy: Participatory Politics for a New Age,* Berkeley: University of California Press.

Berman, E.M. (1995), 'Empowering employees in state agencies: A survey of recent progress', *International Journal of Public Administration, 18,* 833–50.

Box, R.C. (1998), *Citizen Governance: Leading American Communities into the 21st Century,* Thousand Oaks, CA: Sage.

Box, R.C. (1999), 'Running governments like a business: Implications for public administration theory and practice', *American Review of Public Administration, 29,* 19–43.

Bozeman, B. (1993), *Public Management,* San Francisco: Jossey Bass.

Brief, A.P. and Motowidlo, S.J. (1986), 'Prosocial organizational behaviors', *Academy of Management Review, 11,* 710–25.

Brinton, M.H. (1994), 'Nonprofit contracting and the hollow state', *Public Administration Review, 54,* 73–7.

Brudney, J.L. (1990), *Fostering Volunteer Programs in the Public Sector: Planning, Initiating, and Managing Voluntary Activities,* San Francisco: Jossey-Bass.

Brudney, J.L. and Duncombe, W.D. (1992), 'An economic evaluation of paid, volunteer, and mixed staffing options for public services', *Public Administration Review, 52,* 474–81.

Coble, R. (1999), 'The nonprofit sector and state governments: Public policy issues facing nonprofit in North Carolina and other states', *Nonprofit Management and Leadership, 9,* 293–313.

Cohen, A. and Vigoda, E. (1999), 'Politics and the workplace: An empirical examination of the relationship between political behavior and work outcomes', *Public Productivity and Management Review, 22,* 3, 389–406.

Cohen, A. and Vigoda, E. (2000), 'Do good citizens make good organizational citizens? An empirical examination of the effects of citizenship behaviour and orientations on organizational citizenship behavior', *Administration and Society, 32* (5), Forthcoming.

Conover, P.J., Crewe, I., and Searing D.D. (1993), *Citizen identities in the liberal state,* Paper prepared for the annual meeting of the American Political Science Association.

Cotton, J.L., Vollrath, D.A., Froggat, K.L., Lengnick-Hall, M.L., and Jennings, K.R. (1988), 'Employee participation: Diverse forms and different outcomes', *Academy of Management Review, 13,* 8–22.

Etzioni, A. (1994), *The Spirit of Community,* New York: Touchstone.

Etzioni, A. (1995), *New Communitarian Thinking: Persons, Virtues, Institutions, and Communities,* Charlottesville: Virginia University Press.

Fredrickson, H.G. (1997), *The Spirit of Public Administration,* San Francisco: Jossey Bass.

Garson, G.D. and Overman, E.S. (1983), *Public Management Research in the United States,* New York: Praeger.

Gidron, B. and Kramer, R.M. (1992), *Governments and the Third Sector: Emerging Relationships in Welfare States,* San Francisco: Jossey Bass.

Graham, J.W. (1991), 'An essay on Organizational Citizenship Behavior', *Employee Responsibilities and Rights Journal, 4*, 249–70.

Hurd, D. (1989), 'Freedom will flourish where citizens accept responsibility', *The Independent*, 13 September.

Janoski, T. and Wilson, J. (1995), 'Pathways to voluntarism: Family socialization and status transmission model', *Social Forces, 74*, 271–92.

Katz, D. and Kahn, R.L. (1966), *The Social Psychology of Organizations*, New York: Wiley.

Keller, R.T. (1997), 'Job involvement and organizational commitment as longitudinal predictors of job performance: A study of scientists and engineers', *Journal of Applied Psychology, 82*, 539–45.

King, C.S., Feltey, K.M., and Susel, B.O. (1998), 'The question of participation: Toward authentic public participation in public administration', *Public Administration Review, 58*, 317–26.

King, C.M. and Stivers, C. (1998), *Government is Us: Public Administration in an Anti-government Era*, Thousand Oaks, CA: Sage.

Kramer, R. (1999), 'Weaving the public into public administration', *Public Administration Review, 59*, 89–92.

Lum, L., Kervin, J, Clark, K., Reied, F., and Sirola, W. (1998), 'Explaining nursing turnover intent: Job satisfaction, pay satisfaction, or organizational commitment?', *Journal of Organizational Behavior, 19*, 305–20.

Lynn, L.E. (1998), 'The new public management: How to transform a theme into a legacy', *Public Administration Review, 58*, 231–37.

Marshall, D. (1990), 'The restorative qualities of citizenship', *Public Administration Review, 50*, 21–5.

Marshall, T.H. (1950), *Citizenship and Social Class and Other Essays*, Cambridge: Cambridge University Press.

McKevitt, D. (1998), *Managing Core Public Services*, Oxford: Blackwell.

McPherson, J.M. and Rotolo, T. (1996), 'Testing a dynamic model of social composition: Diversity and change in voluntary groups', *American Sociological Review, 61*, 179–202.

Michael, H. (1981), 'Youth, voluntary associations and political socialization', *Social Forces, 60*, 211–23.

Milbrath, L.W. (1965), *Political Participation*, Chicago: Rand McNally.

Monroe, K.R. (1994), 'A fat lady in a corset: Altruism and social theory', *American Journal of Political Science, 38*, 861–93.

Morrison, E.W. (1996), 'Organizational citizenship behavior as a critical link between HRM practices and service quality', *Human Resource Management, 35*, 493–512.

O'Connell, B. (1989), 'What voluntary activity can and cannot do for America', *Public Administration Review, 49*, 486–91.

Organ, D.W. (1988), *Organizational Citizenship Behavior: The Good Soldier Syndrome*, Lexington, MA: Lexington Books.

Organ, D.W. and Konovsky, M. (1989), 'Cognitive versus affective determinants of organizational citizenship behavior', *Journal of Applied Psychology, 74*, 157–64.

Pateman, C. (1970), *Participation and Democratic Theory*, London: Cambridge University Press.

Perry, J.L. and Kraemer, K. (1983), *Public Management: Public and Private Perspectives*, Palo Alto, CA: Mayfield.

Peterson, S.A. (1990), *Political Behavior*, Thousand Oaks, CA: Sage.

Piliavin, J.A. and Charng, H.W. (1990), 'Altruism: A review of recent theory and research', *Annual Review of Sociology, 16*, 27–65.

Podsakoff, P.M. and MacKenzie, S.B. (1997), 'Impact of Organizational Citizenship Behavior on organizational performance: A review and suggestions for future research', *Human Performance, 10*, 133–51.

Pollitt, C. (1988), 'Bringing consumers into performance measurement', *Policy and Politics, 16*, 77–87.

Putnam, R. (1993), *Making Democracy Work: Civic Traditions in Modern Italy*, Princeton, NJ: Princeton University Press.

Rainey, H. (1990), 'Public Management: Recent Development and Current Prospects', in N.B. Lynn and A. Wildavsky (eds), *Public Administration: The State of the Discipline* (pp.157–84), Chatham, New Jersey: Chatham House.

Rimmerman, C.A. (1997), *The New Citizenship: Unconventional Politics, Activism, and Service*, Boulder, CO: Westview Press.

Smith, C.A., Organ, D.W., and Near, J.P. (1983), 'Organizational citizenship behavior: Its nature and antecedents', *Journal of Applied Psychology, 68*, 653–63.

Smith, S.R. and Lipsky, M. (1993), *Non-Profits for Hire: The Welfare State in the Age of Contracting*, Cambridge, MA: Harvard University Press.

Sobel, R. (1993), 'From occupational involvement to political participation: An exploratory analysis', *Political Behavior, 15*, 339–53.

Thomas, J.C. (1999), 'Bringing the public into public administration: The struggle continues', *Public Administration Review, 59*, 83–8.

Van Dyne, L., Graham, J.W., and Dienesch, R.M. (1994), 'Organizational Citizenship Behavior: Construct redefinition, measurement, and validation', *Academy of Management Journal, 37*, 765–802.

Vardi, Y. and Wiener, Y. (1996), 'Misbehavior in organizations: A motivational framework', *Organization Study, 7*, 151–65.

Verba, S. and Nie, N.H. (1972), *Participation in America*, New York: Harper and Row.

Vigoda, E. (2000a), 'Internal politics in public administration systems: An empirical examination of its relationship with job congruence, organizational citizenship behavior and in-role performances', *Public Personnel Management, 29*, 185–210.

Vigoda, E. (2000b), 'Are you being served? The responsiveness of public administration to citizens' demands: An empirical examination in Israel', *Public Administration, 78*, 1, 165–91.

Young, B.S., Worchel, S., and Woehr, D.J. (1998), 'Organizational commitment among public service employees', *Public Personnel Management, 27*, 339–48.

2. From Responsiveness to Collaboration: Governance, Citizens, and the Next Generation of Public Administration[1]

Eran Vigoda-Gadot

INTRODUCTION

Modern public administration involves an inherent tension between better responsiveness to citizens as clients and effective collaboration with them as partners. This tension stems from tangible differences between the nature of responsiveness as opposed to the essence of collaboration. While responsiveness is mostly seen as a passive uni-directional reaction to the people's needs and demands, collaboration represents a more active bi-directional act of participation, involvement and unification of forces between two (or more) parties. Moreover, responsiveness is based on the marketplace view of better service for citizens as clients or customers. Answering their needs is seen as vital for governments and public administration (government and public administration) systems that seek extensive legitimization and high performance. On the other hand, collaboration highlights a moral value of genuine cooperation and teamwork between citizens and government and public administrations while each party is neither a pure servant nor the master, but more of a social player in the theatre of state.

The differences between responsiveness and collaboration/partnership are not merely conceptual or terminological. In fact, they represent an intensifying paradox that emerges in both the theory and the practice of contemporary public sector management. The paradox increases especially due to an ongoing consensus on the necessity of both responsiveness and collaboration for moving government and public administration systems toward future reforms. Thus, it is quite surprising to find that most of the current theoretical thinking in public administration deals with these values separately, somewhat neglecting the mutual benefit of integrating them in a useful manner. An overview of the literature reveals two distinct groups of studies. One group highlights administrative responsiveness to citizens' requests as the most important value of public agencies in a businesslike arena (Keon, 1999; Rourke, 1992; Stivers, 1994; Vigoda, 2000). The other group emphasizes partnership between the sides as a premise for a cultural revolution in contemporary bureaucracies (for example, Nalbandian 1999; Thompson, Tancredi and Kisil, 2000; John et al., 1994; Hart, 1997; Callahan and Holzer, 1994). To date very little literature has consolidated these two prominent themes into one whole to illuminate the theoretical as well as empirical merit of their coexistence (for example, Fredrickson, 1982).

This chapter argues that expanded orientation of government and public administration systems toward responsiveness, as prescribed by new public managerialism, is frequently accompanied by lower willingness for sharing, participation, collaboration and partnership with citizens. This paradox is identified as a theoretical as well as a practical rift in the present array of the new public management (NPM) approach. While the chapter applauds the recent trend in public managerialism that fosters manager–customer relationships in the public arena it also criticizes such leanings for resting solely upon a unidirectional pattern of relationships where citizens are covertly encouraged to remain passive clients of government. A role of 'customer' or 'client' denotes a passive orientation of citizens toward another party (government and public administration) that is more active in trying to satisfy the customer/client's needs. It is suggested that such a pattern of dependency is likely to create serious obstacles to reforms in public agencies and to interrupt the emergence of better public service. The paradox between serving clients and collaborating with citizens needs to be resolved on the way to creating a high-performing type of public organization, of a sort that will work better for societies as well as for individuals in the generations to come.

To promote understanding of the processes that modern societies require and may undergo we advance in three stages. First, several similarities and differences are presented between the ideas of responsiveness and collaboration as developed in public administration studies of recent years. These discussions make use of various disciplinary sources such as democratic theory, comparative political science and political economy, as well as theories of administrative reforms. Second, we provide our analysis and view of 'one lady with two hats', our metaphor for one continuum connecting two current alternatives of the state of the discipline. In light of this we finally suggest a discussion that redefines duties and responsibilities of various players, and also compares our view and other perceptions of the next generation of public administration.

RESPONSIVENESS AND COLLABORATION: TWO DIFFERENT LADIES OR ONE LADY WITH TWO HATS?

Responsiveness to Citizens as Clients

A previous work by Vigoda (2000) identified two approaches to understanding public administration's responsiveness. These approaches can be defined as controversial but also as complementary. They provide distinct views of responsiveness, but in addition each approach contains checks and balances missing in the other. According to one approach, responsiveness is at best a necessary evil that appears to compromise professional effectiveness, and at worst an indication of political expediency if not outright corruption (Rourke, 1992). According to this line of research, responsiveness contradicts the value of professionalism in government and public administration since it forces public servants to satisfy citizens even when such actions run counter to the required public interest. In the name of democracy, professionals are almost obliged to satisfy a vague public will. Short-term considerations and popular decisions are put forward while other long-term issues receive little and unsatisfactory attention. In addition there is a risk that powerful influences of some may ring out loudly, and wrongly pretend to represent the opinions of many. Such influences can result in an anti-democratic decision-making pattern and simply may not represent the true voice of the majority. The other approach to responsiveness suggests that democracy requires administrators who are responsive to the popular will, at least through legislatures and politicians if not directly to the people (Stivers, 1994; Stewart and Ranson, 1994). This approach is more alert to the need to encourage a flexible, sensitive and dynamic public sector. It fact, it argues that only by creating a market-derived environment can government and public administration adopt some necessary reforms that will improve their performance, effectiveness and efficiency.

While responsiveness is occasionally considered a problematic concept in public administration literature it is undoubtedly critical for politicians, bureaucrats and citizens alike. A responsive politician or bureaucrat must be reactive, sympathetic, sensitive and capable of feeling the public's needs and opinions. Since the needs and demands of a heterogeneous society are dynamic, it is vital to develop systematic approaches to understanding it. Undoubtedly, this is one of the most important conditions for securing a fair social contract between citizens and governmental officials. Hence, scholars and practitioners suggest the elaboration of performance indicators based on public opinion. The opinions of service receivers must be seriously considered good indicators of public policy outcomes (Palfrey et al., 1992; Winkler, 1987; National Consumer Council, 1986; DHSS, 1979). This information can help one to: (1) understand and establish public needs; (2) develop, communicate and distribute public services; and (3) assess the degree of satisfaction with services (Palfrey et al., 1992: 128). Consequently, the NPM approach advocated the idea of treating citizens as clients, customers and main beneficiaries of the operation of the public sector that is today more oriented to assessing its performance (Thomas and Palfrey, 1996). In essence, the motivation to meet such demands as raised by citizens is equivalent to satisfying the needs of a regular customer in a regular neighborhood supermarket. According to this view responsiveness in the public arena closely complies with business-oriented statements such as 'the customer is always right' and 'never argue with the clients' needs' that every salesperson memorizes from his/her first day at work.

But what does responsiveness actually mean? How can we best define and operationalize it for dependable social research? In essence responsiveness generally denotes the *speed* and *accuracy* with which a service provider responds to a request for action or for information. According to this definition, speed can refer to the waiting time between a citizen's request for action and the reply of the public agency or the public servant. Accuracy means the extent to which the provider's response meets the needs or wishes of the service user. Yet while speed is a relatively simple factor to measure, accuracy is more complicated. Beyond the recent trends of analysing public arenas in terms appropriate for the marketplace, public service accuracy must take into consideration social welfare, equity, equal opportunities and fair distribution of 'public goods' to all citizens (Vigoda, 2000). These values are additional to efficiency, effectiveness, and service that characterize market-driven processes (Rhodes, 1987; Palfrey et al., 1992). To test the accuracy of government and public administration endeavors, several methods may be applied:

1. Examining citizens' attitudes and feelings when consuming public services; this can be achieved by using satisfaction measures indicating the outcomes of certain activities and the acceptance of public administration actions as fruitful, beneficial, equally shared among a vast population, effective, fast and responding well to public needs.
2. Examining the attitudes and perceptions of others who take part in the process of planning, producing, delivering and evaluating public outcomes. These 'others' include external private and not-for-profit firms, suppliers, manufacturers, constructors, etc.

3. Comparing objective public outcomes with absolute criteria for speed, quality and accuracy. The absolute criteria need to be determined in advance within a strategic process of setting performance indicators (PIs) (Pollitt, 1988). Such a comparison is even more effective when conducted over time, populations, cultures, geographical areas, etc.
4. Comparing the distribution of services and goods with moral and ethical criteria as set forth by academics and professionals.

Subject to several restrictions and balances, responsiveness has a potentially positive effect on social welfare and it improves the process of modernization in the public sector. Recent managerial positions, such as the NPM approach, also suggest that, as in the private sector, increasing external-related outcomes (that is, responsiveness of government and public administration to citizens' demands) will have a profound impact on internal control mechanisms (Smith, 1993). It simply implies that managers and public servants become more sensitive to their duties and highly committed to serving the people.

Collaboration with Citizens as Partners

At first glance collaboration and partnership between government and public administration and citizens seem to contradict the essence of bureaucracy. The ideal type of bureaucracy, as set out by Max Weber, has clearly defined organizational characteristics that have remained relevant down the years. Public organizations have undergone many changes in the last century. But they are still based on the Weberian legacy of clear hierarchical order, concentration of power among senior officials, formal structures with strict rules and regulations, limited channels of communication, confined openness to innovation and change, and non-compliance with the option of being replaceable. These ideas seem to be substantially different from the nature of collaboration, which means negotiation, participation, cooperation, free and unlimited flow of information, innovation, agreements based on compromises and mutual understanding, and a more equal distribution and redistribution of power and resources. According to this utopian analysis, collaboration is an indispensable part of democracy. It means partnership where authorities and state administrators accept the role of leaders who need to run citizens' lives better not because they are more powerful or superior but because this is a mission to which they are obligated. They must see themselves as committed to citizens who have agreed to be led or 'governed' on condition that their lives continuously improve.

In support of the above recognition Thompson (1983) stated that 'democracy does not suffer bureaucracy gladly. Many of the values we associate with democracy – equality, participation, and individuality – stand sharply opposed to hierarchy, specialization, and impersonality we ascribe to modern bureaucracy' (p.235). Bureaucracies, like other organizations, constitute a worksite that is anything but democratic. According to Golembiewski and Vigoda (2000) bureaucracies embody a firm hierarchy of roles and duties, a vertical flow of orders and reports, accountability to highly ranked officers, fear of sanctions and restrictions, and sometimes even lack of sufficient accountability dynamics. All these signal that the 'natural state' in public administration is authoritarian.

Hence, it seems odd to ask for genuine collaboration between those in power and those who delegated power. In many respects, growing citizenry involvement by interest groups, political parties, courts and other democratic institutions may only bother politicians in office and state administrators. Too broad an involvement, in the eyes of elected politicians and appointed public officers, may be perceived as interfering with their administrative work. The freedom of public voice is thus limited and obscured by the need of administrators and politicians to govern. The public consequently lacks sufficient freedom of voice and influence. While mechanisms of direct democracy are designed to show such impediments the door, modern representative democracy lets them back in through the rear entrance. Representative democracy frequently diminishes the motives for partnership with governance. Constitutions, legislatures, federal and local structures as well as electoral institutions are in slow but significant decline in many western societies. They suffer from increasing alienation, distrust and cynicism among citizens; they encourage passivism and raise barriers before original individual involvement in state affairs (Eisinger, 2000; Berman, 1997). Consequently, and as a counter-revolutionary course of action, a swelling current in contemporary public administration seeks to revitalize collaboration between citizens and administrative authorities through various strategies. In fact such trends are not so new. The need to foster certain levels of cooperation among political governmental institutions, professional agencies of PA, and citizens as individuals or groups has been mentioned before, and was advanced in several ways. Among these philosophies and strategies one should mainly consider

1. Greater cooperation with the third sector (Thompson et al., 2000; Gidron, Kramer and Salamon, 1992; Grubbs, 2000).
2. Greater collaboration with the private sector and initiation of plans aimed at supporting communities through various services in the fields of internal security, transport, and education (Glaister, 1999; Collin, 1998; Schneider, 1990).

3. Encouragement of state and local municipality initiatives that foster values of democratic education, participation and involvement among citizens (for example, the local Democratic club established in Culver City, California: http://www.culvercityonline.com/). This pattern also coheres with the idea of a communitarian spirit that transfers some (but not all) responsibility for civic development from central government to local authorities in states and cities, as well as directly to individual citizens (Etzioni, 1994; 1995).

4. Innovation by original citizenry involvement through not-for-profit civic organizations that help to establish a culture of participation and practice of voice (see the examples of 'citizens conventions' in Denmark).

Still, advocates of the NPM approach continue to claim that the main instrument to restore ill-functioning government and public administration systems is better responsiveness to citizens as clients or customers. According to this line, which is rooted in political-economy rationality and social choice theory (Kettl and Milward, 1996; Hughes, 1994), only better compliance with people's wishes can steady the wobbly interface between citizens and rulers in contemporary democracies. But is a market-driven responsiveness really the best answer for crises in governance, or is it only an over-simplification of wider problems in modern society?

Customers or Partners? A Quest for Hats and Ladies

What are the advantages of citizens' being treated as clients/customers over their being perceived as equal partners in the process of governance? A metaphor of ladies and hats may prove useful here to examine two competing options. (1) There are two substantially separated faces of government and public administration (two ladies), one that adopts the idea of responsiveness and one that favors collaboration. (2) The discipline of governance and public administration is more coherent (only one lady) than we might think, and at most it changes colors over time (two hats).

Above we portrayed two themes in current public administration research as separate and dissimilar perspectives. We argued that responsiveness is in the essence of NPM and we further suggested that NPM seems detached from the idea of collaboration. Therefore, it may be suggested that there are two different types of public administration; like two ladies, one is attired by the supporters of responsiveness, the other by supporters of collaboration. These two ladies substantially differ because, as explained earlier, they advocate independent views of the roles of government and public administration and citizens in the process of running states and societies. Yet we may in fact be suggesting only one lady with two hats. One hat, an older styled classic, is more oriented to bureaucratic tyranny and concentration of power in public agencies. It reflects a situation where public administration is the right hand of politicians and thus must preserve power through maximum centralization and control over decisions as well as resources. This hat/attitude implies minimal care for either responsiveness or collaboration because both mean depriving government and public administration of their power. The other hat, however, is newer and more receptive and appreciative of de-concentrated managerial ideas, such as better responsiveness and improved collaboration with citizens, which affect a wider process of modernization. This last hat signals a continuous change in public administration systems, and, maturing with time, it implies more participation of the people in the administrative process. A lady of public administration wearing the newer hat is less concerned about bureaucracy losing power and control but instead favors sharing responsibilities and dialogue with citizens that may lead to cooperation and partnership on a higher level.

In addition, the 'two ladies' version is a more classic approach to the understanding of responsiveness and collaboration in public arenas so it has received wide scholarly attention over the years. As noted earlier, one group of studies has concentrated on the first 'lady' of public administration, namely the idea of responsiveness (for example, Stivers, 1994; Rourke, 1992) while the other group has focused on the other lady, who represents the idea of collaboration and partnership (for example, John et al., 1994; Thompson, Tancredi and Kisil, 2000; Nalbandian, 1999). In fact, hardly any attempt has been made to try to integrate these views or to suggest that they may be better seen stemming from one another. The 'two hats for one lady' image inclines to this integration but it is also less frequently developed and needs more extensive explanation and elaboration. According to this image, responsiveness and collaboration are inherently related. They designate different points on a continuum of government and public administration–citizen interaction that are constantly shifted and re-framed with time and social events. Thus, a framework of interaction with citizens is better presented here by one evolutionary continuum (one lady) of public administration. Along this continuum responsiveness and collaboration are only different 'hats' on one line of symmetry.

Interacting with Citizens: An Evolutionary Continuum

Figure 2.1 presents an evolutionary continuum of the role of citizens, government and public administration authorities, and their reciprocal interaction as it advances with the years. Along this line citizens may be seen as subjects, voters, clients–customers, partners or owners. Moving along the continuum we also (respectively) observe government and public

Continuum 1: The role of citizens

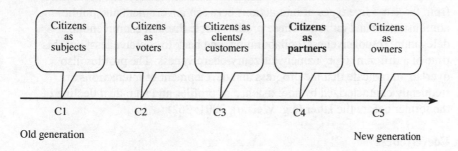

Continuum 2: The role of governance and public administration (G&PA)

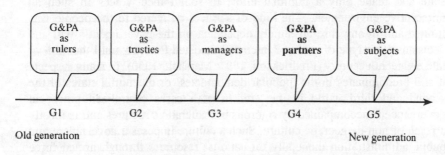

Continuum 3: Type of interaction

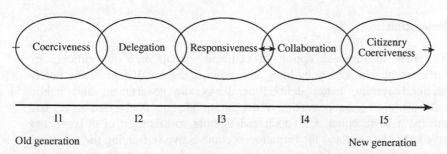

Figure 2.1   An evolutionary continuum of PA–citizen interaction

administration as rulers, trustees, managers, partners or subjects. Stemming from these are five types of interactions between government and public administration and citizens. These profiles circle through coerciveness, delegation, responsiveness, collaboration, and back to coerciveness, but this time of a different type, namely citizenry-coerciveness. The profiles also overlap, to indicate that the progress and development of interactions are frequently characterized by co-existence of profiles and a gradual decline of the former before the latter (e.g. Weikart, 2001: 362).

Coerciveness

The old generation of public administration used to treat *citizens as subjects*, where leaders and administrators held almost absolute power and control over the people. Citizens, for their part, accepted the unlimited tyranny of the state and made only a minimal effort to sound their voices in such an unreceptive environment. The kind of services delivered to the people was limited and in any case absolutely dependent on the government's will and decisions. This type of coercive interaction existed for ages, until the mid- or late eighteenth century (Fredrickson, 1997; Marshall, 1950). In many respects it still predominates in the 'popular democracies' or dictatorial states of the second and third world in our era. In both cases centralized power in governance is accompanied by rigorous bureaucratic structures and is mostly a result of non-democratic culture. Such a culture imposes a government and public administration monopoly on national resources through armed force and dominance of education and socialization systems. The old-orthodox public administration controlled and monitored many, if not all, aspects of citizens' daily lives to create a pattern of coerciveness in the citizen–ruler relationship.

Delegation

The first institutional option for citizens' inputs into the process of government and society building was through the installation of the voter-electoral system, better defined as democratic government and public administration or an interaction of delegation. Without doubt, democracy has created a more equal, fair, open and flexible co-existence of citizens and rulers, and has enabled the former to become active in framing the nature of governance. This is how a *citizens as voters* style emerged, and made a tremendous conceptual and practical change in the understanding of citizen – government relationships. Since the end of the eighteenth century, and more robustly toward the late nineteenth century, developing representative democracies of the western world induced the idea of delegation. In a representative democracy, it was argued, citizens cannot manage their lives but count on the wisdom, experience, and civic goodwill of their representatives. W. Wilson and D. Waldo called for a reform of government and public administration and for an emphasis on specialization, professionalism, merit-based appointment and promotion, and the application of management sciences in local, state and federal agencies. Following this, citizens were given the option of voice but only via representatives and at wide intervals of time (between elections), with no sufficient instruments for an effective in-between influence. Nonetheless, citizens in America and in Europe initiated self-derived attempts to become more involved in administrative actions by interest groups and by political parties. Fredrickson (1997) thus argued that in the 1950s 'pluralism' emerged as the best term to describe the indirect connection between citizens and governments. Yet with the passage of time it also became clear that such attempts were too few, too vague, and too slight in impact on government and public administration. The formal 'open gate' for citizenry involvement did not mean that a widespread atmosphere of original participation by individual citizens or groups actually matured.

As scientific knowledge has accumulated, theory of political participation has clarified that there are people who are unable or unwilling to participate in governmental or political processes, while others are simply not aware of the importance and contribution of this involvement (Verba, Schlozman, and Brady, 1995). In fact, representative democracy highly contradicted the promise of vast spontaneous citizenship involvement. Being remote from decision making centers, by choice or not, citizens developed increased cynicism toward government and toward public administration systems. As argued by Eisinger (2000), 'over the past decades, scholars, political pundits and elected officials have professed that cynicism has spiraled up and down to the point that it has become an endemic part of the psyche in the 1980s [when] a fog of cynicism surrounds American politics, and that the 1990s are a time of unparalleled public cynicism about politics, which has continued and accelerated to this day' (p.55). Hence, this simple delegation type of relationship between rulers and citizens drew heavy fire from academics, professionals, public servants, and even politicians. In many respects, the need for an additional change in the nature of state–citizen interaction drove the NPM movement in the following years.

Responsiveness

Citizens as voters was only one step toward the development of *citizens as clients/customers* model. As suggested by Rainey (1990), the 1960s and the 1970s were characterized by the initiation of unsuccessful public policies in

Europe and in America. Over the years efforts by governments to create extensive changes in education, welfare systems, health programs, internal security and crime control were widely criticized for being ineffective and low-performing, and for misusing public budgets, while responsiveness to the real needs and demands of citizens was paltry. The crisis in practical public policy implementation together with increased cynicism of citizens toward government and public administration generated rich scholarly activity aimed at creating useful alternatives for improved policy in various social fields as well as in the administrative processes in general (Peters, 1999). Voters expressed their dissatisfaction with governors, and hand in hand with the academic community called for extensive reforms in government. This call produced a large number of working papers, articles and books that portrayed and targeted extensive administrative changes. One of the most inspiring works, Osborne and Gaebler's *Reinventing Government* (1992), is frequently mentioned as the unofficial starting point of such reforms, later known as NPM. According to Peters (1996), Terry (1998), and Weikart (2001), NPM is presently increasing in popularity in North America and across the world, and many governments adopt ideas and recommendations that have proven beneficial in the continuous implementation of this strategy.

True enough, the NPM approach suggested a different type of interaction between citizens and rulers in democracies. However, the roots of such interactions can be found around a century ago. For example, Weikart (2001) asserted that 'the ideas behind NPM are not new' and that 'NPM builds on a long history of using business practices in government and reflects a resurgence of old ideas about the form and functions of government' (p.362). During the first years of the twentieth century reformers and business leaders demanded greater accountability in local government, and many politicians as well as public officers turned to business principles to improve governmental activities, invigorate performance and decrease corruption. However, the vision of NPM is also far different from the old business-guided governance due to its aspiration to decrease government size and lower its involvement in citizens' lives. NPM relies on theory of the marketplace and on a businesslike culture in public organizations. For example, in an extensive review of NPM literature Hays and Kearney (1997) found five core principles of this approach: (1) downsizing – reducing the size and scope of government, (2) managerialism – using business protocols in government, (3) decentralization – moving decision making closer to the service recipients, (4) debureaucratization – restructuring government to emphasize results rather than processes, and (5) privatization – directing the allocation of governmental goods and services to outside firms (Weikart, 2001). All these principles are mutually related, relying heavily on theory of the private sector and on business philosophy, but aimed at minimizing the size and scope of governmental activities. Integrated with ideas rooted in political economy, they became applicable for public sector institutions (Farnham and Horton, 1995).

Stemming from the above principles, a major belief of NPM advocates is that government and public administration encourage a view whereby citizens are clients/customers of the public sector while government and public administration are perceived as managers of large bureaucracies. According to this outlook (Aucoin, 1995; Garson and Overman, 1983; Pollitt and Bouckaert, 2000) the state and its bureaucratic subsystems are equivalent to a large private organization operating in an economic environment of supply and demand. In this spirit a major goal of government is to satisfy the needs or demands of citizens, namely to show higher responsiveness to the public as clients. In line with this Savas (1994) argued that modern states must rely more on private institutions and less on government to satisfy societal needs of vast populations. Hence, the goal of satisfying the needs of citizens became central to NPM legacy.

Nevertheless, NPM may be criticized for not doing enough to encourage and infuse the idea of collaboration or partnership between citizens and government and public administration and for failing to apply these themes in modern managerial thinking (Vigoda and Golembiewski, 2001). Unlike traditional public administration, the NPM movement focuses on citizens as sophisticated clients in complex environments. The principles of NPM cohere with theories of political economy such as regulative policy by governments or the trend of transferring responsibilities from the state sector to the third sector. As suggested by Farnham and Horton (1995), 'these ideas, and the governmental policies deriving from them, challenged the social democratic principles and values' (p.3) in Britain, America, and many other western democracies. Public authorities were urged to treat the public well not only because of their presumed administrative responsibility for quality in action but also because of their obligation to marketplace rules and to economic demands, and above all because of their fear of losing clients in an increasingly competitive businesslike arena. In fact, while NPM has proved an advance over more classic views of public administration that saw citizens as subjects or voters, it is still very limited in fostering the idea of vital collaboration between citizens and government and public administration, which is in the essence of democratic civil society.

In line with this, 'Neo-Managerialism' (Terry, 1998) places an additional obstacle before productive partnership that must also be recognized and isolated. According to Terry, Neo-Managerialism fosters the idea that administrative leaders should assume the role of public entrepreneurs. However, 'public entrepreneurs of the neo-managerialist persuasion are oblivious to other values highly prized in the U.S. constitutional democracy.

Values such as fairness, justice, representation, or participation are not on the radar screen (and) this is indeed, troublesome' (p.200). In many respects neo/new managerialism and NPM encourage passivity among the citizenry. They impart to citizens the power of *exit* (which indeed was virtually unavailable in the past) but at the same time they discourage use of the original power of *voice* by citizens who may have much to contribute to their communities (Vigoda and Golembiewski, 2001). Hirschman (1970) in fact suggested that exit is an economic choice while voice is more of a political selection by individuals in and around organizational systems. Exit is also classified as a general destructive behavior while voice is a productive one. According to this rationality, NPM restricts and discourages productive political voices of the people.

Hence, recent developments in the study of NPM have focused on the responsibilities of government and public administration in their interaction with citizens but similarly have paid far less attention to the active roles of citizens and to their obligations in the community. Most of the up-to-date NPM literature favors massive socialization of business management practices in the public sector to provide governments with better tools for policy implementation (for example, Lynn, 1998; Pollitt, 1988; Rosenbloom, Goldman and Ingrahm, 1994). But on the other hand, these orientations and practices have so far just not been integrated with another core-construct of healthy democracies: genuine collaboration and partnership with citizens founded on equal opportunities for participation and massive involvement in running public life more effectively (Peters, 1999). This under-evaluation of the idea of partnership and collaboration, at the expense of good responding management, may be deemed a flaw in contemporary NPM theory.

TOWARD COLLABORATION AND PARTNERSHIP: A MULTI-DIMENSIONAL PERSPECTIVE

Between Clients and Partners

As we have indicated, collaboration is founded on responsiveness. However, it also reaches decidedly beyond. Moreover, while greater collaboration is not a very new idea in PA, it has never fulfilled its promising potential, partly due to the informal competition with businesslike strategies such as NPM. An economic interaction between managers and customers carries some basic deficiencies for modern states. The term client, or customer, that is so applicable in the private sector (that is, rational choice theory or agency theory), contradicts the very basic notion of belonging, altruism, contributing

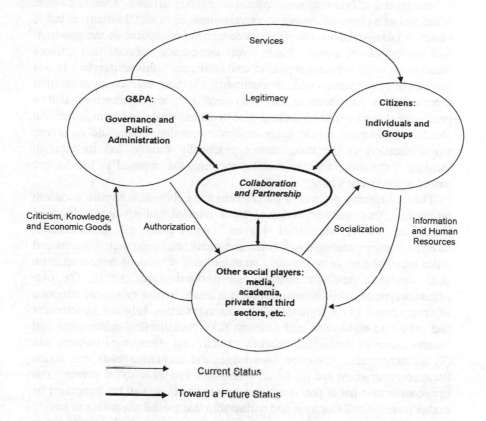

Figure 2.2   Collaboration among social players: an insight into the next generation

to society, and self-derived participation in citizenry actions. When someone is defined as a client he/she is not actively engaged in social initiatives but is merely a passive service (or product) consumer, dependent on the goodwill and interest of the owner. While direct democracy suggests that citizens themselves 'own' the state, representative democracy adds an interface to this ownership by politicians and administrators. Citizens run their lives through representatives only because they also need a 'board of directors' that is professional and capable of making wise decisions for huge communities. An absolute democracy, where every citizen is equally responsible for every single decision of the state, cannot practically survive and function in growing, expanding, and fast-moving societies (as opposed to the limited nature of the Greek's polis).

The evolutionary process of government and public administration–citizen interactions thus must be followed by a rational and applicable level of integration across all social players. As Figure 2.2 demonstrates, interrelationships among government and public administration, citizens and other social players is becoming a strategic goal of modern democracies on their way to a new administrative spirit (Fredrickson, 1997). The old-orthodox type of public administration was characterized by a triple structure of transactions: (1) a legitimacy–services transaction between government and public administration and citizens; (2) a socialization–information and human-resources transaction between citizens and other social players; and (3) an authorization–criticism, knowledge, and economic-goods transaction between government and public administration and other social players. The new-cooperative hat of public administration, however, will be dominated by higher levels of collaboration and partnership that exceed the nature of simple transactions as presented above. In fact, this is one core challenge for future generations. Government and public administration must take a step forward, going beyond elementary exchange relationships and responsiveness to demands.

Our view, as presented above, seeks to expand on future possible trends in public administration scholarship by renewing the values of collaboration and partnership. We argue that civic society is almost unthinkable in purely rational–economic patterns. Thus, following the dimensions of new governance as suggested by John et al. (1994), and somewhat enlarging them for our purposes, the discussion now elaborates on several questions: (1) *What* do collaboration and partnership actually mean? (2) *Where* on the continuum of public administration evolution are they located? (3) *Whose* responsibility is it to make the partnership possible? Consequently (4) *how* can this productive collaboration between government and public administration and citizens be achieved?

The answer to the first question is relatively simple. Three main players are identified. Above all, both government and public administration and citizens have core responsibilities in this process. Contrary to the perception of responsiveness, where government and public administration hold almost exclusive power and authority, and are expected to navigate among various public demands, the collaborative approach asks for extensive responsibilities and involvement on the part of the public. This can take a form of individual initiatives that seek greater participation in administrative decisions and actions, or alternatively various kinds of organized citizenry actions (for example, as represented by semi-organized groups or as formed by the third sector). Hence, both parties (citizens and government and public administration) must be actively engaged in the process of administrative change and reforms, otherwise the very essence of collaboration is spoiled. Still, in addition to these two central players there is much room for the operation of other social units. Among these we have chosen to expand on the role of the media and academia, but other players are relevant here as well (for example, political parties, interest groups, constitutional and electoral institutions, and other bodies of the private sector and the third sector). As will be explained below, the role of these institutions is mostly educative and is directed at enhancing socialization for citizen–government and public administration collaboration.

The second question, as to how this collaboration may be accomplished, is more complex. It can benefit from a practical method of studying public organizations, as suggested by Golembiewski (1995). Accordingly, we will try to define and explain various operative goals to be pursued by each accountable party.

The Role of Government and Public Administration

The present starting point of government and public administration–citizens relationships is not very encouraging. King, Feltey and Susel (1998) argued that 'although many public administrators view close relationships with citizens as both necessary and desirable most of them do not actively seek public involvement. If they do seek it, they do not use public input in making administrative decisions...(and) believe that greater citizen participation increases inefficiency,...delays, and red tape'. Following this Peters (1999) elaborated on the common belief that today public institutions are structured to prevent effective participation. Given this, the implications for collaboration need no further interpretation. They only emphasize the change and challenge facing modern bureaucracies of our era.

In light of this, the prime responsibility of governments and public administration is to define strategic goals that can enhance partnership with and empowerment of citizens. This partnership must also conjoin with resources available in the private and third sectors, which for diverse reasons become more willing to engage in actions for the community and for the public. To respond to the demands for effective participation by the public, these institutions may engage in future structural and cultural changes and extensively use the tool of 'empowerment' by which collaboration develops. Empowerment may encourage authentic voluntary behavior by citizens that is not manipulated by the state. Governments can only stimulate environmental conditions that are necessary to generate spontaneous behavior by citizens as individuals and groups, or as part of organized institutions. Programs of involvement and collaboration need to be governed by citizens and administered by practitioners who understand them. However, public service practitioners will fulfill their duties by becoming citizens' honest advisers and helpers rather than controllers of public organizations (Box, 1998; 1999; Rimmerman, 1997). As suggested in previous studies, several programs and techniques can be applied to achieve these goals.

First, volunteer programs in the fields of health, welfare services, education and security need to receive national and federal support (Brudney, 1990). Adequate training programs of volunteers as well as volunteer leadership and management need to be developed and implemented by professionals. Second, educational efforts that emphasize the importance of individual-level and organized entrepreneurism may start in the very first years of school and create awareness in the very young of the high values of citizenship involvement. Without such an extensive educational effort long-term initiatives will remain limited and incomplete. Governments will also be responsible for coordination of cooperation among different voluntary groups and institutions. This coordination may increase the efficiency of volunteer groups and third-sector organizations to get more value for effort. However, the government and public administration's role must not be coercive but must remain consultative. Using their delegated authority, governments can establish public volunteers' committees to coordinate the voluntary activity at the local and national levels. Government and public administration will maintain their advisory position, providing the citizens with sufficient conditions and experience to work out their spontaneous ideas.

Public administration may also become more active and entrepreneurial in the initiation of partnership between public servants and citizens. In some countries (for example, Britain, Germany and Australia) public servants, in contrast to governments and elected politicians, usually enjoy a less political image in the eyes of citizens, so they may gain more public trust and participation than politicians. In other countries, such as the United States, public trust can be gained differently, perhaps through higher transparency of government and public administration, more involvement of the media, and communal administrative ventures that bring citizens closer to the daily administrative process. The focus of new public management in collaborative spheres will benefit from adjusting more vigorously to include transformation of 'goodwill' into 'effective operations'. Public administration, through its professional cadre, can lead the operative involvement of citizens by improving the partnership between governments and citizens. Investment in spontaneous behavior of the people is low-cost and economic compared with other reform efforts and thus must be encouraged (Brudney and Duncombe, 1992). Another responsibility of public administration is the function of evaluation. All programs of citizens' involvement will benefit from obtaining continuous evaluation by unbiased professionals. These can be found in academia or in the private sector.

The Role of Citizens

Active citizens in modern societies are a minority. Even the most optimistic estimates by scholars in the field of participatory democracy affirm that their proportion is less than 10 percent of the population (Almond and Verba, 1963; Verba, Schlozman and Brady, 1995). Still, the political and social influence of this relatively small group is immense and must not be underestimated. This vanguard practically and ideologically paves the way to potential social changes, whatever these may be. Collaboration of government and public administration with these people, as individuals or as groups, may also lead others to join.

Citizens' participation also includes highly organized and fully institutional collective endeavors. The most obvious representative of this sub-category is the organized third sector, elsewhere defined as nonprofit or voluntary organizations. Collective institutional citizenship derives from ambitious interests of large groups that have undergone a relatively complicated process of institutionalization and formalization. Management and public administration sciences have devoted considerable attention to this field (Brinton, 1994; Coble, 1999; O'Connell, 1989; Smith & Lipsky, 1993). In many ways these organizations represent increased public involvement aimed at providing services in which the state is unable or unwilling to play a significant role.

Organized voluntary activity in modern nations has rapidly expanded in recent decades. With the years, people, organizations, and governments have become aware that the state cannot, or will not, be involved in every field of human life. They have discovered that no bureaucracy is capable of being everywhere, all the time, and with optimal resources and remedies for all social problems. This 'third sector' is distinct from the traditional public and private sectors (Gidron and Kramer, 1992). In recent years voluntary organizations and the third sector constituted about 10 percent of the economic size of all governmental activities in the US (O'Connell, 1989) and their relative size continues to grow. Such figures may indicate that citizens of modern societies have more needs/demands and that they are disappointed with governments' operation and inability to provide satisfactory welfare services. Hence, it seems that today, more than ever before, citizens are willing to engage in collective voluntary actions (both semi-organized and fully organized) to support their needs (King, Feltey and Susel, 1998).

The growing activity of the third sector is perhaps only one positive signal in this direction. According to O'Connell (1989), voluntary organizations and the third sector constituted about 10 percent of the economic volume of all governmental activities in the US, and these numbers (including numbers of volunteers) are in continuous growth.

Supported by rapidly growing academic interest and practical ventures, the promising potential of reciprocal linkage and collaboration between government and public administration and citizens can be further developed. In this linkage, citizens have several roles. The most elementary is active participation in running their lives and managing their communities. This role is momentous, so it should not be left solely in the hands of politicians or even professional public servants. It can be accomplished on several levels, individual, group or institutional (Vigoda and Golembiewski, 2001). Participation in neighborhood associations or voluntary groups to aid the young, the elderly, or other sections of the population, active involvement in citizens' committees as presented earlier in this essay, involvement in parents' committees at schools, donating money, time or effort for charity or equivalent social goals, development of community services in various manners, and encouraging others to take part in such activities – all are worthy missions that allow continuous partnership of the people in administrative processes. In addition, citizens have the duty to voice constructive criticism of the public system to encourage a culture of accountability, and to provide feedback for politicians and public servants, thereby increasing their responsiveness and sense of responsibility. This can be achieved through original civic journalism, letters to newspapers, public officials and politicians calling radio and television programs, and using the computerized media to spread knowledge and attitudes. The education system has the power of teaching the youngest to become more involved and to use these methods more extensively. This way civic involvement may resound when children grow up and become adult citizens with formal rights and duties. Thus, citizens, like other social players, serve as socialization agents of partnership. They have an educational mission to contribute increased motivation and furnish values of involvement in future generations. It is well within their power to promote understanding of shared responsibilities within social life.

Lastly, it would be naïve to seek large-scale political participation (Almond and Verba, 1963; Verba, Schlozman and Brady, 1995) and vast self-derived mobilization by citizens without creating the necessary conditions for such involvement. People have the duty to become engaged in collaborative activities with government and public administration but, as mentioned earlier, government and public administration have the greater duty to create conditions for such involvement by all available means. Moreover, the voyage to increased collaboration between citizens and government and public administration can also become calmer and much more effective when media and academia join in the effort.

The Role of the Media and Academia

Fox and Miller (1997) suggested that 'public policy discourse has entered an era of media-driven hyperreality, becoming detached from the lived experience of the polity' (p.64). The media in free democracies bear responsibility for promoting accountability to citizens. To achieve this goal the media seek increased transparency of governmental institutions. This important task advances a legitimate debate between citizens and government on how public resources are spent and whether responsibilities are properly shared to increase the public good. Despite its considerable limitations, the positive elements of 'loop democracy' (Fox and Miller, 1995) cannot be realistic without active, independent and responsible media.

However, the media have other roles as well. Their primary responsibility is to serve as an effective and reliable communication channel between citizens and governments, one that promotes collaboration and partnership. The media are a powerful tool exercising immense influence over people's attitudes and opinions. This power can be used to encourage citizenship involvement and participation in a variety of ways, but also to extend administrative willingness to consult citizens on relevant policy decisions. The promotion of this goal on public television and radio channels as well as computerized networks is subject to policymakers' decisions. Citizens who are aware of their power may also demand greater involvement by the public media in covering entrepreneurial actions and in generating favorable public opinion about supportive community activities. The media may also encourage public recruitment to collaborative activities by means of educational programs. Regarding private media, newspapers and computer networks, citizens' power may be aimed directly at the business-telecommunication firms, using the collective strength of consumer groups and general public opinion. This is an important way in which responsiveness can work in the service of collaboration.

Another important player in these processes is academia. The contribution of the management and administration sciences to citizen–government and public administration collaboration and partnership is twofold. First, by pointing out theoretical considerations, conceptual grounding and practical means for cooperation, managerial science promotes the understanding of mutual social efforts. This knowledge is crucial for isolating and cultivating the benefits of partnership. It also highlights its advantages over a simple state of competition, which is a major construct of economics-based systems or a responsiveness-based interaction. Second, when reconfirmed by the power of science, the discussion on collaboration acquires priority over other issues in social affairs. The public agenda becomes more sensitive to issues of partnership and their growth value. This way the managerial and administrative sciences also promote legitimization of cooperation and encourage more individuals to participate in public management enterprises. Scientific confirmation of the actual benefits of collaborative actions fosters their acceptance in the eyes of both citizens and rulers, which in the long run may also establish them more solidly in state culture.

THE NEXT GENERATION: COLLABORATION – ONE STEP BEYOND RESPONSIVENESS

Looking toward the future of government and public administration Ott (1998) argued that 'Traditional bureaucracy is not an adequate form of governmental organization' and that 'the questions now are not whether government bureaucracies should be reformed but whether it is possible to govern through traditional bureaucratic government structures, whether traditional bureaucratic structures can be reformed enough so that we could govern through them and, which of the many alternative models being proposed would be best suited to governing the United States' (p.540). This chapter suggests that traditional structures of government and public administration face reforms that are based on an evolutionary continuum. Such reforms will create a different and more flexible model of governing that combines responsiveness, collaboration and the ideal type of citizens' ownership.

So far treating citizens as clients of the public system has definitely worked for the benefit of bureaucracies by illuminating some neglected dimensions in government and public administration–citizen relationships. Among these improvements are (1) the assumption of great responsibility by government and public administration toward citizens; (2) accountability in and transparency of the public sector operation, (3) the idea that governments' action must be continuously monitored to ensure high efficiency, effectiveness and better economic performance; (4) recognition that the government's power must depend principally on citizens' support, voice and satisfaction with the services they receive.

However, in this chapter we have argued that some adjustment must be made in the process of running modern states by the new generation of public administration. In fact, our view is much in line with the discourse theory of Fox and Miller (1995). In their stimulating book on *Postmodern Public Administration: Toward Discourse*, these authors tried to develop an alternative philosophy for both the institutionalist/constitutionalist and communitarianism approaches to government and public administration–citizen relationships. Instead, they rendered a synthetic (not analytic) idea that the public sphere is an energy field where mixed interests and explanations of reality coexist despite deep contradictions. According to Fox and Miller (1995, 101), the discipline of public administration, in theory and in practice, is facing a *paradigm shift* from bureaucracy (the orthodox type) to public energy fields (the future 'new' type). The discourse theory is built upon the public energy explanation, which paves the way for a new model for public administration and policy.

Moreover, while according to Fox and Miller (1995) representative democracy is neither representative nor democratic, it is definitely here to stay for years to come. In such a system citizens cannot and do not want to be in the position of owners in a citizenry-coerciveness type of interaction. Citizens give up ownership of government and public administration because of restraints impelled by the structure and culture of modern states. Thus, citizens as owners, defined on our continuum as 'citizenry-coerciveness' interaction, is an 'ideal type of democracy', one that must remain *ideal* but can never be implemented practically. Citizens are unwilling, perhaps incapable, of becoming practical owners of the state even if they are the real owners by all democratic and business criteria. Still, they resist being treated as subjects or even as simple voters, as is usually accepted in the old-orthodox type of government and public administration. They generally seek practical flexibility between the role of clients/customers and the position of equal partners. Government and public administrations, at the other extreme, move between their roles as managers and their proposed mission as citizens' partners. In the last decade many government and public administration systems in America and abroad have gladly adopted the role of managing citizens' lives, and do so from a businesslike standpoint. In the coming decades they are likely to face citizens' demands to treat them as equal partners. This shift forward is anticipated to be less readily adopted by government and public administration.

Our suggestion, then, is that a better definition of the government and public administration–citizen relationship must rely upon the conception of collaboration and partnership, if not citizenry ownership and control. Put another way, 'government will continue to govern, but the more authentic the encounters with citizens will be, the less will government be *they* and the more will it be *we*' (Fox and Miller, 1995, 128). Hence, this chapter has attempted somewhat to fill a conceptual and practical gap between perceptions of responsiveness and the quest for productive partnership by citizens, state administrators, politicians, and other social players such as the media and academia. We portrayed a normative possible interaction among these players in an evolving marketplace arena that will become even more turbulent in the future. The administrative–democratic turmoil will lead to growing and serious risks of citizens' alienation, disaffection, skepticism and increased cynicism toward governments. Such trends are already intensifying, and only a high level of cooperation among all parties in society may potentially guard against these centrifugal forces. Thus, the new generation of public administration will need a different spirit, perhaps a combination of communitarianism, institutionalism, and energism, but in any case one that successfully fosters *mutual effort*. This movement from a 'they' spirit to a 'we' spirit is perhaps the most important mission of public administration in our era.

NOTE

1. Based on Vigoda (2002), 'From responsiveness to collaboration: Governance, citizens, and the next generation of public administration', *Public Administration Review*, **62** (5) 515–28. Copyrights with permission from Blackwell Publishing.

REFERENCES

Almond, G. A. and Verba, S. (1963), *The Civic Culture: Political Attitudes and Democracy in Five Nations: An Analytic Study*, Boston: Little Brown.

Aucoin, P. (1995), *The New Public Management: Canada in Comparative Perspective*, Montreal: IRPP, Ashgate Publishing Company.

Berman, E. M. (1997), 'Dealing with cynical citizens', *Public Administration Review*, **57**, 105–12.

Box, R. C. (1998), *Citizen Governance: Leading American Communities into the 21st Century*, Thousand Oaks, CA: Sage.

Box, R. C. (1999), 'Running governments like a business: Implications for public administration theory and practice', *American Review of Public Administration*, **29**, 19–43.

Brinton, M.H. (1994), 'Nonprofit contracting and the hollow state', *Public Administration Review*, **54**, 73–77.

Brudney, J. L. (1990), *Fostering Volunteer Programs in the Public Sector: Planning, Initiating, and Managing Voluntary Activities*, San Francisco: Jossey-Bass.

Brudney, J. L. and Duncombe, W. D. (1992), 'An economic evaluation of paid, volunteer, and mixed staffing options for public services', *Public Administration Review, 52*, 474–81.

Callahan, K. and Holzer, M. (1994), 'Rethinking governmental change: New ideas, new partnership', *Public Productivity and Management Review, 17*, 201–14.

Coble, R. (1999), 'The nonprofit sector and state governments: Public policy issues facing nonprofit in North Carolina and other states', *Nonprofit Management and Leadership, 9*, 293-313.

Collin, S. O. (1998), 'In the twilight zone: A Survey of public–private partnership in Sweden', *Public Productivity and Management Review, 21*, 272–83.

DHSS (1979), *Patients First*, London: HMSO.

Eisinger, R. M. (2000), 'Questioning cynicism', *Society, 37*, 55–60.

Etzioni, A. (1994), *The Spirit of Community*, New York: Touchstone.

Etzioni, A. (1995), *New Communitarian Thinking: Persons, Virtues Institutions, and Communities*, Charlottesville: Virginia University Press.

Farnham, D. and Horton, S. (1995), 'The political economy of public sector change' in D. Farnham and S. Horton (eds), *Managing the New Public Services* (pp. 3–26), Basingstoke: Macmillan.

Fox, C. J. and Miller, H. T. (1995), *Postmodern Public Administration: Toward Discourse*, Thousand Oaks, CA: Sage.

Fox, C. J. and Miller, H. T. (1997), 'The depreciating public policy discourse', *American Behavioral Scientist, 41*, 64–89.

Fredrickson, G. H. (1982), 'The recovery of civism in public administration', *Public Administration Review, 42*, 501–9.

Fredrickson, G. II. (1997), *The Spirit of Public Administration*, San Francisco: Jossey-Bass.

Garson, D. G., and Overman, S. E. (1983), *Public Management Research in the United States*, New York: Praeger.

Gidron, B., Kramer, R. M., and Salamon, L. M. (eds) (1992), *Government and the Third Sector*, San Francisco: Jossey-Bass.

Glaister, S. (1999), 'Past abuses and future uses of private finance and public–private partnership in transport', *Public Money and Management, 19*, 29–36.

Golembiewski, R. T. (1995), *Practical Public Management*, New York: Marcel Dekker.

Golembiewski, R. T. and Vigoda, E. (2000), 'Organizational innovation and the science/craft of management' in M. A. Rahim, R.T. Golembiewski, and K.D. Mackenzie (eds), *Current Topics in Management, 5*, (pp. 263–80), Greenwich, CT: JAI Press.

Grubbs, J. W. (2000), 'Can agencies work together? Collaboration in public and nonprofit organizations', *Public Administration Review, 60*, 275–80.

Hart, D. (1997), 'A partnership in virtue among all citizens: The public service and the civic humanist tradition', *International Journal of Public Administration, 20*, 967–80.

Hays, S. W. and Kearney, R. C. (1997), 'Riding the crest of a wave: The national performance review and public management reform', *International Journal of Public Administration, 20*, 11–40.

Hirschman, A. O. (1970), *Exit, Voice and Loyalty*, Cambridge, MA: Harvard University Press.

Hughes, Owen E. (1994), *Public Management and Administration*, London: Macmillan.

John, D., Kettl, D. F., Dyer, B., and Lovan, R. W. (1994), 'What will new governance mean for the federal government?' *Public Administration Review, 54*, 170–76.

Keon, C. S. (1999), 'Improving responsiveness', *Public Administration Review, 59*, 278–80.

Kettl, Donald F. and Milward, Brinton H. (eds) (1996), *The State of Public Management*, Baltimore, MD: Johns Hopkins University Press.

King, C. S., Feltey, K. M., and Susel, B. O. (1998), 'The question of participation: Toward authentic public participation in public administration', *Public Administration Review, 58*, 317–26.

Lynn, L. E. (1998), 'The new public management: How to transform a theme into a legacy', *Public Administration Review, 58*, 231–7.

Marshall, T. H. (1950), *Citizenship and Social Class and Other Essays*, Cambridge: Cambridge University Press.

Nalbandian, J. (1999), 'Facilitating community, enabling democracy: New roles for local government managers', *Public Administration Review, 59*, 187–97.

National Consumer Council (1986), *Measuring Up: Consumer Assessment of Local Authority Services*, London.

O'Connell, B. (1989), 'What voluntary activity can and cannot do for America', *Public Administration Review, 49*, 486–91.

Osborne, D. and Gaebler, T. (1992), *Reinventing Government*. New York: Plume.

Ott, S. (1998). 'Government reform or alternatives to bureaucracy? Thickening, tides and the future of governing', *Public Administration Review, 58*, 540–45.

Palfrey, C., Phillips, C., Thomas, P., and Edward, D. (1992), *Policy Evaluation in the Public Sector: Approaches and Methods*, Hants: Avenbury.

Peters, G. B. (1996), *The Future of Governing: Four Emerging Models*, Kansas City: University Press of Kansas.

Peters, G. B. (1999), *American Public Policy: Promise and Performance*, New York: Seven Bridges.

Pollitt, C. (1988), 'Bringing consumers into performance measurement', *Policy and Politics, 16*, 77–87.

Pollitt, C. and Bouckaert, G. (2000), *Public Management Reform*, Oxford: Oxford University Press.

Rainey, H. (1990), 'Public management: Recent development and current prospects' in N.B. Lynn and A. Wildavsky (eds), *Public Administration: The State of the Discipline*, (pp.157–84), Chatham, New Jersey: Chatham House.

Rhodes, R. A. W. (1987), 'Developing the public service orientation, or let's add a soupçon of political theory', *Local Government Studies*, May-June: 63–73.

Rimmerman, C. A. (1997), *The New Citizenship: Unconventional Politics, Activism, and Service*, Boulder, CO: Westview Press.

Rosenbloom, D. H., Goldman, D. D., and Ingrahm, P. W. (eds) (1994), *Contemporary Public Administration*, New York; McGraw-Hill.

Rourke, F. E. (1992), 'Responsiveness and neutral competence in American bureaucracy', *Public Administration Review, 52*, 539–46.

Savas, E. S. (1994), 'On privatization' in F. Lane (ed.), *Current Issues in Public Administration*, (pp. 404–13), New York: St. Martin's.

Schneider, A.l. (1990), 'Public–private partnership in the U.S. prison system', *American Behavioural Scientist*, 43, 192-208.

Smith, P. (1993), 'Outcome-related performance indicators and organizational control in the public sector', *British Journal of Management, 4*, 135–51.

Smith, S.R., and Lipsky, M. (1993), *Non-Profits for Hire: The Welfare State in the Age of Contracting*, Cambridge, MA: Harvard University Press.

Stewart, J. and Ranson, S. (1994), 'Management in the public domain' in D. McKevitt and A. Lawton (eds), *Public Sector Management*, (pp. 54–70), London: Sage.

Stivers, C. (1994), *Gender Images in Public Administration: Legitimacy and the Administrative State*, Newbury Park, CA: Sage.

Terry, L. D. (1998), 'Administrative leadership, neo-managerialism, and the public management movement', *Public Administration Review, 58*, 194–200.

Thomas, P. and Palfrey, C. (1996), 'Evaluation: Stakeholder-focused criteria', *Social Policy and Administration, 30*, 125–42.

Thompson, A. A., Tancredi, F. B., and Kisil, M. (2000), 'New partnership for social development: Business and the third sector', *International Journal of Public Administration, 23*, 1359–85.

Thompson, D. (1983), 'Bureaucracy and democracy' in G. Duncan (ed.), *Democratic Theory and Practice*, (pp. 235-50), Cambridge: Cambridge University Press.

Verba, S., Schlozman, K. L., and Brady, H. E. (1995), *Voice and Equality: Civic Voluntarism in American Politics*, London: Harvard University Press.

Vigoda, E. (2000), 'Are you being served? The responsiveness of public administration to citizens' demands: An empirical examination in Israel', *Public Administration, 78*, 165–91.

Vigoda, E. and Golembiewski, R T. (2001), 'Citizenship behavior and the spirit of new managerialism: A theoretical framework and challenge for governance', *American Review of Public Administration, 31*, 273–95.

Weikart, L. A. (2001), 'The Giuliani administration and the new public management in New York City', *Urban Affairs Review, 36*, 359–81.

Winkler, F. (1987), 'Consumerism in health care: Beyond the supermarket model', *Policy and Politics, 15*, 1–8.

PART TWO

Citizenship Involvement and the Workplace

Foreword

This part is devoted to an issue that has been rather neglected for many years but has been gaining more attention recently – the relationship between citizenship involvement and the workplace. More specifically we will be addressing how the behavior and attitudes of employees in the workplace are impacted by their participation in civic activities. In fact, some research on this topic was published in the late twentieth century (that is, Peterson, 1990; Sobel, 1993). The main thesis of this research was that the workplace mirrors the political sphere, both with regard to issues of time and type of activity. Work occurs contemporaneously with politics, and both are formally structured. Roles in the political sphere can train individuals to perform workplace roles because experiences of self-direction or conformity in politics inculcate congruent values and orientations.

The main theory of the research on this relationship is described as a spillover effect (Sobel, 1993). The spillover model states that the nature of one's work experiences will carry over into the non-work domain and affect attitudes and behavior there. It posits transference of beliefs, attitudes and values learned in one setting to another. The degree of involvement at work will be directly related to the degree of involvement in social roles outside of work.

The few studies performed on this topic immediately following Sobel's initial research uncovered some interesting findings that supported the relationship between citizenship involvement and work. However, there were very few subsequent studies. Increased attention to the relationship between work and non-work renewed the interest in the relationship between citizenship involvement and work (Brady et al. 1995; Sobel, 1993) But the more recent studies raised the possibility that the relationship between citizenship involvement and work might operate in a direction opposite to the one examined in the early research. The more current research (Sobel, 1993) suggested that there is also a possibility that intense participation in politics might influence work participation. Brady et al. (1995) elaborated on how experiences in politics can be transferred to work. Political participation can provide the individual with civic skills (communication skills, speech-making skills) that can be relevant to the workplace. The research presented in this section follows the more current trend of research. The chapters examine the relationship between citizenship involvement and work from the point of view that it is citizenship involvement that is related to work behavior and attitudes.

The first chapter presented in this part by Aaron Cohen and Eran Vigoda-Gadot provides a good demonstration of the above approach. This chapter examines the relationship between general citizenship (for example, political participation, community involvement, general altruism and disillusionment with government) and two work outcomes (perceived performance and turnover intentions). Two alternative models were proposed in order to test whether the effect of citizenship behavior and orientations was direct or mediated by participation in decision making. The respondents in this survey were 268 nursing personnel from public health organizations in Israel. Path analysis using LISREL VIII showed that the direct model best fit the data. This model supports the notion that the resources acquired by involvement in the civic setting can be utilized in the work setting. One of the main contributions of this paper is the use of an advanced methodology (Structural Equation Modeling – SEM) to test two alternative conceptual models.

The second chapter, also by Cohen and Vigoda-Gadot, is in a way a partial replication of the above study. Using a regression analysis instead of SEM, it found that civic behavior was related to involvement in the job, the latter represented by a combination of three constructs: organizational commitment, turnover intentions and perceived performance. More specifically, general altruism and disillusionment with government had a significant relationship with involvement in the job.

The third chapter in this section, also by Cohen and Vigoda-Gadot, adds several dimensions to the previous chapters. First in addition to attitudinal work outcomes (job satisfaction, organizational commitment and participation in decision making) it examines actual performance as measured by supervisors' evaluations. Second it tests the interaction effect of gender and political participation on the relationship with work outcomes. Such a test is important because the finding that men are more likely to participate in politics than women is one of the most thoroughly substantiated in the social sciences. The respondents in this study were 200 administrative and medical personnel from one of the major public health organizations in Israel. Supervisors in each of the clinics provided the data on the performance of the employees. The findings of regression analysis showed that in general political behavior was related to important behaviors and attitudes in the work setting. The relationship can be defined as modest but consistent. It is modest because the political behavior variables did not explain a large portion of the variance of the four work outcomes. It is consistent because all work outcomes were related to one or more of the political behavior variables, and this relationship held beyond the effect of the control variables. The findings also showed that the relationship between political behavior and performance and organizational commitment is stronger for females than for males.

REFERENCES

Brady, H.E., Verba, S. and Schlozman, K.L. (1995), 'Beyond SES: A resource model of political participation', *American Political Science Review*, *89*, 71–294.
Peterson, S. A., (1990), *Political Behavior*, California: Sage.
Sobel, R. (1993), 'From occupational involvement to political participation: an exploratory analysis', *Political Behavior*, *15*, 339–53.

3. An Empirical Assessment of the Relationship Between General Citizenship and Work Outcomes[1]

Aaron Cohen and Eran Vigoda-Gadot

INTRODUCTION

The relationship between politics and the work setting has received little conceptual and empirical attention in the literature. However, continuing concern for understanding the origins and consequences of political participation, and the growing interest in studying and developing democracy at work, brought the topic into the 1990s (Sobel, 1993). Several writings in political theory advanced the expectation that political behavior relates to behavior at the workplace (Almond and Verba, 1963; Brady, Verba and Schlozman, 1995; Inkeles, 1969; Pateman, 1970; Peterson, 1990; Sobel, 1993). This argument basically holds that work and politics are in fact similar institutions and therefore experiences in one domain can spill over to the other one. Almond and Verba (1963) and Pateman (1970) argued that structures approximate politics and government more closely when they exist at the same time, possess similar degrees of formality of authority, or have similar criteria for authority positions. The 'closer' two social institutions are, the greater the likelihood of congruence between their authority structures. Congruence lies in the generally analogous formal authority patterns between institutional spheres. The more similar two experiences, the more likely a transference from one to the other (Sobel, 1993). The workplace lies close in time and in kind to the political sphere. Work occurs contemporaneously with politics, and both are formally structured. Roles in the political sphere can train occupants to perform workplace roles because experiences of self-direction or conformity in politics inculcate congruent values and orientations (Pateman, 1970; Almond and Verba, 1963). Golembiewski (1989; 1995) also proposed that work and politics are related domains, arguing that external citizenship (political behavior), internal (organizational) citizenship and administration constitute three interacting competencies that can affect each other. Elden's study (1981) provided empirical support for such a relationship, showing that indicators of work and indicators of citizenship behavior had a strong connection.

Brady, Verba and Schlozman (1995) elaborated on how experiences in one domain can be transferred on. When people perform skill-acts in one institution they increase their ability so that they can engage in still more skill-acts in that or some other domain. Political participation can provide the individual with civic skills relevant to the workplace. People use pre-existing civic skills (education-based organizational and communications skills as well as innate skills) or develop them through their involvement in the institutions of adult life to perform skill-acts (planning meetings, making speeches, etc.), and such civic skills potentially transferable to work. In short, political participation is a learned social role acquired by practice in democratic skills. The more individuals participate, the better able they become to do so. Participation breeds participation and intense participation in politics might influence work participation (Pateman, 1970; Sobel, 1993). Moreover, their participation as citizens has probably guided them to more skills and experiences that may assist them in the workplace (Brady, Verba and Schlozman, 1995; Sobel, 1993; Peterson, 1990).

All the above research assumes, however, that work affects politics, namely one's experiences in the workplace affect one's political behavior (Pateman, 1970; Elden, 1981; Sobel, 1993); that the relationship might also work in the opposite direction is rarely considered. Elden (1981) did suggest that the political behavior of employees would affect their behaviors and attitudes at work, with the argument that workers with a high sense of political efficacy prior to beginning work in an organization may respond more favorably to the opportunity for self-management provided by a new organization's design than workers without such a sense of efficacy. Sobel (1993) elaborated on the notion that intense participation in politics might influence work participation, suggesting as one reason for such a relationship that some people with a personal predisposition to seek authority and activity might do so in both spheres. Research increasingly shows bi-directionality in the relationship between work and nonwork (Frone, Russell and Cooper, 1992; Kirchmeyer, 1992); accordingly this study examines the relationship between general citizenship and two work outcomes, perceived performance and turnover intentions.

This issue, almost absent in public administration literature, has both conceptual and practical implications. Conceptually it can increase our understanding of the relationship between work and nonwork in general, and politics and the work setting in particular. We ask if this relationship is uni-directional, the workplace affecting politics as suggested by Peterson (1990), or bi-directional, in that politics also affects the workplace. The long debate on the relationship between political science and public administration (Golembiewski, 1989; 1995; Whicker, Strickland and Olshafski, 1993) imparts particular importance to this question. Golembiewski (1989; 1995) and Whicker et al. (1993) proposed an important research direction at the interface of public administration and political science on how the political environment influences continuity of goals and policy in public organizations. Testing the effect of politics on work outcomes, as will be done here, is one important way to respond to this challenge.

This research, then, tests in a sample of public employees the relationship between general citizenship and two important work outcomes, namely perceived performance and turnover intentions. Its contribution is threefold: first, it examines the relationship between politics and work from a viewpoint overlooked in the literature, that politics affects work. Second, it tests the possibility that the relationship between politics and work is not direct but more complex. For this purpose we propose and test several models of such a relationship, to ascertain whether and how factors from the civic and political setting account for variations in the levels of work outcomes. Does civic behavior relate directly to work outcomes, or is this relationship more complex and mediated by a variable that represents the work setting? Thirdly, it applies valid and established scales to test these research questions against previous research relying on secondary data, and so applies results from one or two items to measure a given variable (Sobel, 1993).

GENERAL CITIZENSHIP AND WORK OUTCOMES: WHAT IS THE LINKAGE?

Several conceptual frameworks seek to explain how general citizenship relates to behavior at work. Most of the research mentioned above (Pateman, 1970; Peterson, 1990; Sobel, 1993; Brady, Verba and Schlozman, 1995) describes the work–politics relationship as a spillover effect where participation in one arena provides an individual with certain skills and the self-confidence to participate in other areas of social life. Golembiewski (1989; 1995) argued that efforts to energize organizational citizenship require – and promote experience in – attitudes and behaviors also appropriate in other citizenship arenas. The concept of spillover holds the key to the relationship between politics and work, so some elaboration on its nature and its relevance to this research is required. Sieber (1974) classified four types of positive spillover from nonwork to work relevant here. First, certain role privileges or rights are institutionalized within each role along with certain duties. Therefore, the greater the number of roles accumulated, the greater the number of privileges which can be enjoyed. For example, a person who has a formal position in a political party might enjoy higher status and informal privileges at the workplace. A second type of positive spillover, overall status security, stems from the idea that role strain can be buffered by participation in another role. Sieber argued that alternative relationships afford compensatory affection, moral support, emergency resources, and perhaps even assistance for renewal of effort in the original role. Resources for status enhancement and role performance are the third type of positive spillover. Namely the by-products of one role are invested in the other roles so that the expanding resources outweigh the costs of meeting role demands. For example, personal contacts made outside work, as in community services, and certain information obtainable only through nonwork experiences, can be valuable resources for successful work functioning. The fourth type of spillover is personality enrichment or development. Among the benefits arising from wide and varied roles Sieber cites tolerance gained through the recognition of discrepant viewpoints, flexibility required in adjusting to the demands of diverse role partners, and the sense of feeling appreciated by these various partners.

Alongside positive nonwork-to-work spillover, interdomain conflict, an expression of negative spillover, has emerged as a popular area of research (Frone, Russell and Cooper, 1992). Examples of this include: time spent in nonwork domains depleting the time available for work; tension and anxiety produced in nonwork domains reducing performance at work; and behaviors required in nonwork domains proving inappropriate for work (Greenhaus and Beutell, 1985). Such negative spillover effects will result in lower levels of work outcomes.

Direct Relationship Between General Citizenship and Work Outcomes

We test four common dimensions of general citizenship. The first is participation in political activities, which is the classic and one of the most researched constructs in political science (Peterson, 1990). People more involved in political activities like voting, sending support/protest messages to politicians, taking part in political demonstrations, or signing petitions on political issues will presumably be more involved in the work setting. This expectation rests on the argument that such spillover provides resources for role performance. Namely the experience and expertise gained by participating in political activities might make it easier to demonstrate higher levels of work outcomes (Brady, Verba and Schlozman, 1995; Sieber, 1974; Peterson, 1990; Sobel, 1993).

The second dimension tested is participation in community activities. Barber (1984) argued that 'political participation in common action is more easily achieved at the neighborhood level, where there is a variety of opportunities for engagement' (p.303). Recent political science and sociological literature has strongly developed the concept of communitarian involvement as a separate and important dimension of political participation (Barber, 1984; Etzioni, 1995; 1994). Community activity is considered more informal participation than national activity (Sobel, 1993). While certain individual characteristics promote both national and local participation, other personal as well as local community characteristics primarily stimulate participation in local politics (Pettersen and Rose, 1996). Some people may decline to participate in political activities because of dislike or indifference. They may prefer a closer, perhaps more personal domain – the community, with activities such as membership of a tenants' committee or of a parents' school committee. People who are active in their community will presumably demonstrate higher levels of work outcomes than those who are not active; the rationale is similar to that for political participation, although Sieber's (1974) explanation of personality enrichment or development might also apply here. For example, tolerance gained through recognition of discrepant viewpoints might be helpful in the work setting.

The third dimension tested is general altruism, behaviors that show care, kindness, compassion and consideration for other citizens, particularly those needing the support of others. Such behaviors match the definition of loyalty because loyal citizens are expected to volunteer extra effort for the common good, for example, assisting other citizens in need of assistance to perform everyday deeds. Citizens who demonstrate such behavior are expected to display higher levels of work outcomes, in particular since civility seems to represent an altruistic behavior outside the work environment. Sieber's (1974) explanation of personality enrichment or development provides a rationale for the way civility relates to work outcomes. The sensitivity, kindness and consideration people gain and learn in the civil setting will reflect in the work setting.

The fourth dimension, disillusionment with government, illuminates how a citizen adopts the cynical view of government as indifferent, perhaps scornful of him or her. In contrast to the above three it represents more an orientation than a behavior. Political orientations are considered an important aspect of citizenship because they help to shape individuals' understanding of the political world and their place in it (Peterson, 1990). Theiss-Morse (1993) argued that most people apparently engage in the political sphere in ways consistent with their citizenship perspective. Measuring people's perspectives on good citizenship offers greater predictive power, thereby providing better specified models to explain behavior. Van Dyne et al. (1994) tested a variable reflecting cynicism and argued that it could have a pervasive and important effect on a variety of behaviors, including those in the workplace. Those generally cynical about others will assess relationships at work in terms of their own personal advantage. Consequently, these individuals will be unlikely to form a covenantal relationship and accordingly will engage in fewer citizenship behaviors.

Disillusionment with government is defined as the way citizens adopt the cynical view of government as indifferent to the citizen (Schussler, 1982), so this variable well represents loyalty. People cynical about the political system and who do not perceive themselves as capable of influencing it will transfer such an orientation to the work setting as well. A spillover of disillusionment with government to the work setting will result in lower levels of activities in the workplace and in fewer attempts to change things there too.

Work Outcomes

Up to now this chapter has treated work outcomes as one general concept. However, as mentioned earlier, we test two dimensions of work outcomes separately. Performance is the most frequently studied concept in literature on management and on public administration. Most of the concepts developed in public administration and management literature were developed to predict and explain levels of performance. Naturally, this research aims to test this behavior. Turnover, which is considered one of the most important indicators of organizational well-being (Mowday, Porter and Steers, 1982), is the second outcome measure examined in this study in its relationship to general citizenship. Employee turnover is one of the aspects most studied in organizational research (Cotton and Tuttle, 1986; Mitra et al., 1992). Yet no firm conclusions exist as to the turnover process (Cotton and Tuttle, 1986), and results concerning the relationship between variables representing individualistic theories (for example, age, gender and job satisfaction) and turnover (Dalton and Todor, 1993) are rather disappointing. Nonwork influences on staying or leaving (Mowday et al. 1982) have received little attention in turnover research. The relationships between individual nonwork-related variables and turnover are often neglected (Mobley et al., 1979).

Direct Model

All this leads to the first model tested in this study. It represents a direct relationship between general citizenship and the two work outcomes. The first model (Model 1a), termed the *direct relationship model* and presented in Figure 3.1, relates each of the above four variables directly to each of the two dimensions of work outcomes; it represents Graham's (1991) and Sobel's (1993) basic arguments of a direct spillover of general citizenship behavior to the work setting. This model expects a direct relationship between each of the four general citizenship variables and the two outcome variables. It expects no mediating effect of the variable participation in decision making presented in this model. Note that all the above explanations rest on a positive nonwork-to-work approach and therefore positive relationships are expected between each of

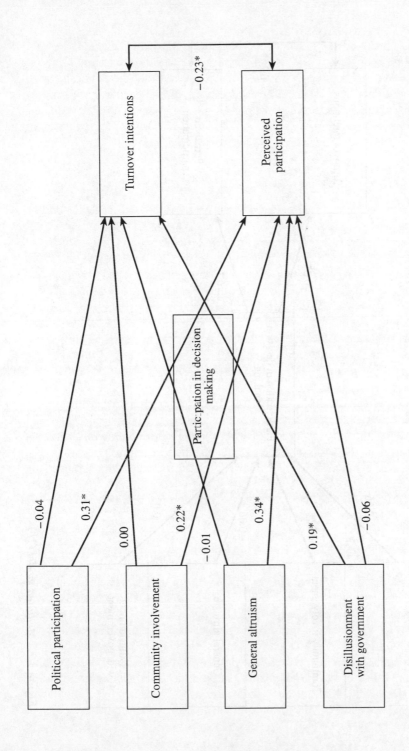

Figure 3.1 Direct model (1a)

67

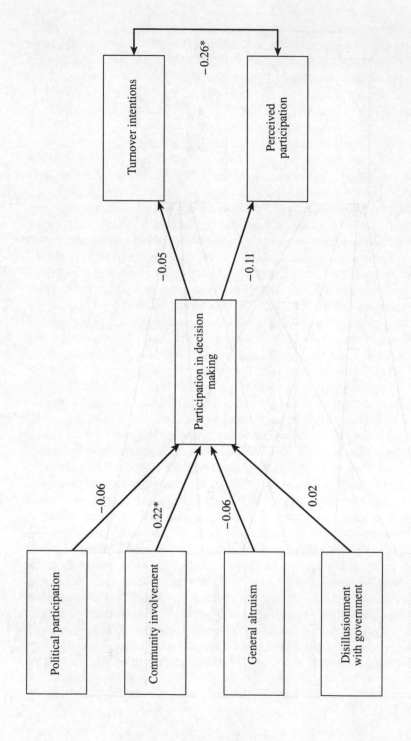

Figure 3.2 Mediated model (1b)

the four general citizenship variables and work outcomes. The present study, based on the findings of previous research (Birnbaum and Somers, 1993; McEvoy and Cascio, 1987; Schwab, 1991) analyses the two work outcomes as distinct but related constructs, as seen in Figure 3.1.

Mediated Model

Political theory also advanced the notion that general citizenship does not relate directly to behavior at work. Brady, Verba and Schlozman (1995) argued that 'the opportunity to practice civic skills in an institution requires both involvement in the institution and a setting that provides the chance to practice some skills' (p.275). Accordingly, citizens as loyal and participating as they may be in the civic setting will not demonstrate similar behavior in the workplace if they feel that the setting is not appropriate. What does an appropriate setting imply in terms of politics-to-work spillover? Van Dyne et al. (1994) made a good attempt to deal with this question. They argued that in the two spheres covenantal relationships are important for sustaining positive relationships between citizens and the state in the political setting and between organizations and their members in the work setting. A covenant is defined as a reciprocal relationship based on ties that bind individuals to their communities and communities to their members (Kanter, 1968). A covenantal relationship differs from a social exchange in that it depends on more than a general notion of fairness. A covenantal relationship requires commitment to the welfare of both parties to the exchange and is also based on values. Political philosophy suggests that the relationship citizens have with their government is critical for their citizenship behavior. The active citizenship syndrome is based on a covenantal relationship, characterized by open-ended commitment, mutual trust and shared values. Van Dyne et al. (1994) stated further that a covenantal relationship is also important in the organizational context. The incompleteness of covenantal contracts, and their emphasis on trust, mutuality and shared values, will lead to high levels of citizenship behavior, perhaps because their open-endedness and lack of specificity elevate motivation and encourage internally driven (intrinsic) motivation. The above arguments showed that a covenantal relationship will enhance political participation in the civic setting and work outcomes in the work setting. Those who participate in politics have developed a covenantal relationship with the government and will probably tend to do the same in the work setting. However, Van Dyne et al.'s (1994) argument suggests that the process of spillover from politics to work might be complex. If the organization does not provide the setting for a covenantal relationship then citizens will not be motivated to contribute in any way. In short, the relationship one has with the organization, or perhaps one's perception of the quality of this relationship, can determine whether one will transfer one's civic skills to a given work setting.

The variable participation in decision making is tested here as representing the type of relationship one has with the organization and therefore as mediator of the relationship between general citizenship and work outcomes. In political theory this variable appears as an essential construct that bridges participation in the civic setting and in the work setting (Elden, 1981; Pateman, 1970; Sobel, 1993). It is also considered a good indicator of fairness and justice in terms of the relationship between an employee and the organization (Farh, Podsakoff and Organ, 1990; Skarlicki and Latham, 1996). The expected relationship between participation in decision making and work outcomes stems from the literature that showed the importance of this construct for the relationship between supervisor and subordinate. Schnake (1991) argued that a leader's supportive behavior may create a need in subordinates to reciprocate. One way to 'pay back' a leader for his or her support is by engaging in citizenship behavior. Employees consider their leader the key representative of the organizational justice process because of his or her frequent contact with them. Thus, a person's sense of fairness would greatly depend on the leader's behavior (Farh, Podsakoff and Organ, 1990; Konovsky and Pugh, 1994; Niehoff and Moorman, 1993; Wayne and Green, 1993). Supervisors can directly influence employees' behaviors by increasing the fairness of their interactions with them (Moorman, 1991). Participation in decision making has proved an important factor contributing to the perception of justice and fairness. Farh, Podsakoff and Organ (1990), for example, applied three indicators to measure subordinates' perceptions of leader fairness; one of them was participative leader's behavior, which measures the degree to which subordinates perceive that their supervisors ask for and use their suggestions in the decision making process. Skarlicki and Latham (1996) proposed increasing participation in decision making as a way to increase perceptions of fairness and justice.

The mediated model, presented in Figure 3.2, relies on political theory (Sobel, 1993) and emphasizes the importance of the variable participation in decision making as the bridge between the civic setting and the work setting (Elden, 1981; Golembiewski, 1985). Accordingly the model expects that the four general citizenship variables will positively affect participation in decision making. Milbrath (1965) described a comparative survey of political participation in five countries that found that in countries with higher levels of political participation there was also a much higher level of social and organizational activity. The same study showed the commutative nature of participation in decisions in nonpolitical organizations: persons participating in decisions in one organization are very likely to participate in decisions in others too. Thus citizens involved in the civic setting will be involved in the decision making process in the organization because of the experiences and the skills they acquired in the former (Brady, Verba and Schlozman, 1995; Pateman, 1970; Peterson, 1990; Sobel, 1993). The following paths demonstrate an exchange relationship. Employees who participate in the decision making process in the organization will feel more involved and reciprocate with positive work outcomes such as higher performance and lower turnover intentions.

METHOD

Subjects and Procedure

Data were collected from a sample of nurses in the north of Israel. The data were collected from three sources that include two hospitals and a group of nurses participating in higher education programs at an Israeli university. A total of 500 questionnaires were distributed; 268 usable questionnaires were returned, a response rate of 54%; 81% of the respondents were females, 60% were married, and 67% had high school education or higher. The average age of the respondents was 34 and the average tenure in the organization was nine years. The demographic characteristics of the samples in the three sources of data are quite similar and therefore it was decided to combine them into one group for the statistical analysis.

Path Analysis

The models regarding the relationships between citizenship behaviors and orientations and work outcomes as presented in Figures 3.1 and 3.2 were assessed by path analysis with LISREL VIII. Estimating a path analysis model for directly observed variables with LISREL differs from the original path analysis technique developed in the 1930s. Rather than estimating each equation separately, LISREL considers the model as a system of equations, and estimates all the structural coefficients directly (Joreskog and Sorbom, 1993). Structural equation programs possess the advantage of their ability to estimate the parameters in a path model while correcting for the biasing effects of random measurement error. Usually structural relationships are estimated among latent variables that are free of measurement errors. This study, however, treated the multi-item scales as single indicators of each construct because of the large number of parameters (46 latent variables) relative to the size of the sample and relative to the structural theoretical parameters (12–20). In view of this decision, we corrected for random measurement errors by equating the random error variance associated with each construct to the product of its variance multiplied by the quantity one minus its estimated reliability (Bollen, 1989). Recent studies adopted this approach (Farkas and Tetrick, 1989; Frone, Russell and Cooper, 1992; Wayne and Ferris, 1990). Moreover, a study (Netemeyer, Johnston and Burton, 1990) supported its use, showing that latent variable analysis yielded virtually identical parameter estimates in terms of direction, magnitude and significance. Results of both of these procedures, however, diverged substantially from the uncorrected single-indicator analysis.

Model Evaluation

Fit indices

Eight indices assessed the fit of the models. The chi-square test is the most basic test and is essential for the nested-model comparison. Because the chi-square test is sensitive to sample size, we used the ratio of the model chi-square to degrees of freedom as another fit index. We considered a ratio of less than 2.0 a fairly good fit for the hypothesized model. Studies report the following fit indices as less sensitive to sample size differences and to the number of indicators per latent variable increase (Medsker, Williams and Holahan, 1994). The relative fit index (RFI) proposed by Bollen (1989) and the comparative fit index (CFI) proposed by Bentler (1990) were developed to facilitate the choice of the best fit among competing models that may differ in degree of parameterization and specification of relations among latent variables, and are recommended as being the best approximation of the population value for a single model. The closer their value to 1 the better the fit. RNI (McDonald and Marsh, 1990) is recommended as more informative in those cases involving model comparison when the RFI (Bollen, 1989) and CFI are not equal. Bentler and Bonett (1980) proposed NFI. Importantly, NFI is additive for the nested-model comparison. The closer its value to 1 the better the fit. NFI has the disadvantage of being affected by sample size. It may not reach 1.0 even when the model is correct, especially in smaller samples. This difficulty was resolved with the modified index called the non-normed fit index (NNFI or TLI) (Bentler and Bonett, 1980), which has the major advantage of reflecting model fit very well at all sample sizes. A value closer to 1 reflects better fit. RMSEA proposed by Browne and Cudeck (1989) tests the null hypothesis of close fit, which is much more meaningful than the null hypothesis of perfect fit. Browne and Cudeck provided the following guidelines: an RMSEA lower than 0.05 indicates 'very good' fit; 0.05 to 0.08 indicates 'fair to mediocre' fit; 0.08 to 0.10 indicates 'poor' fit; an RMSEA greater than 0.10 indicates 'very bad' fit. They deemed RMSEA superior to any of the above goodness-of-fit indexes as a measure of model error.

The magnitude of the path coefficients

The fit of a given model to the data is an important criterion of the quality of the model but it does not necessarily imply that this model is the correct causal model. The path coefficients, their significance, and their magnitude provide an important criterion for model evaluation, termed the plausibility criterion. The plausibility of a model refers to a judgment made about the theoretical argument underlying it. This criterion conditions the decision regarding the correct model also on the theoretical correctness of the model demonstrated by its path coefficients. Accordingly, a model that fits the data well, but many of whose theoretical paths do not support the theoretical arguments of the model, cannot be defined as a correct one. In other words, there has to be some balance between the fit indices and the theoretical predictions regarding the relationships among research variables. The accuracy of the theoretical predictions can be tested by the path coefficients in each of the models. Finally, a correlation matrix among the five commitment forms, using listwise deletion of missing values, formed the input for the path analysis.

FINDINGS

Descriptive Statistics

Table 3.1 presents descriptive statistics and the intercorrelations of the research variables. The data indicate reasonable psychometric properties of the measures used in this study. The correlations among the independent variables are not high except for the correlation between political participation and community involvement (r=0.47; P<0.001) which is very typical of these variables. In general the correlations among the independent variables are quite low and indicate the absence of multicollinearity. This should be noted because although self-report data underlay the variables in this study, with the possibility of source bias or general method variance, the low correlations among the independent variables demonstrate the absence of the latter.

Table 3.2 shows the goodness-of-fit indices for the research models. Model 1a, the direct model, clearly evinces the best fit. The fit indices for this model show a small, non-significant chi-square (1.38); the ratio of chi-square to the degrees of freedom is lower than 2; NFI is 0.98, TLI is 0.94, and CFI is 0.99. The alternative mediated model did not fit the data well. The chi-square is significant (48.20; P< 0.001), indicating lower fit of this model in comparison with the direct model. The other fit indices of the mediated model also indicate a poor fit: NFI is 0.23, TLI is 0.27, and CFI is 0.72.

Figures 3.1 and 3.2 contain the structural coefficients for the models tested. As mentioned in the method section, the path coefficients, their significance, and their magnitude provide the important plausibility criterion for model evaluation. Thus, an additional indication that the direct model was superior to the alternative model appears in its path coefficients in comparison with those of the mediated model. The findings indicate that three of the paths from general citizenship to perceived performance were significant. Political participation had a direct positive relationship with performance (0.31; P<0.05), general altruism also had a positive and significant relationship with perceived performance (0.34; P<0.05). An unexpected finding was the negative path (-0.22; P<0.05) from community involvement to perceived performance, namely higher community involvement led to lower perceived performance. As for turnover intentions, the data indicate that higher disillusionment with government related positively and significantly (0.19; P<0.05) to turnover intentions.

The path coefficients of the mediated model strongly demonstrated the superiority of the direct model. Only one significant path existed in this model, that from community involvement to participation in decision making. All the other path coefficients were not significant, including the two from participation in decision making to perceived performance and turnover intentions. An interesting finding that should be noted is that the significant path from community involvement participation in decision making was positive, in comparison with the negative path it had with perceived performance in the direct model.

DISCUSSION

This chapter has contributed to the testing of important organizational outcomes by using concepts not frequently studied in organizational behavior. Very little research exists on the effects of general citizenship on work outcomes examined from the perspective of political theory. Graham (1991) and Van Dyne et al. (1994) proposed preliminary conceptual arguments for testing such relationships suggesting that some forms of citizenship behaviors can be demonstrated in the organizational setting. This study adopted their argument for the need to look at work outcomes from a political theory perspective. Our findings show in general that good citizens can be good organizational citizens: some forms of general citizenship such as political participation and general altruism have a direct effect on work outcomes. Model 1a, which tested this possibility, showed a very good fit with the data. These, on the other hand, had a poor fit with Model 1b, which argues that the variable participation in decision making strongly filters the effects of general citizenship on work outcomes. The results support the notion that participation in the civic setting furnishes the individual with positive attitudes and valuable skills that are transferred to the work setting. In sum, the findings of this research show the usefulness of concepts adopted from one discipline, political science, to another, organizational behavior.

The literature suggested that the quality of the fit of the models should also be assessed by the magnitude of the individual parameters (Bollen, 1989; Breckler, 1990). Thus, while significant paths are not the only or the main

Table 3.1 Descriptive statistics and intercorrelations for the study variables (reliabilities in parentheses)

Variables	Means	S.D.	1	2	3	4	5	6	7
Independent variables									
1. Political participation	1.87	0.39	(0.73)						
2. Community involvement	1.43	0.47	0.47***	(0.77)					
3. Disillusionment in government	3.06	0.67	−0.18**	−0.01	(0.69)				
4. General altruism	3.77	0.67	0.18**	0.29***	0.12	(0.85)			
5. Participation in decision making	2.17	1.02	0.03	0.15*	0.02	0.02	(0.84)		
Dependent variables									
6. Turnover intentions	2.02	0.99	−0.07	−0.01	0.17*	0.01	−0.04	(0.81)	
7. Perceived performance	4.41	0.64	0.26***	0.04	−0.06	0.30***	−0.09	−0.25***	(0.87)

Notes N = 232– 268 due to missing values; * P ≤ 0.05   ** P ≤ 0.01   *** P ≤ 0.001

75

Table 3.2   Goodness-of-fit summary

Model/Description	df	x^2	x^2/df	RNI	RFI	NFI	TLI	CFI	RMSEA
1. Direct model	2	2.77	1.38	0.99	0.82	0.98	0.94	0.99	0.04
2. Mediated model	8	48.20*	6.02	0.72	0.23	0.71	0.27	0.72	0.15

Note
* $p \leq .001$

criteria for assessing the fit of the models they definitely provide some guidance for future research. This should consider the findings here that indicated significant paths between some forms of general citizenship and work outcomes in the direct model. First, note that general citizenship more strongly relates to perceived performance than to turnover intentions. This is demonstrated in more significant paths between variables representing general citizenship and perceived performance. Overall, general citizenship relates to in-role behavior performed for the sake of the system rather than to behavior aimed at leaving the system. This supports the notion that the spillover relevant to work outcomes is more of the type concerning resources for status enhancement and role performance (Brady, Verba and Schlozman, 1995; Sieber, 1974). Namely the by-products of one role are invested in other roles, so that the resources gained in political participation can be valuable resources for successful work functioning, as found here.

However, the effect of the variables representing general citizenship on work outcomes seems complex and to represent a mixture of both positive and negative spillover. For example, the positive relationship of political participation and general altruism with perceived performance and the expected negative path of disillusionment in government represents more of a positive spillover. That is, skills and attitudes acquired in the civic setting contribute positively to work outcomes. The negative relationship of community involvement with perceived performance represents a negative spillover. This was not expected because we anticipated that skills and experiences acquired by participating in community activities will lead to higher levels of performance. One possible explanation is that this unexpected negative relationship represents conflict stemming from nonwork-to-work spillover, such as time spent in community involvement, which diminishes the time available for work. Namely employees very active in community involvement have less time available for work, and this may cause a lower level of performance and in our case also a lower level of perceived performance.

Among the general citizenship variables, community involvement deserves further attention. The negative relationship between this variable and perceived performance indicates that strictly community involvement seems to have negative consequences for behaviors and attitudes at work. Possible explanations for this finding are of interest. What so differentiates community involvement from the other general citizenship constructs that it results in opposite effects on work attitudes and behaviors? Are people involved in the community because they seek an entirely new role, one to compensate them for what they perceive as negative experiences at work? In this case, is involvement in community so different from political participation? How? A related interesting question stems from the positive path of community involvement to participation in decision making. This leads to the conclusion that community involvement has a more complex relationship with work outcomes. A possible explanation is that community involvement furnishes the individual with skills and attitudes that will increase her/his involvement in the workplace. Namely a person involved in the community will tend to transfer this involvement to the organization. Future research should explore whether or not and in what conditions such involvement will lead to better work outcomes. This study found no support for a positive relationship between participation in decision making and work outcomes. Research on the relationship between citizenship behavior and work outcomes should also consider Putnam's (1993) findings of complex relationships among the dimensions of citizenship. For example, Putnam found that community involvement affects political participation and cynicism. That is, the relationship between some forms of citizenship and work outcomes may not be direct but mediated by other forms of citizenship. Future models should consider and test more complex relationships among citizenship variables in their relationship to work outcomes.

Note too that the data were collected from a homogeneous sample, nursing personnel, in a particular setting, hospitals. Therefore, generalizing beyond the particular work experiences contained in the sample demands caution. With other occupations and/or other organizations the findings might have differed. This is particularly relevant for the variable participation in decision making, the core of the mediated variable. Elden (1981) and Golembiewski (1995) strongly emphasized the importance of this variable for the relationship between citizenship and work. In these data the mean score for participation in decision making was quite low and it provides some indication of rather hierarchical and nonparticipative organizations. Elden (1981) argued that creating a participative environment is a key factor in enhancing participation at work and in civic settings. Thus, the effect of participation in decision making might have been different in more participative organizations. Also, the pattern of the relationships found here will arguably differ in private businesses from public ones like those tested here. For example, employees in private organizations are less secure in their jobs, and this might cause lower levels of participation by them in politics or community. The setting might also affect the relationship between the dependent variables and the two outcome variables. Private organizations operate in a more competitive environment, which may lead to higher levels of performance. Moreover, in private organizations more employees will tend to leave their organization for higher salaries elsewhere. Salaries in public organizations in Israel are stable and job security is the main reward in this sector. All of this might lead to a different pattern of results in private organizations from that in public organizations. These questions should be tested in future research that will compare the models tested here in participative and nonparticipative settings, and in public and private organizations.

Limitations of the Study

Finally, several limitations of this study should be mentioned. First, the use of cross-sectional, correlational data requires that they be interpreted cautiously in terms of the causal inferences concerning the various hypothesized relationships. Second, the study is based on self-report data, incurring the possibility of source bias (for example, social desirability effect) or general method variance. However, we note that the few studies that tested similar concepts as this one (Elden, 1981; Sobel, 1993) were also based on self-report data. This study reported good psychometric properties in terms of reliabilities (Cronbach alphas) and variances of all research variables, which firmly supports the validity of the data and the findings. Third, the data were not collected in a North American setting, although it seems that most research regarding work outcomes has been done in that setting. Therefore, the results might be affected by cultural and structural factors unique to the Israeli setting. For example, the negative effect of community involvement on perceived performance can be partly attributed to cultural and structural characteristics. In addition, the Israeli political system is markedly different from the American, and it is possible that citizenship behaviors will have different effects in different cultures. Therefore, this research should be replicated in other settings before firm conclusions can be made.

Despite its limitations, this study has shown that general citizenship is an important and interesting dimension that should be further explored. Because of the sparse research on the relationship between civic behaviors and work outcomes, future research should further explore this relationship in general and the relationship between civic behavior and work outcomes in particular. The findings of this study have demonstrated the usefulness of examining work outcomes in a conceptual framework developed in another discipline, political science. Research regarding work outcomes has concentrated mostly on contextual work determinants. The relatively low variance encountered in most of that research indicates the need for more work in this area. The contribution of the present study lies in its pointing to some new directions in explaining these important behaviors.

NOTE

1. Based on Cohen and Vigoda (1998), 'An empirical assessment of the relationship between general citizenship and work outcomes', *Public Administration Quarterly*, **21** *(4)*, 401–31. Copyright with permission.

REFERENCES

Almond, G.A. and Verba, S. (1963), *The Civic Culture: Political Attitudes and Democracy in Five Nations: An Analytic Study,* Boston: Little Brown.

Barber, B. (1984), *Strong Democracy: Participatory Politics for a New Age,* Berkeley: University of California Press.

Bentler, P.M. (1990), 'Comparative fit indexes in structural models', *Psychological Bulletin, 107,* 238–46.

Bentler, P.M. and Bonett, D.G. (1980), 'Significance tests and goodness-of-fit in the analysis of covariance structures', *Psychological Bulletin, 88,* 588–606.

Birnbaum, D. and Somers, J.M. (1993), 'Fitting job performance into turnover model: An examination of the form of the job performance-turnover relationship and a path model', *Journal of Management, 19,* 1–11.

Bollen, K.A. (1989), *Structural Equation with Latent Variables,* New York: Wiley.

Brady, H.E., Verba, S., and Schlozman, K.L. (1995), 'Beyond SES: A resource model of political participation', *American Political Science Review, 89,* 271–94.

Breckler, S.J. (1990), 'Applications of covariance structure modelling in psychology: Cause for concern', *Psychological Bulletin, 107,* 260–73.

Browne, M. and Cudeck, R. (1989), 'Single sample cross-validation indices for covariance structure', *Multivariate Behavioral Research, 24,* 445–55.

Cotton, J. L. and Tuttle, J. M. (1986), 'Employee turnover: A meta-analysis and review with implications for research', *Academy of Management Review, 11,* 55–70.

Dalton, D.R. and Todor, W.D. (1993), 'Turnover, transfer, absenteeism: An interdependent perspective', *Journal of Management, 19,* 193–219.

Elden, M. J. (1981), 'Political efficacy at work: The connection between more autonomous forms of workplace organization and a more participatory politics', *American Political Science Review, 75,* 43–58.

Etzioni, A. (1994), *The Spirit of Community,* New York: Touchstone.

Etzioni, A. (1995), *New Communitarian Thinking: Persons, Virtues, Institutions, and Communities,* Charlottesville: University Press of Virginia.

Farh, J.L., Podsakoff, P.M., and Organ, D.W. (1990), 'Accounting for organizational citizenship behavior: Leader fairness and task scope versus satisfaction', *Journal of Management, 16,* 705–21.

Farkas, A.J. and Tetrick, L.E. (1989), 'A three-wave longitudinal analysis of the causal ordering of satisfaction and commitment on turnover decisions', *Journal of Applied Psychology, 74,* 855–68.

Frone, M.R., Russell, M., and Cooper, M.L. (1992), 'Antecedents and outcomes of work–family conflict: Testing a model of the work–family interface', *Journal of Applied Psychology, 77,* 65–78.

Golembiewski, R.T. (1985), *Humanizing Public Organizations,* Mt. Airy, MD: Lomond.

Golembiewski, R.T. (1989), 'Toward a positive and practical public management: Organizational research supporting a fourth critical citizenship', *Administration and Society, 21,* 200–227.

Golembiewski, R.T. (1995), *Practical Public Management,* New York: Marcel Dekker.

Graham, J.W. (1991), 'An essay on Organizational Citizenship Behavior', *Employee Responsibilities and Rights Journal, 4,* 249–70.

Greenhaus, J.H. and Beutell, N.J. (1985), 'Sources of conflict between work and family life', *Academy of Management Review, 10,* 76–88.

Inkeles, A. (1969), 'Participant citizenship in six developing countries', *American Political Science Review, 63*, 1120–41.

Joreskog, K.G. and Sorbom, D. (1993), *Structural Equation Modelling with the SIMPLIS Command Language*, Hillsdale, NJ: Erlbaum.

Kanter, R. M. (1968), 'Commitment and social organization: A study of commitment mechanisms in utopian communities', *American Sociological Review, 33*, 499–517.

Kirchmeyer, C. (1992), 'Nonwork participation and work attitudes: A test of scarcity vs. expansion models of personal resources', *Human Relations, 45*, 775–95.

Konovsky, M.A. and Pugh, S.D. (1994), 'Citizenship behavior and social exchange', *Academy of Management Journal, 37*, 656–69.

McDonald, R. P. and Marsh, H. W. (1990), 'Choosing a multivariate model: Noncentrality and goodness of fit', *Psychological Bulletin, 107*, 247–55.

McEvoy, G.M. and Cascio, W.F. (1987), 'Do good or poor performers leave? A meta-analysis of the relationship between performance and turnover', *Academy of Management Journal, 30*, 744–62.

Medsker, G. J., Williams, L. J., and Holahan, P. J. (1994), 'A review of current practices for evaluating causal models in organizational behavior and human resources management research', *Journal of Management, 20*, 239–64.

Milbrath, L.W. (1965), *Political Participation*, Chicago: Rand McNally.

Mitra, A., Jenkins, G. D., and Gupta, N. (1992), 'A meta-analytic review of the relationship between absence and turnover', *Journal of Applied Psychology, 77*, 879–89.

Mobley, W.H., Rodger, H.G., Hand, H.H. and Meglino, B.M. (1979), 'Review and conceptual analysis of the employee turnover process', *Psychological Bulletin, 86*, 493-537.

Moorman, R.H. (1991), 'Relationship between organizational justice and organizational citizenship behaviors: Do fairness perceptions influence employee citizenship?' *Journal of Applied Psychology, 76*, 845–55.

Mowday, R.T., Porter, L.M., and Steers, R.M. (1982), *Employee–Organization Linkages: The Psychology of Commitment, Absenteeism and Turnover*, New York: Academic Press.

Netemeyer, R.G., Johnston, M.W., and Burton, S. (1990), 'Analysis of role conflict and role ambiguity in a structural equation framework', *Journal of Applied Psychology, 75*, 148 57.

Niehoff, B.P. and Moorman R.H. (1993), 'Justice as a mediator of the relationship between methods of monitoring and organizational citizenship behavior', *Academy of Management Journal, 36*, 527–56.

Pateman, C. (1970), *Participation and Democratic Theory*, London: Cambridge University Press.

Peterson, S. A. (1990), *Political Behavior*, Newbury Park, CA: Sage.

Pettersen, P.A. and Rose, L.E. (1996), 'Participation in local politics in Norway: Some do, some don't, some will, some won't', *Political Behavior, 18*, 51–97.

Putnam, R.D. (1993), *Making Democracy Work*, Princeton: Princeton University Press.

Schnake, M. (1991), 'Organizational citizenship: A review, proposed model, and research agenda', *Human Relations, 44*, 735–59.

Schussler, K.F. (1982), *Measuring Social Life Feelings*, San Francisco: Jossey Bass.

Schwab, D.P. (1991), 'Contextual variables in employee performance–turnover relationships', *Academy of Management Journal, 34*, 966–75.

Sieber, S.D. (1974), 'Toward a theory of role accumulation', *American Sociological Review, 39*, 567–78.

Skarlicki, D.P. and Latham, G.L. (1996), 'Increasing citizenship behavior within a labor union: A test of organizational justice theory', *Journal of Applied Psychology, 81*, 161–9.

Sobel, R. (1993), 'From occupational involvement to political participation: An exploratory analysis', *Political Behavior, 15*, 339–53.

Theiss-Morse, E. (1993), 'Conceptualizations of good citizenship and political participation', *Political Behavior, 15*, 355–80.

Van Dyne, L., Graham, J.W., and Dienesch, R.M. (1994), 'Organizational Citizenship Behavior: Construct redefinition, measurement, and validation', *Academy of Management Journal, 37*, 765–802.

Wayne, S.J. and Ferris, G.R. (1990), 'Influence tactics, affect, and exchange quality in supervisor–subordinate interactions: A laboratory experiment and field study', *Journal of Applied Psychology, 75*, 487–99.

Wayne, S.J. and Green, S.A. (1993), 'The effects of leader–member exchange on employee citizenship and impression management behavior', *Human Relations, 46*, 1431–40.

Whicker, M.L., Strickland, R.A., and Olshafski, D.O. (1993), 'The troublesome cleft: Public administration and political science', *Public Administration Review, 53*, 531–41.

4. The Growth Value of Good Citizenship: An Examination of the Relationship Between Civic Behavior and Orientations and Work Outcomes[1]

Aaron Cohen and Eran Vigoda-Gadot

LOCAL CIVIC BEHAVIOR AND WORK OUTCOMES

This study examined the relation between a set of civic behaviors and employees' work outcomes. The first dimension of citizenship behavior to be discussed and tested is participation in the local setting. Barber (1984) argued that '...political participation in common action is more easily achieved at the neighborhood level, where there is a variety of opportunities for engagement' (p.303). The recent political science and sociological literature has strongly developed the concept of communitarianism as a separate and important dimension of political participation (Barber, 1984; Etzioni, 1995; 1994). Participation in community activities is considered a more informal form of participation than participation in national activities (Sobel, 1993). While participation in local politics depends on certain individual characteristics that serve to promote both national and local participation, there are other personal as well as local community characteristics that primarily stimulate participation in local politics (Pettersen and Rose, 1996). Some people may decline to participate in political activities because they either dislike or are indifferent to politics. They might prefer to participate in a closer, perhaps more personal domain: the community, which can offer them activities such as membership of a tenants' committee or of a parents' school committee. The expectation is that people who are active in their community will demonstrate higher levels of work outcomes than those who are not active. The rationale is similar to that described for political participation, although Sieber's (1974) explanation of personality enrichment or development might also be relevant here. For example, the tolerance gained through the recognition of discrepant viewpoints might be helpful in similar situations in the work setting. Thus, the first hypothesis (H1) suggests that community involvement will be positively related to work outcomes.

The second dimension to be tested is general altruism. The focus here is on civic behaviors that show care, kindness, compassion and consideration toward other citizens, in particular those who need the support of others. Such behaviors match the definition of loyalty because loyal citizens are expected to volunteer extra effort for the common good, for example, assisting other citizens who need assistance in performing daily activities. Citizens who demonstrate such behavior are expected to exert higher levels of work outcomes, in particular since general altruism seems to represent an altruistic behavior outside the work environment. Sieber's (1974) explanation of personality enrichment or development provides a rationale for the way general altruism will be related to work outcomes. The sensitivity, kindness and consideration people acquire and learn in the civil setting will also be reflected in the work setting. Thus, the second hypothesis (H2) suggests that general altruism will be positively related to work outcomes.

The third dimension is community commitment. This variable differs from the previous two in that it represents more of an orientation than a behavior. In this regard the same rationale proposed for the variable disillusionment with government, which is also an attitude, is also relevant for community commitment. As argued by Theiss-Morse (1993), much predictive power is gained by measuring people's perspectives on good citizenship, with the consequent provision of better specified models to explain behavior. The difference is that community commitment concentrates on the local arena, and that it represents a positive attitude to that focus. People who identify with the community are expected to transfer such an orientation to the work setting as well. A spillover of community commitment to the work setting will result in higher levels of positive attitudes toward the workplace. Thus, hypothesis 3 (H3) suggests that community commitment will be positively related to work outcomes.

NATIONAL CIVIC BEHAVIOR AND WORK OUTCOMES

Classical thinking regarding the relationship between politics and work has concentrated on concepts from the national arena as indicators of politics. Three common dimensions of civic behavior in the national arena are tested: political participation, political efficacy and disillusionment with government. Political participation is the classic and one of the most researched constructs in political science (Peterson, 1990). The expectation is that people who are more involved in political activities like voting, sending support/protest messages to politicians, taking part in political demonstrations, or signing petitions on political issues will be more involved in the work setting. This expectation is based on the argument that such spillover provides resources for role performance. That is, the experience and expertise gained by participating in political activities might provide good tools to make it easier to demonstrate higher levels of work outcomes (Brady, Verba and Schlozman, 1995; Sieber, 1974; Peterson, 1990; Sobel, 1993). Thus, hypothesis 4 (H4) suggests that political participation will be positively related to work outcomes.

Niemi, Craig and Mattei (1991) argued that of the different concepts dealing with the individual's attitudes toward politics, political efficacy is the most important; therefore it has received much attention in the literature. Political efficacy refers to the individual's perception of her/his ability to influence political officials and the political system by the belief that with personal effort they can affect the political system (Barner and Rosenwein, 1985). Milbrath and Goel (1977) argued that political efficacy is part of the sense of mastery a child acquires during socialization. Political efficacy includes two related dimensions: internal efficacy and external efficacy (McPherson, Welch and Clark, 1977). Internal efficacy refers to one's belief in one's ability and competence to understand political processes and to take part in them. External efficacy refers to one's belief that the political system and political officials are responsive to one's attempts to influence it and that citizens' demands do affect governance. Conceptually, political efficacy should be related to political participation. Someone with high internal and external efficacy will be highly motivated to participate in the political system. Therefore, there is strong reason to expect that political efficacy will also be related to work outcomes based on the same rationale proposed for political participation. Thus, hypothesis 5 (H5) suggests that political efficacy will be positively related to work outcomes.

Disillusionment with government reflects the way citizens adopt the cynical view of government as indifferent to the citizen, perhaps scornful of him or her. It differs from the above three factors in that it represents more of an orientation than a behavior. Political orientations are considered an important aspect of citizenship because they help to shape individuals' understanding of the political world and their place in it (Peterson, 1990). Theiss-Morse (1993) argued that most people are apparently involved in the political sphere in ways consistent with their citizenship perspective. Her study showed that high predictive power is gained by measuring people's perspectives on good citizenship, with the resulting provision of better specified models to explain behavior. Van Dyne, Graham and Dienesch (1994) tested a variable reflecting cynicism, and argued that it could have a pervasive and important effect on a variety of behaviors, including those in the workplace. They argued that those who are generally cynical about others will assess relationships at work in terms of their own personal advantage. As a result, these individuals will be unlikely to form a covenantal relationship, and accordingly will engage in fewer citizenship behaviors. Disillusionment with government is defined as the way citizens adopt the cynical view of government as indifferent to the citizen (Schussler, 1982). In keeping with the above definition this variable is a good representation of loyalty. People who are cynical about the political system and do not perceive themselves as capable of influencing it will transfer such an orientation to the work setting as well. A spillover of disillusionment with government to the work setting will result in lower levels of activities in the workplace and in fewer attempts to change things there too. Thus, hypothesis 6 (H6) suggests that disillusionment with government will be negatively related to work outcomes.

While the general hypotheses of this research are that the direction and the intensity of the effects of civic behavior and orientations will operate equally in relation to all work outcomes mentioned above, it may be expected that the relationship between local civic behavior and work outcomes will be stronger than the relationship between national civic behavior and work outcomes. This is because one probably participates more in local activities since they are handier and therefore easier to access than national ones. Moreover, issues in the community such as education (school) and neighborhood matters have an immediate effect on one's life and therefore one will be more motivated to become involved in the local setting. Participation in local activities may thus be expected to furnish the individual with more skills and resources that are relevant to the work setting. Thus, hypothesis 7 (H7) suggests that participation in local activities will be more strongly related to work outcomes than participation in national activities.

THE MODERATOR EFFECT OF GENDER, AGE AND EDUCATION

We expect that some of the relationships between civic behavior and work outcomes will not be direct but moderated. Political science literature suggests that civic behavior variables may operate differently for different groups, and this provides the grounds to expect differential relationships of these variables with work outcomes. The finding that men are more likely to participate in politics than women is one of the most thoroughly substantiated in social sciences (Peterson, 1990; Milbrath, 1965). Research has shown that females are less politically effectual and less involved in politics (Peterson, 1990). Data supporting this proposition come from at least nine countries (Milbrath, 1965). Although economic and social modernization is slowly eroding this gender difference (Milbrath, 1965), females are still expected to be found less politically involved, particularly in Israeli society that is generally more conservative than North American society. Therefore, it can be expected that the above relationship will operate differently for males and females. Accordingly the effect of variables representing civic behavior and orientation on work outcomes is expected to be stronger for males than for females. Political science literature also indicates that political participation differs for younger and older citizens (Milbrath, 1965), the latter participating more than the former. Two reasons are suggested for this effect of age. First, integration with the community develops gradually with marriage, job responsibility and acquiring a family. Second, older people have more time available for politics than younger people, who are occupied, for example, by young children and other obligations. This is so especially for young mothers. Research findings also indicate that those with higher education will tend to participate more in politics. Many reasons were advanced for such an effect (Milbrath, 1965; Almond and Verba, 1963; Brady, Verba and Schlozman, 1995), but space limitations allow only some of them to be presented here. First, the more educated person is more aware of the impact of government on the individual than is the person of lesser education. Second, the more educated individual has more political information. Third, the more educated individual has opinions over a wider range of political subjects; the focus of her/his attention to politics is broader. Fourth, the more educated individual is more likely to engage in political discussion. In sum, it can be expected that the relationship between civic behavior and work outcomes will differ by gender, age and level of education in the lines outlined above. Thus, hypothesis 8 (H8) suggests that the effect of civic behavior variables on work outcomes will be stronger for males than for females, for older than for younger employees, and for more educated than for less educated employees.

THE EXAMINATION OF WORK OUTCOMES

Finally, three dimensions of work outcomes are tested here; perceived performance, turnover intentions and organizational commitment. Performance was tested here as it represents one of the most frequently studied variables in literature on management and on public administration.. Turnover, which is considered one of the most important indicators of organizational well-being (Mowday, Porter and Steers, 1982), is another outcome examined in this study in its relationship to general citizenship. Another work attitude that is researched frequently is organizational commitment, defined as the strength of attachment to an organization and reflecting a psychological state more than overt behavior (O'Reilly and Chatman, 1986). Organizational commitment was found to be an important resource of public organizations (Romzek and

Hendricks, 1982; Romzek, 1985), and it is tested as another work outcome in its relationship to civic and political behavior.

METHOD

The data for this study was similar to that in the previous chapter. Research hypotheses were tested by hierarchical regression analysis, conducted in the following steps: first the control variables (age, education, gender and number of children) were entered into the equation. In the second step the three local civic behavior variables (community involvement, general altruism, community commitment) were entered. In the third step the three national civic behavior variables (political participation, political efficacy and disillusionment with government) were entered. Steps 1, 2 and 3 tested hypotheses 1–7. In the fourth step, six two-way interactions were entered into the equation (political participation*gender, political efficacy*gender, disillusionment with government*gender, community involvement*gender, general altruism* gender, community commitment*gender). The same procedure was performed for the variables age and education. Thus, 18 possible interactions were tested for each of the three work outcome variables in order to test hypothesis 8 regarding the interaction effect of gender, education and age. Altogether, 54 possible interactions were tested.

FINDINGS

Table 4.1 presents descriptive statistics and the intercorrelations of the research variables. The data indicate reasonable psychometric properties of the measures used in this study. The correlations among the independent variables are quite low and indicate the absence of multicollinearity. This should be noted because despite the fact that most of the variables in this study were based on self-report data, which allows source bias or general method variance, the low correlations among the independent variables demonstrate the absence of common method variance in these data.

Table 4.2 presents the results of the regression analyses for work outcomes as the dependent variables, and the control variables and civic behavior variables as the independent variables. The control variables were entered into the equations in step 1 in each of the regressions. Note the consistent effect of the control variables: only number of children had a significant effect on organizational commitment and perceived performance, explaining 10% and 7% of the variance respectively. The other control variables had no effect on work outcomes.

In step 2 the three local civic behavior variables were entered into each of the equations. The findings show that two of the three local participation variables had a significant effect on perceived performance, namely community involvement and general altruism. However, the direction of the effect of community involvement was negative and contradicts Hypothesis 1, which expected a positive relationship. That is, the finding here indicated that more community involvement decreased perceived performance. Hypothesis 2 was strongly supported by the strong and positive relationship of general altruism to perceived performance as shown in Table 4.2. The nonsignificant coefficient of community commitment indicates no support for Hypothesis 3, which expected a positive relationship between community commitment and perceived performance. For turnover intentions, the results of step 2 showed a nonsignificant effect by all of the three local civic behavior variables. This finding refutes Hypotheses 1-3 for the variable turnover intentions. For organizational commitment, the results of step 2 show that the variable general altruism had a positive effect on commitment. This finding supports Hypothesis 2 for the variable organizational commitment. No support was found for Hypotheses 1 and 3 because of the nonsignificant coefficients of community involvement and community commitment with organizational commitment.

The three national behavior variables were entered into each of the equations in step 3. The findings show that the variable political participation had a significant effect on perceived performance. Greater political participation increased perceived performance. This finding supports Hypothesis 4. No support was found for Hypotheses 5 and 6, which expected a significant relationship of political efficacy and disillusionment with government perceived performance. None of the coefficients of these variables was significant. For the variables turnover intentions and organizational commitment, the results of step 3 showed a similar pattern of relationship, that is, an expected significant relationship of the variable disillusionment with government with both of them. A stronger perception of disillusionment with government led to a stronger intention to leave the organization and to lower level of organizational commitment. This finding supports Hypothesis 6. No support was found for Hypotheses 4 and 5 for turnover intentions and commitment, as the variables political participation and political efficacy were not related to either of them.

Hypothesis 7 expected that variables representing participation in local activities would be more strongly related to work outcomes than variables representing participation in national activities. This was partly supported only for the variable perceived performance. Two of the local civic behaviors, community involvement and general altruism, were significantly related to this variable, as against only one variable representing national civic behavior, namely political participation. Regarding organizational commitment, one

Table 4.1 Descriptive statistics and intercorrelations among research variables (reliabilities in parentheses)

Variables	Means	S.D.	1	2	3	4	5	6	7	8	9	10	11	12
Dependent variables														
1. Perceived performance	4.41	0.64	(0.87)											
2. Turnover intentions	2.02	0.99	−0.27**	(0.81)										
3. Organizational commitment	3.49	0.74	0.34**	−0.48	(0.82)									
Independent variables														
4. Political participation	1.87	0.37	0.25**	−0.05	0.01	(0.73)								
5. Political efficacy	2.94	0.68	0.07	0.04	0.03	0.40**	(0.64)							
6. Disillusionment with government	3.08	0.67	−0.05	0.14*	−0.15*	−0.19**	0.00	(0.79)						
7. Community involvement	1.43	0.47	0.04	−0.00	0.05	0.48***	0.24**	−0.04	(0.77)					
8. General altruism	3.77	0.67	0.32**	−0.02	0.15*	0.18*	0.11	0.11	0.29**	(0.85)				
9. Community commitment	2.53	0.97	0.14*	−0.01	−0.01	0.39***	0.20**	0.02	0.46***	0.29**	(0.68)			

Table 4.1 *(continued)*

Variables	Means	S.D.	1	2	3	4	5	6	7	8	9	10	11	12
Control variables														
10. Gender (female)	0.81	0.39	0.08	−0.07	0.02	−0.04	−0.18**	0.14*	0.00	0.12	0.09			
11. Age	33.51	10.90	0.8**	−0.21**	0.24**	0.16*	0.05	−0.01	0.11	0.03	−0.02	−0.06		
12. Education	2.82	1.05	0.02	−0.09	−0.09	0.24**	0.28**	−0.09	0.13*	−0.02	0.03	−0.14*	−0.03	
13. Number of children	1.32	1.39	0.24**	−0.18**	0.29**	0.20**	0.07	−0.02	0.018**	0.08	0.09	−0.10	0.62	−0.08

Notes
N = 235–268 due to missing values
*p < 0.05   **p < 0.01   ***p < 0.001

Table 4.2 Multiple regression analyses (standardized coefficients) of civic behavior variables on work outcomes

	Perceived performance			Turnover intentions			Organizational commitment		
	Step 1	Step 2	Step 3	Step 1	Step 2	Step 3	Step 1	Step 2	Step 3
Control variables									
Age	0.05	0.07	0.05	−0.14	−0.14	−0.15	0.09	0.09	0.10
Education	−0.05	−0.07	−0.02	−0.11	−0.12	−0.13	−0.06	−0.05	−0.06
Gender (female)	0.11	0.07	0.08	−0.10	−0.11	−0.11	0.04	0.03	0.06
Number of children	0.21*	0.19*	0.17*	−0.12	−0.13	−0.13	0.24**	0.23**	0.24***
Local civic behavior									
Community involvement		−0.14*	−0.22**		0.06	0.05		−0.01	0.01
General altruism		0.31***	0.31***		−0.02	−0.04		0.15*	0.17*
Community commitment		0.09	0.04		−0.00	−0.02		−0.07	−0.05

Table 4. 2 (continued)

National civic behavior	Perceived performance			Turnover intentions			Organizational commitment		
	Step 1	Step 2	Step 3	Step 1	Step 2	Step 3	Step 1	Step 2	Step 3
Political participation			0.24**			0.02			−0.12
Political efficacy			−0.02			0.06			0.08
Disillusionment with government			−0.06			0.15*			−0.20**
R^2 (Adjusted)	0.07 (0.05)	0.17 (0.14)	0.22 (0.18)	0.07 (0.05)	0.07 (0.04)	0.10 (0.06)	0.10 (0.08)	0.12 (0.09)	0.16 (0.12)
F	4.10**	6.46***	5.92***	4.08**	2.40*	2.78**	6.01***	4.18***	4.06***
ΔR^2		0.10	0.05		0.00	0.03		0.02	0.04
F Change		9.01***	4.05***		0.21	2.08		1.68	3.43*

Notes
N = 235–268 due to missing values
* p ≤0.05   ** p ≤0.01   *** p ≤0.001

93

Table 4.3 Interaction findings (standardized coefficients)

Interaction	Perceived performance		Turnover intentions		Organizational commitment	
	Political efficacy × Gender	Disillusionment with government × Education	Political participation × Gender	Disillusionment with government × Age	Political efficacy × Gender	Political efficacy × Age
Control variables						
Age	0.08	0.03	−0.10	0.14	0.13	−0.63*
Education	0.01	−0.03	−0.13	−0.14*	−0.07	−0.05
Gender (female)	0.13*	0.09	−0.10	−0.13	0.11	0.08
Number of children	0.17*	0.18*	−0.17*	−0.14	0.23**	0.25**
Local civic behavior						
Community involvement	−0.22**	−0.20**	0.02	0.05	0.00	0.02
General altruism	0.33***	0.31***	−0.01	−0.05	0.18**	0.16*
Community commitment	0.02	0.04	−0.01	−0.01	−0.07	−0.04

Table 4.3 (continued)

Interaction	Perceived performance		Turnover intentions		Organizational commitment	
	Political efficacy × Gender	Disillusionment with government × Education	Political participation × Gender	Disillusionment with government × Age	Political efficacy × Gender	Political efficacy × Age
National civic behavior						
Political participation	0.24**	0.24**	0.39*	0.02	−0.12	−0.15
Political efficacy	0.37*	−0.03	0.07	0.06	0.47**	0.08
Disillusionment with government	−0.05	−0.10	0.14*	0.18**	−0.19**	−0.21**
Interaction	−0.41***	0.22**	−0.42**	0.17**	−0.42**	0.55**
R^2 (Adjusted)	0.24(0.20)	0.26(0.22)	0.13(0.09)	0.12(0.08)	0.18(0.14)	0.17(0.13)
F	6.22***	6.86***	2.92**	2.78**	4.43***	4.08***

Notes
N = 235–268 due to missing values
* $p \leq 0.05$ ** $p \leq 0.01$ *** $p \leq 0.001$

variable from each category was related to it. Regarding turnover intentions only one variable representing national civic behavior was related to it.

INTERACTION EFFECTS

In the final step the interaction variables were entered. As mentioned in the method section, a possible interaction of each of the six civic behavior variables with gender, age and education was tested for each of the outcome variables, that is, 18 possible interactions for each outcome variable, hence 54 together.

General Overview of the Interaction Effects

The findings revealed six significant interactions out of the 54 possible that were tested. These six are presented in Table 4.3. As may be seen, two interactions were found for each of the outcome variables. An interesting finding in that regard is that only for the national civic behavior variables were significant interactions found. No significant interaction was found with any of the local civic behavior variables.

Table 4.3 shows that two interactions were found for perceived performance. The first one is political efficacy*gender, and the second one is disillusionment with government * education. A detailed examination of the first interaction generated by plotting it (Aiken and West, 1991) revealed that for males stronger political efficacy increased perceived performance, while this variable did not affect perceived performance for females.

The pattern of the second interaction revealed that for employees with lower levels of education, stronger perception of disillusionment with government increased perceived performance more than it did for employees with higher levels of education. The first interaction for turnover intentions was political participation*gender. The pattern of this interaction revealed that stronger political participation increased turnover intentions more for males than for females.

The pattern of the second interaction, disillusionment with government*age, revealed that stronger perceptions of disillusionment with government increased turnover intentions much more for older employees than for younger ones.

The two interactions for the variable organizational commitment involve political efficacy. They showed that stronger political efficacy increased organizational commitment more for males and for older employees than for females and younger employees.

Summary of the Interaction Effects

Overall, the findings of Tables 4.2 and 4.3 show that variance explained by the independent variables varied for each of the dependent variables. Relatively high variance was explained for perceived performance, 22%. The lowest explained variance was for turnover intentions, 10%. The explained variance for organizational commitment was 16%. The findings also showed that the civic behavior variables had basically a main effect on outcomes, as demonstrated by only six significant interactions out of the 54 that were possible.

DISCUSSION

The findings of this study show in general that civic behavior is related to important attitudes in the work setting. They support the notion that participation in the civic setting furnishes the individual with positive attitudes and valuable skills that can be transferred to the work setting.

The relationship found here can be defined as modest but consistent. It is modest because the political behavior variables did not explain a large portion of the variance of the three work outcomes. It is consistent because all work outcomes were related to one or more of the political behavior variables, and this relationship held beyond the effect of the control variables.

Note that the political behavior variables were not expected to explain a large portion of the variance because research shows that the three outcome variables studied here are related more strongly to work situational variables (Mowday, Porter and Steers, 1982; Griffin and Bateman, 1986; Wayne and Ferris, 1990; Wayne and Green, 1993). Yet the findings here show that variables representing political behavior should be included in future models of work outcomes because they do add to our understanding of behavior at work.

Contribution of the Study

One of the contributions of this chapter was the testing of important work outcomes by using concepts not frequently applied in management research. There is very little research on the effects of political behaviors and orientations on work outcomes examined from the perspective of political theory. Preliminary conceptual arguments for testing such relationships were proposed by Graham (1991), who suggested that some forms of citizenship behaviors can be demonstrated in the organizational setting.

The findings here showing that variables representing political behavior were useful in predicting important work outcomes are in line with those of

Kirchmeyer (1992), who found that resources made available for work by participation in community activities positively affected organizational commitment, and time commitment to community activities positively affected job satisfaction. These findings, together with the findings of this research, support the expansion or the spillover hypothesis, according to which individuals tend to cope with increasing organizational and extra-organizational role demands by responding positively to those demands (Randall, 1988). Adding new roles liberates a source of energy for the individual, and rather than having to pay for extensive social involvements, individuals may come away from new involvements more enriched and vitalized. The positive relationships between political behavior variables and work outcomes indicate that more political involvement increases perceived performance and organizational commitment, and reduces turnover intentions.

In sum, the findings of this research show the usefulness of concepts adopted from one discipline, political science, for another, organizational behavior. However, the relationship between political behavior and work outcomes seems to be complex, as demonstrated in two important findings. The first concerns the interaction effects. This study showed that while most of the relationships between civic behavior and work outcomes are direct, some of them are more complex, in particular the national civic outcomes. The fact that only the national civic behavior variables had a more complex effect on outcomes is interesting and deserves attention in future research.

A possible explanation is that issues in the community such as education (school) and neighborhood matters have a more immediate effect on one's life, and therefore one will be more motivated to become involved in the local setting. As a result, most people experience this or some other form of local civic behavior. Therefore these constructs exert more of a main effect.

However, fewer people participate, are involved, or even care for issues regarding the national level, and the effect of national civic behavior will vary depending on aspects that determine lower or higher participation on the national level such as age, gender and education. This explanation should be tested in future research.

Second, the findings here seem to represent a mixture of both positive and negative spillover. While the positive relationship of general altruism and political participation with work outcomes represents positive spillover, the negative relationship of community involvement with performance represents negative spillover. This negative effect shows that strictly community involvement seems to have negative consequences for behaviors and attitudes at work.

It would be interesting to explore possible explanations for this finding. In what way does community involvement differ from the other civic behaviors and orientations so that it results in opposite effects on work outcomes? Is it that people are involved in the community because they are looking for an entirely new role, one that will compensate them for what they perceive as negative experiences at work? And in that case, is involvement in the community so different from political participation? If so, how? Future research should deal with these questions conceptually and empirically.

Limitations of the Study

Finally, this study is not free of limitations. First and most importantly, the data were not collected in a North American setting, while it seems that most research regarding work outcomes has been done in that setting. Therefore, the results might be affected by cultural and structural factors unique to the Israeli setting. For example, the Israeli political system is quite distinct from the American, and it is possible that political behavior will have different effects in different cultures.

Therefore, this research should be replicated in other settings before firm conclusions can be made. Second, the design of this research is cross-sectional and any conclusions regarding causality should be treated with caution. Future research regarding the relationship between politics and work would benefit from a longitudinal research design able to illuminate the nature of this relationship. That is, do civic and political behaviors affect work more strongly than the reverse, or is the relationship perhaps bi-directional?

FINAL COMMENTS

Despite its limitations, the findings of this study have demonstrated the usefulness of examining work outcomes from a non-conventional perspective. The results of this study support Kirchmeyer's (1992) conclusion that to truly understand the individual at work, one must consider not only her or his work life but also her or his life away from work too.

Near, Rice and Hunt (1980) concluded that extra-work conditions greatly affect reactions to work. So far, research regarding work outcomes has concentrated mostly on situational determinants. The relatively low variance that has been accounted for in most of this research showed that more work is needed in this area. The contribution of this research lies in its pointing out some new directions for better explaining these important behaviors.

NOTE

1. Based on Cohen and Vigoda (1998), 'The growth value of good citizenship: An examination of the relationship between civic behavior and involvement in the job', *Applied Psychology: An International Review*, **47**, 559–70. Copyright with permission from the International Association of Applied Psychology.

REFERENCES

Aiken, L.S. and West, S.G. (1991), *Multiple Regression: Testing and Interpreting Interactions*, Newbury Park, CA: Sage Publications.

Almond, G.A. and Verba, S. (1963), *The Civic Culture: Political Attitudes and Democracy in Five Nations: An Analytic Study*, Boston: Little Brown.

Barber, B. (1984), *Strong Democracy: Participatory Politics for a New Age*, Berkeley: University of California Press.

Barner, C. and Rosenwein, F. E. (1985), *Psychological Perspectives on Politics*, Englewood, NJ: Prentice Hall.

Brady, H.E., Verba, S., and Schlozman, K.L. (1995), 'Beyond SES: A resource model of political participation', *American Political Science Review*, **89**, 271–94.

Etzioni, A. (1994), *The Spirit of Community*, New York: Touchstone.

Etzioni, A. (1995), *New Communitarian Thinking: Persons, Virtues, Institutions, and Communities*, Charlottesville: University Press of Virginia.

Graham, J.W. (1991), 'An essay on organizational citizenship behavior', *Employee Responsibilities and Rights Journal*, **4**, 249–70.

Griffin, R. W. and Bateman, T. S. (1986), 'Job satisfaction and organizational commitment' in C. L. Cooper and I. Robertson (eds), *International Review of Industrial and Organizational Psychology* (pp. 157–88), New York: John Wiley and Sons Ltd.

Kirchmeyer, C. (1992), 'Nonwork participation and work attitudes: A test of scarcity vs. expansion models of personal resources', *Human Relations*, **45**, 775–95.

McPherson, J., Welch, S., and Clark, C. (1977), 'The stability and reliability of political efficacy, using path analysis to test alternative models', *Political Science Review*, **71**, 509–21.

Milbrath, L.W. (1965), *Political Participation*, Chicago: Rand McNally and Company.

Milbrath, L.W. and Goel M. L. (1977), *Political Participation: How and Why Do People Get Involved in Politics* (2nd edn), Chicago: Rand McNally College Pub. Co.

Mowday, R. T., Porter, L. M., and Steers, R. M. (1982), *Employee–Organizational Linkage*, New York: Academic Press.

Near, J.P., Rice, R.W. and Hunt, R.G. (1980), 'The relationship between work and nonwork domains: A review of empirical research', *Academy of Management Review*, **5**, 415–29.

Niemi, R.G., Craig, S.C., and Mattei, F. (1991), 'Measuring internal political efficacy in the 1988 national election study', *American Political Science Review*, **85**, 1407–13.

O'Reilly, C. A. and Chatman, J. (1986), 'Organizational commitment and psychological attachment: The effects of compliance, identification and internalization on prosocial behavior', *Journal of Applied Psychology*, 71, 492–9.

Peterson, S.A. (1990), *Political Behavior*, Newbury Park, CA: Sage.

Pettersen, P.A. and Rose, L.E. (1996), 'Participation in local politics in Norway: Some do, some don't some will, some won't', *Political Behavior*, 18, 51–97.

Randall, D.M. (1988), 'Multiple roles and organizational commitment', *Journal of Organizational Behavior*, 9, 309–17.

Romzek, B. S. (1985), 'The effects of public service recognition, job security and staff reductions of organizational involvement', *Public Administration Review*, 45, 282–91.

Romzek, B.S. and Hendricks, J.S. (1982), 'Organizational involvement and representative bureaucracy: Can we have it both ways?', *The American Political Science Review*, 76, 75–82.

Schussler, K.F. (1982), *Measuring Social Life Feelings*, San Francisco: Jossey Bass.

Sieber, S.D. (1974), 'Toward a theory of role accumulation', *American Sociological Review*, 39, 567–78.

Sobel, R. (1993), 'From occupational involvement to political participation: An exploratory analysis', *Political Behavior*, 15, 339–53.

Theiss-Morse, E. (1993), 'Conceptualizations of good citizenship and political participation', *Political Behavior*, 15, 355–80.

Van Dyne, L., Graham, J.W., and Dienesch, R.M. (1994), 'Organizational Citizenship Behavior: Construct redefinition, measurement, and validation', *Academy of Management Journal*, 37, 765–802.

Wayne, S.J. and Ferris, G.R. (1990), 'Influence tactics, affect, and exchange quality in supervisor–subordinate interactions: A laboratory experiment and field study', *Journal of Applied Psychology*, 75, 487–99.

Wayne, S.J. and Green, S.A. (1993), 'The effects of leader–member exchange on employee citizenship and impression management behavior', *Human Relations*, 46, 1431–40.

5.   Politics and the Workplace: An Empirical Examination of the Relationship Between Political Behavior and Work Outcomes[1]

Aaron Cohen and Eran Vigoda-Gadot

INTRODUCTION

Several conceptual frameworks have been proposed for the relationship between political behavior and behavior at work. One line of argument is based on the relationship between work and nonwork domains. Accordingly, one's attitudes and behaviors regarding nonwork aspects such as family, leisure activities, and membership of social clubs can affect one's attitudes and behaviors in the work setting (Near, Rice, and Hunt, 1980). Following this line, Peterson (1990) and Sobel (1993) described the relationship between work and politics as based on a spillover effect where participation in one arena allows an individual to gain certain skills and the self-confidence necessary to participate in other areas of social life.

Sobel (1993) argued that political participation is a learned social role whose educative function consists of practice in democratic skills. The more individuals participate, the better able they become to do so. In short, participation breeds participation and intense participation in politics may influence participation in work. Sobel's findings (1993) from a national American sample supported the above argument by showing positive and modest relationships between forms of political participation and variables such as job and work participation, supervisory responsibility, and authority.

The 'spillover effect' has particular importance in light of the long debate regarding the relationship between political science and public administration as reflected in a recent paper of Whicker, Strickland, and Olshfski (1993). One of the important research directions at the interface of public administration and political science proposed by Whicker et al. (1993) is to learn how the political environment influences continuity of goals and policy in public organizations. In line with this, a recent study of Wilson (1995) found support for the relationship between politics and organizational commitment of top executives in the federal government. Testing the relationship between politics and work outcomes, as was done in the present study, is one important way to respond to this challenging research question.

LITERATURE REVIEW AND HYPOTHESES

Political Participation and Orientations

Graham (1986, 1991) summarized and presented a typology of political behavior and orientations. It is based on three categories of citizenship behaviors formulated by classical philosophy and modern political theory (Aristotle, 1962; Cary, 1977; Janowitz, 1980; Pateman, 1970; Plato, 1892; Walzer, 1970), and it is applied here. The first category is *obedience*, or respect for orderly structures and processes. Citizens are responsible for obeying existing laws, which also protect them. For example, laws may require that citizens pay taxes, drive on a designated side of the road, refrain from violating another's rights, and at times even risk their lives in military service. Because behavior and attitudes at work represent more of an informal contribution the expectation is that it will be affected more by informal behaviors. Therefore, this study did not deal with obedience, which is a formal aspect of political behavior.

The second category is *loyalty,* which involves the expansion of individual welfare functions to include the interests of others, the state as a whole, and the values it embodies. This category includes uncompensated contributions of effort, money or property; protecting and/or enhancing a state's good reputation in the eyes of outsiders; and cooperating with others to serve the common interest, rather than seeking a free ride.

The third category, *participation*, concerns participation in governance. Citizens-as-rulers assist in implementing the law (for example, by holding or electing others to executive positions) and in adjudicating violations (for example, by serving on juries). They also participate (directly or through representatives) in changing laws to respond to new facts and in evolving an understanding of the common interest. As a result, political behavior includes devoting time and effort to the responsibilities of governance, keeping well informed, sharing information and ideas with others, engaging in discussions about controversial issues, voting in whatever manner is provided under the law, and encouraging others to do likewise.

Based on the above typology, four dimensions of political behavior were tested. The first is participation in political activities. Here the expectation was that people who are more involved in political activities such as voting, sending support/protest messages to politicians, taking part in political demonstrations, or signing petitions on political issues will be more involved in the work setting. This expectation is based on Sieber's (1974) argument that such spillover provides resources for role performance. That is, the experience and expertise that are gained by participating in political activities might provide good tools to make it easier to demonstrate higher levels of performance at work (Sieber, 1974; Peterson, 1990; Sobel, 1993). Also, following the trait explanation, it is be argued that people who are politically active evince a personality type: they are more involved, they care, and they are committed to their environment. People who do more than is formally required in their civic setting will probably be more active in organizational life, and consequently demonstrate higher levels of work performance. Thus, hypothesis 1 (H1) suggests that *Political* participation will be positively related to work outcomes.

The second dimension of political behavior tested is participation in community activities. This form is considered as an important dimension of the political sphere (Almond and Verba, 1963). Some people may possibly decline to participate in political activities because they dislike or are indifferent to politics. Such people might direct their tendencies toward a closer, perhaps more personal domain, such as the community. The expectation is that people who are active in their community will demonstrate higher levels of performance than those who are not active. The rationale is similar to the one described for political participation, although Sieber's (1974) explanation of personality enrichment or development might also be relevant here. For example, the tolerance gained through the recognition of discrepant viewpoints might be helpful in similar situations in the work setting. Thus, hypothesis 2 (H2) suggests that community involvement will be positively related to work outcomes.

A third dimension of political behavior to be tested is civility. Here the focus is on behaviors that show care, kindness, compassion and consideration toward other citizens, in particular those who need the support of others. People who demonstrate such civil behavior are expected to exert higher levels of performance, in particular since civility seems to represent an altruistic behavior outside the work environment. Sieber's (1974) explanation of personality enrichment or development provides a rationale for the way civility will be related to performance. The sensitivity, kindness and consideration people gain and learn in the civil setting will be reflected also in the work setting. Thus, hypothesis 3 (H3) suggests that civility will be positively related to work outcomes.

The fourth dimension, namely faith in citizen involvement, is different from the previous three in that it represents more of an orientation than a behavior. But as Peterson (1990) argued, political orientations are an important dimension of political behavior because they shape people's political attitudes and actions. Faith in citizen involvement is defined here as the extent to which people believe that by being involved they can influence the political system (Schussler, 1982). Those who believe that they can have some say in the political system and are capable of influencing it may be expected to transfer such an orientation to the work setting as well. A spillover of faith in citizen involvement to the work setting will result in higher levels of activities in the workplace in an attempt to change things there, too; work performance represents such a set of activities. Thus, hypothesis 4 (H4) suggests that faith in citizenship involvement will be positively related to work outcomes.

The Effect of Gender on the Relationship Between Political Behavior and Work Outcomes

The finding that men are more likely to participate in politics than women is one of the most thoroughly substantiated in social sciences (Peterson, 1990; Milbrath, 1965). Research has shown that females are less politically effectual and less involved in politics (Peterson, 1990). Data supporting this proposition come from at least nine countries (Milbrath, 1965). Although economic and social modernization is slowly eroding this sex difference (Milbrath, 1965), females are still expected to be found less politically involved, particularly in Israeli society that is generally more conservative than North American society. Therefore, it can be expected that the above relationship will operate differently for males and females. Accordingly, the relationship between variables representing political participation and work outcomes is expected to be stronger for males than for females. Thus, hypothesis 5 (H5) suggests that the relationship between political behavior variables and work outcomes will be stronger for males than for females.

Work Outcomes

Four dimensions of work outcomes are tested separately in this study. Each of them is an established and frequently studied concept in management literature. The main difference among the four outcomes is that one of them represents actual behavior, namely performance, and the other three are important work attitudes such as participation in decision making, job satisfaction and organizational commitment.

In addition, three important work attitudes are tested here also. As noted above, participation in decision making was presented by Sobel (1993) as a key concept that connects work and politics. Therefore, such participation seems to be a concept that can be related to political participation and orientations. People who are involved in their civil setting will probably be involved in their organizational setting too, and this involvement will be demonstrated in their higher involvement in the decision making process in the organization. Moreover, their participation as citizens has probably provided them with more skills and experiences which may assist them in decision making processes in the organization (Sobel, 1993; Peterson, 1990).

Locke (1976) defined job satisfaction in a general sense as a 'pleasurable or positive emotional state resulting from the appraisal of one's job or job experiences'. Job satisfaction has emerged as the most studied work attitude (Griffin and Bateman, 1986) mainly because it was and still is assumed to be related to important work behaviors such as turnover, absenteeism, and performance (Mowday, Porter and Steers, 1982). While much research has tested a variety of antecedents to job satisfaction, very little has tested the relationship between political behavior and this important attitude. A possible relationship between political behavior and attitudes and job satisfaction was proposed by Peterson (1990), who explained such a relationship by the spillover effect. Our study empirically tested the relationship between political behavior and job satisfaction.

Another work attitude that is frequently researched is organizational commitment, defined as the strength of attachment to an organization and reflecting a psychological state more than overt behavior (O'Reilly and Chatman, 1986). Organizational commitment was found to be an important resource of public organizations (Romzek and Hendricks, 1982; Romzek, 1985) and is tested as another work outcome in its relationship to political behavior.

While the general hypothesis of this research is that the direction and the intensity of the effects of political participation and orientations will be equal for all work outcomes mentioned above, political behavior is expected to be more firmly related to the three attitudes than to actual performance. The reasons are, first, that attitudes are usually better explained than actual behaviors, and second, that the three attitudes examined here are in themselves important determinants of performance (Mowday, Porter and Steers, 1982; Griffin and Bateman, 1986) and sometimes are considered as mediators between given antecedents and work outcomes (Mowday, Porter and Steers, 1982). Therefore, it may be expected that they will be affected by political behavior more strongly than performance, which is affected very strongly by variables such as job satisfaction, organizational commitment and participation in decision making. Hence, hypothesis 6 (H6) suggests that political behavior will be more strongly related to work attitudes than to actual performance.

METHOD

Subjects and Procedure

Data were collected from a sample of employees in one of the major public health organizations in Israel that agreed to our request to take part in this study. Some of the clinics in the north of Israel that had not participated in any other study during the previous year were asked by the organization's head office to cooperate. A total of 345 questionnaires were distributed in 16 clinics to administrative and medical personnel; 200 usable questionnaires were returned, a response rate of 58%. Supervisors in each of the clinics provided the performance data for each employee who completed a questionnaire about a month after the survey. A breakdown of respondents by occupation showed 31% of the sample to be physicians, 35% nurses, and 34% clerical and administrative workers; 82% of the sample were female, and 84% married. The average age of the respondents was 45 years (s.d.= 10.3); average tenure in the clinics and in the organization was 10.26 (s.d.= 7.1) and 14.9 (s.d.= 8.5), respectively; finally 38% held a BA degree or higher. The demographic characteristics of the sample are quite similar to those of the employees of all the clinics in the north of Israel: 79% females, 82% married, average age 45, average tenure in the organization 15 years, and 40% with BA or higher.

Data Analysis

The research hypotheses were tested by hierarchical regression analysis, conducted in the following steps: first the control variables (education, origin, gender, and age) were entered into the equation. In the second step the four political behavior variables (political participation, community involvement, civility, and faith in citizen involvement) were entered. Steps 1 and 2 tested hypotheses 1–4. In the third step, four two-way interactions were entered into the equation (political participation*gender; community involvement*gender; civility*gender; faith in citizen involvement*gender) to test hypothesis 5 regarding the interaction effect of gender. The final equations tested hypothesis 6.

FINDINGS

Table 5.1 presents descriptive statistics and the intercorrelations of the research variables. The data indicate reasonable psychometric properties of the measures used in this study. The somewhat low reliability of the variables political participation, community involvement and civility could be attributed to the fact that they measure reported behaviors in a given domain, not attitudes. When factor analyses of the political participation and community involvement variables were performed, the reliability of the full scales was found to be higher than any combination of their factors. The correlations among the independent variables are quite low and indicate the absence of multicollinearity. This should be noted because despite the fact that most of the variables in this study were based on self-report data, which allows source bias or general method variance, the low correlations among the independent variables demonstrate the absence of common method variance in these data.

Table 5.2 presents the results of the regression analyses for work outcomes as the dependent variables, and the control variables and political behavior variables as the independent variables. In step 1 in each of the regressions the control variables were entered into the equations. Note the inconsistent effect of the control variables: they had a strong effect on organizational commitment – three of them, education, origin and age, having a significant effect and alone explaining 21% of the variance; on the other hand, the control variables had no effect on participation in decision making and a weak effect on performance and job satisfaction. Only gender had a significant effect on performance, and origin on job satisfaction, explaining 5% and 6% of the variance respectively.

In step 2 the four political participation variables were entered into each of the equations. The findings show that none of the four political participation variables had a significant effect on performance. This finding rejects hypotheses 1–4 for the variable performance. For job satisfaction, the results of step 2 showed a positive and significant effect of faith in citizenship involvement; namely those with higher faith in citizenship involvement had higher job satisfaction. This finding supports hypothesis 4 for the variable job satisfaction. For organizational commitment, the results of step 2 show that two political participation variables, civility and faith in citizenship involvement, had a positive effect on commitment. This finding supports hypotheses 3 and 4 for the variable organizational commitment. In the case of participation in decision making, the results of step 2 show a significant and positive effect of two variables: community involvement and faith in citizenship involvement. This finding supports hypotheses 2 and 4 for participation in decision making. Note that the contribution of the political participation variables is beyond the effect of the control demographic variables.

In the final step the interaction variables were entered. With two outcome variables an interaction effect was found. The more interesting one was with the variable political participation. While none of the political variables was significant in step 2, the inclusion of the interaction variables caused a significant main effect of the variable political participation and a significant interaction effect of gender*faith in citizenship involvement. More interesting was the direction of the effect of the variable political participation, which was negative, namely more political participation decreased level of performance. This finding was not anticipated in hypothesis 1 and in fact contradicts it for the variable performance. The interaction effect shows that the relationship between faith in citizenship involvement and performance was stronger for females and quite constant for males. This finding contradicts hypothesis 5, which predicted the opposite. Another interaction effect was found for the variable organizational commitment. In this case the interaction of gender was with the variable political participation. The pattern of this interaction is similar to the previous one and indicates a closer relationship between political participation and organizational commitment for females. This interaction also contradicts hypothesis 5. Overall, the findings of Table 5.2 showed that variance explained by the independent variables varied for each of the depended variables. Relatively high variance was explained for organizational commitment, 32%. The lowest explained variance was for actual performance, 12%, as expected in hypothesis 6. The explained variance for job satisfaction was 14%, and for participation in decision making 15%.

Finally, it should be noted that all data analyses were performed separately for males and females in order to control for the possibility of gender bias. Since the research sample consisted of a large proportion of females (n=164; 83%), we decided to conduct separate regression analyses for males and for females. The regression analysis for females yielded similar results to those based on the total research sample. For example, political participation was positively related to employee performance (β=-0.17; $p<0.05$ for females and β=-0.16; $p<0.05$ for the total sample), community involvement was positively related to participation in decision making (β=0.22; $p<0.01$ for females and β=0.23; $p<0.01$ for the total sample), and faith in citizenship involvement was positively related to job satisfaction (β=0.25; $p<0.01$ for females and β=0.27; $p<0.001$ for the total sample) and to organizational commitment (β=0.22; $p<0.01$ for females and β=0.25; $p<0.01$ for the total sample). The separate analysis for males yielded nonsignificant relationships between variables representing political behavior and work outcomes, probably because the number of males in the sample was low (n=36; 17%).

Furthermore, we decided to perform t-tests for the differences between males and females with the political behavior and dependent variables. The findings revealed one significant difference between males and females in the political behavior variables; males participated more in politics than females (mean=1.8 versus 1.6; $p<0.001$). As for the dependent variables, the findings revealed that females were more committed than males (mean=3.7 versus 3.4; $p<0.01$); participated more in decision making (mean=4.4 versus 4.0; $p<0.05$); were more satisfied with work (mean=3.7 versus 3.4; $p<0.05$); and performed better at work (mean=4.4 versus 4.1; $p<0.05$). The differences found in the t-test findings imply that perhaps in a larger male sample significant differences

Table 5.1   *Means, standard deviation, Cronbach's alpha, Pearson's r correlations for the variables*

Variable	Mean	S. D.	1	2	3	4	5	6	7	8	9	10	11	12
1. Education	3.11	1.5	1.00											
2. Origin	0.57	0.50		1.00										
3. Gender	0.82	0.38	-0.33***	0.00	1.00									
4. Age	44.95	10.31	0.14	0.38***	-0.14*	1.00								
5. Political participation	1.64	0.35	0.14	-0.10	-0.29***	-0.00	(0.67)							
6. Community involvement	1.43	0.42	-0.06	0.00	-0.11	-0.05	0.35***	(0.71)						
7. Civility	4.21	0.75	-0.18*	0.09	-0.00	0.02	-0.05	0.05	(0.63)					
8. Faith in citizenship involvement	2.80	0.52	-0.15*	0.03	0.05	0.01	0.14	0.26***	0.19**	(0.72)				
9. Job satisfaction	3.62	0.61	-0.12	0.16*	0.14*	0.08	-0.08	0.06	0.06	0.28***	(0.71)			
10. Organizational commitment	3.68	0.67	0.30***	0.21**	0.16*	0.23***	-0.10	0.08	0.25***	0.33***	0.57***	(0.84)		
11. Participation in decision making	4.11	0.81	-0.09	-0.08	0.15*	0.10	0.06	0.27	0.05	0.27***	0.14*	0.21**	(0.75)	
12. Performance	4.31	0.66	-0.00	-0.10	0.16*	-0.14*	-0.12	0.03	-0.12	0.02	0.04	0.10	-0.21**	(0.93)

Note
*P < 0.05   **P < 0.01   ***P < 0.001

111

Table 5.2 *Multiple Hierarchic Regression Analyses (Standardized Coefficients) between independent variables set and dependent variables set*

Step	Performance			Job Satisfaction			Organizational Commitment			Participation in Decision Making		
	1	2	3	1	2	3	1	2	3	1	2	3
Control variables												
1. Education	0.07 (0.95)	0.07 (0.93)	0.09 (1.22)	−0.12 (−1.53)	−0.07 (−0.91)	−0.06 (−0.82)	−0.34*** (−4.90)	−0.26*** (−3.79)	−0.26*** (−3.72)	−0.03 (−0.36)	0.04 (0.50)	0.05 (0.60)
2. Origin (born outside Israel)	−0.07 (−0.91)	−0.08 (−1.00)	−0.07 (0.85)	0.17* (2.14)	0.14 (1.86)	0.13 (1.74)	0.19** (2.74)	0.15* (2.22)	0.16* (2.34)	−0.06 (−0.71)	−0.08 (−1.12)	−0.08 (−1.11)
3. Gender (women)	0.17* (2.21)	0.13 (1.70)	0.15 (1.84)	0.11 (1.49)	0.10 (1.26)	0.11 (1.36)	0.07 (1.06)	0.07 (1.06)	0.12 (1.59)	0.13 (1.71)	0.17* (2.20)	0.21* (2.52)
4. Age	−0.10 (−1.31)	−0.10 (−1.26)	−0.09 (−1.18)	0.05 (0.64)	0.05 (0.63)	0.05 (0.64)	0.22** (3.06)	0.22** (3.21)	0.21** (3.18)	−0.05 (−0.67)	−0.04 (−0.50)	−0.04 (−0.49)
Political behavior												
5. Political participation		−0.15 (−1.84)	−0.16* (−1.98)		−0.08 (−1.00)	−0.08 (0.097)		−0.07 (−0.96)	−0.07 (−0.97)		−0.02 (−0.28)	−0.02 (−0.26)
6. Community involvement		0.09 (1.09)	0.08 (1.07)		0.03 (0.33)	0.01 (0.18)		0.03 (0.39)	0.02 (0.24)		0.24** (3.20)	0.23** (3.00)
7. Civility		−0.12 (−1.64)	−0.12 (−1.60)		−0.02 (−0.34)	−0.03 (−0.42)		0.13* (2.10)	0.11 (1.70)		0.01 (0.13)	−0.01 (−0.15)
8. Faith in citizenship involvement		0.05 (0.68)	0.04 (0.58)		0.27*** (3.69)	0.27*** (3.72)		0.25*** (3.89)	0.25**** (3.79)		0.21** (2.88)	0.21** (2.82)

Table 5.2 (continued)

Step	Performance			Job Satisfaction			Organizational Commitment			Participation in Decision Making		
	1	2	3	1	2	3	1	2	3	1	2	3
Interactions												
9. Gender × political participation			-0.16 (-1.98)			0.00 (0.03)			-0.17* (-2.08)			-0.11 (-1.21)
10. Gender × community involvement			-0.03 (-0.31)			-0.08 (-0.92)			0.12 (1.59)			0.03 (0.33)
11. Gender × civility			0.05 (0.74)			0.05 (0.67)			0.03 (0.51)			0.07 (1.02)
12. Gender × faith in citizenship involvement			-0.17* (-2.33)			0.07 (0.91)			-0.03 (-0.41)			0.01 (0.146)
R^2	0.05	0.08	0.12	0.06	0.13	0.14	0.21	0.30	0.32	0.03	0.15	0.16
Adj. R^2	0.03	0.04	0.06	0.04	0.09	0.08	0.19	0.27	0.27	0.01	0.11	0.10
F	2.34	1.96*	2.02*	3.07	3.50***	2.50**	12.39***	9.94***	7.08***	1.52	4.10***	2.89**
ΔR^2	–	0.03	0.04	–	0.07	0.01	–	0.09	0.02	–	0.12	0.01
F for ΔR^2	–	1.56	2.13	–	3.75**	0.55	–	6.14***	1.26	–	6.51***	0.54

Notes
N = 200
$P <^*0.05$ $P <^{**}0.01$ $P <^{***}0.001$

would have been found in the regression analyses. Future research should consider this possibility.

DISCUSSION

The findings of this study showed in general that political behavior is related to important behaviors and attitudes in the work setting. The relationship can be defined as modest but consistent. It is modest because the political behavior variables did not explain a large portion of the variance of the four work outcomes. It is consistent because all work outcomes were related to one or more of the political behavior variables, and this relationship held beyond the effect of the control variables. One should note that the political behavior variables were not expected to explain a large portion of the variance because research shows that the four outcome variables studied here are more strongly related to work situational variables (Mowday, Porter and Steers, 1982; Griffin and Bateman, 1986). Yet the findings here show that variables that represent political behavior should be included in future models of work outcomes because they do add to our understanding of behavior at work.

One of the contributions of this chapter was the testing of important work outcomes by using concepts not frequently used in management research. Very little research exists on the relationship between political behavior and work outcomes examined from the perspective of political theory. Preliminary conceptual arguments for testing such relationships were proposed by Graham (1991), who suggested that some forms of citizenship behaviors can be demonstrated in the organizational setting. The findings here showed that variables representing political behavior were useful in predicting important work outcomes. These findings are in line with those of Kirchmeyer (1992), who found that resources made available for work by participating in community activity positively affected organizational commitment. Kirchmeyer also found that time commitment to community work positively affected job satisfaction. The above findings together with the findings of this research support the expansion or the spillover hypothesis, according to which individuals tend to cope with increasing organizational and extra-organizational role demands by responding positively to them (Randall, 1988). Adding new roles liberates a source of energy for the individual, and rather than having to pay for extensive social involvements, individuals may come away from new involvements more enriched and vitalized. The positive relationships between political behavior variables and work outcomes indicate that more political involvement increases job satisfaction, organizational commitment, and participation in decision making. In sum, the findings of this study show the usefulness of concepts adopted from one discipline, political science, to another, organizational behavior.

However, the relationship between political behavior and work outcomes seems to be complex, as demonstrated in two important findings. First, the findings here seem to represent a mixture of positive and negative spillover. While the positive relationship of civility, community involvement, and faith in citizenship involvement with all work outcomes except performance represents positive spillover, the negative relationship of political participation with performance represents a negative one. This negative effect shows that strictly political involvement seems to have negative consequences for behaviors and attitudes at work. It would be interesting to explore possible explanations for this finding. What is so different in political involvement from community involvement and from faith in citizenship involvement that it results in opposite effects on work attitudes and behaviors? Is it that people are involved in politics because they are looking for an entirely new role, one that will compensate them for what they perceive as negative experiences at work? In such a case, is involvement in politics so different from community involvement? How? Future research should deal with these questions conceptually and empirically.

Second are the findings regarding the interaction effects. Performance is one of the most studied outcomes in management and administration literature. This study showed that the relationship between political behavior and performance is not direct but a complex interaction effect. Performance was affected by an interaction of gender with faith in citizenship involvement and by a main effect of political participation, as can be seen in Table 5.2, step 3. The moderator effect of gender was quite obvious in light of the strong theories and findings that show that political behavior differs for males and females. However, the direction of this effect was unpredictable. While the expectation was that the relationship between political behavior and work outcomes would be stronger for males, it was found to be stronger for females, and the weak slope for males indicates that this relationship was consistent for males. This finding shows that the spillover effect operated more strongly for females. The skills, confidence and experiences females acquire in the political setting are more helpful for them in the work setting than they are for males. In light of this interesting finding, future research should attempt to replicate it and to develop and test theories that consider other possible moderators that might interact with political behavior in their effect on work outcomes.

The results of this study support Kirchmeyer's (1992) conclusion that to truly understand the individual at work, one must consider not only her or his work life but also his or her life away from work too. Near, Rice and Hunt (1980) concluded that extra-work conditions greatly affect reactions to work. Our study supports their conclusion and their argument that if living conditions directly affect attitudinal/behavioral reactions to the job, then efforts to improve reactions to the job by improving working conditions may have limited success. It may be necessary to consider changes in off-the-job conditions to improve the experienced quality of working life. Future research should further explore the effect of nonwork on work. While the work outcomes studied here are important, research should also test the relationship between political behavior and other outcomes. For example, the strong relationship between political behavior and organizational commitment suggests that turnover should be tested as one of the outcomes. The reason is that organizational commitment is strongly related to turnover and one can expect that turnover will also be related to political behavior. Absenteeism is another outcome that should be tested in the future in its relationship to political behavior.

NOTE

1. Based on Cohen and Vigoda (1999), 'Politics and the workplace: An empirical examination of the relationship between political behavior and work outcomes', *Public Productivity and Management Review*, **22**, (3), 389–406. Copyright with permission from Sage Publishing.

REFERENCES

Almond, G.A. and Verba, S. (1963), *The Civic Culture: Political Attitudes and Democracy in Five Nations: An Analytic Study*, Boston: Little Brown.
Aristotle (1962), *The Politics*, Harmondsworth: Penguin.
Cary, C.D. (1977), 'The goals of citizenship training in American and Soviet schools', *Studies in Comparative Communism*, *10*, 281–97.
Graham, J.W. (1986), *Organizational citizenship informed by political theory*, Paper presented at the meeting of the Academy of Management Journal.
Graham, J.W. (1991), 'An essay on Organizational Citizenship Behavior', *Employee Responsibilities and Rights Journal*, *4*, 249–70.
Griffin, R. W. and Bateman, T. S. (1986), 'Job satisfaction and organizational commitment', in C. L. Cooper and I. Robertson (eds), *International Review of Industrial and Organizational Psychology* (pp. 157–88), New York: Wiley.
Janowitz, M. (1980), 'Observations on the sociology of citizenship rights and obligations', *Social Forces*, *59*, 1–24.
Kirchmeyer, C. (1992), 'Nonwork participation and work attitudes: A test of scarcity vs. expansion models of personal resources', *Human Relations*, *45*, 775–95.
Locke, E.A. (1976), 'The nature and causes of job satisfaction', in M.D. Dunnette (ed.), *Handbook of Industrial and Organizational Psychology* (pp. 1297–1349). Chicago: Rand McNally.
Milbrath, L.W. (1965), *Political Participation*, Chicago: Rand McNally.
Mowday, R. T., Porter, L. M., and Steers, R. M. (1982), *Employee–Organizational Linkage*, New York: Academic Press.
Near, J.P., Rice, R.W. and Hunt, R.G. (1980), 'The relationship between work and nonwork domains: A review of empirical research', *Academy of Management*

Review, 5, 415–29.

O'Reilly, C. A. and Chatman, J. (1986), 'Organizational commitment and psychological attachment: The effects of compliance, identification and internalization on prosocial behavior', *Journal of Applied Psychology, 71*, 492–9.

Pateman, C. (1970), *Participation and Democratic Theory*, London: Cambridge University Press.

Peterson, S. A. (1990), *Political Behavior,* Newbury Park, CA: Sage.

Plato (1892), *The Republic,* in B. Jowett (trans.), *The Dialogues of Plato I* (pp. 591–879), New York: Random House (original work composed in the 4th century BC).

Randall, D.M. (1988), 'Multiple roles of organizational commitment', *Journal of Organizational Behavior, 9*, 309–17.

Romzek, B. S. (1985), 'The effects of public service recognition, job security and staff reductions on organizational involvement', *Public Administration Review, 45*, 282–91.

Romzek, B. S. and Hendricks, J. S. (1982), 'Organizational involvement and representative bureaucracy: Can we have it both ways?' *The American Political Science Review, 76*, 75–82.

Schussler, K.F. (1982), *Measuring Social Life Feelings,* San Francisco: Jossey Bass.

Sieber, S.D. (1974), 'Toward a theory of role accumulation', *American Sociological Review, 39*, 567–78.

Sobel, R. (1993), 'From occupational involvement to political participation: An exploratory analysis', *Political Behavior, 15*, 339–53.

Walzer, M. (1970), *Obligations: Essays on Disobedience, War and Citizenship.* Cambridge, MA: Harvard University Press

Whicker, M.L., Strickland, R.A., and Olshfski, D.O. (1993), 'The troublesome cleft: Public administration and political science', *Public Administration Review, 53*, 531–41.

Wilson, P.A. (1995), 'The effects of politics and power on the organizational commitment of federal executives', *Journal of Management, 21*, 101–18.

PART THREE

Organizational Citizenship Behaviors in Public
Domains

Foreword

The third part of this book focuses on organizational citizenship behaviors (OCB) and on their unique meaning in public sector worksites. Organizational citizenship behavior is a relatively new concept in management literature but in fact represents an old and enduring phenomenon of human altruistic behavior. Citizenship behavior in organizations has its roots in many earlier works. For example, Katz and Kahn (1966) suggested that effective functioning of an organization is highly dependent on innovative and spontaneous activities that are beyond the prescribed role requirement. This behavior was termed extra-role behavior by Katz (1964) or organizational citizenship behavior (OCB) by Bateman and Organ (1983), who proposed this term to denote organizationally beneficial behaviors and gestures that can neither be enforced on the basis of formal role obligations nor elicited by a contractual guarantee of compensation. According to Organ's definition, 'OCB represents individual behavior that is discretionary, not directly or explicitly recognized by the formal reward system, and in the aggregate promotes the efficient and effective functioning of the organization' (Organ, 1988:4). Thus, OCB consists of informal contributions that participants can choose to make or withhold, without regard to considerations of sanctions or formal incentives. OCB derives its practical importance from the premise that it represents contributions that are not part of formal role obligations. The presumption is that many of these contributions, aggregated over time and individuals, enhance organizational effectiveness (Organ and Konovsky, 1989).

As studies have shown, OCB is not a uni-dimensional construct. Smith, Organ, and Near (1983) developed a list of items inspired by interviews conducted with supervisory personnel in two organizations. The interviewers asked the supervisors to describe subordinates' actions that they appreciated and regarded as helpful, but could not demand on the basis of supervisory authority or promise of remuneration. When the measure was pre-tested in several samples, two fairly clear-cut factors emerged. One factor suggested the quality of altruism. The items comprising this factor all had to do with helping a specific person, whether the supervisor, a co-worker, or a client. The other factor, at the time labeled general compliance, appeared to represent a more impersonal sort of OCB – conscientiousness in attendance, use of work time, and adherence to various rules, but a conscientiousness that far surpassed any enforceable minimum standards. Smith, Organ and Near (1983) argued that compliance emerged as a class of citizenship behavior factorially distinct from altruism. Whereas altruism appeared to represent the help accorded to specific persons as the situation prompted it, generalized compliance was a factor defined by a more impersonal sort of conscientiousness. It implied more of a 'good soldier' or 'good citizen' syndrome of doing things that were 'right and proper', but doing them for the sake of the system rather than for specific individuals. In the view of Smith, Organ and Near (1983), the two elements represent distinct classes of citizenship behavior, and therefore should be analysed separately.

Since the development of the concept, much research has been conducted to explore possible determinants of OCB, and two related explanations have been posited for their effect. The first explanation about the emergence of OCB is based on social exchange theory, which predicts that given certain conditions, people seek to requite those who benefit them. To the extent that a person's satisfaction results from the efforts of organizational officials, and such efforts are interpreted as volitional and non-manipulative in intent, one will seek to reciprocate those efforts. Citizenship behaviors of the sort described above are more likely to be under an individual's control, and thus more likely to be a salient mode of reciprocation (Organ, 1990). A variable that seems to represent this contention the best is job satisfaction, one of the main determinants of OCB. Wayne and Green (1993), for example, found that leader–member exchange was related to altruism, but not to compliance behavior, supporting the social exchange explanation for the relationship between leader–member exchange and employee behavior. To examine this idea, the first chapter in Part 3 deals with the transferring of citizenry ideas, attitudes and behaviors from public work domains to non-work domains. We suggest that a social exchange theory may explain the dynamic of spillover effect where good general citizenship is rewarded and appreciated, and may eventually lead to additional citizenship behaviors, this time in the intra-organizational sphere. This empirical study was conducted in a public health care organization and may further imply that citizenry behaviors are transferable from the general social context into the intra-organizational landscape of public sector and bureaucracies.

The second explanation suggests that OCB stems from one's perceptions of fairness or unfairness (Organ, 1988; 1990; Schnake, 1991). Organ (1990) postulated a general tendency for people to presume initially that they had a social exchange relationship with the organization. This presumption lasts until the weight of interpreted evidence indicates that such a relationship is not viable, because of unfairness. Confirmation of the lack of fairness in social exchange, which is accompanied by dissatisfaction, prompts a redefinition of the relationship as one of economic exchange. Such a perception can be based on a social comparison, a promise or imagined promise, past experience, the going rate, or on one's image of 'the way the world should be'. Thus, persons who perceive inequity are likely to withhold discretionary behaviors and to limit their contributions to the organization to those behaviors that are formally prescribed. Konovsky and Pugh (1994) found that procedural justice (the use of procedurally fair supervisory practices that affect higher-order issues like employees' commitment to a system) and distributive justice (the fairness of transactional contracts and economic exchange) positively affect an employee's trust in a supervisor, which in turn leads to higher levels of OCB. As a result, the majority of research regarding OCB has concentrated on variables that reflect an exchange of perceptions of fairness or equity in the workplace. The second chapter in this part is dedicated to the examination of this idea. Vigoda's work retests the relationship between OCB and levels of fairness or justice in the workplace as represented by perceptions of organizational politics. Internal politics in public organizations is considered a good representative of fairness and justice in the work environment, and its impact on OCB is examined using a structural equation modeling strategy and two alternative models.

Finally, the third chapter in this part is dedicated to the discussion on OCB in the context of the emerging non-profit and voluntary sector and in relation with the concepts of 'work congruence' and 'human resource management'. As with the previous chapters in this part, here again we examine OCB as a possible result of an individual's expectations and fit with the organization. Nonetheless, the present chapter uses two separate samples, one from the public sector and the other from the voluntary sector, to support a set of hypotheses about the relationship of OCB and various other work attitudes such as job satisfaction, organizational commitment, intentions of leaving the organization (exit), intentions of raising one's voice in order to change and improve the functioning of the organization, intentions of neglecting one's job duties, and as suggested in the first chapter, perceptions of organizational politics. Thus, this chapter may be treated as a simultaneous examination of both explanations of OCB that were suggested in the previous chapters: (1) the expectancy/fit/congruence theory and, (2) the fairness/justice/politics theory. The chapter concludes that in both studies the most conspicuous relationship was found between met expectations and OCB. It goes on to argue that the findings of this research may contribute to OCB theory by suggesting that one way of enhancing this positive behavior is to improve the interface between individuals and their work environment by means of continuous assessments of fit and expectations as well as by paying greater attention to questions of fairness and internal politics. OCB may therefore be reinforced by improvements in strategies of human resource management such as sophisticated recruitment, selection or job development programs that promote the fit of individuals to their organizational environment and the fulfillment of their expectations.

REFERENCES

Batemen, T.S. and Organ, D.W. (1983), 'Job satisfaction and the good soldier: The relationship between affect and employee citizenship', *Academy of Management Journal, 26*, 587–95.

Katz, D. (1964), 'The motivational basis of organizational behavior', *Behavior Science, 9*, 131–3.

Katz, D. and Kahn, R.L. (1966), *The Social Psychology of Organizations,* New York: Wiley.

Konovsky, M.A. and Pugh, S.D. (1994), 'Citizenship behavior and social exchange', *Academy of Management Journal, 37*, 656–69.

Organ, D.W. (1988), *Organizational Citizenship Behavior: The Good Soldier Syndrome,* Lexington, MA: Lexington Books.

Organ, D.W. (1990), 'The motivational basis of organizational citizenship behavior', *Research in Organizational Behavior, 12*, 43–72.

Organ, D.W. and Konovsky, M. (1989), 'Cognitive versus affective determinants of organizational citizenship behavior', *Journal of Applied Psychology, 74*, 157–64.

Schnake, M. (1991), 'Organizational citizenship: A review, proposed model, and research agenda', *Human Relations, 44*, 735–59.

Smith, C.A., Organ, D.W., and Near, J.P. (1983), 'Organizational citizenship behavior: Its nature and antecedents', *Journal of Applied Psychology, 68*, 653–63.

Wayne, S.J. and Green, S.A. (1993), 'The effects of leader–member exchange on employee citizenship and impression management behavior', *Human Relations, 46* 1431–40.

6. Do Good Citizens make Good Organizational Citizens? An Empirical Examination of the Relationship Between Good Citizenship and Organizational Citizenship Behavior in Israel[1]

Aaron Cohen and Eran Vigoda-Gadot

INTRODUCTION

Organizational citizenship behavior (OCB) has received considerable attention in management research during the past decade. This concept had its roots in the work of Katz and Kahn (1966), who argued that an important behavior required of employees for the effective functioning of an organization is their undertaking innovative and spontaneous activities beyond the prescribed role requirement. OCB consists of informal contributions that participants can choose to make or withhold, without regard to sanctions or formal incentives. Many of these contributions, aggregated over time and persons, were thought to enhance organizational effectiveness (Organ and Konovsky, 1989). Up to now, OCB has drawn sustenance from social psychology, some classical writings on management, and organizational psychology. However, although the word *citizenship* carries social and political implications, little enrichment of the concept has been derived from political theory. Apart from Graham (1986, 1991) and Van Dyne, Graham and Dienesch (1994), no study has tried to explain OCB from a more general perspective of the global concept of *citizenship*.

This study argues that OCB is conceptually a good representation of voluntary work behaviors that can be related to general citizenship and civic orientations in the wider society. Previous studies mentioned the relationship between workplace values and behaviors and political domains (for example, Brady, Verba and Schlozman, 1995; Pateman, 1970; Sobel, 1993). Most of these view the workplace as a potential determinant of a wider political culture. However, empirical evidence as to causality is scarce. Does the work setting affect politics, or does the political environment account for changes in the workplace? It is also possible that a mutual relationship exists between these spheres, or that no relationship can be elicited between them.

The present research, however, focuses on the effect of general citizenship on OCB. In the last decade, the topic of voluntary behavior received growing attention by political scientists and organizational behavior scholars alike. Political scientists, especially those concerned with the state of public administration, claim that an independent form of voluntary behavior is already structured in the very basic construct of modern societies. They refer to the third sector as one example of this behavior, which supports the state and its public administration agencies in fulfilling elementary commitments to the citizens (Brudney, 1990; Powell, 1987). This line of research promotes our understanding on how society in general may benefit from spontaneous behaviors of ordinary citizens. We think that issues of citizenship, voluntary activities, and spontaneous involvement of the people in the administrative process are among the most significant topics in contemporary writing on public administration. Taking a somewhat different perspective, organizational behaviorists are more interested in the advantages of spontaneous/voluntary behavior in organizations, namely OCB, for improving organizational outcomes and responsiveness. For example, Podsakoff and MacKenzie (1997) mention the potential relationship between OCB and COB (Customer-Oriented Behavior). Thus, OCB may be very useful especially in public organizations that serve wide populations. The new public management approach (NPM) argues that to improve its functioning, the public sector must become more responsive to citizens' demands and encourage flexibility, creativity and spontaneous behavior by its employees (Pollitt, 1988; 1990; Stewart and Ranson, 1994). Hence, a better understanding of the general environment and the antecedents of OCB can contribute to higher quality of services and better productivity of public agencies that serve citizens in modern societies.

Inspired by several disciplines (political science, public administration, management and organizational behavior), this study tried to find a linkage between different constructs of citizenship behavior. Why is this relationship so important? On the grounds of previous studies (for example, Podsakoff and MacKenzie, 1997) it is assumed that better OCB in the public sector contributes to improved productivity and higher performance rates of public personnel. It also advances quality services and high responsiveness to citizens' demands. Studies found positive relationships between good citizenship in the workplace and work outcomes. Good organizational citizenship expresses extra-role behaviors and a better psychological contract between organizations and employees (Organ, 1988). General good citizenship is important for every society. However, for citizens as clients of the public system it is organizational citizenship that matters more. This study argues that OCB has indispensable merit for organizations in general and mainly for the public arena. Satisfaction of the public with public agencies should be related to the *immediate* environment of administration and to public personnel, and is only indirectly affiliated with general good citizenship behavior. The public may be satisfied or dissatisfied with the services provided by governmental institutions. At least part of this satisfaction level is gained through the extra-role behavior of public servants. Public personnel's citizenship behavior may influence citizens' attitudes to public agencies, improve their legitimacy, and increase citizens' trust in democracy. It is a momentous construct of workplace activities that must be further explored.

Building on the positive effect that OCB may have on public sector performance (a relationship which is not tested here) we believe it is important to explore the antecedents of OCB. If one seeks better knowledge on quality performances by the public sector, one must be aware of the value of OCB and explore possible facets that may influence it. While organizational behavior theory has concentrated on intra-organizational antecedents of OCB we suggest a slightly different perspective. A basic hypothesis of this study is that good general citizenship behavior is positively related to good OCB and may enhance it directly or indirectly. To support our propositions several competitive hypotheses and models were developed and examined to show how factors from the civic/political setting may account for variations in the levels of OCB, and hence influence public sector outcomes.

The Socio-Political Heritage of OCB

To establish a socio-political heritage of organizational citizenship a clear linkage must first be established between internal and external voluntary actions of individuals. Graham (1991) is one of the few researchers who attempted to conceptualize OCB by starting from the political inheritance of citizenship rather than extra-role/organizationally functional defining criteria. Graham's typology is based on three categories of citizenship behaviors revealed by classical philosophy and modern political theory (Aristotle, 1962; Cary, 1977; Inkeles, 1969; Pateman, 1970; Plato, 1892; Walzer, 1970). Together these categories comprise what Inkeles (1969: 1139) termed the 'active citizenship syndrome'. The first category is *obedience*, or respect for orderly structures and processes. Citizens are responsible for obeying existing laws, which also protect them. Because OCB represents informal organizational contributions, the expectation is that it will be affected more by informal citizenship behaviors than by formal demonstrations of citizenship such as obedience. Therefore, this chapter does not deal with obedience. The second category is *loyalty*, namely the expansion of individual welfare functions to include the interests of others, the state as a whole, and the values it embodies. Loyal citizens promote and protect their communities and volunteer extra effort for the common good. The third category, *participation*, concerns participation in governance, keeping well informed, sharing information and ideas with others, engaging in discussions about controversial issues, voting in constitutional elections, and encouraging others to do likewise (Graham, 1991; Van Dyne, Graham and Dienesch, 1994). Graham (1991) argued that these three citizenship categories could be used in organizational settings. Participation in civic activities, both inside and outside organizations, is basically a voluntary behavior. People may or may not choose to participate in civic activities such as voting or involvement in community ventures. OCB is also a voluntary behavior because it is not formally required from employees. Moreover, good organizational citizens are not directly rewarded for such activities. Involvement in voluntary behavior in the civic sphere may thus encourage similar behavior in the work setting, namely OCB. Van Dyne et al. (1994) empirically tested Graham's typology, and concluded that while two forms of citizenship, participation and loyalty, could be applied to measure OCB, the inclusion of obedience as an OCB dimension was not empirically supported.

This expectation is noted in several studies in political theory (Almond and Verba, 1963; Brady, Verba and Schlozman, 1995; Inkeles, 1969; Peterson, 1990; Sobel, 1993). The basic argument is that work and politics are similar institutions so experiences in one domain can spill over to the other. Almond and Verba (1963) argued that institutions are closer to politics and government when they exist at the same time, are similar in degree of formal authority, or have similar criteria for authority positions. The 'closer' two social institutions are, the greater is the likelihood of congruence between their authority structures. The workplace is closer in time and in kind to the political sphere. Work exists contemporaneously with politics, and work and politics are formally structured. Roles in the political sphere can train occupants to perform workplace roles because experiences of self-direction or conformity in politics inculcate congruent values and orientations. Congruence lies in the generally analogous formal authority patterns between institutional spheres. The more closely two experiences approximate each other, the more likely is transference from one experience to the other (Sobel, 1993).

A more recent study by Brady, Verba and Schlozman (1995) also shows how experiences in one domain can be transferred further. Their study suggests a resource model of civic skills (that is, institutional involvement, skill opportunities, and skill acts) that can provide 'a powerful explanation of political participation' (p.272). People use pre-existing civic skills (education-based organizational and communications skills as well as innate skills) or develop civic skills through their involvement in the institutions of adult life to perform skill-acts. In turn, when individuals perform skill-acts in one institution, political or non-political, they increase their skills so that they can engage in still more skill-acts in that or in some other domain (p.278). The study by Brady, Verba and Schlozman (1995) tries to go beyond SES (socio-economic status) by emphasizing the unique effect of some social institutions (for example, church and workplace) on political participation. However, resources and skills can also be transferred from the political environment to other organizations. As noted by Brady and his colleagues, 'civic skills could be the result as well as the cause of political activity' (pp. 278-79) and generate different types of citizenship behavior. Hence, political participation and general citizenship traits can provide the individual with civic skills relevant to the workplace. Practicing skill-acts (planning meetings, making speeches, participating in debates, being involved in communal life, etc.) develops civic skills that are potentially transferable to work and may be used to enhance organizational performances.

Dimensions of General Citizenship and OCB

Four dimensions of general citizenship can be mentioned. Participation in political activities and community involvement best represent the participation category. As for loyalty, civility is a good example of such behavior. Faith in citizen involvement is more of an orientation that represents loyalty and willingness to participate in a democratic process.

The first dimension is participation in political activities, which is classic and one of the most researched constructs in political science (Peterson, 1990). People who are more involved in political activities like voting, sending support/protest messages to politicians, taking part in political demonstrations, or signing petitions on political issues are expected to be more involved in the work setting. This expectation derives from a positive spillover effect. Experience, expertise and resources gained in political activities might facilitate higher levels of job performance and OCB (Brady, Verba and Schlozman, 1995; Peterson, 1990; Sieber, 1974; Sobel, 1993).

The second dimension is participation in community activities. Barber (1984) argued that 'political participation in common action is more easily achieved at the neighborhood level, where there is a variety of opportunities for engagement' (p.303). Recent political science and sociology literature has strongly developed the concept of communitarianism as a separate and important dimension of political participation. For example, Etzioni (1994; 1995) views communitarianism as a necessary behavior of citizens that should be encouraged by modern societies. More community involvement can help the state and its public administration agencies in fulfilling their duties and commitment to the citizens. Citizens' demands from the state, as well as the obligation of the state to fulfill these demands, have dramatically increased in recent decades. Public agencies are sometimes incapable of providing adequate responses to citizens' needs, so citizens themselves become responsible and must react by enhanced communitariansm. The more willing citizens are to initiate voluntary behaviors (for example, in fields such as education or local administration) the better the state operates and society prospers (Brudney, 1990).

Community activity is also considered a more informal way of participation than national activity (Sobel, 1993). Certain individual characteristics serve to promote both national and local participation, but other personal and local community characteristics primarily stimulate participation in local politics (Pettersen and Rose, 1996). Some people may avoid political activities because they dislike or are indifferent to politics. They may prefer a closer-knit, perhaps more personal domain, such as the community, which offers membership of a tenants' committee or of a school parents' committee. People active in their community are expected to show higher levels of OCB than those who are not active. The rationale is similar to that for political participation, although Sieber's (1974) explanation of personality enrichment or development might also be relevant here. For example, tolerance gained through recognition of discrepant viewpoints might be helpful in similar situations in the work setting.

The following two dimensions represent the loyalty category of citizens' behavior. Civility focuses on daily behaviors that show care, kindness, compassion and consideration toward other citizens, in particular those who need such support. These behaviors match the definition of loyalty because loyal citizens are expected to volunteer extra effort for the common good. They are also expected to display higher levels of OCB since civility seems to represent an altruistic behavior outside the work environment. Sieber's (1974) explanation of personality enrichment or development provides a rationale for the way civility will be related to OCB. The sensitivity, kindness and consideration that people gain and learn in the civil setting will be reflected in the work setting. The fourth dimension, faith in citizen involvement, differs from the above three in that it is more an orientation than a behavior. Political orientations are considered an important aspect of citizenship because they help to shape individuals' understanding of the political world and their place in it (Peterson, 1990). Theiss-Morse (1993) argues that most people are apparently involved in the political sphere in ways consistent with their citizenship perspective. Her study shows that greater predictive power is gained by measurement of people's perspectives on good citizenship, producing better specified models to explain behavior. Faith in citizen involvement is defined as the extent to which people believe that the average citizen can effect changes in the political system and that by being involved they can influence the political system (Schussler, 1982). Hence, this variable is a good representation of loyalty and trust in the political system. People who believe that they can have some say in the political system will transfer such an orientation to the work setting, resulting in higher levels of OCB.

The Relationship Between General Citizenship and OCB

Two alternative relationships, direct and indirect, are proposed to describe the effect of general citizenship on OCB. A direct relationship is relatively simple. It implies that characteristics of political participation, community involvement, civility and faith in citizens' involvement account for variations in OCB. This idea is straightforward and suggests that the organizational environment has no effect on the willingness of employees to take part in intra-organizational voluntary actions. The alternative, however, is an indirect relationship. This model elaborates on job attitudes as possible mediators between general citizenship and organizational citizenship. An indirect relationship reflects the cardinal role of workplace constructs in shaping OCB. A gradual influence is assumed here of the effect of general citizenship on organizational citizenship. General citizenship has a role in framing employees' job attitudes, which in return has an effect on OCB. Job satisfaction, organizational commitment and participation in decision making are among the most important constructs of job attitudes that have received impressive attention in OB literature during the years. These job attitudes express employees' perceptions of the immediate work sphere, which is so related to OCB. They are also frequently mentioned in organization studies as related to formal and informal performances. Moreover, job satisfaction and organizational commitment have been extensively examined in relation to OCB and found to be positively correlated with its constructs.

Participation in decision making and forms of commitment are mentioned in political science theory as components of citizenship behavior, loyalty and involvement in society (for example, Pateman, 1970). For example, commitment to the job may be compared to commitment to other social structures and values (for example, commitment to democracy). Participation in decision making reflects a willingness to participate in collective efforts both inside and outside the workplace (for example, in the community or neighborhood). The next section develops a rationale for the direct and indirect relationships, as well as competitive hypotheses and models aimed at testing them.

Direct Relationship
The direct relationship derives mainly from political science theory. Graham (1991) and Sobel (1993) promote the idea of direct spillover of general citizenship behavior to the work setting. This expectation is based on the argument that such spillover provides resources for role performance (Brady, Verba and Schlozman, 1995) when experience and expertise gained in political activities might facilitate higher levels of OCB. Pateman (1970) and Peterson (1990) also support a direct relationship between these spheres, arguing that a reciprocal relationship may exist. People who tend to perform more good citizenship behavior in the communal or national sphere are also more likely to do so in the workplace. According to this relationship, transformation of civic behaviors and orientations is rooted in personality and is less affected by contextual work attitudes. The fourth type of positive spillover mentioned by Sieber (1974) considers personality enrichment or development, and further supports the direct relationship.

The direct relationship model expected a direct relationship between each of the four general citizenship variables and OCB. It did not expect a mediating effect by the three contextual work attitudes (job satisfaction, organizational commitment and participation in decision making). The above explanations are based on a positive nonwork-to-work approach. Hence, positive relationships were expected between each of the four general citizenship factors and OCB. The first competitive hypothesis (H1) is therefore that OCB is directly and positively related to general citizenship behavior.

Indirect Relationship
Several scholars have argued that the relationship between determinants and OCB is not direct but mediated (Konovsky and Pugh, 1994; Latham and Skarlicki, 1995; Moorman, 1991; Organ, 1988; 1990; 1994). The notion that general citizenship is not related to behavior at work directly was also advanced by political theory. Brady, Verba and Schlozman (1995) argued that 'the opportunity to practice civic skills in an institution requires both involvement in the institution and a setting that provides the chance to practice some skills' (p.275). The relationship one has with the organization can determine whether one will transfer one's civic skills to a given work setting. Individuals' attitudes to the organization thus comprise a significant source of knowledge on the chances of using civic skills as a positive work

input.

In search of a reliable description of individual–organizational relationships we turned to three well-studied contextual work attitudes: job satisfaction, organizational commitment and participation in decisions. These variables were tested as mediators of the relationship between general citizenship and OCB. Job satisfaction and organizational commitment are good examples of employees' attitudes in the workplace that were found to relate to OCB (Organ and Ryan, 1995; Williams and Anderson, 1991). Highly satisfied and committed employees are more likely to engage in organizational citizenship behaviors because of reciprocal exchange relationships and better attachment they have with the work environment. Participation in decisions in nonpolitical organizations was found to be cumulative: persons participating in decisions in one organization were likely to do so in others. Political participation is also a learned social role acquired by practice in democratic skills. The more individuals participate, the better able they become at it (Pateman, 1970). Participation breeds participation, and intense participation in politics might influence work participation (Sobel, 1993). Accordingly, citizens involved in the civic setting will be involved in the decision making process in the organization because of the experiences and the skills they acquired (Brady, Verba and Schlozman, 1995; Peterson, 1990). Employees who participate in extra-organizational decision making processes will tend to participate similarly within the organization. Consequently, they will show higher job satisfaction and organizational commitment (DeCotiis and Summers, 1987; Zeffane, 1994). Committed, satisfied, and involved employees will thus reciprocate with higher levels of OCB. This idea was supported by Organ and Ryan (1995). Their findings showed comparable effect sizes between satisfaction, fairness, organizational commitment, leader supportiveness and OCB. Participation in decision making has not been tested frequently for its relationship to OCB, but it is presented in political theory as an essential construct that bridges participation in the civic setting to the work setting (Pateman, 1970; Sobel, 1993). It is also considered a good indicator of fairness and justice in the relationship between an employee and the organization (Farh, Podsakoff, and Organ, 1990; Skarlicki and Latham, 1996). Milbrath (1965) described the findings of a comparative survey of political participation in five countries. In those with higher levels of political participation there was also a much higher level of social and organizational activity. According to this relationship, all three mediators will be affected by citizenship behaviors, and all will affect OCB. Committed and satisfied employees who are involved in the organization will reciprocate with higher levels of OCB. Therefore, the second competitive hypothesis (H2) is that job satisfaction, organizational commitment, and participation in decision making mediate the relationship between general citizenship behavior and OCB.

Models

Two models are presented in Figure 6.1, and they examine the competitive hypotheses. Model 1 follows hypothesis H1. It presents a direct relationship, and thus is named the *direct relationship model*. It suggests that each of the general citizenship variables is related directly to each of the two dimensions of OCB. Model 2 follows hypothesis H2, and is termed the *mediated model*. Here, general citizenship is related to OCB indirectly, via the three contextual work attitudes. A path from job satisfaction to organizational commitment is included in all the models tested here. The main reason is that job satisfaction is viewed as one of the determinants of organizational commitment (Mowday, Porter and Steers, 1982).

THE CITIZENSHIP BEHAVIOR STUDY

Data were collected from a sample of employees at a major public health organization in Israel. The organization agreed to our request that it take part in this study. Out of the 32 clinics of the organization in the north of Israel, 22 had not participated in any other study during the previous year. We contacted the 16 largest clinics out of the available 22. A total of 345 questionnaires were distributed in the 16 clinics to administrative and medical personnel; 200 usable questionnaires were returned, a response rate of 58%.

To overcome the self-assessment error extensively mentioned by Brady, Verba and Schlozman (1995) we asked supervisors at each clinic to provide the OCB data for each employee who completed a questionnaire. A breakdown of respondents by occupation showed 31% of the sample to be physicians, 35% nurses, and 34% clerical and administrative workers; 82% of the sample were female, and 84% were married. The average age of the respondents was 45 years (s.d.= 10.3); average tenure in the clinics and in the organization was 10.26 (s.d.= 7.1) and 14.9 (s.d.= 8.5), respectively. Finally, 38% held a bachelor's degree or higher. The demographic characteristics of the sample are similar to those of the employees of all the clinics in the north of Israel: 79% females, 82% married, average age 45, average tenure in the organization 15 years, and 40% with a bachelor's degree or higher.

Model 1: Direct relationship model

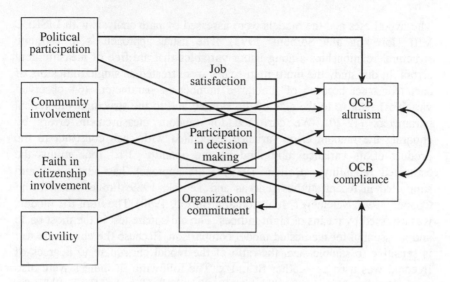

Model 2: Mediated model

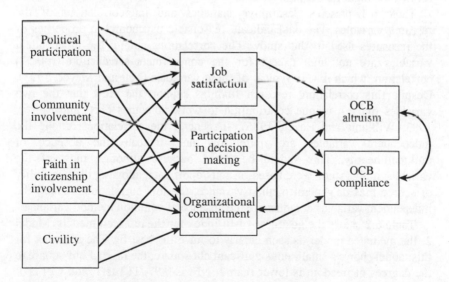

Figure 6.1   The research models

EXAMINATION OF MODELS

The hypotheses and the models were assessed by path analysis with LISREL VIII (Joreskog and Sorbom, 1993). The usual approach is to estimate structural relationships among latent variables that are free of measurement errors. In our study the multi-item scales were treated as single indicators of each construct because of the large number of parameters (64 observed variables) relative to the size of the sample and to the structural theoretical parameters (12-20). We corrected for random measurement errors by equating the random error variance associated with each construct to the product of its variance multiplied by the quantity '$1-\alpha$' (one minus the estimated reliability: Bollen, 1989). This approach has been used and supported in recent studies (Farkas and Tetrick, 1989; Frone, Russell and Cooper, 1992; Netemeyer, Johnston and Burton, 1990). The fit of the models was assessed by means of eight indices. The chi-square test is the most basic and is essential for the nested model comparison. Because the chi-square test is sensitive to sample size, the ratio of the model chi-square to degrees of freedom was used as another fit index. The following fit indices were also used (Medsker, Williams and Holahan, 1994): RFI, CFI, RNI, NFI, NNFI (or TLI), and RMSEA. Finally, a covariance matrix among the research variables formed the input for the path analysis.

Table 6.1 presents descriptive statistics and intercorrelations of the research variables. The data indicate reasonable psychometric properties of the measures used in this study. The correlations among the independent variables are not high except for the commitment–satisfaction ($r=0.57$) correlation, which is very typical of these variables (Tett and Meyer, 1993). Despite this correlation, research findings support the view that the two variables make a unique contribution to work outcomes (Tett and Meyer, 1993; Williams and Hazer, 1986). In general the correlations among the independent variables are quite low and indicate the absence of multicollinearity. This should be noted because although most of the variables in this study were based on self-report data, allowing the possibility of source bias or general method variance, the low correlations among the independent variables demonstrate the absence of common method variance.

Table 6.2 shows the goodness-of-fit index for the research models. Model 2, the mediated model, is seen clearly to have the best fit. The fit index for this model shows a small, nonsignificant chi-square; the ratio of chi-square to the degrees of freedom is lower than 2; NFI is 0.97, TLI is 1, and CFI is 1. The direct model has a significant chi-square, indicating lower fit with the data. All its other fit indices are also inferior in comparison with those of the mediated model. These findings support the competitive hypothesis H2 and reject hypothesis H1.

Table 6.3 contains the structural coefficients and squared multiple correlations for the models. An additional indication that the mediated model was superior to the direct relationship models is demonstrated in the R^2 for OCB, which is the highest for this model (Model 2). It is 0.15 for OCB altruism and 0.19 for OCB compliance. Naturally, main attention is drawn to the structural coefficients of Model 2, which had the best fit with the data. In general, the model supports the notion that the effect of citizenship behaviors and orientations on OCB is strongly mediated by characteristics of the work setting. In terms of the structural coefficients, the findings show no significant effect of political participation on any of the mediated variables. Community involvement had a positive effect on participation in decision making (0.33). People who were more involved in their community tended to participate more in the decision making process in the organization (see Table 6.3). Civility had a positive effect on organizational commitment (0.24). People who demonstrated courtesy in their behavior toward other people in society were more committed to their organization. Finally, those who had more faith in citizen involvement participated more in the organizational decision making process (0.27) and were more satisfied with their job (0.40).

As Table 6.3 shows, there are important differences in the effects of the mediated variables on the two OCB dimensions. Job satisfaction had a strong positive effect on OCB altruism (0.41) and a non-significant effect on OCB compliance. Organizational commitment had a strong negative effect on OCB compliance (-0.49) and a weaker, yet still significant, negative effect on OCB altruism (-0.33). These findings support hypothesis H2. However, the direction of the effect of commitment was unexpected. The data show negative effects for the two dimensions instead of the expected positive effect. Participation in decision making was quite consistent in its effect. The path from participation in decision making to OCB altruism was 0.27, and slightly stronger for OCB compliance (0.32). Both paths were significant and further support hypothesis H2.

DISCUSSION

Do good citizens make good organizational citizens? The findings here show that good citizens can be good organizational citizens, but forms of general citizenship do not have a direct effect on OCB. Model 1, which tested this possibility, showed a poor fit with the data. The data, on the other hand, had a very good fit with Model 2, which argues that one's work experiences strongly filter the effects of citizenship behaviors on OCB. The results support the idea that participation in the civic setting furnishes the individual

Table 6.1 Descriptive statistics and intercorrelations for the study variables (reliabilities in parentheses)

Variables	Means	S.D.	1	2	3	4	5	6	7	8	9	10	11	12	13
Independent variables															
1. Political participation	1.96	0.27	(0.66)												
2. Community involvement	1.43	0.42	0.36***	(0.70)											
3. Faith in citizen involvement	2.80	0.52	0.13	0.26***	(0.72)										
4. Civility	4.21	0.75	−0.06	0.05	0.20**	(0.63)									
5. Participation in decision making	1.90	0.82	0.27***	0.29***	0.04	0.04	(0.75)								
6. Job satisfaction	3.62	0.61	−0.05	0.05	0.26***	0.06	0.16*	(0.71)							
7. Organizational commitment	3.68	0.67	−0.08	0.06	0.32***	0.25***	0.21**	0.57***	(0.84)						
Dependent variables															
8. OCB altruistic	3.31	0.89	−0.10	0.07	0.08	0.00	0.24***	0.18**	0.04	(0.94)					
9. OCB compliance	3.79	0.87	−0.07	0.07	−0.04	−0.15*	0.19**	−0.04	−0.16*	0.55***	(0.75)				

Table 6.1 (continued)

Variables	Means	S.D.	1	2	3	4	5	6	7	8	9	10	11	12	13
Criterion variables															
10. Gender (female)	0.82	0.39	-0.29^{***}	-0.11	0.04	0.00	0.15^*	0.15^*	0.16^*	0.16^*	0.03				
11. Age	44.91	10.37	0.01	-0.06	0.00	0.03	-0.10	0.07	0.23^{**}	-0.13	-0.15^*	-0.14^*			
12. Tenure	15.00	8.51	0.10	0.00	0.07	0.02	0.05	0.08	0.22^{**}	-0.01	-0.08	0.02	0.68^{***}		
13. Center–periphery residence (periphery)	0.23	0.42	0.09	0.16^*	0.03	0.03	-0.04	0.16^*	0.08	-0.01	-0.12	0.00	0.03	0.05	
14. Job status (not permanent)	0.12	0.33	-0.16^*	-0.04	0.05	-0.03	-0.07	-0.02	-0.12	0.16^*	0.23^{***}	0.13	-0.56^{***}	-0.53^{***}	-0.09

Notes
N = 192
*P ≤ 0.05 **P ≤ 0.01 ***P ≤ 0.001

Table 6.2 Goodness-of-fit summary[1]

Model/Description	df	χ^2	df	χ^2/df	RNI	RFI	NFI	TLI	CFI	RMSEA
1. Model 1 – Direct relationship model	11	39.80***	9	3.62	0.89	0.58	0.87	0.66	0.89	0.11
2. Model 2 – Mediated model	10	10.27	8	1.03	1.00	0.88	0.97	1.00	1.00	0.012

Notes
* p ≤ 0.05   ** p ≤ 0.01   *** p ≤ 0.001
1. RNI: Relative No centrality Index
RFI: Relative Fit Index
NFI: Normed Fit Index
TLI: Non-Normed Fit Index
CFI: Comparative Fit Index
RMSEA: Root Mean Square Error of Approximation

with positive attitudes and valuable skills that can be transferred to the work setting. However, the extent to which an individual perceives a relationship with the work setting as fair and satisfactory will determine whether these civic skills will be transferred to it. Model 2 supports the notion that the three contextual work attitudes mediate the effect of general citizenship behavior on OCB. The organization thus has an important role in determining whether external skills and attitudes acquired elsewhere and having the potential to contribute in the work setting will be applied. The practical implication of this is that participation in nonwork activities in general and in citizenship activities in particular can contribute to the organization by increasing levels of OCB. It is much in line with the conclusions of Brady, Verba and Schlozman (1995:285) who argued that the civic skills that facilitate participation are not only acquired in childhood but cultivated throughout the life cycle in the major secondary institutions of adult life. In this way the institutions of civil society operate, as Tocqueville noted, as the school of democracy. Therefore, organizations may benefit from hiring employees with high citizenship values. They should consider candidates' good records in such values an advantage in the selection process, and similarly encourage the adoption of such values by their current employees.

Prior to discussing further implications of the study it is highly important to mention the cultural context in which the findings should be interpreted. The data in this study were not collected in a North American setting, although most OCB research has apparently been done there. This study provides information on different aspects of citizenship behavior in Israel and therefore it encourages future comparisons with findings from other cultures. It is possible however that the relationship between general citizenship and OCB will be different in the North American setting or in any other culture which has other political values. In the present study, voluntary and citizenship behaviors might be affected by cultural and structural factors unique to the Israeli public sector and to the special characteristics of Israeli society. Despite some reforms originating in the late 1970s and extended during the last decade, this sector is still facing some critical difficulties. For more than 50 years large parts of the health system had been under the control of the Histadrut, which is the largest labor union in Israel. Our data were collected precisely when this monopoly was coming to an end and a national health law was being legislated. These substantial changes affected the intra-organizational structure and led to a new management style (Kirkman and Bradford, 1996). They also yielded employee–management conflicts that rocked the entire system for a considerable period of time (mainly between late 1993 and early 1995). All this should be taken into consideration when our findings are examined in a cross-cultural perspective.

Table 6.3   Structural coefficients and squared multiple correlations for OCB altruism and OCB compliance[1]

Parameters (*Path coefficients*)	Model 1 Direct relationship model	Model 2 Mediated model
Political participation → Participation in decision making		−0.20
Political participation → Job satisfaction		−0.22
Political participation → Organizational commitment		−0.04
Political participation → OCB altruism	−0.26*	
Political participation → OCB compliance	−0.26*	
Community involvement → Participation in decision making		0.33*
Community involvement → Job satisfaction		0.01
Community involvement → Organizational commitment		0.02
Community involvement → OCB altruism	0.17	
Community involvement → OCB compliance	0.27*	
Civility → Participation in decision making		0.06
Civility → Job satisfaction		−0.06
Civility → Organizational commitment		0.24*
Civility → OCB altruism	−0.09	
Civility → OCB compliance	−0.27*	
Faith in citizen involvement → Participation in decision making		0.27*
Faith in citizen involvement → Job satisfaction		0.40*
Faith in citizen involvement → Organizational commitment		0.14
Faith in citizen involvement → OCB altruism	0.12	

Table 6.3 (continued)

Parameters (*Path coefficients*)	Model 1 Direct relationship model	Model 2 Mediated model
Faith in citizen involvement → OCB compliance	−0.06	
Participation in decision making → OCB altruism		0.27*
Participation in decision making → OCB compliance		0.32*
Organizational commitment → OCB altruism		−0.33*
Organizational commitment → OCB compliance		−0.49*
Job satisfaction → OCB altruism		0.41*
Job satisfaction → OCB compliance		0.27
Job satisfaction → Organizational commitment	0.77*	0.67*
OCB altruism → OCB compliance	0.56*	0.54*
R^2		
Participation in decision making		0.20
Job satisfaction		0.16
Organizational commitment	0.60	0.64
OCB altruism	0.07	0.15
OCB compliance	0.12	0.19

Notes
*$p < 0.05$
1. R^2 is calculated only for the dependent variables in the model

The application of our findings in the North American context is questionable for another reason. The Israeli political system is different from the American. As suggested often in the past (for example, Almond and Verba, 1963; Barber, 1984), citizenship behaviors will possibly have different consequences in different cultures. Citizenship behavior in Israel is different from what it is in North America. For example, voting rates in Israel are very high in general and in local elections (around 70-75%), and the feeling of collectivism in Israeli society is relatively strong. The somewhat nonliberal characteristics of parts of Israeli society may also influence citizenship behavior in Israel (for example, Ben-Eliezer, 1993). Hence, future studies should develop the socio-cultural aspects of general and organizational citizenship behavior and their mutual relationship.

Beyond the cultural context of our findings some implications of the study deserve more attention. The prime question in this regard concerns the implications of enhanced OCB for the performances of public organizations and for society in general. Podsakoff and MacKenzie (1997) summarize some of the most important influences of OCB on organizational success: (a) enhancing co-worker and managerial productivity, (b) freeing up resources so they can be used for more productive purposes, (c) reducing the need to devote scarce resources to purely maintenance functions, (d) helping to coordinate the activities both within and across groups, (e) strengthening the organization's ability to attract and retain the best employees, (f) increasing the stability of the organization's performance, and (g) enabling the organization to adapt more effectively to environmental change. In the public sector however, these contributions directly affect citizens as customers. OCB represents spontaneous behavior, entrepreneurial activities and creative ideas that are vital for the development of a prosperous society and a healthy public administration. A discouragement of OCB may lead to inferior services and low levels of responsiveness to citizens' demands (low Customer-Oriented Behavior – COB). When public officials show hampered outcomes, the citizens/clients are negatively affected (Pollitt, 1988). They obtain poor services from unmotivated public servants, and as a result may develop negative perceptions toward the public system, its efficiency and legitimacy. Thus, public organizations that ignore the importance of OCB and its antecedents contradict the very basic notion of communitarianism (Etzioni, 1994; 1995). They also run counter to modern approaches in contemporary public management. Both the quality management movement of the 1980s and 1990s and the new public management approach (NPM) emphasize spontaneous behavior of employees that is aimed at enhancing the satisfaction of citizens as clients (Brudney, 1990; Stewart and Ranson, 1994).

Naturally, dissatisfied citizens should be the concern of modern societies and new ways should be found to improve the relationship between societies and citizens. In many ways this relationship can be viewed as bi-directional since democratic values may initiate OCB, but they also derive from it. For example, empirical evidence of the relationship between citizens' attitudes toward political democracy and other external values like perceptions of a market economy can be found in the work of Gibson (1996). In this study Gibson suggests a causal association of the two sets of values where citizenship and democratic values are mostly a function of the wish for a more productive economic system. In other words, better production and high performance of organizations positively contribute to democratic values and to better citizenship behavior. The findings imply however that high general citizenship behavior and orientations positively affect OCB in the public sector. Public agencies in which OCB is encouraged are more productive and responsive to the public's needs (Podsakoff and MacKenzie, 1997). Their contribution to society grows, and a healthier interaction develops between governments and citizens. Furthermore, the present findings show that the relationship between general citizenship behavior and OCB was mediated by several work attitudes. Hence, the public sphere was found to have a significant role in buffering the effect of good citizenship behavior and OCB.

General Citizenship and the Work Setting

The strong support for the mediated model indicates no direct spillover of behavior from the civic to the organizational setting. However, the literature suggests that the fit of the models should also be assessed by the magnitude of the individual parameters (Bollen, 1989; Breckler, 1990). Significant paths are not the only or the main criteria for assessing the fit of the models, but they can definitely provide some guidance for future research. The findings here indicated significant paths between general citizenship and OCB in the direct relationship model and significant paths between general citizenship and important work attitudes and behaviors such as commitment, job satisfaction, and participation in decision making in the mediating model. This finding may imply other types of citizenship–workplace relationships, mainly those that represent more complex explanations and that examined different cultural samples.

First, general citizenship is more strongly related to OCB compliance than to OCB altruism. This is demonstrated in the higher multiple correlation for OCB compliance (R^2 =0.12 for OCB compliance compared with 0.07 for OCB altruism) and in more significant paths between variables representing general citizenship and OCB compliance. General citizenship is thus related to extra-role behaviors aimed at the system rather than at specific persons. This supports the notion mentioned in previous studies (for example, Brady, Verba and Schlozman, 1995; Sieber, 1974) that the resources gained in community involvement can be valuable resources for successful work functioning.

The effect of the variables representing general citizenship on OCB seems to be complex and to represent a mixture of positive and negative spillover. The positive relationship of community involvement represents a more positive spillover, and the negative relationship of political participation and civility with OCB altruism represents a negative spillover. This shows in conflict stemming from nonwork-to-work spillover, such as time spent in political participation, which diminishes time available for work; and behaviors required in nonwork domains, such as civility, are inappropriate for work (Greenhaus and Beutell, 1985). Such negative spillover effects lead to lower levels of OCB. Among the general citizenship variables, political participation deserves further attention. It is more consistently negatively related to work attitudes and behaviors than the other general citizenship variables: strictly political involvement seems to have negative consequences for behaviors and attitudes at work. It is interesting to ask what so differentiates political involvement from community involvement, to result in opposite effects on work attitudes and behaviors. Do people get involved in politics because they seek an entirely new role, one that will compensate them for what they perceive as negative experiences at work? Is involvement in politics so different from involvement in community? How? A related question stems from the positive and relatively strong relationships of community involvement with participation in decision making and OCB compliance. Is this the most appropriate behavior in general citizenship-to-work spillover? Considering previously observed and surprising relationships of community involvement with job satisfaction (Iverson and Roy, 1994; Kirchmeyer, 1992) and organizational commitment (Kirchmeyer, 1992), community involvement deserves more attention than it has received. Future research should deal with all these questions conceptually and empirically.

The findings also show that the variables representing general citizenship were useful in predicting important work attitudes such as organizational commitment and job satisfaction, as well as reported participation in decision making. For example, community involvement was related to participation in decision making, civility to organizational commitment and faith in citizen involvement to job satisfaction and participation in decision making. Empirical and conceptual support for such relationships was previously indicated in the literature examining the relationship between work and nonwork (Iverson and Roy, 1994; Kirchmeyer, 1992). All the significant paths in Model 2 indicate that greater citizenship involvement increased job satisfaction, organizational commitment, and participation in decision making. The findings thus show the usefulness of concepts adopted from one discipline, political science, to others, organizational behavior and public management. Moreover, future research should test the possibility that organizational commitment, job satisfaction and participation in decision making mediate but also moderate the relationship between general citizenship and OCB. Namely each of these variables might represent conditions in the workplace that might lead to a differential relationship between general citizenship and OCB.

Finally, this study has shown that general citizenship is an important and interesting dimension that should be further explored. The relationship between civic behaviors and work outcomes has hardly ever been examined, so future studies should explore it as well as the relationship between civic behavior and OCB. The findings of this study have demonstrated the usefulness of examining OCB in a conceptual framework developed in another discipline, political science. It has also shown the potential of structural determinants in affecting OCB levels. Research on OCB has concentrated mostly on contextual work determinants. The relatively low variance encountered in most of that research means that more work is needed. The contribution of the present study lies in its pointing out some new directions in explaining these important behaviors and the potential benefit for public administration in modern societies.

NOTE

1. Cohen, A. and Vigoda, E. (2000), 'Do good citizens make good organizational citizens? An empirical examination of the relationship between general citizenship and organizational citizenship behavior in Israel' *Administration and Society*, **32** (5), 596–624. Copyright with permission from Sage Publishing.

REFERENCES

Almond, G.A. and Verba, S. (1963), *The Civic Culture: Political Attitudes and Democracy in Five Nations: An Analytic Study*, Boston: Little Brown.

Aristotle (1962), *The Politics*, Harmondsworth: Penguin.

Barber, B. (1984), *Strong Democracy: Participatory Politics for a New Age*, Berkeley: University of California Press.

Ben-Eliezer, U. (1993), 'The meaning of political participation in a nonliberal democracy: The Israeli experience', *Comparative Politics, 25*, 397–412.

Bollen, K.A. (1989), *Structural Equation with Latent Variables*, New York: Wiley.

Brady, H.E., Verba, S., and Schlozman, K.L. (1995), 'Beyond SES: A resource model of political participation', *American Political Science Review, 89*, 271–94.

Breckler, S.J. (1990), 'Applications of covariance structure modeling in psychology: Cause for concern', *Psychological Bulletin, 107*, 260–73.

Brudney, J. (1990), *Fostering Volunteer Programs in the Public Sector: Planning, Initiating and Managing Voluntary Activities*, San Francisco: Jossey Bass.

Cary, C.D. (1977), 'The goals of citizenship training in American and Soviet schools', *Studies in Comparative Communism, 10*, 281–97.

DeCotiis, T. A. and Sommers, T. P. (1987), 'A path analysis of a model of the antecedents and consequences of organizational commitment', *Human Relations, 40*, 445–70.

Etzioni, A. (1994), *The Spirit of Community*, New York: Touchstone.

Etzioni, A. (1995), *New Communitarian Thinking: Persons, Virtues, Institutions, and Communities*, Charlottesville: Virginia University Press.

Farh, J.L., Podsakoff, P.M., and Organ, D.W. (1990), 'Accounting for organizational citizenship behavior: Leader fairness and task scope versus satisfaction', *Journal of Management, 16*, 705–21.

Farkas, A.J. and Tetrick, L.E. (1989), 'A three-wave longitudinal analysis of the causal ordering of satisfaction and commitment on turnover decisions', *Journal of Applied Psychology, 74*, 855–68.

Frone, M.R., Russell, M., and Cooper, M.L. (1992), 'Antecedents and outcomes of work–family conflict: Testing a model of the work–family interface', *Journal of Applied Psychology, 77*, 65–78.

Gibson, J.L. (1996), 'Political and economic markets: Changes in the connections between attitudes toward political democracy and a market economy within the mass culture of Russia and Ukraine', *The Journal of Politics, 58*, 954–84.

Graham, J.W. (1986), *Organizational citizenship informed by political theory*, Paper presented at the meeting of the Academy of Management Meetings.

Graham, J.W. (1991), 'An essay on Organizational Citizenship Behavior', *Employee Responsibilities and Rights Journal, 4*, 249–70.

Greenhaus, J.H. and Beutell, N.J. (1985), 'Sources of conflict between work and family life', *Academy of Management Review, 10*, 76–88.

Inkeles, A. (1969), 'Participant citizenship in six developing countries', *American Political Science Review, 63*, 1120–41.

Iverson, R.D. and Roy, P. (1994), 'A causal model of behavioral commitment: Evidence from a study of Australian blue-collar employees', *Journal of Management, 20*, 15–41.

Joreskog, K.G. and Sorbom, D. (1993), *Structural Equation Modeling with the SIMPLIS Command Language*, Hillsdale, NJ: Erlbaum.

Katz, D. and Kahn, R.L. (1966), *The Social Psychology of Organizations*, New York: Wiley.

Kirchmeyer, C. (1992), 'Nonwork participation and work attitudes: A test of scarcity vs. expansion models of personal resources', *Human Relations, 45*, 775–95.

Kirkman, L., Bradford, L. (1996), 'Health care reform in the Netherlands, Israel, Germany, England, and Sweden', *Generations, 20* , 65–70.

Konovsky, M.A. and Pugh, S.D. (1994), 'Citizenship behavior and social exchange', *Academy of Management Journal, 37*, 656–69.

Latham, G.P. and Skarlicki, D.P. (1995), 'Criterion-related validity of the situational and patterned behavior description interviews with organizational citizenship behavior', *Human Performance, 8*, 67–80.

Medsker, G. J., Williams, L. J., and Holahan, P. J. (1994), 'A review of current practices for evaluating causal models in organizational behavior and human resources management research', *Journal of Management, 20*, 239–64.

Milbrath, L.W. (1965), *Political Participation*, Chicago: Rand McNally.

Moorman, R.H. (1991), 'Relationship between organizational justice and organizational citizenship behaviors: Do fairness perceptions influence employee citizenship?' *Journal of Applied Psychology, 76*, 845–55.

Mowday, R.T., Porter, L.M., and Steers, R.M. (1982), *Employee–Organization Linkages: The Psychology of Commitment, Absenteeism and Turnover,* New York: Academic Press.

Netemeyer, R.G., Johnston, M.W., and Burton, S. (1990), 'Analysis of role conflict and role ambiguity in a structural equation framework', *Journal of Applied Psychology, 75*, 148–57.

Organ, D.W. (1988), *Organizational Behavior Citizenship: The Good Soldier Syndrome*, Lexington, MA: Lexington Books.

Organ, D.W. (1990), 'The motivational basis of organizational citizenship behavior', *Research in Organizational Behavior, 12*, 43–72.

Organ, D.W. (1994), 'Personality and Organizational Citizenship Behavior', *Journal of Management, 20*, 465–78.

Organ, D.W. and Konovsky, M. (1989), 'Cognitive versus affective determinants of organizational citizenship behavior', *Journal of Applied Psychology, 74*, 157–64.

Organ, D.W. and Ryan, K. (1995), 'A meta-analytic review of attitudinal and dispositional predictors of organizational citizenship behavior', *Personnel Psychology, 48*, 775–802.

Pateman, C. (1970), *Participation and Democratic Theory,* London: Cambridge University Press.

Peterson, S. A. (1990), *Political Behavior.* Palo Alto, CA: Sage.

Pettersen, P.A. and Rose, L.E. (1996), 'Participation in local politics in Norway: Some do, some don't, some will, some won't', *Political Behavior, 18*, 51–97.

Plato (1892), 'The republic', in B. Jowett (trans.), *The Dialogues of Plato* (pp. 591–879), New York: Random House.

Podsakoff, P.M. and MacKenzie, S.B. (1997), 'Impact of Organizational Citizenship Behavior on organizational performance. A review and suggestions for future research', *Human Performance, 10*, 133–51.

Pollitt, C. (1988), 'Bringing consumers into performance measurement', *Policy and Politics, 16*, 77–87.

Pollitt, C. (1990), 'Performance indicators, root and branch', in M. Cave, M. Kogan, and R. Smith (eds), *Output and Performance Measurement in Government: The State of the Art* (pp. 167–78), London: Jessica Kingsley.

Powell, W. W. (ed.) (1987), *The Non-Profit Sector: A Research Handbook,* New Haven: Yale University Press.

Schussler, K.F. (1982), *Measuring Social Life Feelings,* San Francisco: Jossey Bass.

Sieber, S.D. (1974), 'Toward a theory of role accumulation', *American Sociological Review, 39*, 567–78.

Skarlicki, D. P. and Latham, G. L. (1996), 'Increasing citizenship behavior within a labor union: A test of organizational justice theory', *Journal of Applied Psychology, 81*, 161–9.

Sobel, R. (1993), 'From occupational involvement to political participation: An exploratory analysis', *Political Behavior, 15*, 339–53.

Stewart, J. and Ranson, R. (1994), 'Management in the public domain', in D. McKevitt and A. Lawton (eds), *Public Sector Management* (pp. 54–70), London: Sage.

Tett, R.P. and Meyer, J.P. (1993), 'Job satisfaction, organizational commitment, turnover intention, and turnover: Path analyses based on meta-analytic findings',

Personnel Psychology, 46, 259–93.

Theiss-Morse, E. (1993), 'Conceptualizations of good citizenship and political participation', *Political Behavior, 15*, 355–80.

Van Dyne, L., Graham, J.W., and Dienesch, R.M. (1994), 'Organizational Citizenship Behavior: Construct redefinition, measurement, and validation', *Academy of Management Journal, 37*, 765–802.

Walzer, M. (1970), *Obligations: Essays on Disobedience, War and Citizenship*, Cambridge, MA: Harvard University Press.

Williams, L.J. and Anderson, S.E. (1991), 'Job satisfaction and organizational commitment as predictors of organizational citizenship and in-role behaviors', *Journal of Management, 17*, 601–17.

Williams, L. J. and Hazer, J. T. (1986), 'Antecedents and consequences of satisfaction and commitment in turnover models: A re-analysis using latent variables equation methods', Journal of Applied Psychology, *71*, 219–31.

Zeffane, R. (1994), 'Patterns of organizational commitment and perceived management style: A comparison of public and private sector employees', *Human Relations, 47*, 977–1010.

7. Internal Politics in Public Administration Systems: An Empirical Examination of its Relationship with Job Congruence, Organizational Citizenship Behavior, and In-role Performance[1]

Eran Vigoda-Gadot

INTRODUCTION

During the last two decades the concept of Organizational Politics (OP) has received increased attention in management literature. This attention relied partly on the expectation of finding new answers to some old questions, such as what (dis)motivates individuals at work and how can we better explain variations in employees' behavior and productivity? As a result, studies became particularly interested in the potential relationship between workplace politics and individuals' performances. The primary goal of these attempts was to examine whether internal politics plays a significant role in setting organizational outcomes, and if so, what the nature and characteristics of this relationship are.

Politics and political behavior in organizations seemed a promising field for theoretical inquiry not only because of its practical implications but for some other reasons as well. First, modern societies searched for better efficiency and effectiveness in organizations in order to successfully respond to the increasing demands of their citizens. Scholars were urged to provide new explanations of and remedies for the decline in organizational outcomes in both the business and the public sector. Internal politics and power relations between organizational members appeared to account at least for some of these problems. Second, politics represented a creative approach to the understanding of organizational dynamics, which for many years had been particularly overlooked. Many scholars agreed that politics was a common phenomenon in every organization (for example, Bozeman et al., 1996; Cropanzano et al., 1997; Ferris and Kacmar, 1992; Ferris and King, 1991; Mayes and Allen, 1977; Mintzberg, 1983; Pfeffer, 1992; Zhou and Ferris, 1995;) yet only few comprehensive attempts were made to fully understand it. Studies were preoccupied with other, mainly formal, aspects of workplace activities, and preferred categorizing the political arena as a less significant dimension of the organizational nature. Consequently, the field was much understudied until the 1970s and 1980s. Third, this approach was interdisciplinary, and employed classic terminology rooted in conventional political science and sociological theory. The common perception was that politics in the workplace was a necessary evil that no individual or society could avoid, but no different from many other difficulties that had to be borne. Therefore, management literature consistently considered politics, power and influence relations among stakeholders as illegitimate, informal and dysfunctional, as against authority and formal organizational design, which were described as apolitical and functional (Hardy, 1995). Scholars like Block (1988:5) stated bluntly that 'politics (in organizations) is basically a negative process. If I told you you were a very political person, you would take it either as an insult or at best as a mixed blessing'. OP was presumed to describe a dark and exceptional aspect of workplace activity (Ferris and King, 1991).

With the continuous growing interest in workplace politics, some studies have suggested promoting a more empirical approach to the examination of its outcomes. However, only recently have a few scholars responded positively to this challenge (Bozeman et al., 1996; Ferris et al., 1996; Ferris, Harrell-Cook, and Dulebohn, 1998) and most of them have focused on employees' attitudes as the prime outcomes of OP. As a result, scant empirical evidence exists today that can support the (negative?) effect of internal workplace politics on employees' outcomes, and especially on objective performance evaluations. The main goal of this study is to contribute to the development of theoretical thinking on OP, and more specifically to demonstrate the relationship between job congruence, perception of organizational politics, and two constructs of employees' reactions: in-role performances and organizational citizenship behavior (OCB). The thesis developed here is that employees respond to the political climate of their work environment both formally and informally. Job congruence is expected to affect individuals' perception of politics and both politics and congruence with the work sphere are presumed to have an influence on employees' performances. Note that while the focus of this study is on *public* personnel management, much of the theory developed, as well as the findings and the conclusions, are relevant also to the private sector.

THEORY, HYPOTHESES AND MODELS

OP is a complex phenomenon that appears to have no clear definition. Scholars have treated this slippery concept in many ways. They described it as ways to get ahead in an organization (Wallace and Szilagyi, 1982:181), as dynamic processes of influence that produce organizationally relevant outcomes beyond the simple performance of job tasks, or as the management of influence to obtain ends not sanctioned by the organization or to obtain sanctioned ends through non-sanctioned influence means (Mayes and Allen, 1977:675). Ferris et al. (1989) suggest that OP is a social influence process in which behavior is strategically designed to maximize short-term or long-term self-interests, which is either consistent with or at the expense of others' interests. Pfeffer (1981:4-5) defined OP as those activities carried out by people to acquire, enhance and use power and other resources to obtain their preferred outcomes in a situation where there is uncertainty or disagreement. This perception is much in line with Mintzberg (1983:172) who argued that politics refer to 'individual or group behavior that is informal, ostensibly parochial, typically divisive, and above all, in a technical sense, illegitimate – sanctioned neither by formal authority, accepted ideology, nor certified expertise'. Most of these definitions correlate OP with personal struggles, conflicts, influential activities, and most important inequity and unfairness, which result from the strong ambitions or aspirations of those who hold power in the workplace.

Perception of Organizational Politics

A variety of perspectives and methods were advanced to understand politics in organizations (for example, Bacharach and Lawler, 1980; Brass, 1984; Burns, 1961; DuBrin, 1988; Erez and Rim, 1982; Gandz and Murray, 1980; Izraeli, 1987; Kipnis, Schmidt and Wilkinson, 1980; Mayes and Allen, 1977; Mintzberg, 1983; Pfeffer, 1981; 1992; Yukl and Tracy, 1992). One of the most common approaches is relatively new and began to flourish at the end of the 1980s. Progress was made with the works of Ferris, Kacmar and their colleagues, who focused on employees' subjective *perception* of organizational politics rather than on political behavior or influence tactics per se. Concentration on perception of politics instead of actual political behavior appeared to stem from the fact that the former is more easily defined, explained and empirically measured. However, perception reflects individuals' opinion of the social-political atmosphere of a work unit, and as such it can be categorized as an indirect measure of OP. Not surprisingly, this variable faced some criticism regarding its ability to represent the entire political environment in organizations (Vigoda and Cohen, 1998). Nevertheless, a consensus exists that it embodies an important dimension of the intraorganizational climate created by power struggles and influence tactics of all organizational members.

As was elaborated more specifically by Kacmar and Ferris (1991:193-94) and Ferris and Kacmar (1992:93), perception of organizational politics represents the degree to which respondents view their work environment as political in nature, promoting the self-interests of others, hence unjust and unfair from the individual point of view. This approach is rooted in Kurt Lewin's (1936) argument that people respond to their perception of reality, not to reality itself. Politics in organizations should similarly be understood in terms of what people think rather than what it actually represents. This idea yielded a scale for the measurement of political perception termed the 'Perception of Organizational Politics Scale' (POPS). Different studies resulted in several versions of this scale (Ferris et al., 1989; Ferris and Kacmar, 1992; Ferris, Russ and Fandt, 1989; Kacmar and Carlson, 1994; Kacmar and Ferris, 1991) that proved very useful for other studies during the 1990s (Bozeman et al., 1996; Cropanzano et al., 1997; Ferris et al., 1996; Ferris, Fedor and King, 1994; Ferris et al., 1991).

Several of these studies sought to examine the antecedents of POPS. Ferris, Russ and Fandt (1989) and Ferris and Kacmar (1992) argued the existence of three groups of influences. The first group consisted of general *personal influences* like age, sex and self monitoring. The second group was termed *organization influences* and included variables like centralization, formalization, hierarchical level and span of control. The third group of antecedents, named *job/work environment influences*, was based on variables such as job autonomy, job variety, feedback, advancement opportunity and interaction with others. Most studies accepted this theoretical framework and showed its usefulness for the understanding of workplace politics. However, only a few tried to elaborate on other factors that may be important in that regard. This should be noted, since the ratio of explained variance in most of these studies was moderate and ranged around 0.30–0.41 (Ferris et al., 1996; Ferris and Kacmar, 1992). Therefore, some further efforts in pointing out other predictors of politics perceptions may contribute to our knowledge of this intriguing manifestation.

Relying on the above, the present study suggests taking a step forward, and examining the effect of job congruence on perception of organizational politics and employees' performance. Studies have mentioned job congruence as an important determinant of employees' productivity and performance. For example, Elchanan, Esformes and Friedland (1994) found job congruence to be related to job stability/persistence and to performance evaluations in 774 employees in Israel. Other studies also mentioned the importance of job congruence, organizational climate and general culture as crucial factors that may facilitate employees' coping abilities in a new work environment and during the initial integration stages in organizations (Ferris, Harrell-Cook and Dulebohn, 1998). Schein (1968; 1978) suggested that newcomers are aware of the ongoing politics within the organization but must go through a learning process of gaining the acceptance of others. Job congruence can help them to successfully cope during this period and adapt to the political environment. Therefore, it is only natural to try to relate job congruence to organizational politics, which represents a meaningful domain of workplace atmosphere.

Job Congruence and Organizational Politics

Job congruence generally refers to the basic compatibility of an employee with his/her workplace and specific job. It also reflects a level of fulfilled aspirations and expectations of the work environment in its broad sense. This study treats job congruence as comprised of two constructs: employees' level of met expectations (ME) and person–organization fit (POF). These are two well established factors reflecting the adaptability of an individual to his/her work surroundings. Wanous et al. (1992) defined ME as the discrepancy between what a person encounters on the job in the way of positive and negative experiences and what he/she expected to encounter. Bretz and Judge (1994) defined POF as the degree to which individuals (skills, needs, values and personality) match job requirements. The higher ME and POF are, the higher the congruence of the individual's characteristics and expectations with the organizational environments and demands.

The congruence between an individual and the workplace is expected to have a negative effect on employees' perception of organizational politics. The rationale for this relationship is based on Cropanzano et al. (1997:163) and Hulin (1991), who argued that individuals are more likely to have a positive evaluation of an organization when their goals are met than when their aspirations are threatened. The basic model of Ferris et al. (1989) and Ferris and Kacmar (1992) also mentioned the job/work environment influences as potential predictors of politics perceptions. Variables like job autonomy, job variety, feedback, advancement opportunity and interaction with others represent one's level of fit and compatibility with the workplace. This fit may reduce employees' perception of organizational politics. Those who better fit the organization and have more realistic expectations are presumed to view the environment as less aggressive, less power seeking, more fair and equal, and thus apolitical.

The importance of fit and expectations in social life and their implications for the study of politics was further advanced by Molm (1997:4), according to whom actors in every social political system are motivated by the cost and benefits of their activities and the mutual political exchange relations with the environment. Those who better fit the organization and succeed in fulfilling self aspirations will tend to develop positive perceptions toward their social and work environment. When such congruence exists, employees will perceive the organization as less political and well responding to their needs and aspirations. They will probably attribute their success to factors other than politics, such as their own qualifications and level of performance at work. However, individuals who do not fit a specific job or work unit are expected to perceive the organization more negatively. When job congruence is low it is more likely that employees will feel disappointed and frustrated, and will develop alienation from the organization and their surroundings. Such feelings may broaden the emotional as well as the functional gap between a person and her/his job. Consequently, employees will tend to attribute their failure to achieve their goals to the political system of the organization rather than to themselves.

The relationship between job congruence and performance at work is even more established in management theory. Vroom (1964) developed the expectancy theory, which argued that expectations significantly affect employees' motivation, perceptions and performance in the workplace. The expectancy theory suggests that a better fit between individuals and their work environment enhances employees' met expectations. When one's personal characteristics and attitudes are close to those of the workplace a better fit can be expected between one and one's job/work. Those organizations which employ better fitted individuals have significant advantages over other organizations. They show high levels of production and improved quality of performances, and they encounter only minor problems of absenteeism and turnover.

Empirical evidence exists today to support these claims. An extensive meta-analysis of 31 studies and 17,241 people was conducted by Wanous et al. (1992), who found correlation of -0.29 between met expectations (ME) and intentions to leave the organization. A correlation of 0.19 was reported between ME and job survival, and of 0.11 between ME and job performance. Bretz and Judge (1994) examined person–organization fit (POF) as a construct of work adjustment. They affirmed a positive effect of POF on tenure, satisfaction and other constructs of career success. These arguments led to the first hypothesis in this study (H1) that job congruence is negatively related with perception of organizational politics and positively related with employees' performances.

Consequences of Organizational Politics

Most studies on organizational politics naturally expected to find it related with poor performance by employees (Eisenhardt and Bourgeois, 1988; Cropanzano et al., 1997) or as a potential source of work stress (Ferris et al., 1996). However, this relationship seems far more complex. Bozeman et al. (1996) elaborated on the effect of perception of politics on four outcome variables: organizational commitment, job satisfaction, intention to turnover, and job stress. No direct relationships were found in this two-study investigation, yet some interactive relationships were found between perception of organizational politics, feelings of self-efficacy, and the outcome variables. Specifically, individuals with high job self-efficacy perceived organizational politics as a threat, and thus exhibited lower levels of organizational outcomes (organizational commitment and job satisfaction) than persons with low job self-efficacy. Ferris and King (1991) found that influence tactics of employees contributed to being liked by the supervisor, which led the supervisor to rate the employees' job performance more favorably. Tziner et al. (1996) further developed and supported this idea, and thus promoted the Janus-face image of OP which was proposed by Mintzberg (1985) and Rollinson, Broadfield and Edwards (1998).

A more balanced approach to OP was adopted in other studies. In a survey conducted by Gandz and Murray (1980), over half of the respondents thought that politics in an organization means unfair, bad, irrational and unhealthy behavior. Nonetheless, many believed that political behavior is necessary if one wants to be a good employee or a successful manager and get ahead in the organization. An early work of Hirschman (1970) suggested that political behavior is a legitimate fight response to different conflicts or to a decline in organizations. It was also argued that OP is a legitimate way for people to take effective action in the organizational context by having control over information, flexibility and statecraft (Hirschman, 1970; Ryan, 1989). These studies imply that OP is not necessarily related to negative work outcomes. Ferris et al. (1989) and Kumar and Ghadially (1989) stated that OP is a natural social influence process. Workplace politics may have functional as well as dysfunctional consequences, and can be helpful or harmful for members of the organization. OP may have several positive outcomes (for example, career advancement, recognition and status, enhanced power and position, accomplishment of personal goals, control, and success). It may also result in harmful outcomes (for example, loss of strategic power, position credibility, negative feeling toward others, internal feelings of guilt). More important for our study, a majority of these works argued that organizations with extremely high levels of internal politics will eventually have to face hampered job performance of their members.

Theories of organizational conflict may also be useful in analysing the possible consequences of OP. These ideas (for example, Putnam, 1995) view organizations as rife with power struggles and political processes. Conflict in organizations may have negative effects on the aggregate ability of organizations to function efficiently. Conflict in the workplace is almost inevitable and operative measures have to be taken to prevent its negative effect on employees' performances. Nevertheless, conflict can also balance power relationships, promote flexibility and adaptability, and prevent stagnation of work units. It has a potential of enhancing growth and stability, guarding against groupthink, and facilitating effective decision making. This can be achieved only if conflict and internal politics are wisely used by the organizational leadership to create a feeling of productive competition under fair terms among all players. Note, however, that only a few studies have provided sound empirical support for this theoretical rationale and therefore the relationship between OP and employees' performances remains vague.

Employees' Performances

So far this chapter has discussed employees' performances as one construct. However, we examined both formal (in-role) and informal (extra-role) performances of individuals. In-role performances usually refer to duties and responsibilities one executes as an integral part of one's job assignments. Extra-role behavior describes some activities beyond formal job requirements that one chooses to do without expecting any direct reward. These formal and informal activities contribute to the general health and prosperity of the work unit. Among them, organizational citizenship behavior (OCB) is the one that has received considerable attention in management literature during the past decade. OCB had its roots in the work of Katz and Kahn (1966), who argued that an important type of behavior required of employees for the effective functioning of an organization is the undertaking of innovative and spontaneous activities beyond the prescribed role requirement. OCB consists of informal contributions that participants can choose to make or withhold, without regard to sanctions or formal incentives. For example, this behavior may show exceptional willingness to assist others with their work duties, helping new employees, or using the organizational resources only when necessary. Many of these contributions, aggregated over time and persons, were thought to enhance organizational effectiveness (Organ and Konovsky, 1989). OCB was described by Organ (1988) as the 'good soldier syndrome' which every organization must foster.

Further suggested was the idea that better measurement of OCB should also include items representing in-role behaviors because such an analysis would clarify whether the respondents differentiated intra-role and extra-role behaviors (Williams and Anderson, 1991). This recommendation was strongly supported by Morrison (1994), who found that the boundary between intra-role and extra-role behavior was ill-defined and varied from one employee to the next and between employees and supervisors. While OCB refers to informal behaviors aimed at enhancing organizational outcomes, in-role performances refer to a set of required behaviors one is expected to display in one's job and for which one is directly rewarded. These activities comprise duties, routine tasks, and ad hoc requests of the immediate supervisor. Sometimes they are part of the organizational formal procedures and regulations but they are always perceived as an essential part of the contiguous production process. For this reason, the present study has undertaken an integrative approach to the measurement of OCB, using both in-role and extra-role behaviors in one scale.

Perception of organizational politics is predicted to be negatively related to OCB and in-role performance. High levels of OP usually reflect an unfair organizational environment in which those who hold more political power determine criteria of resource allocation and distribution. This is generally done with only minor concern for objective standards, fair priorities, and actual needs of the rest of the organization members. Ferris et al. (1996) suggested a relationship between constructs of procedural justice (for example, time since last promotion or time since last appraisal) and perception of politics. Arguments that support the relationship between justice and performance in the workplace can also be found in numerous other studies (Farh, Podsakoff, and Organ, 1990; Konovsky and Pugh, 1994; Moorman, 1991; Niehoff and Moorman, 1993; Schnake, 1991; Tansky, 1993; Wayne and Green, 1993). For example, Schnake (1991) argued that a leader's fair or supportive behavior may create a need in subordinates to reciprocate. One way to 'pay back' a leader for his/her supportive and fair behavior is by performing better or engaging in citizenship behavior. Employees consider their leader the key representative of the organizational justice process because of his/her frequent contact with them. A person's sense of fairness would depend very much on the leader's behavior and fairness values. Moorman (1991) found that supervisors have a direct influence on subordinates' behavior by increasing the fairness of interactions with them. This idea can be extended to include other organizational members as well. Managers and co-workers are continuously responsible for the formation of the political climate in the workplace. Organizations rife with political maneuvering and power struggles usually have less concern with fairness and equity values. They enable the powerful ones to gain more advantages and benefits than others. Therefore, in-role performance, and especially OCB, may be negatively related with the general political atmosphere in a given work unit. The study of Farh, Podsakoff and Organ

(1990) partially supported this notion. These authors found that higher levels of justice and fairness (lower levels of organizational politics) encourage employees to respond with higher levels of OCB. Building on the exchange approach, employees with high job congruence will perceive their environment as more fair, and therefore will reciprocate with better performances. That is, organizations that create a culture and atmosphere of better equity, and a fair distribution of social and political resources may increase employees' formal performances as well as willingness to engage in OCB. Thus, a second hypothesis (H2) suggests that perception of organizational politics is negatively related to in-role performance and organizational citizenship behavior.

Since perception of organizational politics largely reflects attitudes toward fairness and equity in the organizational arena (Ferris and Kacmar, 1992; Kacmar and Ferris, 1991) it is also expected to mediate the relationship between individuals' congruence with the job/work environment and personal performances. Schein (1968; 1978) argued that employees may be expected to develop attitudes to the political climate of the work unit only after they spent a reasonable period of time in the organization. During the first stages of entering the organization they experience political events only as bystanders. However, with time they are bound to actively enter into situations where their personal power and influence abilities are confronted with other employees' ambitious. The results of such confrontations can be translated to positive or negative work outcomes.

The proposition that perception of organizational politics is a mediator between job congruence and employees' performances is based on previous studies (Bozeman et al, 1996; Cropanzano et al., 1997; Ferris et al., 1996; Ferris and Kacmar, 1992; Parker, Dipboye and Jackson, 1995). These studies argued that perception of politics mediates the relationship between some job/work influences and individuals' outcomes such as job anxiety, job stress and burnout, organizational withdrawal, turnover, absenteeism, job satisfaction, effectiveness, loyalty and commitment. Perception of politics was found to have a negative relationship with job satisfaction and with organizational commitment. It was also positively related to job stress and burnout. However, to our knowledge, almost no evidence exists today as to how politics affects formal and informal performance evaluations of employees' by their supervisors. Relying on these findings, and mainly on the mediating role of perception of politics recently found by Ferris et al. (1996), the third hypothesis (H3) suggests that perception of organizational politics mediates the relationship between job congruence and employees' performances.

Models

Two models are suggested to test the contribution of organizational politics to the understanding of variations in employees' performances. These models have the advantage of examining the entire theoretical conception of the study as one integrative view. They extend the implications of the hypotheses that elaborate on some meaningful, yet specific and relatively limited relationships between OP, job congruence and performances.

The Indirect/ Research Model

This model relies on the literature of perception of organizational politics. It assumes that OP does make a difference and can affect employees' performances. The general conception is that internal politics mediates the relationship between job congruence and employees' performances. High job congruence results in low perception of organizational politics and a perception of fair resource distribution. In this environment employees feel equally treated and as having reasonable chances of achieving interests and ambitions. Also expected is an increase of job performance, which is the reaction to such positive attitudes toward the organization, managers and co-workers. Thus, it is anticipated that low perception of organizational politics leads to an increase in formal outcomes (in-role performance) as well as informal outcomes (OCB).

The Direct/ Alternative Model

This model excludes organizational politics from the analysis of individuals' performances at the workplace and expects to find that job congruence is directly related to employees' performances. Thus, organizational politics, fairness and justice in the workplace have only a minor effect, or no effect at all, on employees' performances. The alternative model must be examined in comparison with the research model in order to more strongly support the latter (Joreskog and Sorbom, 1994). It also represents the null hypothesis in our study and if supported, it implies that analysing perception of organizational politics makes no meaningful contribution to the understanding of employees' performances.

METHOD

Sample and Procedure

A two-phase survey of 411 employees in two local municipalities located in northern Israel was conducted between May 1996 and January 1997. The employees had not taken part in any other study during the previous two years. Participation in the entire research was voluntary and employees were assured of full confidentiality in the data analysis. To ensure this process, the research staff distributed the questionnaires in the departments and collected them directly from the respondents after they had been completed. Alternatively, employees had the option of returning the questionnaires by mail in a sealed envelope provided by the researcher.

At time 1 (T1) employees were asked to provide information about their feelings regarding fit with the organization and their level of met expectations. They also provided information on their perception of organizational politics. At time 2 (T2) which took place six months later supervisors completed a detailed questionnaire on the formal and informal performances of their employees. This information was obtained only for those who completed the questionnaires at T1. A total of 303 questionnaires (return rate of 73.7%) were used in the final analysis. A breakdown by occupation showed that 17% of the sample were blue-collar employees, 43% clerical and administrative workers, 20% high-technical workers, and 29% engineers, architects and other professionals; 56% of the sample were female, 77% married, 89% had a full-time job, and 33% were low-level or middle-level managers. Average age was 44.2 years (s.d.= 10.3); average tenure in the organizations was 11.8 (s.d.= 8.6); 32% of the respondents held a BA degree or higher. The demographic characteristics of the sample were quite similar to those of the total population in the two organizations that participated in the study: 57% females, 74% married, average age 45, average tenure in the organization 9 years, and 31% with BA degree or higher.

Path Analysis and Evaluation of the Models

The two models were assessed using path analysis with LISREL VIII. A covariance matrix among the research variables, using listwise deletion of missing values, formed the input for the path analysis. The common approach is to estimate structural relationships among variables that are free of measurement errors. However, we implemented another technique. Here the multi-item scales were treated as single indicators of each construct because of the large number of parameters (54 observed variables) relative to the size of the sample and to the structural theoretical parameters (9-10). As was mentioned by Bollen (1989), the ratio of the number of observed variables to the sample size should be at least 1:5 in order to allow the common estimation approach. Otherwise, the alternative method should be implemented, as was done here.

To correct for random measurement errors the random error variance associated with each construct was equated to the value of its variance multiplied by the quantity one minus its estimated reliability (Bollen, 1989). Other studies have also used this approach (Farkas and Tetrick, 1989; Frone, Russell and Cooper, 1992). Moreover, the utility of the approach was supported in another study (Netemeyer, Johnston and Burton, 1990) which showed that latent variable analysis yielded virtually identical parameter estimates of direction, magnitude and significance. Results of this procedure, however, diverged substantially from the uncorrected single-indicator analysis.

FINDINGS

Descriptive Statistics

The descriptive statistics and intercorrelations of the research variables are presented in Table 7.1. Reasonable psychometric properties were found for all the measures. The correlations between the OCB constructs and in-role performance were relatively high ($r=0.36$ to $r=0.58$; $P<0.001$) yet still typical for such variables. More important, they did not exceed the critical point of 0.60. These findings reduce the possibility of multicollinearity among the independent variables. Other correlations among the variables indicate that POPS was negatively related to ME and POF ($r=-0.46$; $P<0.001$ and $r=-0.53$; $P<0.001$ respectively). POPS was also found to be negatively related to OCB altruistic and to OCB compliance ($r=-0.16$; $P<0.01$ and $r=-0.14$; $P<0.01$ respectively). These conditions are mentioned by Baron and Kenny (1986) and James and Brett (1984) as necessary for the support of a mediating effect, and therefore imply that POPS may indeed play a mediating role in the research model.

Confirmatory Factor Analysis

A confirmatory factor analysis (CFA) using LISREL VII was performed to estimate the internal dimensionality of the dependent variables. This was done to support more strongly the use of formal and informal measures of performance in one model. It also confirmed the assumption that the two OCB constructs (altruistic and compliance) substantially differ from each other and deserve a separate representation in the models. The three-factor model placed the 20 indicators of OCB altruistic, OCB compliance, and in-role performance on separate latent factors. This model was compared with three two-factor models that forced the indicators of two subscales into a single factor, and forced the remaining indicators of the remaining subscale into a single factor. The three-factor model was also compared with a single-factor model where all 20 indicators were forced into a single latent factor.

The findings, presented in Table 7.2, reveal that the three-factor model fitted the data better than any of the two-factor models or the single-factor model. A chi-square difference test (Bollen, 1989) shows that the restrictions added to all the alternative models significantly reduced the fit of these models in comparison with the three-factor one. Another analysis was performed to test the dimensionality of the two OCB subscales. In this analysis only the indicators of the two OCB subscales were tested. The two-factor model placed the 13 indicators of OCB altruistic and OCB compliance on separate latent factors. It was compared with a single-factor model, which placed all 13 indicators on a single latent factor. The findings presented in the lower portion of Table 7.2 reveal a better fit with the data of the two-factor model than the single-factor model. The chi-square difference test also shows that the single-factor model reduced the fit with the data. The above analyses reconfirm the examination of both formal and informal performances, as well as the separate use of OCB altruistic and OCB compliance in one model.

Summary of Models' Evaluation

Table 7.3 estimates the goodness-of-fit statistics for the models. As Table 7.3 shows, the indirect model clearly provides the best fit. The fit indices for this model show a small, non-significant chi-square (6.89); the ratio of chi-square to the degrees of freedom is lower than 2 (1.15); RFI is 0.96, NNFI is 0.99, CFI is 1.00, AGFI is 0.97, ECVI is 0.12, and RMSEA is 0.02. The alternative direct model provides a relatively inferior fit with the data. The chi-square is significant (42.07; P<0.001), indicating lower fit of this model than the mediating model. Other fit indices of the direct model also show a meager fit with the data: RFI is 0.63, NNFI is 0.65, CFI is 0.91, AGFI is 0.77, ECVI is 0.25, and RMSEA is 0.18. These findings provide some support for hypothesis 3, which expected to find that perception of organizational politics mediates the relationship between job congruence and performances.

The path coefficients, their significance and their magnitude furnish the important plausibility criterion for model evaluation. Thus, an additional indication that the mediated model is better than the alternative/ direct model can be found in the path coefficients. All the paths in the mediated model (6 out of 6) were significant, as compared with only 3 out of 7 in the direct model. Needless to say, the mediated model also contained a lower total number of paths and therefore was more parsimonious than the direct model. All these further support hypothesis 3.

In line with the theory, ME and POF showed a negative relationship with perception of organizational politics (-0.40; P<0.05 and -0.31; P<0.05 respectively). These findings support hypothesis 1, which suggests that employees with high job congruence perceive their work environment as less

Table 7.1 Descriptive statistics and intercorrelations for the study variables (reliabilities in parentheses)

Variable	Means	S.D.	1	2	3	4	5	6
1. Person–Organization Fit (POF)	3.36	0.67	(0.78)					
2. Met Expectations (ME)	3.05	0.67	0.45***	(0.83)				
3. Perceptions of Organizational Politics Scale (POPS)	3.06	0.60	–0.46***	–0.53***	(0.77)			
4. OCB Altruistic	3.40	0.80	0.01	0.12*	–0.16**	(0.93)		
5. OCB Compliance	3.77	0.68	0.11	0.09	–0.14**	0.36***	(0.80)	
6. In-Role Performance	4.19	0.66	0.12*	0.03	–0.14*	0.55***	0.58***	(0.92)

Notes
N = 298–303 due to missing values
*P<0.05   **P<0.01   ***P<0.001

Table 7.2   Confirmatory factor analysis for employees' performances (20 items of OCB and in-role behavior)

Model/Description	df	X^2	Model Comparison	X^2	df	$X/^2$df
All variables						
Three-factors						
1. OCBA vs. OCBC vs. INR#	149	411.25*	–	–	–	2.76
Two-factors						
2. OCBA & OCBC vs. INR	151	846.77*	1 vs. 2	435.52*	2	5.61
3. OCBA & INR vs. OCBC	151	1267.51*	1 vs. 3	856.26*	2	8.39
4. OCBC & INR vs. OCBA	151	612.94*	1 vs. 4	201.69*	2	4.06
One-factor						
5. OCBA & OCBC & INR	152	1470.94*	1 vs. 5	1059.69*	3	9.68
OCB constructs						
Two-factors						
6. OCBA vs. OCBC	64	219.27*	–	–	–	3.42
One-factor						
7. OCBA & OCBC	65	567.55*	6 vs. 7	348.28*	1	8.73

Notes
OCBA = OCB altruistic, OCBC = OCB compliance, INR = in-role performance
*$p < 0.001$

Table 7.2 (continued)

RFI	NFI	NNFI	CFI	GFI	AGFI	ECVI	RMSEA
0.88	0.90	0.92	0.93	0.87	0.84	1.63	0.076
0.76	0.79	0.79	0.82	0.71	0.63	3.06	0.120
0.64	0.68	0.67	0.71	0.56	0.45	4.46	0.160
0.83	0.85	0.86	0.88	0.79	0.73	2.29	0.100
0.59	0.63	0.61	0.65	0.53	0.42	5.12	0.170
0.88	0.91	0.92	0.93	0.90	0.85	0.90	0.090
0.71	0.76	0.73	0.78	0.71	0.60	2.05	0.160

Table 7.3 Goodness-of-fit summary for the research models

Model/Description	df	X^2	X^2/df	RFI	NFI	NNFI	CFI	GFI	AGFI	ECVI	RMSEA
1a. Perceptions of organizational politics and performance: An indirect model	6	6.89	1.15	0.96	0.98	0.99	1.00	0.99	0.97	0.12	0.02
1b. Perceptions of organizational politics and performance: A direct model	4	42.07*	10.52	0.63	0.90	0.65	0.91	0.96	0.77	0.25	0.18

Note
* P<0.001

political and more fair. In addition, perception of organizational politics was negatively related to job performance. It was negatively related to the two OCB constructs (-0.24; P<0.05 with OCB altruistic and -0.23; P<0.05 with OCB compliance), and also to in-role performance (-0.16; P<0.05). These findings support hypothesis 2, which expected to find a negative relationship between perception of organizational politics and employees' performances. In addition, these relationships support the positive relationship between job congruence and job performance as was suggested in hypothesis 1. Further support for this hypothesis can be found in the positive relationship between ME and OCB altruistic, and ME and in-role performance (0.20; P<0.05 and 0.17; P<0.05 respectively) as described in model 1b. Note that these paths, together with the path between POF and ME (0.59; P<0.05), were the only significant relationship found in the direct model. In sum, the path coefficients of the mediated model strongly demonstrate its superiority over the alternative/direct model.

DISCUSSION

This study tried to support the idea that internal politics should be considered a prominent behavior with significant consequences for employees' performances in public administration systems. Building on other studies that found a relationship between politics and performance, the current study supported the notion that perception of organizational politics is a good mediator between constructs of job congruence and employees' performances. These findings affirm the complex relationship between politics and performance that was mentioned by Drory (1993).

Recent findings of Maslyn and Fedor (1998) and Witt (1998) are also in line with this research. For example, the study of Maslyn and Fedor (1998) found different levels of organizational politics (work-group and organizational) and indicated that they are related to different outcomes in the workplace. Witt (1998) tested the assertion that the efforts of first-line supervisors to enhance agreement on organizational goal priorities among their employees would decrease the impact of organizational politics on outcomes for those employees. Having examined five organizations, Witt supported the notion that individual-level performance may be an outcome of organizational politics. The study also demonstrated that perceptions of politics and actual employee–boss goal congruence have interactive effects on organizational commitment and job performance. As one may observe, the concept of congruence is mentioned as a critical element that relates organizational politics with performances. For individuals holding priorities different from those of their boss, politics may have had some impact on commitment and job performance. For those holding priorities similar to those of the boss, politics had comparatively little impact. Drawing on the above, future studies that examine attitudes and behaviors at the workplace must not neglect the effect of job congruence and political perceptions on employees' performances.

Moreover, studies have overlooked the relationships between these constructs in the public sector, and only scarce empirical evidence exists today on the nature of internal politics in public administration systems. What may the reason for this be? As mentioned earlier, studies on OP started to flourish only in the late 1970s and were conducted mostly in private organizations. Since the public sector represents classic bureaucracy with high formal structures, many scholars assumed that internal politics played only a secondary role in these organizations and hence paid little attention to the examination of this sector. Another reasonable cause for the lack of studies on OP in public organizations may be rooted in the environment of modern societies. In a recent study, Ferris, Harrell-Cook and Dulebohn (1998) argued that the magnitude and rapidity of technological change occurring within industry has created an environment rife with ambiguity, hence rife with political behavior. Thus, many studies examined OP in the private-industrial sector but somehow have neglected its investigation in public organizations, which have also undergone fundamental changes in the recent years. Many scholars also presumed that internal politics in public administration systems is extremely sensitive and highly difficult to measure by conventional methods of the social sciences. This speculative assumption discouraged many from obtaining original field data on this behavior. Limitations of time, heavy bureaucracy, and the small likelihood of finding willingness to cooperate in such studies also restrained the advancement of knowledge in this field.

Despite the above obstacles, this study has succeeded in obtaining useful information regarding internal politics in two public organizations. Since these data were collected in two phases (T1, T2) and from two different sources (employees and supervisors), they have stronger validity and reliability than has been evinced so far in other studies, which mostly applied self-reported data. Job congruence, especially ME and POF, were found to be good predictors of perceptions of politics. These findings contribute to the basic model of Ferris and his colleagues by adding two new constructs not mentioned up to now in the study of OP. These variables are based on the expectancy theory of Vroom (1964), and they reconfirmed its usefulness for the understanding of power relations, politics and influence in organizations. Thus, ME, POF and other factors that may better reflect job congruence deserve further inquiry in other studies. Furthermore, perception of politics was successfully related to the objective information on formal and informal performances of public personnel. The CFA that was conducted for the OCB and in-role behaviors certified the use of separate measures for every one of the performance constructs in this study. The findings also provided support for the idea of mediation that has been recently promoted by Ferris et al. (1996) and Ferris, Harrell-Cook and Dulebohn (1998).

The present findings reveal that politics contributes to our understanding of organizational dynamics and outcomes. The most profound finding of this study is that internal politics extensively exists and does make a difference in public administration systems. The significant paths of the indirect/research model showed that politics had a modest negative effect on formal performances (in-role behavior). It also maintained a stronger negative influence on informal performances as represented by the two OCB dimensions. These findings contradict a recent study of Cropanzano et al. (1997) who found an insignificant relationship between perception of politics and OCB among manufacturing employees and students who were working part-time. The findings here imply that politics may function as the *silent enemy* within organizations and can be even more destructive for public administration systems than for private organizations. According to Hirschman (1970) the option of exit is more realistic for employees in the private sector. Public sector employees do not tend to give up work security and tenure even if they feel that politics is all around and sometimes personally harms them. Normally, they choose to respond with more passive behaviors like neglect or apathy, which are less risky. Today, most of the public sector still does not reward employees according to their performances at work. The absence of direct linkage between performances and compensation may lead public employees to show more neglect of job assignments and duties in comparison with employees from private organizations. In many cases, labor unions provide some informal legitimacy for such behaviors and protect even the lower performing employees. As a result of internal politics, the public sector may comprise more 'unsatisfied-neglecting types' than 'unsatisfied-leaving types' of employees. Another aspect of neglect in the workplace is the informal way of decreased motivation to engage in volunteer and spontaneous behaviors like OCB. This lack of motivation functions as a silent enemy because it is usually not measured by existing performance evaluations that apply mostly to formal outcomes. However, organizations with lower levels of OCB lose some elementary parts of internal health and recreation capabilities, and thus are considerably harmed (Katz and Kahn, 1966).

It is also important to note that the silent effect of internal politics can spill over beyond the formal boundaries of public organizations. Attitudes and behaviors of public servants toward citizens/clients partially reflect the effectiveness and efficiency of public administration. Higher levels of internal politics may lead employees to exercise lower levels of performances. When public officials show hampered formal or informal outcomes, the citizens are negatively affected. They obtain inferior services from discouraged public servants, and as a result may develop negative perception toward the entire public system. Thus, internal politics highly contradicts modern approaches to the management of public agencies (for example, the quality movement of the 1980s and 1990s and the new public management approach (NPM)). Together with the discouragement of service orientations of public personnel, internal politics may have a negative effect on entrepreneurial activities and spontaneous and creative ideas that are vital for the prosperity of modern society and a healthy public administration. Practitioners and managers in the public sector must not ignore internal politics and should be aware of its hazardous consequences on both public personnel and citizens. Of course, these implications deserve further examination in future studies that will be able to compare the current results with findings from the private arena.

Limitations and Suggestions for Further Study

Three main limitations of this study must be considered. First, it focused on perception of organizational politics but did not examine the entire political environment of public organizations. Perception of organizational politics is an important construct of OP but it does not fully describe other political rituals inside and outside organizations (for example, influence tactics between internal and external stakeholders). To do this, other measures should be developed and examined more thoroughly. Among these constructs, it is highly recommended to evaluate actual political behaviors, influence tactics and power strategies, and to relate them to perceptions of organizational politics. As was suggested by Vigoda and Cohen (1998), this line of research will be able to provide insights into the relationship between perception of politics and actual political behavior, and the way they relate to organizational outcomes. While some literature exists on this topic (Ferris, Harrell-Cook and Dulebohn, 1998) it is still a vague domain waiting to be explored.

Another limitation of this study is the fact that it was conducted in a non-American culture, which makes the comparison with other studies more problematic. Nevertheless, other studies can benefit from a fresh source of data on OP. An examination of internal politics in a non-American environment can advance our understanding of the differences in political behavior across cultures. It may also help create a more robust theory of the field. This line of research is important since studies have shown the significant role of culture in shaping the political behavior of individuals and institutions outside organizations (Almond and Verba, 1963; Kavanagh, 1972).

The third limitation of this study lies in its relatively narrow examination of other variables that are thought to affect politics and performance in the workplace. The basic theory of Ferris and his colleagues, as well as studies which followed it, mentioned many constructs that should be taken into consideration in this regard. However, as in other studies in the field of organizational behavior, it is impossible to test all of them in a single effort. Nevertheless, the theoretical model suggested here emphasized the functionality of job congruence in explaining perception of politics and employees' performance. The findings demonstrated the usefulness of this idea so further studies should follow it and examine the job congruence–politics relationship more extensively. The theoretical conception, as well as the findings may also provide such studies with a new point of departure for proclaiming and establishing the central role of internal politics in public administration systems.

NOTE

1. Based on Vigoda (2000), 'Internal politics in public administration systems: An empirical examination of its relationship with job congruence, organizational citizenship behavior and in-role performances', *Public Personnel Management*, **29** (2), 185–210. Copyright with permission from IPMA: International Personnel Management Association.

REFERENCES

Almond, G.A. and Verba, S. (1963), *The Civic Culture: Political Attitudes and Democracy in Five Nations: An Analytic Study*, Boston: Little Brown.

Bacharach, S.B. and Lawler, E.J. (1980), *Power and Politics in Organizations*, San Francisco, CA: Jossey-Bass.

Baron, R.M. and Kenny, D.A. (1986), 'The moderator–mediator variable distinction in social psychological research: Conceptual, strategic, and statistical considerations', *Journal of Personality and Social Psychology*, *6*, 1173–82.

Block, P. (1988), *The Empowered Manager: Positive Political Skills at Work*, San Francisco, CA: Jossey-Bass.

Bollen, K.A. (1989), *Structural Equation with Latent Variables*, New York: Wiley.

Bozeman, D.P., Perrewe, P.L., Kacmar, K.M., Hochwarter, W.A., and Brymer, R.A. (1996), *An examination of reactions to perceptions of organizational politics*, Paper presented at the 1996 Southern Management Association Meetings, New Orleans.

Brass, D.J. (1984), 'Being in the right place: A structural analysis of individual influence in an organization', *Administrative Science Quarterly*, *29*, 518–39.

Bretz, R.D. and Judge, T.A. (1994), 'Person–organization fit and the theory of work adjustment: Implications for satisfaction, tenure, and career success', *Journal of Vocational Behavior*, *44*, 32–54.

Burns, T. (1961), 'Micropolitics: Mechanisms of institutional change', *Administrative Science Quarterly*, *6*, 257–81.

Cropanzano, R., Howes, J.C., Grandey, A.A., and Toth, P. (1997), 'The relationship of organizational politics and support to work behaviors, attitudes, and stress', *Journal of Organizational Behavior*, *18*, 159–80.

Drory, A. (1993), 'Perceived political climate and job attitudes', *Organizational Studies*, *14*, 59–71.

DuBrin, A.J. (1988), 'Career maturity, organizational rank and political behavior tendencies: A correlational analysis of organizational politics and career experience', *Psychological Reports*, *63*, 531–7.

Eisenhardt, K.M. and Bourgeois, L.J. (1988), 'Politics of strategic decision making in high-velocity environments: Toward a midrange theory', *Academy of Management Journal*, *31*, 737–70.

Elchanan, M., Esformes, Y., and Friedland, N. (1994), 'Congruence and differentiation as predictors of worker's occupational stability and job performance', *Journal of Career Assessment*, *2*, 40–54.

Erez, M. and Rim, Y. (1982), 'The relationship between goals, influence tactics and personal and organizational variables', *Human Relations*, *35*, 877–8.

Farh, J.L., Podsakoff, P.M., and Organ, D.W. (1990), 'Accounting for organizational citizenship behavior: Leader fairness and task scope versus satisfaction', *Journal of Management*, *16*, 705–21.

Farkas, A.J. and Tetrick, L.E. (1989), 'A three-wave longitudinal analysis of the causal ordering of satisfaction and commitment on turnover decisions', *Journal of Applied Psychology*, *74*, 855–68.

Ferris, G.R., Fedor, D.B., Chachere, J.G., and Pondy, L.R. (1989), 'Myths and politics in organizational context', *Group and Organization Studies*, *14*, 83–103.

Ferris, G.R., Fedor, D.B., and King, T.R. (1994), 'A political conceptualization of managerial behavior', *Human Resource Management Review*, *4*, 1–34.

Ferris, G.R., Frink, D.D., Galang, M.C., Zhou, J., Kacmar, K.M., and Howard, J.L. (1996), 'Perceptions of organizational politics: Prediction, stress-related implications, and outcomes', *Human Relations*, *49*, 233–66.

Ferris, G.R., Harrell-Cook, G., and Dulebohn, J.H. (1998), 'Organizational Politics: The nature of the relationship between politics perceptions and political behavior', in S.B. Bacharach and E.J. Lawler (eds), *Research in the Sociology of Organizations*, CT: JAI Press.

Ferris, G.R. and Kacmar, K.M. (1992), 'Perceptions of organizational politics', *Journal of Management*, *18*, 93–116.

Ferris, G.R. and King, T.R. (1991), 'Politics in human resources decisions: A walk on the dark side', *Organizational Dynamics*, *20*, 59–71.

Ferris, G.R., King, T.R., Judge, T.A., and Kacmar, K.M. (1991), 'The management of shared meaning in organizations', in R.A. Giacalone and P. Rosenfeld (eds), *Applied Impression Management* (pp.41–64), Newbury Park, CA: Sage.

Ferris, G.R., Russ, G.S., and Fandt, P.M. (1989), 'Politics in organizations', in R.A. Giacalone and P. Rosenfeld (eds), *Impression Management in the Organization* (pp.143–70), Hillsdale, NJ: Lawrence Erlbaum.

Frone, M.R., Russell, M., and Cooper, M.L. (1992), 'Antecedents and outcomes of work–family conflict: Testing a model of the work–family interface', *Journal of Applied Psychology, 77*, 65–78.

Gandz, J. and Murray, V.V. (1980), 'The experience of workplace politics', *Academy of Management Journal, 23*, 237–51.

Hardy, C. (ed.) (1995), *Power and Politics in Organizations*, Cambridge, MA: Harvard University Press.

Hirschman, A.O. (1970), *Exit, Voice and Loyalty*, Cambridge, MA: Harvard University Press.

Hulin, C.L. (1991), 'Adaptation, persistence, and commitment in organizations', in M.D. Dunnette and L.M. Hough (eds), *Handbook of Industrial and Organizational Psychology* (Vol. 2, pp. 445–506), Palo Alto, CA: Consulting Psychologistics Press.

Izraeli, D. (1987), 'Sex effects in the evaluation of influence tactics', *Journal of Occupational Behavior, 8*, 79–86.

James, L.R. and Brett, J.M. (1984), 'Mediators, moderators, and tests for mediation', *Journal of Applied Psychology, 69*, 307–21

Joreskog, K. and Sorbom, D. (1994), *Structural Equation Modeling with the SIMPLIS Command Language*, Chicago: Scientific Software International.

Kacmar, K.M. and Carlson, D.S. (1994), *Further validation of the perceptions of politics scale (POPS): A multiple sample investigation*, Paper presented at the annual meeting of the Academy of Management, Dallas, Texas.

Kacmar, K.M. and Ferris, G.R. (1991), 'Perceptions of organizational politics scale (POPS): Development and construct validation', *Educational and Psychological Measurement, 51*, 193–205.

Katz, D. and Kahn, R.L. (1966), *The Social Psychology of Organizations*, New York: Wiley.

Kavanagh, D. (1972), *Political Culture*, London: Macmillan.

Kipnis, D., Schmidt, S.M., and Wilkinson, I. (1980), 'Intraorganizational influence tactics: Exploration in getting one's way', *Journal of Applied Psychology, 65*, 440–52.

Konovsky, M.A. and Pugh, S.D. (1994), 'Citizenship behavior and social exchange', *Academy of Management Journal, 37*, 656–69.

Kumar, P. and Ghadially, R. (1989), 'Organizational politics and its effects on members of organizations', *Human Relations, 42*, 305–14.

Lewin, K. (1936), *Principles of Topological Psychology*, New York: McGraw-Hill.

Maslyn, J.M. and Fedor, D.B. (1998), 'Perceptions of politics: Does measuring different foci matter?' *Journal of Applied Psychology, 83*, 645–53.

Mayes, B.T. and Allen, R.W. (1977), 'Toward a definition of organizational politics', *Academy of Management Review, 2*, 672–8.

Mintzberg, H. (1983), *Power in and Around Organizations*, Englewood Cliffs, NJ: Prentice Hall.

Mintzberg, H. (1985), 'The organization as political arena', *Journal of Management Studies, 22*, 133–54.

Molm, L.D. (1997), *Coercive Power in Social Exchange*, Cambridge: Cambridge University Press.

Moorman, R.H. (1991), 'Relationship between organizational justice and organizational citizenship behaviors: Do fairness perceptions influence employee citizenship?' *Journal of Applied Psychology, 76*, 845–55.

Morrison, W.E. (1994), 'Role definition and organizational citizenship behavior: The importance of the employees' perspective', *Academy of Management Journal, 37,* 1543–67.

Netemeyer, R.G., Johnston, M.W., and Burton, S. (1990), 'Analysis of role conflict and role ambiguity in a structural equation framework', *Journal of Applied Psychology, 75,* 148–57.

Niehoff, B.P. and Moorman R.H. (1993), 'Justice as a mediator of the relationship between methods of monitoring and organizational citizenship behavior', *Academy of Management Journal, 36,* 527–56.

Organ, D.W. (1988), *Organizational Citizenship Behavior: The Good Soldier Syndrome,* Lexington, MA: Lexington Books.

Organ, D.W. and Konovsky, M. (1989), 'Cognitive versus affective determinants of organizational citizenship behavior', *Journal of Applied Psychology, 74,* 157–64.

Parker, C.P., Dipboye, R.L., and Jackson, S.L. (1995), 'Perceptions of organizational politics: An investigation of antecedents and consequences', *Journal of Management, 21,* 891–912.

Pfeffer, J. (1981), *Power in Organizations,* Marshfield, MA: Pitman Publishing.

Pfeffer, J. (1992), *Management with Power,* Boston, MA: Harvard Business School Press.

Putnam, L.L. (1995), 'Formal negotiations: The productive side of organizational conflict', in A.M. Nicotera (ed.), *Conflict and Organizations: Communicative Processes* (pp.183–200), New York: State University of New York Press.

Rollinson, D., Broadfield, A., and Edwards, D.J. (1998), *Organizational Behavior and Analysis* (pp. 375–414), New York: Addison Wesley Longman.

Ryan, M. (1989), 'Political behavior and management development. Special issue: Politics and management development', *Management Education and Development, 20,* 238–53.

Schein, E.H. (1968), 'Organizational socialization and the profession of management', *Industrial Management Review, 2,* 59–77.

Schein, E.H. (1978), *Career Dynamics: Matching Individual and Organizational Needs,* Reading, MA: Addison Wesley.

Schnake, M. (1991), 'Organizational citizenship: A review, proposed model, and research agenda', *Human Relations, 44,* 735–59.

Tansky, J.W. (1993), 'Justice and organizational citizenship behavior: What is the relationship?', *Employees Responsibilities and Rights Journal, 6,* 195–207.

Tziner, A., Latham, G.P., Price, B.S., and Haccoun, R. (1996), 'Development and validation of questionnaires for measuring perceived political considerations in performance appraisal', *Journal of Organizational Behavior, 17,* 179–90.

Vigoda, E. and Cohen, A. (1998), 'Organizational politics and employee performances: A review and theoretical model', *Journal of Management Systems, 10,* 59–72.

Vroom, V.H. (1964), *Work and Motivation,* New York: Wiley.

Wallace, M. and Szilagyi, A. (1982), *Managing Behavior in Organizations,* Glenview, IL: Scott, Foresman.

Wanous, J.P., Poland, T.D., Premack, S.L., and Davis, K.S. (1992), 'The effect of met expectations on newcomer attitudes and behaviors: A review and meta-analysis', *Journal of Applied Psychology, 77,* 288–97.

Wayne, S.J. and Green, S.A. (1993), 'The effects of leader–member exchange on employee citizenship and impression management behavior', *Human Relations*, *46*, 1431–40.

Williams, L.J. and Anderson, S.E. (1991), 'Job satisfaction and organizational commitment as predictors of organizational citizenship and in-role behaviors', *Journal of Management*, *17*, 601–17.

Witt, L. A. (1998), 'Enhancing organizational goal congruence: A solution to organizational politics', *Journal of Applied Psychology*, *83*, 666–74.

Yukl, G. and Tracey, J.B. (1992), 'Consequences of influence tactics used with subordinates, peers, and the boss', *Journal of Applied Psychology*, *77*, 525–35.

Zhou, J. and Ferris, G.R. (1995), 'The dimensions and consequences of organizational politics perceptions: A confirmatory analysis', *Journal of Applied Social Psychology*, *25*, 1747–64.

8. Work Congruence and Excellence in Human Resource Management: Empirical Evidence from the Israeli Non-Profit Sector[1]

Eran Vigoda-Gadot and Aaron Cohen

INTRODUCTION

What is the secret of organizational excellence and success? What are the conditions that foster performance and make some organizations better than others? The scientific community has so far suggested many competing answers for these questions, for example, better goal setting (Hollensbe and Guthrie, 2000), effective organizational structure (O'Toole and Meier, 1999), greater creativity and innovation (Golembiewski and Vigoda, 2000), improved flexibility and adherence to dynamic environments (Priem et al., 1995), and more intelligent leadership (Gerstner and Day, 1997). However, no one disputes that excellent human resource is a momentous element, which is inherently built into the fabric of all the various answers. Good human resource is a crucial and elementary construct of the successful organization, be it private, public, voluntary or other. But should we always and under all conditions focus on bringing the best qualified human forces into organizations? This question is not as simple as it might seem. It carries economic and social implications related to cost–benefit considerations of purchasing the most expensive product in the labor market, with no assurance that it suits the organizational needs. This question also illuminates a dilemma before many organizations, and even more human resource (HR) managers, in exceedingly productive markets where competition over quality employees is exacting.

Excellence in contemporary human resource systems is a precondition that allows modern organizations to grow and prosper. Organizations have undoubtedly always searched for the finest and most expert employees available in the labor market, and will continue to do so. Nevertheless, today many organizations face another pressing need that somehow competes with the goal of employing only the best human resource. This is the necessity to identify, locate, recruit and retain the best *fitted* and most *congruent* individuals for specific work, job and organization; the craft of creating congruence between people and organizations proves to be the foremost mission for modern human resource systems.

The goal of this study was thus threefold: (1) to develop a better understanding of the meaning of congruence in the workplace and to suggest one way of measuring it; (2) to explore the relationship between aspects of work congruence and a variety of work outcomes in two non-profit organizations; and (3) to draw conclusions on possible implications of these relationships for organizations in general and for the non-profit sector especially.

THE ESSENCE OF WORK CONGRUENCE AND ITS MEANING IN THE NON-PROFIT SECTOR

Congruence between individuals and organizations generally refers to the basic compatibility of an employee with his/her workplace and specific job. It also reflects one's level of fulfilled aspirations and expectations from various constructs of the work sphere such as co-workers, supervisors, physical conditions, rewards, career development, or social relations (Blau, 1964; Vroom, 1964). More specifically, theory has suggested two core aspects of individual–organizational congruence: person–organization fit (POF) and employees' level of met expectations (ME). Bretz and Judge (1994: 37-8) suggest that POF reflects the interface between people and institutions. They propose four different perspectives of such a fit. The first assesses the degree to which individual knowledge, skills and abilities match job requirements. The second determines the degree of congruence between individual needs and organizational reinforcement system and structure. The third matches patterns of organizational values and patterns of individual values. The fourth perspective concerns individual personality and perceived organizational image as key constructs of POF. According to Wanous et al., (1992:288) employees' ME represent the discrepancy between what a person encounters on the job in the way of positive and negative experiences and what he/she expected to encounter. However, expectations also reflect a set of anticipations one believes one is able to fulfill in the workplace, and more importantly the actual senses of personal capability of making these aspirations real.

The classic works of Vroom (1964) and Blau (1964) prepared the ground for our theoretical understanding and inquiry of fit and expectations in the workplace. In fact, one of the most significant assumptions by these researchers was that fit and expectations are mutually related. When one's personal characteristics and attitudes are close to those of the workplace a better fit is achieved between the employee and her/his organization. Moreover, people need to fit their work environment as much as organizations need to fit the people. Such a better fit enhances employees' met expectations while expectations significantly affect employees' motivation, perceptions and performance in the workplace. Vroom (1964) thus concluded that fit and expectations are essential for motivating people at work. Hence expectations, and more importantly actual capability to fulfill expectations, are elementary for appropriately matching an employee with a particular job or work environment. They represent a psychological state of mind differently framed by each individual according to his/her ambitions and personal characteristics, which need to cohere with the collective demands and expectations in a wider organizational context. Managers who do a better job in successfully matching individuals with their workplace also promote levels of met expectations and increase the general congruence, which is so essential for a successful organizational process (Chatman, 1989).

Up to this point, work congruence, fit and expectations have been mentioned in their general organizational context. However, the current study focuses on work congruence in non-profit organizations and that is for two reasons, which somehow contradict. The first relies on similarities between non-profit and for-profit organizations while the second draws substance from inherent differences between them.

As suggested by Herman and Renz (1999), non-profit and for-profit organizations have a wide range of managerial similarities, and this calls for better applicability of theories from the more established field (the for-profit) to the relatively new field (the non-profit). To increase effectiveness and attain higher performance, non-profit organizations need to use correct management knowledge, methods and skills, previously tested and supported in for-profit firms. Here the general theory of work congruence, basically rooted in business management, organizational behavior and human resource management (for example, Chatman, 1989; 1991; O'Reilly, Chatman, and Caldwell, 1991), may be transferable to the non-profit sector and contribute to its exploration and good managerial development. According to this view our study re-examines conventional knowledge in an unconventional arena.

The other view may suggest that work congruence deserves special attention and consideration in the non-profit sector precisely for its being markedly different from for-profit agencies. While every employee must have a certain level of fit and adherence with his/her organizational climate and atmosphere, the environment of non-profit organizations is unique and highly distinguished from ordinary for-profit companies where materialistic values take the lead in individual–organizational relationships. Recent studies have suggested that employees in the non-profit sector face a substantially different organizational atmosphere and culture from that encountered by employees in for-profit organizations. For example, Brower and Shrader (2000) found that profit and non-profit boards differ in types of ethical climates; and Armstrong (1992) argued that voluntary and non-profit organizations frequently apply different styles for management of commitment and diversity among personnel. These studies and others promote the idea that the non-profit sector consists of a more cooperative culture than the culture of other organizations and that its internal managerial processes deserve special examination and consideration.

In line with this, the meaning of fit as well as the nature of expectations may also take substantially different courses in for-profit and non-profit organizations. For example, employees in for-profit firms are first of all expected to respond properly to market demands and economic transitions that may affect the firm's stability, profitability and competitiveness. They are encouraged to put the client first, and the more significant client even ahead of others. In addition, they work under consistent and continuous pressure to comply with any decision that may potentially increase the economic outputs of the firm. Compared with the for-profit sector, employees in modern non-profit organizations are expected to adjust to an even more complex and demanding environment. Such an environment has always emphasized social goals and transference of services to vast and highly heterogeneous populations, but in recent years it has also become highly committed to better economic outputs.

On the social side employees in the non-profit sector, unlike their counterparts in for-profit companies, are not allowed, at least formally, to put a wealthy or important client first or to provide him/her with any special treatment. This is especially relevant to public organizations, which are expected to use their 'public capital' only for the purpose of enhancing 'public goods'. Such organizations are encouraged to treat every client equally, according to strict rules of fairness and equity, and under more demanding ethical norms (DeLeon, 1996). Consequently, they are obliged to work under fairly strict regulations of compensation, they meet a different style of managerial leadership, and most importantly, they are subject to heavier pressure due to the demands of accountability. This makes the worksite in public and other non-profit agencies more formal, slow to adjust to the environment, and highly centralized in various respects (Golembiewski and Vigoda, 2000).

Progress on the economic side is even more evident. Indeed, until recent years non-profit organizations were simply seen as 'working, but not for profit'. They were deemed natural spending authorities that could not (and perhaps should not) be analysed by simple terminology or knowledge relevant to the free market. Moreover, it was accepted that public and third-sector organizations be directed by the state, or by voluntary entrepreneurials as proxies of the state, to spend the people's money on (good) public causes as they saw fit. Therefore, a prevalent, albeit informally anchored perception was that these systems should not bother too much with traditional cost and benefit dilemmas or other economic calculations that private companies confront daily. However, new trends in theory and practice of managing the public sector (for example, new public management: Lynn, 1998; Stewart and Ranson, 1994) as well as the growing share and influence of third sector organizations in modern economics (for example, O'Connell, 1989; Gidron and Kramer, 1992), have reframed our understanding and perceptions of these systems. One of the most consequential results was a quest for employees of a different type better to meet the needs of non-profit agencies. Today this new generation of employees is expected to be both capable and ready to work under multi-directional, and sometimes even conflicting demands. On the one hand they are encouraged to pay more attention to business requirements such as improved effectiveness and efficiency, compliance with proper economic demands, and spending collective resources wisely. On the other hand they are also required to sustain a high level of social norms such as accountability, transparency and strict standards of morality, as well as sound equality and fairness criteria in treating all citizens. Integrating these demands (the social and the economic) is undoubtedly a complex mission. It can be fulfilled only with highly fitted personnel and more responsive and flexible organizations that invest effort into human resource management processes and improve their strategies of person–organization adaptation. The question of congruence between employees and their non-profit working sites has accordingly become more complicated, and has emerged as important and meaningful for non-profit organizations of the modern age. Growing pressures to improve the performance of such agencies and the possibility that more knowledge on work congruence can advance these goals directed us in the present study. They stimulated us to investigate the meaning and nature of work congruence in one public and one third-sector agency, and more specifically, to explore the relationship of work congruence with employees' performance.

WORK CONGRUENCE AND PERFORMANCE IN THE NON-PROFIT SECTOR: A DOUBLE CHALLENGE

Human resource management of our era faces the double challenge of bringing better fitted individuals into organizations as well as making organizational arenas highly compatible with individuals' needs and expectations. There is a compelling demand to develop ideas, theory, strategies and practical guidelines to improve the interface between employees, employers and their work environment, and to elaborate comprehensive insight that can help human resource managers get better results and improved performance. Undoubtedly, this challenge must also be met by the growing number of non-profit organizations in modern societies. They serve large numbers of citizens and their contribution to society is enormous. Therefore theory must suggest better explanations for the predictors and determinants of performance in these arenas as well as practically assist in staffing these systems with more qualified, sensitive and highly productive professionals who are more adaptive and sensitive to citizens' needs and requests (Rourke, 1992). One way is to rely more heavily on current knowledge available in business management studies, human resource and organizational behavior (OB) theory.

Figure 8.1 presents the general flow of relationships between work congruence and work performance as stemming from these research fields. Empirical evidence exists in support of the idea that work congruence is related to various work outcomes. First, it has a potential effect on work attitudes and behavioral intentions, and in the longer run it may result in transformations in actual performance of employees and organizations. For example, an early study by O'Reilly (1977) found that lack of personality–job congruence is related in complex ways to a less positive affect toward work. In a more recent study O'Reilly, Chatman and Caldwell (1991) found that POF represents an Organizational Culture Profile (OCP) that predicts job satisfaction and organizational commitment a year after fit is measured, and actual turnover two years after. Chatman (1991) supported these findings and concluded that employees whose values most closely match the firm's feel most satisfied and intend to and actually remain with the organization longer. Bretz and Judge (1994) added that POF has a positive effect on tenure, job satisfaction, and several aspects of career success. These findings were reconfirmed in numerous more recent studies and replications (for example, Mueller, Iverson and Jo, 1999; Saks and Ashforth, 1997; Vandenberghe, 2000). In addition, an examination of employees' met expectations as a construct of work congruence yielded quite similar results. Wanous et al. (1992) conducted an extensive meta-analysis of 31 studies and 17,241 people, and found that ME was negatively related to intentions to leave the organization and positively related to job survival and job performance. A study by Hom et al. (1998) found that ME have direct and indirect effects through other mediators on turnover precursors, namely job satisfaction and organizational commitment. Using path analysis and LISREL VIII, Vigoda (2000a) examined the relationships among POF, ME, Perceptions of Organizational Politics Scale (POPS), in-role performance, and Organizational Citizenship Behavior (OCB) in the public sector. Findings revealed that job congruence was negatively related to POPS and positively related to employee performance. Moreover, POF positively affected ME while POPS mediated the relationship between job congruence and employee performance as represented by in-role and extra-role (OCB) behaviors.

Therefore, we argue that high work congruence as represented by better POF and high ME denotes a more effective and adaptive human resource management, which contributes to more job satisfaction, better organizational commitment and lower intentions of exit. Furthermore, the general idea fostered here suggests that higher work congruence in the non-profit sector increases individual, and consequently organizational performance across a wider set of organizational variables, such as greater willingness of voice, lower tendencies of negligent behavior, and lower levels of perceived organizational politics (POPS). With time these may also enhance in-role performance and organizational citizenship behavior (OCB). Note, however, that with the exception of Vigoda (2000a) all the studies mentioned above were conducted in a general organizational context. As far as we could find, no study so far has tried closely to examine these relationships in the wider sphere of the non-profit sector or to single out specific implications that may allow comparative views with for-profit arenas. As shown earlier, beyond some similarities between non-profit and for-profit organizations, the former still operate in a unique atmosphere and climate. The non-profit sector differs considerably from the for-profit in many cultural aspects such as duties, goals, values, compensation and style of leadership (Brower and Sharder, 2000; Armstrong, 1992; Rainey, 1991). From the above, it seems worth examining a wider congruence–excellence set of relationships in non-profit systems where economic and market forces increasingly compound with social values of better serving the public. Accordingly, we elaborated the following three hypotheses, intended to test a variety of relationships between work congruence and performance specifically in the non-profit sector.

The first hypothesis (H1) suggests that POF and ME of employees in the non-profit sector are positively related to job satisfaction, organizational commitment and intentions of voice. The second hypothesis (H2) suggests that POF and ME of employees in the non-profit sector are negatively related to intentions of exit and neglect and to perceptions of organizational politics.

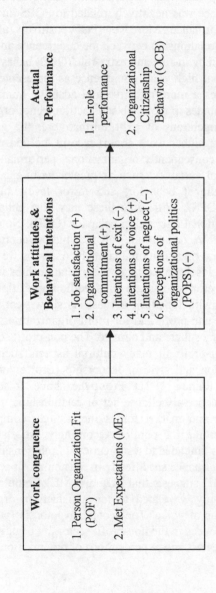

Work congruence

1. Person Organization Fit (POF)

2. Met Expectations (ME)

Work attitudes & Behavioral Intentions

1. Job satisfaction (+)
2. Organizational commitment (+)
3. Intentions of exit (−)
4. Intentions of voice (+)
5. Intentions of neglect (−)
6. Perceptions of organizational politics (POPS) (−)

Actual Performance

1. In-role performance

2. Organizational Citizenship Behavior (OCB)

Figure 8.1 A general relationship between work congruence and work performance

The third hypothesis (H3) suggests that POF and ME of employees in the non-profit sector are positively related to in-role performance and organizational citizenship behavior (OCB) as reported by supervisors.

METHOD

Sample and Procedure

Two samples were used to test the hypotheses. The first (n1=244) consisted of employees from one large public sector agency dealing with local governance services, the second (n2=155) of employees from a smaller third-sector organization which provides day-care services for children. Data from these samples were collected between 1997 and 1998 in the northern area of Israel. Return rate was 86.5% for n1 and 77.5% for n2. Employees in the first sample were asked to provide information about organizational, structural and personal variables, ME, POF, and a variety of work outcomes. The second sample served for a deeper investigation of the relationship between ME and work outcomes, and a measure of POF was not included. Participation in the entire research was voluntary and employees were assured full confidentiality in the data analysis. In addition, beyond self-reported data, supervisors in the two organizations were asked to provide information on employees' in-role performance as well as organizational citizenship behavior (OCB). Thus, this chapter has the advantage of presenting two separate sources of information (self-reports and objective reports) coming from two non-profit organizations (one public and one third-sector).

Table 8.1 presents a list of the research measures and several descriptive characteristics of the two samples. Means and standard deviation values were found close or similar to the general values in the overall population of the two studied organizations. This finding increases the representative power of our samples. Alpha Cronbach values were good, and mostly well above the minimal requirement of 0.60 as suggested by Nunnaly (1967). All these testify on the appropriate construction of the research samples.

FINDINGS

Table 8.2 shows Pearson's r correlations among the research variables. With the exception of voice in study 2, ME in both studies showed a significant and consistent relationship with most of the outcome variables. It was positively related to job satisfaction in study 1 and in study 2 (r=0.50;

p<0.001 and r=0.66; p<0.001 respectively), organizational commitment (r=0.47; p<-0.001 and r=0.49; p<0.001 respectively), voice (r=0.18; p<0.01 in study 1), in-role performance (r=0.13; p<0.05; and r=0.26; p<0.01 respectively), and OCB (r=0.19; p<0.01 and 0.25; p<0.01 respectively). It was also negatively related to intentions of exit (r=-0.44; p<0.001 and -0.41; p<0.001 respectively), neglect (r=-0.30; p<0.001 in both studies), and POPS (r=-0.56; p<0.001 and -0.46; p<0.001 respectively). Beyond these, study 1 showed that POF was positively related to job satisfaction, organizational commitment, and OCB (r=0.34; p>0.001, r=0.32; p<0.001, and r=0.13; p<0.05 respectively) and negatively related to intentions of exit and POPS (r=-0.18; p<0.01 and r=-0.50; p<0.001 respectively). Study 1 also found a strong and positive relationship between POF and ME (r=0.48; p<0.001). These findings provided a preliminary indication that the research hypotheses were oriented in reasonable directions.

Tables 8.3 and 8.4 present separate regression analyses of the two samples. These analyses provide limited yet noteworthy support for the relationship between POF and ME and a series of other work outcomes among employees from the non-profit sector as suggested in the research hypotheses. According to study 1, POF and ME were positively related to job satisfaction (β=0.15; p<0.05 and β=0.43; p<0.001 respectively) and organizational commitment (β=0.15; p<0.05 and β=0.39; p<0.001 respectively). ME was also positively related to behaviors of voice and OCB (β=0.25; p<0.01 and β=0.17; p<0.05 respectively). These findings are in line with H1 and H3. In addition, POF was negatively related to POPS (β=-0.31; p<0.001) while ME was negatively related to intentions of exit, neglect, and POPS (β=-0.44; p<0.001, β=-0.33; p<0.001, and β=-0.40; p<0.001 respectively). These findings strongly support H2 for the variable ME and to a lesser extent for the variable POF. Hypothesis H2 was not supported regarding the relationship between POF and intentions of exit, voice and neglect. Furthermore, no relationship was found between ME and in-role performance or between POF and in-role performance. POF was not related to OCB, although ME showed a weak positive relationship with OCB (β=0.17; p<0.05). Hence we concluded that H3 was generally not supported except for the relationship between ME and OCB.

Findings of the second study reconfirmed the positive relationships between ME and several work outcomes such as job satisfaction, organizational commitment, intentions of exit, neglect, POPS, and OCB (β=0.67; p<0.001, β=0.50; p<0.001, β=-0.42; p<0.001, β=-0.30; p<0.001, β=-0.45; p<0.001, and β=0.27; p<0.01 respectively). These findings provided additional support for H1 and H2 regarding the variable ME. In addition, study 2 also found a positive relationship between ME and in-role performance as reported by supervisors (β=0.26; p<0.01) and again, a positive relationship between ME and OCB ($\beta=0.27$; $p<0.01$). These findings supported H3 regarding the variable ME.

Note also that the achieved explained variance (R^2) in both studies for most of the outcome variables was relatively high. For example, POF and ME accounted for most of the explained variance in job satisfaction (28%), organizational commitment (28%), and POPS (41%) as found in study 1. Furthermore, in that study ME alone accounted for most of the explained variance in intentions of exit (20%), voice (6%), neglect (10%), and OCB (5%). In study 2 ME accounted for most of the explained variance in job satisfaction (46%), organizational commitment (33%), intentions of exit (26%), neglect (10%), POPS (21%), in-role performance (23%), and OCB (10%). These findings provide additional support for the effect of POF, and especially for the important effect of ME, in determining performances of employees from the non-profit sector.

DISCUSSION

The basic goal of this study was to explore the meaning of work congruence and its relationship with employees' performance in an organizational sphere outside the profit sector. Work congruence was suggested to embody a certain level of person–organization fit and met expectations, and the study examined the effect of these constructs on various aspects of performance. The study also tried to elaborate farther on the special meaning of work congruence for the non-profit sector. We argued that the task of better matching individuals and organizations in this sector grows more complex and more challenging with the years. The findings provided some empirical support for the research hypotheses. Work congruence had an effect on work attitudes and behavior dispositions as well as on actual performance measures. According to the relatively high (but not so high as to cause multicollinearity) correlation found between ME and POF ($r=0.48$; $p<0.001$) we further suggest that these constructs represent different but related dimensions of work congruence worthy of examination and deliberation in the special context of non-profit organizations.

What is the added value of our study to OB literature, in particular the study of human resource management in the non-profit sector? First, the findings presented here reconfirmed existing knowledge on the positive relationship between POF and ME, and several work outcomes such as job satisfaction, organizational commitment, and intentions of exit or turnover (O'Reilly, Chatman and Caldwell, 1991; Mueller, Iverson and Jo, 1999; Saks and Ashforth, 1997; Vandenberghe, 2000). Here, existing knowledge from the for-profit sector proved relevant and useful.

Table 8.1 Descriptive statistics and reliabilities of the research variables

Variable	Study 1 (Public Sector)			Study 2 (Third Sector)		
	Mean	S.D.	α	Mean	S.D.	α
Research variables						
1. Person–Organization Fit (POF)	3.41	0.65	0.77	–	–	–
2. Met-Expectations (ME)	3.07	0.66	0.83	3.21	0.75	0.85
3. Job satisfaction	3.55	0.70	0.76	3.75	0.66	0.70
4. Organizational commitment	3.69	0.78	0.89	4.05	0.87	0.90
5. Intentions of Exit	2.00	0.82	0.83	1.78	0.92	0.84
6. Voice	3.19	0.73	0.77	2.78	0.80	0.62
7. Neglect	1.90	0.65	0.70	1.79	0.66	0.63
8. Perceptions of Organizational Politics (POPS)	3.04	0.59	0.76	2.69	0.78	0.77
9. In-role performance	4.22	0.63	0.92	4.38	0.54	0.91
10. Organizational Citizenship Behavior (OCB)	3.61	0.61	0.90	3.62	0.65	0.81
Demographic variables						
11. Age	44.86	10.23	–	46.05	9.80	–
12. Education	2.73	1.44	–	1.64	1.19	–

Notes
N for study 1 ranges between 217 and 244 due to missing values; N for study 2 ranges between 125 and 155 due to missing values

Table 8.2   Pearson's r correlations among the research variables

	Study 1 (Public Sector)		Study 2 (Third Sector)
	POF	ME	ME
1. Job satisfaction	0.34***	0.50***	0.66***
2. Organizational commitment	0.32***	0.47***	0.49***
3. Intentions of Exit	-0.18**	-0.44***	-0.41***
4. Voice	N.S.	0.18**	N.S.
5. Neglect	N.S.	-0.30***	-0.30***
6. Perceptions of Organizational Politics (POPS)	-0.50***	-0.56***	-0.46***
7. In-role performance	N.S.	0.13*	0.26**
8. Organizational Citizenship Behavior (OCB)	0.13*	0.19***	0.25**
9. Person–Organization Fit (POF)	–	0.48***	–

Notes
N for study 1 ranges between 217 and 244 due to missing values
N for study 2 ranges between 125 and 155 due to missing values
*P≤0.05   **P≤0.01   ***P≤0.001
N.S. = Not significant

Table 8.3 Regression for Study 1 (Public Sector): The effect of POF and ME on work outcomes (standardized coefficients)

Variables	Job satisfaction	Organizational commitment	Intentions of exit	Voice	Neglect	Perceptions of organizational politics	In-role performance	Organizational citizenship behavior
1. Person-organization fit (POF)	0.15*	0.15*	0.02	-0.14	0.09	-0.31***	0.01	0.04
2. Met expectations (ME)	0.43***	0.39***	-0.44***	0.25**	-0.33***	-0.40***	0.13	0.17*
3. Age	0.02	-0.03	-0.01	-0.03	-0.04	0.01	0.06	0.10
4. Education	0.01	-0.13*	0.08	0.11	0.03	-0.13*	-0.08	-0.06
5. Marital status (1=married)	0.12*	0.19**	-0.07	-0.03	0.01	-0.10	-0.03	-0.06
R^2	0.28	0.28	0.20	0.06	0.10	0.41	0.03	0.05
Adjusted R^2	0.26	0.26	0.18	0.03	0.07	0.39	0.01	0.03
F	15.34***	15.46***	9.87***	2.42*	4.12***	27.07***	N.S.	2.20*

Notes
N for study 1 ranges between 217 and 244 due to missing values; N for study 2 ranges between 125 and 155 due to missing values;
*$P \leq 0.05$ **$P \leq 0.01$ ***$P \leq 0.001$; N.S. = Not significant

Table 8.4 Regression for Study 2 (Third Sector): The effect of ME on work outcomes (standardized coefficients)

Variables	Job satisfaction	Organizational commitment	Intentions of exit	Voice	Neglect	Perceptions of organizational politics	In-role performance	Organization al citizenship behavior
1. Met expectations (ME)	0.57***	0.50***	-0.42***	-0.03	-0.30***	-0.45***	0.26**	-0.27**
2. Age	0.10	0.21**	-0.29***	0.01	-0.03	0.03	0.14	-0.02
3. Education	-0.06	-0.15*	-0.01	-0.04	0.08	0.05	0.23*	-0.01
4. Marital status (1=married)	0.03	-0.02	-0.01	-0.03	0.04	0.02	0.10	0.19*
R^2	0.46	0.33	0.26	0.01	0.10	0.21	0.13	0.10
Adjusted R^2	0.44	0.31	0.23	0.01	0.07	0.19	0.10	0.07
F	26.74***	15.56***	10.89***	N.S.	3.55**	8.47***	4.05**	2.99*

Notes

N for study 1 ranges between 217 and 244 due to missing values; N for study 2 ranges between 125 and 155 due to missing values

*$P \leq 0.05$ **$P \leq 0.01$ ***$P \leq 0.001$; N.S. = Not significant

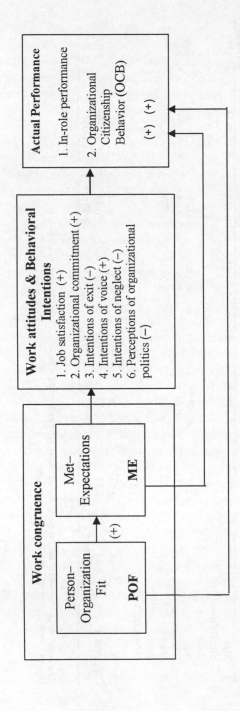

Figure 8.2 A suggested specific model for the relationship between work congruence (POF and ME) and work performance

According to these findings we suggest that at least some of the relationships between work congruence and work outcomes are transferable and generalizable across the private, public and third sectors. However, in an attempt to extend this knowledge we further examined additional relationships between POF and ME and various dimensions of employees' performance that were overlooked in past studies. Among the variables found meaningful here, and not investigated so far, are neglect, POPS and OCB.

The negative effect of ME on employees' tendencies to neglect job duties was consistent and relatively strong in both studies. The findings for POPS were even stronger and more impressive, and in addition were supported by the relatively strong negative relationship between POF and POPS. In fact, both neglect and POPS represent a general negative perception of an individual's worksite (Ferris and Kacmar, 1992; Vigoda, 2000a; 2000b). When an employee does not fit the organization or when he/she is incapable of fulfilling a minimum level of expectations in the workplace the organization may well be perceived as political in nature, unfair, and as treating its members unequally. This may influence employees to react with negative attitudes to their surroundings and to the organization in general. As suggested by Vigoda (2000a) such attitudes and behavioral intentions may be especially dangerous and harmful for public or non-profit organizations. In these arenas alternative reactions to job disapproval (for example, voice or exit) are less acceptable and less realistic for most employees, who are usually greatly concerned with job security and tenure. To the best of our knowledge, no additional empirical evidence exists today on the effect of work congruence (ME or POF) on these variables in the non-profit sector. Hence, another contribution of this study is its pointing to intentions of negligence and to POPS as possible outcomes of work incongruence. Future studies are thus encouraged to examine these relationships in other settings beyond the private sector. Such studies will also benefit from comparing their results with ours.

Note also that this study examined the relationship between work congruence and two objective measures of performance as reported by supervisors. This is a significant contribution that deserves further elaboration. The most conspicuous relationship was found between ME and OCB across the two studies. Theories accumulated over recent decades (for example, Organ, 1988; Van Dyne, Graham and Dienesch, 1994; Podsakoff and MacKenzie, 1997) have treated the concept of OCB in various ways, but as far as we could find never closely investigated the possibility that OCB is related to work congruence. The findings of this research may contribute to OCB theory by suggesting that one way of improving this positive behavior is to improve the interface between individuals and their work sphere using continuous assessments of fit and expectations. OCB may therefore be reinforced by improvements in strategies of human resource management such as sophisticated recruitment, selection or job development programs that promote the fit of individuals to their organizational environment and the fulfillment of their expectations. Again, the findings of our study are especially relevant to the non-profit sector but should attract attention in for-profit firms as well since most of them face fairly similar HR problems and dilemmas.

In light of the above we believe it is important to elaborate on another question stemming from our findings that is related to the exact nature of the relationship between POF and ME and employees' performance. Theory suggests that fit and expectations rely heavily on each other when better fitted employees are more likely to meet their expectations in the workplace, and on the other hand higher met expectations enhance the fit and adaptability to a certain worksite. According to our analyses, ME in the public sector are more closely related to the outcome variables than is the variable POF. Because POF was not included in study 2 we could not deduce its overall relationship with the outcome variables in the third-sector organization that was studied there. Nevertheless, it is reasonable to suggest that the general relationships among all constructs examined here is *POF* → *ME* → *Performance*. Essentially this implies that POF leads to ME more than ME leads to POF. More specifically, Figure 8.2 suggests the specific pattern of relationships among the research variables.

Still, this question of complex relationships was beyond the scope of the current study. It was not tested empirically here, so it must remain a suggestion deserving comprehensive examination in future studies. One way of doing this is to apply mediation analysis strategy as suggested by Baron and Kenny (1986) and James and Brett (1984). Another is to use Structural Equation Modeling (SEM), which is specifically designed to test such hypotheses as well as to render causality implications based on comparison of competing research models in the social sciences.

Although not directly related to the research hypotheses, several findings on the effect of the control variables on performance also deserve some attention. Age had a positive effect on organizational commitment and a negative effect on intentions of exit. Employees with a low level of education showed a weaker tendency to be more committed to the organization than higher educated employees. Married employees showed a higher level of job satisfaction and organizational commitment, as well as stronger orientation toward OCB, than unmarried employees. Nevertheless, as none of the control/demographic variables proved a significant relationship with work congruence (POF or ME) our study confirmed the results of Posner (1992), who found no mediating effect of demographic variables on the work congruence–work outcomes relationship.

No study, this one included, is free of limitations. First, although we tried to explain the meaning and importance of work congruence for the non-profit sector our two samples investigated a relatively narrow expression of this phenomenon. We used only two measures (POF and ME), and in fact the second sample could testify only on ME and its relationship with employees' performance. Further studies should try to develop the meaning of work congruence beyond ME and POF. It may also be useful to extend our view and to examine the relationship between work congruence and additional aspects of performance such as actual turnover or absenteeism. Second, despite our attempt to provide empirical evidence on one public and one third-sector organization, the external validity of our findings should be treated with caution. The two samples are not cross-sectional and refer to only one culture, the Israeli one. Future studies will benefit from more cross-sectional and cross-cultural data that may also foster progress toward comparative examinations. Such data will undoubtedly yield better understanding of the actual meaning of work congruence in the non-profit sector, its relationship with performance, and differences across sectors and cultures.

Beyond the limitations of this study lies a wider value for organizations in general and for human resource management in the non-profit sector in particular. While the harmony of values, expectations and perceptions of individuals and organizations is not a new issue in the general theory of organizational behavior (Vroom, 1964; Blau, 1964; Wanous et al., 1992; Bretz and Judge, 1994), our study generally supports its desirability beyond the profit sector to public and third-sector organizations. More congruence between individuals and organizations is especially important for non-profit organizations, which work in a different atmosphere from for-profit organizations and in a distinct cultural environment. While companies usually seek employees who directly contribute economical inputs into the work sphere, non-profit organizations may even gain added benefits by recruiting and encouraging better fitted employees who share the organizational values in their wider context. Recruiting and retaining better fitted employees and maintaining a satisfactory level of met-expectations is without doubt good for organizations of all sectors. Nevertheless, while it is a recommended option for for-profit companies, it is a greater *necessity* for non-profit agencies, whose culture is more heterogeneous and vague, and whose structure, work tradition, values, position and role in society are more complex. Hence, advancing congruence in the non-profit sector is an ambitious challenge, which has expediency beyond simple economic outputs.

Finally, the importance of work congruence for public and third-sector organizations has communal, ecological, educational and civic–cultural outputs that can be shared by all citizens and are relevant for the society in general. Our study implies the importance of such congruence, yet future endeavors should be dedicated to comparing these findings with similar data in the private sector. All in all, this chapter suggests that fit and expectations should be taken more seriously by human resource managers in the non-profit sector on account of their influential and important role in determining multiple aspects of organizational performance.

NOTE

1. Based on Vigoda and Cohen (2003), 'Work congruence and excellence in human resource management: Empirical evidence from the Israeli non-profit sector' *The Review of Public Personnel Administration*, **23**, (3), 192–216. Copyright with permission from Sage Publishing.

REFERENCES

Armstrong, M. (1992), 'A charitable approach to personnel', *Personnel Management*, *24*, 28–32.
Baron, R.M. and Kenny, D.A. (1986), 'The moderator–mediator variable distinction in social psychological research: Conceptual, strategic, and statistical considerations', *Journal of Personality and Social Psychology*, *6*, 1173–82.
Blau, P.M. (1964), *Power and Exchange in Social Life,* New York: Wiley.
Bretz, R.D. and Judge, T.A. (1994), 'Person–organization fit and the theory of work adjustment: Implications for satisfaction, tenure, and career success', *Journal of Vocational Behavior*, *44*, 32–54.
Brower, H.H. and Shrader, C.B. (2000), 'Moral reasoning and ethical climate: Not-for-profit vs. for-profit boards of directors', *Journal of Business Ethics, 36*, 147–67.
Chatman, J.A. (1989), 'Improving interactional organizational research: A model of person–organization fit', *Academy of Management Review*, *14*, 333–49.
Chatman, J.A. (1991), 'Matching people and organizations: Selection and socialization in public accounting firms', *Administrative Science Quarterly*, *36*, 459–84.
DeLeon, L. (1996), 'Ethics and entrepreneurship', *Policy Studies Journal*, *24*, 495–510.
Ferris, G.R. and Kacmar, K.M. (1992), 'Perceptions of organizational politics', *Journal of Management*, *18*, 93–116.
Gerstner, R.C. and Day, D. (1997), 'Meta-analytic review of leader–member exchange theory: Correlates and construct issues', *Journal of Applied Psychology*, *82*, 827–44.
Gidron, B. and Kramer, R.M. (1992), *Governments and the Third Sector: Emerging Relationships in Welfare States,* San Francisco: Jossey Bass.
Golembiewski, R.T. and Vigoda, E. (2000), 'Organizational innovation and the science/craft of management', in M. A. Rahim, R.T. Golembiewski, and K.D.

Mackenzie (eds), *Current Topics in Management* (Vol. 5, pp. 263–80), Greenwich, CT: JAI Press.

Herman, R.D. and Renz, D.O. (1999), 'Theses on non-profit organizational effectiveness', *Non-profit and Voluntary Sector Quarterly, 28*, 107–26.

Hollensbe, E.C. and Guthrie, J.P. (2000), 'Group pay-for-performance plans: The role of spontaneous goal setting', *Academy of Management Review, 25*, 864–72.

Hom, P.W., Griffeth, R.W., Palich, L.E. and Bracker, J.S. (1998), 'An exploratory investigation into theoretical mechanisms underlying realistic job previews', *Personnel Psychology, 51*, 421–51.

James, L.R. and Brett, J.M. (1984), 'Mediators, moderators, and tests for mediation', *Journal of Applied Psychology, 69*, 307–21.

Lynn, L.E. (1998), 'The new public management: How to transform a theme into a legacy', *Public Administration Review, 58*, 231–7.

Mueller, C.W., Iverson, R.D., and Jo, D.G. (1999), 'Distributive justice evaluations in two cultural contexts: A comparison of U.S. and South Korean teachers', *Human Relations, 52*, 869–93.

Nunnaly, J.C. (1967), *Psychometric Theory,* New York: McGraw Hill.

O'Connell, B. (1989), 'What voluntary activity can and cannot do for America', *Public Administration Review, 49*, 486–91.

O'Reilly, C.A. (1977), 'Personality job fit – implications for individual attitudes and performance', *Organizational Behavior and Human Performance, 18*, 36.

O'Reilly, C.A., Chatman, J., and Caldwell, D.F. (1991), 'People and organizational culture: A profile comparison appraisal', *Academy of Management Journal, 34*, 487–516.

Organ, D.W. (1988), *Organizational Citizenship Behavior: The Good Soldier Syndrome*, Lexington, MA: Lexington Books.

O'Toole, L.J. and Meier, K. (1999), 'Modeling the impact of public management: Implications of structural context', *Journal of Public Administration Research and Theory, 9*, 505–26.

Podsakoff, P.M. and MacKenzie, S.B. (1997), 'Impact of Organizational Citizenship Behavior on organizational performance: A review and suggestions for future research', *Human Performance, 10*, 133–51.

Posner, B.Z. (1992), 'Person–organization values congruence: No support for individual differences as a moderating influence', *Human Relations, 45*, 351–61.

Priem, R.L., Rasheed, A.M.A., and Kotulic, A.G. (1995), 'Rationality in strategic decision processes, environmental dynamism and firm performance', *Journal of Management, 21*, 913–29.

Rainey, H.G. (1991), *Understanding and Managing Public Organization* (Chapter 1, pp. 15–36), San Francisco: Jossey Bass.

Rourke, F.E. (1992), 'Responsiveness and neutral competence in American bureaucracy', *Public Administration Review, 52*, 539–46.

Saks, A.M., and Ashforth, B.E. (1997), 'A longitudinal investigation of the relationships between job information sources, applicant perceptions of fit, and work outcomes', *Personnel Psychology, 50*, 395–426.

Stewart, J. and Ranson, R. (1994), 'Management in the public domain', in D. McKevitt, and A. Lawton (eds), *Public Sector Management* (pp. 54–70), London: Sage.

Vandenberghe, C. (2000), 'Organizational culture, person–culture fit, and turnover: A replication in the health care industry', *Journal of Organizational Behavior, 20,* 175–84.

Van Dyne, L., Graham, J.W., and Dienesch, R.M. (1994), 'Organizational Citizenship Behavior: Construct redefinition, measurement, and validation', *Academy of Management Journal, 37,* 765–802.

Vigoda, E. (2000a), 'Internal politics in public administration systems: An empirical examination of its relationship with job congruence, organizational citizenship behavior and in-role performances', *Public Personnel Management, 29,* 185–210.

Vigoda, E. (2000b), 'The relationship between organizational politics, job attitudes, and work outcomes: Exploration and implications for the public sector', *Journal of Vocational Behavior, 57,* 326–47.

Vroom, V.H. (1964), *Work and Motivation,* New York: Wiley.

Wanous, J.P., Poland, T.D., Premack, S.L., and Davis, K.S. (1992), 'The effect of met expectations on newcomer attitudes and behaviors: A review and meta-analysis', *Journal of Applied Psychology, 77,* 288–97.

PART FOUR

Dilemmas and New Directions in the Study
of Citizenship and Modern Bureaucracies

Foreword

This part of the book includes works that represent new directions and challenges in the research regarding citizenship involvement and work. What seems to unite the three chapters in this part is a more macro perspective on the relationship between citizenship involvement and work. Broad concepts such as democracy, workplace politics, and the image of the public sector in general are utilized in this part in an attempt to encourage more research on these concepts and their effects on the relationship between citizenship involvement and work.

One issue that is raised in these chapters is the citizen's control over the operation of public agencies, a core necessity in every democracy. There is an implied contract that governments are elected to serve the people and may not be re-elected if they fail to function at a minimally acceptable standard. Today citizens of stable democracies are committed to this contract. Yet the question of how governments fulfill their part of the contract and how sensitive they are to citizens' needs is unclear.

The first chapter in this section by Eran Vigoda-Gadot deals with questions such as, do governments and public officials really work hard for the public money entrusted to them? Do public officials misuse these resources? What do citizens think of the quality and quantity of the services they receive? Do they really believe that they are being served properly? Vigoda's research addresses the above questions and proposes an empirical examination of the public administration–citizens' contract. The participants in the study were 281 residents of a large Israeli city. The findings indicate that perceptions of public administration's responsiveness were affected by both policy and cultural factors, by the quality of the human resource system, and by the quality of the public servants.

The second study in this part by Aaron Cohen et al. deals with an interesting and unique aspect of the relationship between citizens and bureaucracies. It examines the process and determinants by which a potential employee decides whether or not to seek employment in the public sector. This issue received some attention in the mid-twentieth century, but interest in it has since lagged. One goal of this study is to stimulate more research that may make conceptual as well as practical contributions to the field. Cohen et al. adopted several ideas from two earlier studies. Kilpatrick, Cummings and Jennings' (1964) notion of the importance of the image of the public sector is applied here by using the concept of public sector image as one of the main components of the decision to work in the public sector. This concept is a good demonstration of the interaction between citizens and bureaucracies. Blank's (1985) study was the first to propose a model of factors that influences whether one becomes a public or private sector employee. Some of the determinants proposed by Blank are applied in Cohen et al.'s study. While Blank's model is based on demographic determinants, Cohen et al.'s model includes psychological as well as experiential variables together with the public sector image variables.

This study of Israeli students in their last year before graduation examines three research questions: first, what are the determinants of public sector image; second, what are the determinants underlying the decision to work in the public sector; and third, are these determinants mediated directly or indirectly by the citizens' image of the public sector. The research model consists of three groups of independent variables: demographic, experiential, and personal–psychological. Questionnaires were distributed by mail to 1640 students, and 660 usable questionnaires were returned, a response rate of 40%. The findings showed that the consideration to seek employment in the public sector and public sector image were related and that the image of the public sector mediated the relationship between the proposed determinants and the propensity for working in the public sector.

The third study, by Eran Vigoda-Gadot, is a continuation of the research begun by him in the chapter mentioned previously. This study examined the relationship between public sector performance and several aspects of citizenship involvement. Participants reported their perceptions about the operation of a local municipality in areas such as the humanity of the public servants, the initiative and creativity of the municipality, and its morality and ethical standards. The study's subjects also commented on their satisfaction with the organization's operation and the services provided, and indicated their faith in the efficacy of citizenship involvement and their level of active citizenship involvement. Five alternative models were suggested to test the relationship, and path-analysis of latent variables was used to test the models. A structural equation modeling (SEM) using LISREL VIII showed the superiority of one model, in which (1) perceptions of public service operation positively affected performance and faith in citizenship involvement, and (2) active citizenship involvement was positively affected by faith in citizenship involvement, and, simultaneously, was negatively affected by public sector performance.

REFERENCES

Blank, M. R. (1985), 'An analysis of workers' choice between employment in the public and private sectors', *Industrial and Labor Relations Review*, *38*, 211–24.

Kilpatrick , F., Cummings, M. and Jennings , K. (1964), *Source Book of a Study of Occupational Values and the Image of the Federal Service,* Washington: The Brookings Institution.

9. Are You Being Served? The Responsiveness of Public Administration to Citizens' Demands: An Empirical Examination in Israel[1]

Eran Vigoda-Gadot

INTRODUCTION

Citizens' control over the operation of public agencies is a core necessity in every democracy. It cannot be attained when there is insufficient knowledge on the fit between what citizens desire and what governments offer. European theoreticians of the seventeenth and eighteenth centuries like Hobbes, Locke, and Rousseau argued that citizens and rulers have a hidden agreement or 'social contract'. By electing a government, people lend, alienate or give up their power to political rulers on condition that it be used to satisfy certain of their most important needs (Hampton, 1986: 256). Under such an arrangement, these needs, such as personal security, social order, welfare and prosperity must be delivered by governmental authorities and by the public administration. Governments are elected to serve the people and may not be re-elected if they fail to accomplish minimum requirements. Thus, theoretically, nothing should be more important, either for citizens, politicians or public servants, than to work faithfully and diligently for the sake of society and its members. Alternatively, the social contract becomes useless since some basic domains of democratic regimes no longer exist.

Considering the fact that today, citizens of stable democracies are still committed to this ancient contract, the question of how governments fulfill their part of the deal and how sensitive they are to citizens' needs remains unclear. Do governments and public officials really work hard for the public money delivered to them continuously and in increasing amounts? Alternatively, do public officials misuse these resources? What do citizens/clients think of the quality and quantity of the services they receive? Do they really believe that they are being served properly? Answers to these descriptive questions may lead toward meaningful explanations of how citizens evaluate the responsiveness of public administration. More importantly, they may illuminate the main causes leading to changes in such evaluations.

The present study seeks to address these questions and to propose an empirical examination of the public administration–citizens' contract. To do this, some plausible explanations for change in public administrations' responsiveness and in citizens' satisfaction are suggested. The first explanation is based on policy and cultural factors. The second emphasizes human resource considerations and the quality of public servants. Moreover, an attempt is made to estimate the relative contribution of all factors – policy and culture and human resources – to understanding public administrations' responsiveness. This will provide some insights into the question of what is important for citizens when contacting public agencies. Is it policy and cultural motives or alternatively the quality of public servants and the human system that back up this policy?

THEORETICAL OVERVIEW

Responsiveness to Citizens' Demands

Approaches to the understanding of public administrations' responsiveness are controversial. Some studies describe responsiveness as, at best, a necessary evil that appears to compromise professional effectiveness and, at worst, an indication of political expediency if not outright corruption (Rourke, 1992). According to this line of research, responsiveness damages professionalism since it forces public servants to satisfy citizens even when such actions contradict the collective public interest. To satisfy the public will, short-term considerations and popular decisions are overemphasized, while other long-term issues receive little or no attention. However, other studies suggest that democracy would seem to require administrators who are responsive to the popular will, at least through legislatures and politicians if not directly to the people (Stivers, 1994; Stewart and Ranson, 1994). While responsiveness is occasionally considered a problematic concept in public administration literature it is undoubtedly critical to politicians, bureaucrats and citizens alike. A responsive politician or bureaucrat must be reactive, sympathetic, sensitive and capable of feeling the public's needs and opinions. Since the needs and demands of a heterogeneous society are dynamic, it is vital to develop systematic approaches for its understanding. In many ways this is the key for securing a fair social contract between citizens and rulers.

A clear consensus exists among many scholars and practitioners that the opinions of service receivers need to be taken seriously by policy makers (Palfrey et al., 1992; Winkler, 1987; National Consumer Council, 1986; DHSS, 1979). This information can help to: (1) understand and establish public needs; (2) develop, communicate and distribute public services and; (3) assess the degree of satisfaction with services (Palfrey et al., 1992: 128). Thomas and Palfrey (1996) argue that citizens are the clients and main beneficiaries of public sector operation and thereby should be involved in every process of performance evaluation. In their study, responsiveness of the public sector to citizens' demands is mentioned as an important part of performance *control* since it refers to the speed and accuracy with which a service provider replies to a request for action or for information. According to this definition, speed can refer to the waiting time between citizens' request for action and the reply of the public agency. Accuracy means the extent to which the response of the provider is appropriate to the needs or wishes of the service user. Nonetheless, while speed is relatively a simple factor to measure, accuracy is a more complicated one.

Contrary to the private sector, public service accuracy must take into consideration social welfare, equity, equal opportunities and fair distribution of 'public goods' to all citizens. Rhodes (1987) and Palfrey et al. (1992) suggested these criteria among the values that are additional to efficiency, effectiveness, and service that characterize market-driven processes. To test for accuracy of governmental endeavours one must examine how citizens feel when consuming public services. A well accepted method is to use satisfaction measures indicating the outcomes of certain activities and the acceptance of public administration actions as fruitful, contributing, equally shared among a vast population, and responding well to public needs.

Responsiveness, accountability, and performance in the public sector
While it is not obvious that the accumulated wisdom of the private sector is transferable to the public sector (Pollitt, 1988; Smith, 1993), still inevitable interactions between the two spheres are productive for both. The main interest of this study, however, is how the public sector can benefit from the experience of private organizations in managing the process of performance control and evaluation in large bureaucracies. This question has received much attention in the new public management literature that has been rapidly developed in Western societies since the 1980s (Stewart and Ranson, 1994). A considerable effort was dedicated to recognizing and defining new criteria that may help in determining the extent to which public agencies succeed in adhering growing needs of the public. As a result, new public management trends have increased the interest in specific Performance Indicators (PIs) used in private organizations. It has recommended that they be applied in the

public sector (for example, Smith, 1993: Carter, 1989). It was also argued that these indicators can function as milestones on the way to better efficiency and effectiveness of public administration.

For example, Smith (1993) mentions two different indicators for measuring public sector performance: Internal and external to the organization. Measures of internal performance, such as managerial process, routines and formal procedures, are of limited interest to ordinary citizens yet are also those which attract more attention in management literature. Their main objective is to enable the central government to secure closer control of devolved management teams (Carter, 1989). However, Smith (1993) argues that these studies are less concerned with external indicators (outcome-related) that are intended to enhance the *accountability* of public organizations to external interested parties (for example, service users, the electorate, taxpayers, the central government). The role of such outcome indicators is to furnish external users with information about the consequences of public sector activity so that citizens can make better judgments about the organization's performance.

In line with this, Anthony and Young (1984: 649) claimed that more active interest in the effective and efficient functioning of public organizations by its governing boards is essential for the improvement of management in non-profit organizations. Citizens' awareness of the performance of local services will increase the political pressure placed on elected and appointed representatives on governing boards, thereby enhancing both managerial and allocation efficiency in the public sector. Smith (1993) compares this process of public accountability to stakeholders/ citizens, to the role adopted by financial reporting in the private/corporate sector. As in the private sector, increasing external-related outcomes, such as responsiveness of public authorities to citizens' demands, will have a profound impact on internal control mechanisms, as managers and public servants become more sensitive to their duties and are highly committed to serve the people.

Management theory, as well as political science theory, defines this process of 'controlling' or 'monitoring' as the collection and analysis of relevant data about organizations' achievements and the implementation of actions to improve future performance (Thomas and Palfrey, 1996). Control and monitoring is frequently identical with accountability when public needs and interests are involved. As was argued by Stewart and Ranson (1994), organizations in the public domain exercise substantial power for which they are accountable. Public accountability must involve a political process that responds to the many voices of citizens/clients. The option of 'voice' is defined by Hirschman (1980) as a pure political action compared with 'exit' which represents more of an economical action. Since citizens generally don't have the alternative of exit in a public market, the option of voice becomes more relevant and eminent. Moreover, it seems that western democracies are facing pressures for greater rather than less accountability on behalf of their clients. Traditionally, large public bureaucracies use a variety of formal control systems (for example, general and internal auditing, accounting and special departments which deal with citizens' requests and complaints) that are aimed at providing the organization with better information on which to base internal performance indicators. However, hardly any effort has been made to actively obtain external performance indicators such as citizens' external opinion of public operation. Moreover, even when such steps are taken, the main motive is political rather than professional or administrative.

Politics and performance in public administration
The political environment of public organizations restricts its professional flexibility and capability to appropriately responding to citizens' demands. As was noted by Palfrey et al. (1992:133) 'enhanced awareness of consumers' views offers elected members the opportunity to increase their chances of re-election and prospective members of being elected'. It seems that the political sphere is responsible for the somewhat negative image of responsiveness in the eyes of many administrators and scholars. Since the strongest motive of politicians in every democracy is to be (re)elected, outcomes of public activity are normally being examined and stand for citizens' criticism only prior to the coming elections. It is only when elections become relevant that citizens' satisfaction turns to be important for politicians and worthy of evaluation. Frequently, these assessments do not rely on objective or scientific databases and serve only the politicians' narrow interests. Moreover, Winkler (1987) has criticized the superficiality of current consumerism in the public sector for being little more than a public relations exercise. This public relations largely involves politics and politicians who find consumerism to be a good vote recruiter. When consumerism and consumers become a tool in the political game the reliability of public surveys made for political purposes is damaged and its implications should be treated with considerable suspicion.

For these reasons, it is unsurprising to find that almost no western democracy evaluates the responsiveness of public administration to citizens' demands on a continuous basis, relying on scientific and well-grounded research methods, and with sufficient independence and separation from the political system. This should be noted since almost every western state maintains and develops special bureaux that specialize in statistical evaluation. Unfortunately, they are usually not engaged in the evaluation process of citizens' demands and preferences regarding the activity of public agencies. While private organizations must always be aware of clients' satisfaction in order to adjust for better self-responsiveness, public organizations are less concerned with citizens' demands since usually the former do not have a real exit alternative for getting the necessary services such as security, transportation, ecology, health, education, etc. Even when such alternatives exist they are usually partial, limited in quantity, relatively more expensive and beyond the pocket of ordinary citizens.

Nevertheless, as new public management evolves, public administration is urged to become more active and initiative-taking in measuring self-performance. For example, Pollitt (1990) suggested a taxonomy for measuring performance in the public sector: (a) measuring performance as an activity aimed at renewing or reinforcing political and public legitimacy, and (consequently) as attracting political allocations of resources; (b) measuring performance as a decision aid to management in adjusting organizational structure and processes, and internal resource allocation to support these; and (c) measuring performance in order to provide customers and clients with information on the quality, effectiveness, accessibility or efficiency of the services being provided (Kanter and Summers, 1987:158). It is argued that while the two first types of performance measurements remain the dominant concern of the literature, the third is a long way back. New public management argues that citizens/consumers represent a new actor – and a most important one – in the performance evaluation 'game'. Understanding their demands and satisfactions can contribute not only to the stock of public management information and continuous improvement but also to the process of public education. According to Pollitt (1990), the public have often been underquestioned in the past. They can learn more analytically about their experiences in the use of schools, higher education, clinics, hospitals and government offices.

Public management and responsiveness
The new public management perspective toward public administrations' responsiveness may be understood in different ways. For example, Gunn (1984) mentions four major aspects of public management: (1) public management as public administration, (2) public management as business management, (3) public management as public policy, (4) public management as managing people. Parsons (1995:554) suggests that contemporary literature in public policy 'is for the most part concerned with the evaluation of programmes and policies. However, in a managerial framework it also encompasses the evaluation of people *qua Human Resources*'. Thus, the knowledge gained through the understanding of Human Resource Management (HRM) and Organizational Development (OD) is most important and emphasizes *the evaluation of People* as opposed

to programs and policy. Using these techniques, people are changed so as to become more committed, competent, cost-effective, and in sympathy with the aims of the organization which is to bring better services to the citizens (Thompson, 1990:307).

These aspects of new public management represent a holistic approach toward the goals of public services in modern democracies. Such an approach can be defined as *an Integration of ideas from different disciplines on the operation of large bureaucracies which function under political pressures, using general management wisdom and business considerations to implement innovatory policies and ideologies for the public interest.* Building on the above, responsiveness in public organizations is a synthesis of business considerations, public policy and human determinants that better describe the complex environment of public administration. Thus, we suggest two main groups of antecedents which may affect responsiveness to the public needs: (1) public policy and cultural causes, and (2) human resource determinants and quality of public servants.

Public policy and culture
Welfare state ideology, which flourished in Europe after the Second World War, was mainly a result of post-war solidarity and common faith in the growing power of democracy (Gladstone, 1995) but at the same time reflected an attempt to respond to citizens' increasing demands for better services and an improved quality of life. The greatest challenge to public administration during the late 1940s and until the 1960s was to bring more services to the people and to re-build a new European society. However, no welfare state can ignore economic and business considerations that heavily determine its efficiency and stability. Thus, since the late 1960s and early 1970s, public administration was urged to become more effective, efficient and business oriented. To achieve these goals scholars suggested ideas of better flexibility, entrepreneurship and willingness to adopt creative new ideas. The concepts of Management by Objectives (MBO), Total Quality Management (TQM), and International Organization for Standardization (ISO) became more applicable in public agencies. A philosophy of privatization was implemented under the Thatcher administration in Britain. Innovatory ideas of rebuilding public sector budgets (for example, Zero Based Budgeting), reinventing government, outsourcing and reengineering of public administration were suggested in America. These ideas have tried to respond to the growing strain between democracy and market forces. The environment of public administration had started to change and called for the establishment of new standards of operation in the public services of western societies (Osborne and Gaebler, 1992; Bozeman, 1993; Farnham and Horton, 1993). It was agreed that a responsive, effective and efficient public policy

must adopt a balanced strategy that synthesizes economic and budgetary factors with social and human care considerations.

While today, the debate continues in every modern society regarding how to successfully balance these two factors, almost no one disputes the fact that citizens as clients have much to say about public policy. Since governmental policy directly affects the society, the public have the right to democratically influence public policy. Thus, policy is assumed to have an impact on citizens' perceptions of public sector responsiveness. When policy agrees with public demands, citizens are more willing to accept administrative actions as responding to their needs and to show more support in the entire democratic process. Public policy considerations and operation affect citizens' day to day life. They can thus be hypothesized to affect public perceptions of the responsiveness of public authorities. It is worth noting that generating public policy that works, and at the same time obtaining citizens' support, is a complex, some say almost impossible mission. However, citizens' support of or opposition to governments' policy must be reflected through a continuous measure of attitudes toward public administration and by satisfaction indicators in a variety of fields. Unfortunately, until now only a few initiatives have been suggested to respond to this challenge.

Beyond the limits of policy determination and implementation, policy plays an essential role in framing administrative culture, norms, and the behaviors of public servants. For example, hand-in-hand with governmental operation, questions of ethical standards, integrity, fair and equal treatment to clients, or appropriate criteria for rewards to public servants become more relevant. Today, public services in Europe are wider than ever before (Gladstone, 1995). As a result, public servants are taking care of growing budgets. They control the transference of more capital to and from the state treasury. This exposes many of them to ethical dilemmas as to how to properly manage, distribute and redistribute economical wealth. Other ethical difficulties arise as a result of the instability between business and social requirements in the public environment. For example, when the cost of certain medicine is too high for citizens to purchase, should the state take responsibility and help them? When state prisons are full of convicted prisoners, should the state release some of them to create more places for others? Responding to such moral issues is difficult. However, public policy which neglects considerations of ethics, equal treatment of the public, or basic justice and fairness among its members is initiating a self-destructive process which may damage its functioning in the long run (Wilenski, 1980).

The last two decades have witnessed a growing interest in issues of administrative ethics and fairness (Gawthrop, 1976; Wilenski, 1980; Richardson and Nigro, 1991; Suzuki, 1995; DeLeon, 1996; Lui and Cooper, 1997). Generally, citizens are sensitive to and aware of such unhealthy processes although having almost no opportunity to use their collective opinion in order to influence decision makers. While the media, the auditing system, the state comptroller, and even the legal authorities in western societies are those which should play an important part in criticizing public policy and administrative culture, citizens themselves are rarely questioned about their feelings and attitudes on such topics. Do they feel that public administration operates effectively and ethically? Are they being treated fairly by public servants? Nonetheless, the absence of a direct and sound public voice does not imply that citizens give up their potential power. Citizens seem to have their personal attitudes and impressions of internal processes in public agencies (for example, do they work to high standards of morality and ethics, do they treat all citizens fairly?). Citizens as clients increasingly develop independent perspectives toward issues such as what kind of culture public administration encourages and how this culture corresponds with Woodrow Wilson's ideal type of a general morality in public administration. It is argued in this study that the policy and culture of public administration affect citizens' feelings and beliefs regarding the responsiveness of public agencies.

Drawing on the above, it was decided to focus on four factors that represent public policy and cultural characteristics: business or social orientation of the public authority, entrepreneurship and initiation of changes, internal ethics, and internal politics among civil servants. All these factors refer to policy perceptions, orientations, and the administrative culture of public organizations. They consist of declared objectives and operative actions that public authorities choose to take, stand for, or alternatively withhold. No personal affiliation is relevant here and the public system as one integrative whole is under evaluation.

Human Resources and the Quality of Public Servants

A second group of variables that is hypothesized to affect citizens' satisfaction and perceptions toward the responsiveness of the public sector is more related to the human side of organizations. Compared with the policy and cultural elements that reflect more macro level constructs, the traits of public servants are rooted in the micro level of organizations and in HRM theory and practice. This approach often describes the employees as the 'organizational core' and views the quality of human staff as even more significant in public administration systems where there is a direct confrontation between the taxpayers and the civil servants.

Many studies have elaborated on the importance of creating an efficient, skilful, professional and committed public service to assist the government in its functioning (for example, Staats, 1988; Hart and Grant, 1989; Holzer,

1989; Holzer and Rabin, 1987). However, the quality of public servants is frequently criticized by scholars and practitioners. For example, Holzer and Rabin (1987) claimed that sustained attacks on the public service encourage many top students to pursue careers in the private sector, lower the morale and increase attrition of public servants. As a result, elected officials try to minimize pay rises for career officials and thereby discourage recruitment and retention of the most able public servants.

The quality of leadership and management significantly influence the success or failure of every organization. Lane (1988) argues that leadership in the public sector has become more important especially since the 1980s. Its growing importance is related to the fiscal crisis of the state that has emerged since about 1975, as well as to the attempt to insert more private sector principles into the public sector. Modern organizations in the private and in the public sector put a great deal of effort into improving managers' skills and developing business as well as human vocations among the internal leadership. Since this layer of employees is responsible for the continuous, long-range operation and healthy functioning of the organization, it is of major value to test its image in the eyes of citizens. Despite the fact that citizens do not always have sufficient knowledge about the abilities and professionalism of public managers, still they operate as objective and 'honest' evaluators of services they are entitled to receive. Do they trust public servants and have faith in their leadership? Do they believe in their professionalism and capability to implement public policy as required? These are important questions. A supplementary step must include the assessment of employees as qualified and effective in fulfilling their duties. While managers have a most influential effect on the operation of public administration, employees are generally those who directly confront the public and need to provide immediate answers to their requests. Being in the 'front lines', employees must demonstrate service-orientation, professionalism, knowledge, patience and understanding of the citizens' changing needs. In contrast to the assessment of managers' operation this research asserts that the public is even more capable of evaluating the functioning of employees.

However, one must also be aware of another point of view. What are the citizens' reactions when contacting public administrations' agencies? Do they feel burdened and stressed or alternatively relieved and untroubled? While the last decades have witnessed a growing interest in the issues of stress and strain of public employees in the fields of education, health care and welfare (for example, Crank, 1991; Friesen and Sarros, 1989; Israel et al., 1989) almost no attention has been given to citizens'/clients' stress in their relationship with public institutions. When public servants are skilled and professional, citizens are expected to feel more comfortable and to have less stress and strain caused by confrontation with public officials. On the other hand, a non-qualified, passionless, or apathetic public servant may treat citizens insensitively and thus encourage reactions of dissatisfaction, helplessness or even anger toward the public system as a whole. One should note that this is much in line with contemporary psychological theory. Studies have long argued and empirically validated a negative relationship between a supportive environment and reduced levels of stress and strain in organizations (for example, Jayaratne and Chess, 1984; Punch and Tuetteman, 1996; El-Bassel et al., 1998). When the individual is surrounded with an emphatic and supporting environment, levels of stress, strain and anxiety dramatically decrease. Therefore, citizens' stress when contacting public agencies is expected to contribute to a better understanding of the human side of public administration. Relying on the above, this research focuses on three aspects of public servants and their characteristics in public organizations: quality of leadership and management as perceived by clients/citizens, quality of employees who directly address public needs and citizens' reported stress when contacting public administration and public officials. The human factor is examined in this study together with policy and cultural variables and is expected to have significant effect on attitudes toward the responsiveness of public administration.

METHOD

Sample and Procedures

The study was based on a survey of 330 residents from a large Israeli city with a population of approximately 280,000. A total of 281 usable questionnaires (return rate of 85.2%) were used in the final analysis. The city is located in northern Israel and has six main neighborhoods from which the respondents were randomly chosen. Data collection was conducted between April and May 1998. Participants were asked to provide information concerning their attitudes toward public policy and culture, public servants in different city departments, as well as the responsiveness of public agencies and satisfaction from the services provided by the local municipality. Participation in the research was voluntary and citizens were assured of full confidentiality through the entire process. A breakdown by neighborhood shows that 27.0% lived in low class neighborhoods, 32.0% lived in average class neighborhoods, and 41.0% lived in high class areas; 57.3% of the sample were female, 55.6% married, and 65.7% had an income which is equal to or less than the average salary in Israel. Average age was 35.6 years (s.d.= 14.0); average tenure in the city was 24.1 years (s.d.=15.8). A university or college degree was held by 57.7% of the respondents with an additional 8.8% with partly academic or higher education studies. The demographic characteristics of the sample were quite similar to those of the total population in the city as reported by the city's research and statistics department: average age 35.6; 52% female; 46% married; 63.1% with 13+ school years or any academic degree.

Data Analysis

To test the relationships between the independent variables and public responsiveness we used a multiple hierarchical regression method. Three regression models were tested to examine general responsiveness, satisfaction from service and satisfaction from operation. In each of the regression models we examined both the individual relationship of the independent variables with the dependent, and the overall contribution of a group of variables (policy and culture vs. human resource and quality of public servants) to the explanation of responsiveness and satisfaction.

FINDINGS

Table 9.1 presents descriptive statistics, intercorrelations, and reliabilities of the research variables. Reliabilities and psychometric properties of all the variables are good and show normal distribution of the research sample. The correlation matrix shows some significant relationships between general responsiveness and a series of independent variables ($r=-0.36$; $p<0.001$ with business orientation, $r=0.50$; $p<0.001$ with ethics, $r=0.59$; $p<0.001$ with entrepreneurship, $r=-0.40$; $p<0.001$ with interpersonal politics, $r=0.65$; $p<0.001$ with quality of leadership and management and, $r=0.54$; $p<0.001$ with quality of employees). Satisfaction from service was positively related to ethics and entrepreneurship ($r=0.40$; $p<0.001$), quality of leadership and management ($r=0.46$; $p<0.001$), and quality of employees ($r=0.58$; $p<0.001$). It was also negatively related to business orientation ($r=-0.17$; $p<0.01$), interpersonal politics ($r=-0.31$; $p<0.001$), and stress when contacting public administration ($r=-0.25$; $p<0.001$). Satisfaction from operation was positively related to ethics ($r=0.29$; $p<0.001$), entrepreneurship ($r=0.58$; $p<0.001$), quality of leadership and management ($r=0.52$; $p<0.001$), and quality of employees ($r=0.36$; $p<0.001$). In addition it was negatively related to business orientation ($r=-0.29$; $p<0.001$), interpersonal politics ($r=-0.35$; $p<0.001$), and stress when contacting public administration ($r=-0.14$; $p<0.05$).

One may notice that some of these correlations are relatively high. However, all except one (general responsiveness, and quality of leadership and management) do not exceed the level of 0.60. Therefore, the possibility of multicollinearity or 'concept redundancy', as mentioned by Cohen and Cohen (1983), is significantly low. These findings provide some indication for a relatively strong and meaningful relationship between the independent variables and the three types of responsiveness examined in the study. The correlations thus suggest some support for the research model.

Table 9.2 describes the findings of three multiple hierarchical regressions. In each of the regressions the dependant variable was regressed on the independent variables using a three step method. Every step added one group of variables into the equation. In the first step, only variables of the first group (policy and culture) were entered into the equation. This was followed by entering the second group of variables (human resource and quality of public servants). In the third and final step we added the control variables that created the final regression model.

The first regression examined changes in general responsiveness of public administration as perceived by the public. After step 1, all four variables of the policy and culture group were significantly related to general responsiveness. As expected, general responsiveness was positively related to ethics and entrepreneurship (β=0.23; p<0.001 and β=0.39; p<0.001 respectively) and negatively related to business orientations and interpersonal politics (β=-0.18; p<0.001 and β=-0.13; p<0.05 respectively). Step 2 and 3 caused some decrease in these values. However only interpersonal politics became insignificant in the final model. Step 2 showed a positive relationship between quality of leadership and management, and responsiveness (β=0.31; p<0.001) and step 3 induced a positive relationship between quality of employees and responsiveness (β=0.12; p<0.05). In addition, those with high income perceived public administration as less responsive compared with those with low income. These findings support the relationship between the above variables and general responsiveness. Explained variance after step 1 was 46%. Step 2 contributed 8% to this value and an additional 2% of step 3 brought the total explained variance of the entire regression model to 56%. This value is high and implies that the prediction of general responsiveness by the suggested set of independent variables is good and meaningful. Moreover, variables from the first group (policy and culture) were dominant and contributed a higher proportion of variance compared with the other variables. This finding emphasizes the importance of policy and culture variables in explaining general responsiveness.

The second regression examined predictors of citizens' satisfaction from service. Step 1 yielded three significant relationships. Satisfaction from service was positively related to ethics and entrepreneurship (β=0.24; p<0.001 for each of the variables) and negatively related to interpersonal politics (β=-0.13; p<0.05). Step 2 added the human resource variables into

Table 9.1 Descriptive statistics, reliabilities and intercorrelations among research variables (reliabilities in parentheses)

Variables	Mean	S.D.	1	2	3	4	5	6	7	8	9	10	11	12
Policy and culture														
1. Business or social orientation (business)	3.44	0.78	(0.70)											
2. Ethics	2.79	0.77	−0.23***	(0.75)										
3. Entrepreneurship	2.71	0.71	−0.24***	0.47***	(0.80)									
4. Organizational politics	3.46	0.67	0.31***	−0.38***	−0.35***	(0.77)								
Human resource and quality of public servants														
5. Quality of leadership & managers	2.58	0.84	−0.32***	0.51***	0.60***	−0.44***	(0.80)							
6. Quality of employees	2.64	0.77	−0.23***	0.52***	0.49***	−0.44***	0.63***	(0.81)						
7. Stress when contacting PA	2.96	0.97	0.15*	−0.17**	−0.09	0.19***	−0.11	−0.20***	(0.80)					

Table 9.1 (continued)

Variables	Mean	S.D.	1	2	3	4	5	6	7	8	9	10	11	12
Perceptions of PAs' responsiveness														
8. General responsiveness	2.58	0.79	−0.36***	0.50***	0.59***	−0.40***	0.65***	0.54***	−0.08	(0.70)				
9. Satisfaction from service	2.77	0.74	−0.17**	0.40***	0.40***	−0.31***	0.46***	0.58***	−0.25***	0.43***	(0.86)			
10. Satisfaction from operation	2.69	0.64	−0.29***	0.29***	0.58***	−0.35***	0.52***	0.36***	−0.14*	0.51***	0.39***	(0.80)		
Control variables														
11. Gender (female)	0.57	0.50	−0.02	−0.04	0.01	−0.04	0.04	−0.03	0.02	−0.03	−0.05	−0.06	(−)	
12. Income	2.90	1.59	0.10	−0.03	−018**	0.09	−0.15*	−0.03	−0.04	−0.19**	0.00	−0.21***	−0.30***	(−)
13. Neighborhood (high class)	0.61	0.49	−0.09	0.01	−0.08	−0.09	0.01	−0.02	0.00	0.06	−0.10	−0.05	−0.01	0.02

Notes
N = 248–281 due to missing values
* $p \leq 0.05$ ** $p \leq 0.01$*** $p \leq 0.001$

221

Table 9.2 Findings of multiple hierarchical regression analysis (standardized coefficients) for the effect of independent variables on PA's responsiveness (t test in parentheses)

Variable	General responsiveness			Satisfaction from service			Satisfaction from operation		
	Step 1	Step 2	Step 3	Step 1	Step 2	Step 3	Step 1	Step 2	Step 3
Policy and culture									
1. Business or social orientation (business)	−0.18 (−3.53***)	−0.14 (−3.03**)	−0.13 (−2.80**)	−0.02 (−0.31)	0.01 (0.23)	0.00 (0.06)	−0.13 (−2.49*)	−0.10 (−1.89)	0.10 (1.84)
2. Ethics	0.23 (4.12***)	0.13 (2.45*)	0.14 (2.50*)	0.24 (3.56***)	0.08 (1.24)	0.08 (1.20)	−0.03 (−0.55)	−0.08 (−1.23)	−0.07 (−1.21)
3. Entrepreneurship	0.39 (7.26***)	0.24 (4.13***)	0.23 (3.98***)	0.24 (3.68***)	0.10 (1.51)	0.09 (1.40)	0.52 (8.82***)	0.43 (6.70***)	0.41 (6.27***)
4. Organizational politics	−0.13 (−2.34*)	−0.05 (−0.97)	−0.04 (−0.80)	−0.13 (−2.05*)	−0.01 (−0.05)	−0.02 (−0.26)	−0.14 (−2.42*)	−0.10 (−1.68)	−0.10 (−1.78)
Human resource and quality of public servants									
5. Quality of leadership & managers		0.31 (4.67***)	0.30 (4.57***)		0.07 (0.96)	0.08 (1.09)		0.25 (3.32**)	0.25 (3.33***)
6. Quality of employees		0.11 (1.86)	0.12 (2.03*)		0.42 (5.95***)	0.41 (5.77***)		−0.06 (−0.84)	−0.06 (−0.82)
7. Stress when contacting PA		0.06 (1.25)	0.05 (1.15)		−0.13 (−2.50*)	−0.13 (−2.44*)		−0.06 (−1.26)	−0.07 (−1.34)

Table 9.2 (continued)

Variable	General responsiveness			Satisfaction from service			Satisfaction from operation		
	Step 1	Step 2	Step 3	Step 1	Step 2	Step 3	Step 1	Step 2	Step 3
Control variables									
8. Gender (female)			−0.06 (−1.39)			−0.02 (−0.42)			−0.12 (−2.31*)
9. Income			−0.10 (−2.11*)			0.03 (0.63)			−0.12 (−2.26*)
10. Neighborhood (high class)			0.07 (1.59)			−0.09 (−1.65)			−0.04 (−0.76)
R^2	0.46	0.54	0.56	0.24	0.39	0.39	0.38	0.41	0.44
Adjusted R^2	0.45	0.53	0.54	0.22	0.37	0.37	0.37	0.40	0.41
F	52.48***	40.02***	29.31***	18.59***	21.28***	15.26***	37.37***	23.98***	18.07***
ΔR^2		0.08	0.02		0.15	0.00		0.03	0.03
F for ΔR^2		16.53***	4.13**		22.73***			4.63***	4.83**

Notes
N = 248–281 due to missing values
* p ≤0.05 ** p ≤0.01 *** p ≤0.001

the equation. This caused the disappearance of all previous significant relationships. In addition, satisfaction from service became positively related to quality of employees (β=0.42; p<0.001) and negatively related to stress when contacting public administration (β=-0.13; p<0.05). The effect of step 3 on the final model was minor. These findings partially support the relationships between satisfaction from service, and ethics, entrepreneurship and interpersonal politics. While these relationships were quite strong after step 1, they were also inconsistent and became insignificant in the following steps. However the relationships between satisfaction from service, quality of employees and stress were consistent. The explained variance after step 1 was 24% and increased up to 39% after steps 2 and 3. This finding shows that human resource constructs significantly contribute to the explanation of satisfaction from service in public administration.

The third regression tested satisfaction from the operation of public administration. After step 1, this variable was found to have a strong and positive relationship with entrepreneurship (β=0.52; p<0.001) and negative relationship with business orientation and interpersonal politics (β=-0.13; p<0.05 and β=-0.14; p<0.05 respectively). However, only the relationship between entrepreneurship and satisfaction from operation remained consistent after step 2 (β=0.43; p<0.001) while an additional relationship appeared between satisfaction from operation, and quality of leadership and management (β=0.25; p<0.01). These relationships remained stable even after step 3 in which gender and income showed a negative relationship with satisfaction from operation (β=-0.12; p<0.05 for each of the variables). In the third equation, step 1 contributed 38% of the total explained variance while each one of step 2 and 3 contributed an additional 3%. Thus, the total explained variance for the variable satisfaction from operation by all the independent variables summed at 44%. These findings provide support for the relationships between citizens' satisfaction from the operation of public administration, entrepreneurship, and quality of leadership and management.

The findings also show that each of the independent groups of variables significantly contributes to the understanding of public administrations' responsiveness. In all the three regression models described up till now, policy and cultural factors were more important than human resource and quality of public servants. However, at the same time, all of the regression models showed that the importance of policy and culture also dropped when human resource factors and quality of staff considerations were involved. The implications of all these findings will be discussed in the last section of this chapter.

DISCUSSION

While Perry and Kraemer (1983) find the roots of public management as lying in Woodrow Wilson's essay on *The Study of Public Administration (1887)*, it was only a century later that business orientation in public administration became of major interest for governments, politicians, media and citizens. Wilson looked to a new 'science of administration' which would make the practice of government 'less unbusiness-like'. However, it was Wilson himself who showed a normative concern with the need for public administration to be more accountable and more responsive to the public and their needs. In many respects, this normative approach has not changed much and a lack of empirical studies still constrains public administration from becoming more scientific in terms of social/behavioral science. In line with this, factors that may affect the responsiveness of public administration have not been systematically analysed up till now and thus deserve re-evaluation.

The main goal of this study was to try and narrow the gap between the normative and the positive approach to public administration, and to suggest some plausible explanations for citizens' perceptions of responsiveness in public organizations. The findings generally support a basic assertion that different variables are involved in this process. The study also implies that public administration theory may benefit from the separation of these variables into two different groups: policy and culture, and human resource and quality of public servants.

It is clear that on the edge of a new millennium, modern democracies cannot prosper without minimum standards of efficiency, economy and cost–benefit of internal operation in public administration. However, the findings of this study show that the business orientations of a city's agencies have some negative effects on perceptions of general responsiveness, and almost no effect on citizens' satisfaction from services or operation. These findings may be interpreted in two ways. First, high or sometimes excessive business orientations of public administration may lead toward a decrease in responsiveness capabilities in terms of speed and accuracy. When economic considerations are dominant and dictate a rapid business-like operation of public administration, quality and accuracy of human services may be damaged. On the other hand, taking a more realistic view suggests that business orientations do not necessarily conflict with citizens' demands as reflected in satisfaction indicators. They may even conform to citizens' requirements for an effective and efficient public administration, or careful spending of taxpayers' money as long as public administration remains sensitive and aware of citizens' social needs.

While previous studies provided theoretical reasoning for the relationship between ethics and performance in public administration (Balk, 1985; Cohen and Eimicke, 1995), this study is suggesting some empirical evidence in that direction. As well as business orientations, ethics in public administration showed a consistently positive relationship with general responsiveness but not with the satisfaction indicators. The findings show that citizens who believe that public policy is implemented according to clear ethical standards also perceive public administration as more responsive and sensitive to their demands. No support was found for a relationship between ethics and satisfaction from operation, yet some relationship was found between ethics and satisfaction from service. This is also relevant for the variable interpersonal politics. Citizens who believe that public administration involves internal political manoeuvring which contradicts fairness and equity standards, also reported lower responsiveness of public administration, lower satisfaction from service and operation. The findings regarding the negative relationship between internal politics and performance are consistent with much evidence from organizational behavior theory which found this variable to be a good predictor of negative behavioral intentions and low satisfaction levels among employees in private and public organizations (Bozeman et al., 1996; Ferris and King, 1991; Drory, 1993). However, since both relationships disappeared in the second and third steps of the equation, the implication may be that they are not stable and are heavily influenced by other factors in the environment such as human resource and quality of staff. Therefore, the findings regarding these variables should be treated with caution.

The fact that entrepreneurship showed a more consistent relationship with responsiveness and satisfaction is noteworthy. This finding indicates the importance of flexibility, creativity and acceptance of change in public agencies and is much in line with recent literature on new public management which calls for the encouragement of such processes (Du-Gay, 1994; DeLeon, 1996; Bozeman, 1993; Osborne and Gaebler, 1992; Farnham and Horton, 1993). According to the current findings, citizens show concern with stagnation in public administration. They may interpret lack of initiation or entrepreneurship as 'walking back in time' and feel that it damages public administration capability to respond to their needs.

Among the human resource factors it was found that citizens' perceptions on the quality of leadership and management were more related to general responsiveness and to satisfaction from operation while perceptions on employees and feelings of stress were more related to satisfaction from service. The relationship between quality of employees, stress, and satisfaction from service is not surprising and can be explained by the more intimate connections that employees have with the public. When services are delivered by well qualified employees who have faith and trust in the operation of the public organization, citizens receive a more adequate treatment which is directly reflected in satisfaction from service. These findings may also have another explanation. According to this view, citizens draw a clear line between quality of services and quality of operation in public administration. It may suggest that public administration can operate efficiently, effectively and respond directly to citizens' needs yet at the same time provide poor services in its offices by inadequate employees. The relationship between stress and satisfaction from service may also imply that more responsiveness and satisfaction can be obtained by narrowing the psychological gap between public institutions and individuals. While political, structural and cultural restraints will always continue to dominate the operation of large bureaucracies they still should try and reduce formality when possible and create a more supportive environment for those of the citizens who need it. An overly stressful environment in public agencies may lead to citizens making use of them only when absolutely necessary. Such a situation may result in lower levels of satisfaction from service and unnecessary tension that benefits neither the individual nor the entire public system.

To explain the importance of public leadership and management we referred to Lane (1988) who compared leadership in private and public organizations. Lane claims that leadership in public management is more difficult than in business and complicated in many respects. This is the result of different organizational design, structure, objectives, evaluation, openness of procedures, rules, predictability, technology and professionalism. Leadership style in public organizations is also less innovative and based on unique motivation (Jonsson, 1985). It is highly stable (Kaufman, 1976), powerful (Olsen, 1983), and less entrepreneurial. Even more important is the relationship between public leadership and citizens as consumers/clients. Lane's theoretical argument is that public leadership shows less sensitivity to citizens/consumers' demands simply because the latter do not have the option of exit (Hirschman, 1980). While private sector leadership is dependent on an exchange relationship with the consumer, public leadership relates to citizens on the basis of authority. That makes private managers more sensitive to short-term changes in consumers' demands while public leadership remains less responsive in the short-run.

The comparison between leadership in private and public organizations is based on sound theoretical grounding. Nonetheless, empirical evidence in this regard is scarce. The findings of this study provide some support for the notion that quality of leadership and management in public organizations is more related to citizens' satisfaction from public administrations' operation and to general responsiveness, than to satisfaction from service. A strong positive relationship exists between senior managers' professionalism, citizens' satisfaction from operation, and public administrations' responsiveness. Thus, the findings emphasize the need for better recruiting and training systems for senior administrators in the public service.

In this study an estimate was made of the relative contribution of each one of the independent group of variables to the explanation of public administrations' responsiveness. As the findings show, policy and cultural factors were more effective in explaining responsiveness and satisfaction in comparison with human resource and quality of public servants. However, the human resource variables considerably and consistently raised the total explained variance in all of the dependent variables. More important is the fact that human resource variables caused a moderation in the effect of policy and culture on responsiveness and satisfaction.

These findings are much in line with the contemporary HRM approach that encourages the integration of *personnel* management into the corporate strategy of the public organization. The HRM approach stresses that performance is related to the commitment of each employee which can be achieved through better recruiting procedures, emphasis on training in all levels, regular staff appraisal and rewarding performances (Parsons, 1995:555). This study argues that another important way for developing commitment among public personnel is by providing them feedback to check on their quality. A necessary source for such a feedback lies in citizens' evaluation of the responsiveness of public administration as an organization as well as the responsiveness of its members. The suggestion is that while policy and culture continue to play a crucial part in postulating citizens' satisfaction and perceptions of public administration responsiveness, the human side of public administration makes its own independent and important contribution. Therefore, public administration would benefit from an integrative strategy that considers quality of policy, programs and culture, as well as the quality of leadership and employees. Public servants' qualifications may create a helpful and kind environment that sometimes can cover for errors or problems in public policy or equivalent cultural characteristics.

Another contribution of this research is the suggestion of some operative measures for further empirical study of public administration. While an effort was made to find established scales for the measurement of the research variables, such scales could not be relied upon. Thus, an attempt was made to use scales that are well grounded on theoretical definitions and similar variables from general management literature. That was the case in examining general responsiveness, satisfaction, ethics, entrepreneurship, stress, and quality of public servants. However, the scales chosen showed good validity and reliability which imply that they can be used in further studies as well. These studies will also benefit from trying to extend the conceptual operationalization and more comprehensively allow the investigation of each variable.

As was argued by Wildawski (1979), public organizations tend to have goals that are difficult to quantify, meaning that it is difficult to measure their outcomes. Considering this, measuring responsiveness of the public sector as perceived by its own clients/citizens is more of a necessity than just another option of measuring performances in public administration. Drawing on a document from the Local Government Training Board (LGTB) in Britain, Palfrey et al. (1992:132) suggested that responsiveness and the idea of 'getting closer to the public' must involve a profound examination of the public's views on a range of issues. For example, it is necessary to find out public preferences and priorities, the kind of services they want, expect and need, their views on the quality of service and their experience as customers, the image they have of the local authority and the things they would like to be done better or differently. This information, when used appropriately, is valuable for every public agency. It can help to improve future policy and administrative actions while providing citizens with better 'value for money'. For this purpose, it is important that administrators and scholars alike will look for reasons of variation in the public will. Questions such as what affects citizens' perceptions of public administrations' responsiveness and how citizens satisfaction transforms during policy determination and implementation may help in: (1) initiating a more effective and service-oriented public bureaucracy, (2) improving decision making processes and the management styles of administrators, and (3) establishing some well grounded criteria for better responsiveness in the public sector.

Limitations of the Study and Recommendations for Further Research

Several limitations of this study should also be noted. First, and most importantly, the data were collected in an Israeli setting that is different from the North American or even the European setting. Therefore, the results might be affected by cultural and structural factors unique to Israel. For example, the Israeli public sector is markedly different from the American and European. It is more conservative and centralized, and for many years it faced problems typical of relatively new democracies. Thus, this research should be replicated in other settings before firm conclusions can be made. Second, the design of this research is based mainly on self-report data, which are subject to measurement biases such as common method error. While this approach is not infrequent in public sector analyses it has its advantages as well as weaknesses. Therefore, future research on the responsiveness in public administration would benefit from more objective measures of public administrations' responsiveness (for example, examining public spending or evaluating the way in which distribution of goods and services is made). Third, this study examined citizens' perceptions at one point in time and should be replicated to reveal trends and developments in public opinion on public administration. This is recommended also for theoretical purposes as well as for the practical objectives of public administrators and policy makers alike.

Despite its limitations, the findings of this study have demonstrated the usefulness of examining two groups of variables as antecedents of responsiveness in public administration. Up to now, research on responsiveness has followed a normative approach. This study expanded on the advantages of using an empirical method. However, more work is needed in this area. Questions on the relative effect of policy, culture and human resource considerations should include more variables to better represent the contextual setting for defining the antecedents of responsiveness. In this study only seven variables were used. These may be replaced in future studies with other variables that reflect more reliable and valid measures required for understanding the causes of responsiveness. Moreover, a sample of residents in one city allows us to draw upon specific implications in a particular local government. More studies are needed to compare these findings with other public organizations. Thus, the contribution of the study lies in its pointing some new directions to better explain the responsiveness of public agencies to citizens/consumers' demands in light of the new public management approach.

NOTE

1. Vigoda, E. (2000), 'Are you being served? The responsiveness of public administration to citizens' demands: An empirical examination in Israel', *Public Administration*, **78** (1), 165–91. Copyright with permission from Blackwell Publishers.

REFERENCES

Anthony, R.N. and Young, D.W. (1984), *Management Control in Non-profit Organizations* (3rd edn), Homewood: Richard D. Irwin.
Balk, W.K. (1985), 'Productivity improvement in government agencies: An ethical perspective', *Policy Studies Review*, *4*, 475–83.
Bozeman, B. (1993), *Public Management,* San Francisco: Jossey Bass.
Bozeman, D.P., Perrewe, P.L., Kacmar, K.M., Hochwarter, W.A., and Brymer, R.A. (1996), *An examination of reactions to perceptions of organizational politics,* Paper presented at the 1996 Southern Management Association Meetings, New Orleans.

Carter, N. (1989), 'Performance indicators: 'Backseat driving' or 'hands off' control?', *Policy and Politics, 17*, 131–38.

Cohen, J. and Cohen, P. (1983), *Applied Multiple Regression/Correlation Analyses for the Behavioral Sciences* (2nd edn), Hillsdale, NJ: Lawrence Erlbaum.

Cohen, S. and Eimicke, W.B. (1995), 'Ethics and the public administrator', *Annals of the American Academy of Political and Social Science, 537*, 96–108.

Crank, J. (1991), 'Work stress and job dissatisfaction in the public sector: An examination of public safety directors', *Social Science Journal, 28*, 85–100.

DeLeon, L. (1996), 'Ethics and entrepreneurship', *Policy Studies Journal, 24*, 495–510.

DHSS (1979), *Patients First,* London: HMSO.

Drory, A. (1993), 'Perceived political climate and job attitudes', *Organizational Studies, 14*, 59–71.

Du-Gay, P. (1994). 'Making up managers: Bureaucracy, enterprise and the liberal art of separation', *British Journal of Sociology, 45*, 655–74.

El-Bassel, N., Guterman, N., Bargal, D., and Su-Kuo, H. (1998), 'Main and buffering effects of emotional support on job and health related strains: A national survey of Israeli social workers', *Employee Assistance Quarterly, 13*, 1–18.

Farnham, D. and Horton, S. (eds) (1993), *Managing the New Public Services,* Basingstoke: Macmillan.

Ferris, G.R. and King, T.R. (1991), 'Politics in human resource decisions: A walk on the dark side', *Organizational Dynamics, 20*, 59–71.

Friesen, D. and Sarros, J.C. (1989), 'Sources of burnout among educators', *Journal of Organizational Behavior, 10*, 179–88.

Gawthrop, L.C. (1976), 'Administrative responsibility: public policy and the Wilsonian Legacy', *Policy Studies Journal, 5*, 108–13.

Gladstone, D. (ed.) (1995), *British Social Welfare: Past, Present and Future,* London: UCL Press.

Gunn, L. (1984), 'Conceptions of public management', Paper presented at the Conference on Public Management, The Hague.

Hampton, J. (1986), *Hobbes and the Social Contract Tradition,* Cambridge: Cambridge University Press.

Hart, D.K. and Grant, N.K. (1989), 'A partnership in virtue among all citizens: the public service and civic humanism; response to David Kirk Hart', *Public Administration Review, 49*, 101–7.

Hirschman, A.O. (1980), *Exit, Voice and Loyalty: Responses to Decline in Firms, Organizations and States,* Cambridge: Harvard University Press.

Holzer, M. (1989), 'Public service: present problems, future prospects', *International Journal of Public Administration, 12*, 585–93.

Holzer, M. and Rabin, J. (1987), 'Public service: problems, professionalism, and policy recommendations', *Public Productivity Review, 43*, 3–13.

Israel, B., House, J.S., Schurman, S.J., Heaney, C.A., Mero, R.P. (1989), 'The relation of personal resources, participation, influence, interpersonal relationship and coping strategies to occupational stress, job strains and health: a multivariate analysis', *Work and Stress, 3*, 163–94.

Jayaratne, S. and Chess, W.A. (1984), 'The effects of emotional support on perceived job stress and strain', *Journal of Applied Behavioral Science, 20*, 141–53.

Jonsson, E. (1985), 'A model of a non-budget-maximizing bureau', in J.E. Lane (ed.) *State and Market,* London: Sage.

Kanter, R.M. and Summers, D.V. (1987), 'Doing well while doing good: Dilemmas of performance measurement in non-profit organizations and the need for a multiple-constituency approach', in W.W. Powell (ed.), *The Non-Profit Sector: A Research Handbook* (pp. 98–110), New Haven: Yale University Press.

Kaufman, H. (1976), *Are Government Organizations Immortal?*, Washington DC: Brookings Institution.

Lane, J.E. (1988), 'Public and private leadership', in J. Kooiman and K.A. Eliassen (eds), *Managing Public Organizations* (pp. 47–64), London: Sage.

Lui, T.T. and Cooper, T.L. (1997), 'Values in flux: Administrative ethics and the Hong Kong public servant', *Administration and Society, 29*, 301–24.

National Consumer Council (1986), *Measuring Up: Consumer Assessment of Local Authority Services,* London.

Olsen, J.P. (1983), *Organized Democracy,* Oslo: Universitetsforlaget.

Osborne, D. and Gaebler, T. (1992), *Reinventing Government,* New York: Plume.

Palfrey, C., Phillips, C., Thomas, P., and Edward, D. (1992), *Policy Evaluation in the Public Sector,* Hants: Avebury.

Parsons, D.W. (1995), *Public Policy,* Cheltenham, UK and Brookfield, US: Edward Elgar.

Perry, J.l. and Kraemer, K.L. (eds) (1983), *Public Management: Public and Private Perspectives,* CA: Mayfield Publishing Co.

Pollitt, C. (1988), 'Bringing consumers into performance measurement', *Policy and Politics, 16,* 77–87.

Pollitt, C. (1990), 'Performance indicators, root and branch', in M. Cave, M. Kogan, and R. Smith (eds), *Output and Performance Measurement in Government: The State of the Art* (pp. 167–78), London: Jessica Kingsley.

Punch, K. and Tuetteman, E. (1996), 'Reducing teacher stress: The effect of support in the work environment', *Research in Education, 56,* 63–72.

Rhodes, R.A.W. (1987), 'Developing the public service orientation, or let's add a soupçon of political theory', *Local Government Studies, May-June,* 63–73.

Richardson, W.D. and Nigro, L.G. (1991), 'The constitution and administrative ethics in America', *Administration and Society, 23,* 275–87.

Rourke, F.E. (1992), 'Responsiveness and neutral competence in American bureaucracy', *Public Administration Review, 52,* 539–46.

Smith, P. (1993), 'Outcome-related performance indicators and organizational control in the public sector', *British Journal of Management, 4,* 135–51.

Staats, E.B., (1988), 'Public service and public interest', *Public Administration Review, 48,* 601–5.

Stewart, J. and Ranson, R. (1994), 'Management in the public domain', in D. McKevitt, and A. Lawton (eds), *Public Sector Management* (pp. 54–70), London: Sage.

Stivers, C. (1994), *Gender Images in Public Administration: Legitimacy and the Administrative State,* Newbury Park, CA: Sage.

Suzuki, P.T. (1995), 'Public sector ethics in comparative perspective', *Annals of the American Academy of Political and Social Science, 537,* 173–83.

Thomas, P. and Palfrey, C. (1996), 'Evaluation: Stakeholder-focused criteria', *Social Policy and Administration, 30,* 125–42.

Thompson, J.L. (1990), *Strategic Management: Awareness and Change,* London: Chapman and Hall.

Wildawski, A. (1979), *Speaking Truth to Power,* Boston: Little, Brown, and Co.

Wilenski, P. (1980), 'Efficiency or equity: Competing values in administrative reform', *Policy Studies Journal*, *9*, 1239–49.

Wilson, W. (1887), 'The study of administration', *Political Science Quarterly*, *2*, 197–222.

Winkler, F. (1987), 'Consumerism in health care: Beyond the supermarket model', *Policy and Politics*, *15*, 1–8.

10. The Role of Public Sector Image and Personal Characteristics in Determining Tendency to Work in the Public Sector[1]

Aaron Cohen, Yair Zalmanovitch, and Hani Davidesko

INTRODUCTION

Job search is a concept that has attracted a lot of attention from scholars and practitioners (Blau, 1994; Gatewood, Gowan and Lautenschlager, 1993; Moos and Frieze, 1993). Most of the research on this issue has focused on processes and causes that determine the organizational choices of job searchers. Less research has attempted to examine the processes and determinants of what can be termed sectorial choice, namely choices between working in the public or the private sector regardless of the specific organization. The issue of sectorial choice is an important one both for individuals seeking jobs and for policy makers in the public sector in search of qualified applicants. Yet, very little research has investigated the process of job search by looking at the sector rather than the organization as the main concept of inquiry. Two works are exceptional in this regard. Kilpatrick, Cummings and Jennings (1964) examined work values and image of employees in the Federal Service. Their book attempted to shed some light on the issue of sectorial choice, but limited research directly followed the issues raised by it. A more recent work by Blank (1985) examined and compared demographic characteristics of employees in the public and private sectors. The main finding of that paper was that groups protected by federal laws, such as minorities and veterans, tended to work in the public sector.

One goal of this study is to stimulate more research that may make conceptual as well as practical contributions. Instead of elaborating on the limitations of research on this topic, we use some of the ideas of the two studies mentioned above. Kilpatrick, Cummings and Jennings' (1964) notion of the importance of the image of the public sector is applied here by using the concept of public sector image as one of the main determinants of tendency to work in the public sector. Blank's (1985) study was the first to propose a model of factors that determines whether one is a public or private sector employee. Some of the determinants proposed by Blank are applied here. While Blank's model is based on demographic determinants, our model includes psychological as well as experience variables together in addition to the public sector image variables.

Although this study of final-year Israeli students was exploratory, three specific research questions were advanced and tested. First, what are the determinants of public sector image; second, what are the determinants of the tendency to work in the public sector; third, do the determinants of tendency to work in the public sector relate to it directly or indirectly through the mediating effect of the public sector image? The answers to these research questions were expected to contribute to the literature by providing new data about an issue that has been inadequately examined. Beside the expectation that the findings of this study will stimulate more research on the issue, the data provided here may provide policy makers in the public sector with new ideas and ways to attract qualified applicants to the public sector.

CONCEPTUAL FRAMEWORK

The concept explained here is the tendency to work in the public sector. Ajzen and Fishbein (1977) and Ryan (1970) argued that intention to behave in a certain way is the linkage between attitudes and behavior. That is, understanding the reasons for high versus low tendency to work in the public sector has important implications for understanding the actual decisions of applicants whether or not to work in a public sector organization. A concept advanced by Perry and Wise (1990), the closest concept to tendency to work in the public sector, is motivation to work in the public sector. Perry and Wise (1990) proposed three categories of reasons that are related to such motivation: rational motives, such as participation in the process of policy design, normative motives, such as willingness to serve the public interest, and emotional motives, such as commitment to the public sector resulting from an inner belief in its social importance. The concept examined here, tendency to work in the public sector, is similar to the one proposed by Perry and Wise but is more suitable for our target population, namely final-year students. Because our interest here is what causes prospective employees to decide to work or not to work in the public sector, tendency to work in this sector seems to be a more appropriate concept for examination. Another reason to prefer this concept is that the relationship between tendencies toward a given behavior and the actual behavior is not always close. Thus one may have a low tendency to work in the public sector, but in the absence of any real alternative in the private sector may decide to work in the public sector regardless. Note that a person may choose a job not in accordance with his or her preferences because when the organizational choice had to be made no employment alternatives existed in the preferred sector. In this research we were particularly interested in the tendencies, not necessarily on the actual behavior. We wished to explore possible reasons why jobs in the public sector seemed attractive. As stated, this in itself can provide scholars and policy makers with important information on how to attract employees to the public sector.

Once we determined that the concept under investigation here was the tendency to work in the public sector, it was only natural that the conceptual framework for developing a model of proposed determinants of this tendency would be based on the literature of job search and job choice. Moos and Frieze (1993) contended that the process of job choice has two main parts: first, early socialization, when the individual develops expectations and accumulates information on alternative jobs; second, the actual job search and job choice. Lord and Kerman (1987) argued that information on the prospective job and organization is collected before the entry into the organization. Individuals collect and process information on different jobs from childhood onward. Gatewood, Gowan and Lautenschlager (1993) explained that the process of job choice is one of information evaluation. Individuals collect information from two main sources to decide whether to seek work in a given organization: (1) informal, such as family and friends; (2) formal, such as newspaper ads and employment agencies. Gatewood et al. argued that information from informal sources is more important for people than that from formal sources. The above studies suggest that the roots of decisions on employment in the public sector might be found very early in a person's life. An interesting research question in this regard is how the process of accumulation of information on employment alternatives affects one's image of the public sector. The role of socialization mentioned by Gatewood et al. seemed to be closely relevant to the research subject at hand, namely tendency to employment in the public sector, so aspects of socialization were examined in this respect.

The literature on job search and job choice has naturally concentrated on the organizational level (Kilduff, 1992; Osborn, 1990; Schneider, 1987). Two concepts from this research seemed to be most relevant to this research and were integrated into its conceptual model. The first is the concept of person–organization fit (Chatman, 1991; Bowen, Ledford and Nathan, 1991), which refers to the fit between one's personality, values and beliefs and the strategic needs, norms, and values of the organization. The fit is created partly by the organization in the selection process and partly by the organizational socialization process. The literature has emphasized several aspects of fit between the individual and the organization: fit between one's knowledge, qualifications, and abilities and one's job requirements (Caldwell and O'Reilly, 1990); fit between one's needs and the organizational structure as well as its support systems (Moos, 1987); fit between one's values and the organization's culture and values (Chatman, 1989); fit between one's personality and the organizational perceived image or personality (Bowen et al., 1991). The concept of person–organization fit provides the conceptual framework for this research. It leads to the idea that prospective employees gather information about the public sector and evaluate the fit between their characteristics and those of the public sector. The outcomes of this evaluation affect their decisions whether to consider the public sector as an employment alternative favorably or not. This assumption is in line with the assumption that theory of person–organization fit can explain employment decisions of prospective employees. Bowen, Ledford and Nathan's (1991) approach to the concept of person–organization fit emphasizes the organizational image as an important component of the fit.

Organizational image is the second important concept adopted for this research from the job-choice literature. Rynes (1991) defined organizational image as a general impression of the attractiveness of the organization. This impression is based on the amount of information the applicants have at the first stages of their job search, and it affects their preliminary decisions. The importance of the organizational image on employment decisions was emphasized by several scholars (Rynes, Bretz and Gerhart, 1991; Fombrun and Shanley, 1990). The organizational image is determined by social and cultural processes. People are prepared for a realistic level of expectations of the job, and this preparation is accomplished by a variety of socialization agencies such as school, home, community and the media (Gatewood, Gowan and Lautenschlager, 1993).

We are interested not so much in the organizational image as in the sectorial one, more specifically, in the image of the public sector. The literature on this issue is sparse, so some reliance on the organizational image literature was necessary. In analogy with Rynes's (1991) definition of organizational image, we defined sectorial image as a general impression of the attractiveness of the public sector, which affects employment decision. The few studies that have looked into the issue of sectorial image are quite old, and rather limited in their methods (Kilpatrick, Cummings and Jennings, 1964; Jasper, 1961; Janowitz, Wright and Delany, 1958). In some of these studies the public sector image was measured by one item and not by scales tested for their reliabilities and validated for their psychometric properties. Yet despite their limitations, the studies on sectorial image found in general that the image of the public sector was not favorable among American employees. Jasper (1961), who examined engineering graduates and novice engineers, concluded that the general feeling of the group appeared to be that government employment carried a stigma. The students pictured the engineer working for the government as primarily interested in security and felt that employees hired by the government were generally mediocre in ability. The above studies found what seems to be a prevalent negative image/reputation of the public sector, particularly regarding its employees and work in its organizations.

RESEARCH MODEL AND HYPOTHESES

Following the literature, we anticipated that our research population, students before graduation, would develop expectations and gather information on various jobs. This stage is preparatory to the next, which is the actual selection. This study focused on one specific and defined question out of the many possible here, namely if there is a sectorial choice, and if so, what some of its determinants are. Here we set out the research model and its hypotheses. Two of the main concepts of the model have been discussed above: the dependent variable, tendency to work in the public sector, and the mediating variable, public sector image. The independent variables will be described below, together with our hypotheses regarding their relationships with the mediator and the dependent variables. The model consists of three groups of independent variables: demographic variables, background and experience variables, and personal–psychological variables. The first group of hypotheses concerns the relationship between the independent variables and the dependent variable, tendency to work in the public sector. Because we anticipated that public sector image would be positively related to tendency to work in the public sector, we expected the same pattern of relationship between the independent variables and tendency to work in the public sector to prevail for the relationship between the independent variables and public sector image. Therefore, in the hypotheses section we do not elaborate on the relationship between the dependent variables and public sector image but we analyse these relationships in the results section and discuss their implications in the discussion. The main hypothesis of this research was the anticipation of a mediating relationship. That is, sectorial image will mediate the relationship between the independent variables and the tendency to work in the public sector.

Demographic Variables

The main rationale to expect demographic characteristics to be related to tendency to work in the public sector is that deprived groups in society, such as minorities and women, will tend to work in an employment environment where they are more protected and less discriminated against (Blank, 1985). The public sector is considered to be such an environment (Greene and Rogers, 1994). Arabs are a deprived minority in Israel and work in the public sector was found to assist them in earning higher wages and suffering less discrimination than in the private one (Lewin-Epstein and Semyonov, 1994). It was thus logical to expect a greater tendency to work in the public sector among Arab students than among Jewish students, and for Arab students to hold a more positive image of this sector. By the same token it could be argued that immigrant students, those not born in Israel, would also prefer employment in the public sector. Immigrants constitute an unprotected social group that will search for employment that can provide them with more job security and less discrimination, namely employment in the public sector.

Dolton, Makepeace and Inchley (1990) argued that the public sector is one of the more popular employment choices among women. Their income there is higher than in the private sector and they are less discriminated against there than in the private sector. Women may be expected to demonstrate a more positive image of the public sector and a higher tendency to work there than men. Following this logic it could also be expected that married students would prefer employment in the public sector. Blank (1985) argued that the public sector attracts employees looking for job security, and married people are more vulnerable in terms of the costs of losing their jobs. Therefore the public sector can be an attractive alternative for them. Finally it could be expected that older students would tend to work in a more stable environment and be less willing to take risks in their career than younger students. Job security would be a stronger consideration for older students and this would impel them toward employment in the public sector. Thus, according to hypothesis 1 (H1) Arabs, immigrants, females, married and older students will have a more positive image of the public sector and higher tendency to work there.

Background and Experience Variables

The literature has emphasized the role of socialization in determining one's organizational choice (Gatewood, Gowan and Lautenschlager, 1993). Most of the variables that follow represent earlier experiences of students that could shape and affect their attitudes to employment in the public sector. One of them is the major discipline studied by the student. The difference will be between students whose major is in the social sciences and those whose major is in humanities. The importance of this factor was advanced by Kilpatrick, Cummings and Jennings (1964). The rationale is that social sciences students feel that they have studied something of practical value that makes them more attractive in the job market and can assist them in finding a job. Students in humanities feel that what they have studied has less practical value and relatively little to offer in the private sector, so they will prefer employment in the public sector, with its reputation of being less selective than the private. Kilpatrick, Cummings and Jennings (1964) also argued that the average grades of students also affect their decision to choose employment in the private or public sector. Students with higher grades have more alternatives and are more valuable in the employment market, considering that new graduates generally have no work experience. This fact makes the average grades the main measure of quality graduates as job applicants. Those with higher grades will feel more competent and confident to search for a job in the private rather than the public sector, so they will have a lower tendency to work in the latter.

Treadwell and Harrison (1994) emphasized the role of work experience as one of the main socialization agents. Students who have worked at part-time jobs in the public sector acquired a more realistic perception of the employment there, which will probably be more positive than they had before working in it. They will have acquired more accurate information about employment there, including the sector's advantages and benefits. It was thus expected that students who had worked in the public sector would have a stronger tendency to work there and a more positive image of the employment there. By the same token we also posited that students with work experience but with higher income have experienced its benefits, and because higher income is commonly associated with employment in the private sector, such students may be expected to prefer employment in that sector. They would avoid the public sector, which is certainly not associated with high income.

The role of the perception of alternative employment opportunities has been mentioned in the literature as an important criterion in the process of job search (Maehr and Braskamp, 1986). Individuals who perceive that they have fewer employment alternatives and opportunities, regardless of the reasons, will tend to look for a job with more security. In that way they will not have to go back to the job market, which is not promising for them as job seekers. Thus, according to hypothesis 2 (H2) students whose major is in the social sciences, whose average grades are lower, who have had more work experience in the public sector, and a lower income, and who perceive that they have fewer alternatives in the job market, will have a more positive image of the public sector and will have a stronger tendency to work there.

Personal Psychological Variables

Leary, Wheeler and Jenkins (1986) argued that personal characteristics are related to employment choices. Moos and Frieze (1993) explained that individuals look for jobs that will best meet their personal needs and/or values, and choose the one that has the best fit with their needs. The rationale of person–organization fit, the main conceptual framework of this research, also supports the inclusion of personal–psychological variables as determinants of tendency to work in the public sector. Several personal variables are included here.

Kilduff (1992) argued that people with low self-monitoring will feel more comfortable in a work environment that emphasizes more autonomy, and more personal freedom, in comparison with people with high self-monitoring who will prefer a more conformist environment. Those with low self-monitoring will prefer an environment that has clear and formal expectations of their role in the organization. Accordingly, we expected students with low self-monitoring to prefer an environment with more autonomy and tolerating more self-expression, while students with high self-monitoring would prefer employment in the public sector, which is considered a more conformist environment than that which they would probably find in the private sector. It was also expected here that students with external locus of control would prefer employment in the public sector. Students with internal locus of control would attribute success to ability and performance. This would strengthen their preference for employment in the private sector, which seems to emphasize effort and results. A person with external locus of control attributes his or her success to external causes, and will prefer stable employment where the compensation and promotion systems are regulated by laws and formal procedures generated by the government. A person with external locus of control will feel less vulnerable in employment in the public sector.

Two needs variables were also included in the group of personal–psychological determinants. First, students with low need for achievement would prefer employment in the public sector. The rationale is similar to the one outlined in the psychological variables mentioned above. Students with high need for achievement are more ambitious and value competition in order to achieve their goals (Burke and Deszca, 1982). Those with low need for achievement would prefer stability and security over competition, and the public sector is considered a stable and secure environment. Finally, it was strongly expected that students with high need for security would prefer employment in the public sector. Blank (1985) argued that because the goal of the public sector is not profit it attracts job seekers with higher need for security. Employees in the public sector are and feel more secure in terms of losing their job and it could be expected that students with a high need for security would prefer employment in the public sector. Thus according to hypothesis 3 (H3) students with high self-monitoring, external locus of control, low need for achievement and high need for security will have a positive image of the public sector and higher tendency to work there.

The Mediating Role of Public Sector Image

The research model suggests that the relationship between the above-mentioned determinants and tendency to work in the public sector is not direct but mediated by the image of the public sector. Kilpatrick, Cummings and Jennings (1964) were among the very few researchers who examined and emphasized the concept of public sector image. Rynes (1991) in a more recent work defined public sector image as a general impression of the attractiveness of the sector, which affects employment choice. Krau and Ziv (1990) argued that the image of employment in the public service mediates the relationship between the characteristics of employment there and the employment choice of individuals. The expectation here for a mediated relationship is based on the following rationale. Average students are in their early stages of job search, and without stable and permanent employment all they have developed is an image of different aspects of the public sector. Thus, the determinants mentioned above are related first to the perceived image of the public sector. Demographic, work experience, and personal–psychological characteristics all function to shape the image of the public sector starting from childhood and during the years of study at university. The importance of the image is emphasized by the person–organization fit theory. Prospective employees evaluate their characteristics and those of the organization, and choose the one that has the best fit with their characteristics. The image that is the result of these determinants is directly related to the tendency to work in the public sector. Thus according to hypothesis 4 (H4) the relationship between the determinants and the tendency to work in the public sector will be mediated by the image of the public sector.

METHOD

Subjects and Procedure

The target population of this study was 1640 third-year undergraduate students of most of the departments at an Israeli university (University of Haifa). Departments that were not included in the sample were Law, Social work, Art, Nursing, Occupational therapy, Department of Teaching and Teacher education. The reason for not including them is because in the Israeli setting the graduates of these departments do not have much of a sectorial choice. Most of the available jobs for students in Law and Art departments are in the private sector and most of the available jobs for students in Social work, Occupational therapy, Teaching and Teacher education are in the public sector. In all the other departments graduates have more available jobs in both sectors and therefore it was decided to include in the sample only students from such departments. Therefore, all 1640 third-year students from these departments were defined as the target population and were asked to participate in the study.

Questionnaires were distributed by mail to the home address of each of them. After two waves of distributions, 660 usable questionnaires were returned, a response rate of 40%, which was acceptable considering that this was a mail survey. A breakdown of respondents by their major subject showed that 76% of the sample were social sciences students, 64% were females, 86% were Jews, and 14% were Arabs. Respondents' average age was 25.8 years (s.d.= 4.1); 84% of them were born in Israel, 22% were married, 70% had a part-time or a full-time job, and 50% had some experience in working in the public sector. A comparison of the sample with some characteristics of the entire population as provided by the university administration, revealed that 64% were female in the target population, a percentage identical to that in the sample; 76% were Jews in the target population, compared with 86% in the sample; 57% were social sciences students in the target population, compared with 76% in the sample. The differences are reasonable, so we may generalize from the sample to the target population.

Data Analysis

The main statistical analyses in this study were multiple and hierarchical regressions. To support the hypotheses regarding the mediated relationship between the independent variables and the dependent variable, we followed Baron and Kenny (1986) and James and Brett (1984). According to them, a mediating relationship can be supported by one or more of the following methods: (1) regression analysis, (2) ANOVA or MANOVA, (3) testing for interactions. Nevertheless, Baron and Kenny (1986) elaborated on the simplicity and the effectiveness of regression analysis, compared with the limited test for mediation in other methods such as ANOVA. Accordingly, we applied the regression analysis method, in which, as described by Baron and Kenny (1986:1177), to test for mediation one estimates the following three regression equations. First, the mediator is regressed on the independent variable, whereby the independent variable must affect the mediator. Second, the dependent variable is regressed on the independent variable, whereby the independent variable must affect the dependent variable. Third, the dependent variable is regressed on both the independent variable and on the mediator, whereby the mediator must affect the dependent variable. If these conditions all hold in the predicted direction, then the effect of the independent variable on the dependent variable must be less in the third equation than in the second.

FINDINGS

First we examined the two scales for the public sector image to find whether the items of the two scales should be treated as multi-dimensional or uni-dimensional. Exploratory factor analysis of the 32 items of the two scales was performed, and produced three factors; 14 of the 15 items of the image of public sector employee loaded strongly on the first factor, and 13 of the 17 items of image of public sector employment loaded strongly on the second factor. Three items of the employment image loaded on a third factor, and one item of employee image did not load on any of the factors. This finding supported in general the existence of two separate dimensions. But two other indications supported the treatment of the two dimensions as one scale. One of these was the relatively high correlation between the two scales (r=0.66). Note, however, that a correlation of 0.66 is still acceptable in terms of treating the two constructs as separate dimensions. The other indication was that the reliability of the 32 items was very high (0.97) and supported the notion that the two scales were in fact one construct. One can see that the findings above are not conclusive in terms of making a clear decision whether to treat public sector image as a uni-dimensional or a multi-dimensional construct. Therefore, we decided to analyse and present the data with the public sector image as a uni-dimensional and a multi-dimensional construct.

Table 10.1 presents descriptive statistics, intercorrelations, and reliabilities of the research variables. The findings show good reliabilities and good psychometric properties of research variables. The correlations among the independent variables were not high except for the correlation between employment status and income (r=0.61; p<0.001). These findings support the absence of multicollinearity. Note that although the variables in this study were based on self-report data, allowing source bias or general method variance, the low correlations among the independent variables demonstrate the absence of common method error.

The correlation matrix shows negative relationships between tendency to work in the public sector and the three public sector image scales (employee r=-0.45, employment r=-0.44, and total r=-0.37; p<0.01 in all the three correlations). Some consistency can be found in the relationships between the demographic variables and the public sector image variables as well as the tendency to work in the public sector. This is strongly supported for the variables ethnicity, country of origin, major studies and average grade. The variable experience in the public sector is also related significantly to the image variables and to the variable tendency to work in the public sector. Note, too, the lack of relationship between the personal–psychological variables and the image variables. Tendency to work in the public sector was related to two psychological variables (self-monitoring and need for security). In short, the correlations provide some support for hypotheses 1 and 2 and weaker support for hypothesis 3.

Table 10.2 shows the result of four multiple regressions which were conducted following the first and the second terms for mediation of Baron and Kenny (1986), namely significant relationship between the dependent and the independent variables and between the mediator(s) and the independent variable. In each of the equations the mediating variables (public sector image of employment, employee and the total scale) were regressed on the independent variables. Also, the dependent variable was regressed on the independent variables. The findings in Table 10.2 generally support the two terms for mediation mentioned above. First, significant relationships existed between the independent variables and the dependent variable. Variables representing each group of the independent variables (demographic, experiences and psychological) were related to tendency to work in the public sector. As for the relationships between the mediating and the dependent variable, the findings showed significant relationships between the two that support the second term of mediation. These relationships were stronger for the image of employee and for the total scale of image than for the image of employment. The general conclusion is that the findings of Table 10.2 meet the first and second requirement for mediation as described by Baron and Kenny (1986).

Conceptually, the findings in Table 10.2 provide stronger support for hypotheses 1 and 2 than for hypothesis 3. Hypothesis 1 predicted that demographic variables would be related to public sector image and to tendency to work in the public sector. While the demographic variables were not related to the image of employment in the public sector, the findings in Table 10.2 show that males and Arabs had a more positive image of employees in the public sector, and Arabs had a stronger tendency to work there than Jews. This provides some support for hypothesis 1. Stronger support was found for hypothesis 2. Three of the experience variables were related to the image of the public sector. Students whose major was humanities had a more positive image of the public sector in all the three dimensions tested here. Students with higher grades had a more *negative* image of the public sector in all the dimensions. Students with some work experience in the public sector had a more positive image of employees in the public sector. The above significant relationship was found for the total image scale but not the image of employment. Two of the experience variables were related to tendency to work in the public sector. Students whose major was in humanities and students with some work experience in the public sector had a stronger tendency to work there. Altogether, the findings seem to provide solid support for hypothesis 2.

Hypothesis 3 predicted that the psychological variables would be related to image of the public sector and to the tendency to work there, and it received partial support by the data. None of the psychological variables was related to any of the public sector images, and this finding was not expected. Hypothesis 3 was supported by the relationship of two of the psychological variables to tendency to work in the public sector. As expected, students with low self-monitoring, and with high need for security, had a stronger tendency to work in the public sector. The variables locus of control and need for achievement were not related to the image variables or to tendency to work in the public sector. In all it may be concluded that hypothesis 3 was only partially supported by the data.

Table 10.3 contains the data for the third requirement for mediation described by Baron and Kenny (1986). The data in Table 10.3, together with some of the data in Table 10.2, provide stronger information for the third requirement for mediation, namely regressing the dependent variable on both the independent variables and the mediators. In Table 10.3 we performed a two-step regression analysis, where in the first step the dependent variable was regressed on the mediators and in the second step the dependent variable was regressed on both the independent variables and the mediators. This two-step regression was proposed by Ferris et al. (1996) to allow a more sensitive evaluation of the third condition for mediation: the mediators must affect the dependent variable, and, more importantly, the effect of the independent variables on the dependent variable must be less in the last equation of Table 10.2 (the relationship between the independent variables and the dependent variable) than in the second steps of Table 10.3. As mentioned this was done twice, when first public sector was treated as multi-dimensional and when in a second set of equations the public sector image was analysed as one scale. The mediating factors were entered into the equation in the first step while all other independent variables were entered in the second one. The findings in Tables 10.2 and 10.3 provide empirical support for condition 3. First, the data strongly show that public sector image was strongly related to tendency to work in the public sector. Most of the variance in tendency to work in the public sector was due to the effect of public sector image (R^2=19% as a multi-dimensional and 18% as a uni-dimensional construct), while all other variables contributed 10% or 11% to the total explained variance. Although this estimation was not part of the research hypotheses one should note the significant effect of the mediators on tendency to work in the public sector. This finding supports the rationale of hypothesis 4, which expected strong relationships between public sector image, as mediating factors, and the dependent variable, tendency to work in the public sector. The data in Table 10.3 strongly support hypothesis 4 when we compare the last equation in Table 10.2 with the two second step equations in Table 10.3. The data clearly show that the effect of the independent variables was less in the regression equation in Table 10.2 (0.16) than in the two regressions of Table 10.3 (0.29). All these findings are much in line with the third condition for mediation of Baron and Kenny (1986). In short, the findings in Tables 10.2 and 10.3 provide empirical support for hypothesis 4, namely public sector image mediated the relationship between all the independent variables and tendency to work in the public sector.

DISCUSSION

One of the goals of this study was to draw more attention by scholars to an issue that has been overlooked for many years and to stimulate more research on this important topic. The findings of this study support most of the basic arguments advanced by this chapter. First, tendency to work in the public sector is a construct that has a meaning for students who are exploring their possibilities in the job market. The same can be said about the concept of public sector image that was also advanced here. Moreover, the two concepts are related, and the image of the public sector mediated the relationship between the proposed determinants and tendency to work in the public sector. Thus, despite the somewhat exploratory nature of this study since very little research has been conducted on the issue, the findings show that the topic examined offers a promising and challenging research agenda for the future.

The findings of this study provide general support to the very few and somewhat old studies on this issue. Kilpatrick, Cummings and Jennings

(1964) set out the notion that the image one has about the public sector can affect one's attitudes and behavior. This idea was elaborated here and tested by use of valid and reliable scales with more advanced methodology than that employed by Kilpatrick, Cummings and Jennings (1964). The scales we proposed and tested captured two important dimensions of the public sector image: the image of its employees and the image of employment in the public sector. The findings were not conclusive in determining whether public sector image is a multi-dimensional or uni-dimensional construct. While the relatively high correlation between the two (r=0.66) suggests that perhaps they should be treated as uni-dimensional it seems that a multi-dimensional perspective was better supported by the data. Some interesting differences between their determinants supported the notion that they are distinct. For example image of employment was related only to two experience variables while image of employee was related also to gender ethnicity and country of origin. Future research should test the scales proposed here to arrive at a more definite conclusion whether image of the public sector is a uni-dimensional or a multi-dimensional construct.

Regardless of this methodological aspect in both its uni-dimensional and multi-dimensional form, the findings here showed the potential of image of the public sector as a concept able to increase understanding of prospective employees' decision whether or not to work in the public sector. The findings strongly supported the notion that public sector image mediates the relationship between determinants and tendency to work in the public sector. That is, demographic, background and experience variables work to shape the image one has of the public sector, and this image determines one's tendency to work in that sector. This process emphasizes the role of socialization in shaping one's image of the public sector, and supports Moos and Frieze's (1993) argument that socialization is an important component in the job search and job choice processes. The relationship between work experience in the public sector and the image of the public sector supports Lord and Kerman's (1987) argument that the information on the prospective job and organization is collected before entry into the organization. The findings here show, as suggested by Gatewood, Gowan and Lautenschlager (1993), that the process of sectorial choice is one of information evaluation. Individuals collect information that helps them decide whether to get a job in a given organization, in this case the public sector.

The findings of this study also support earlier findings of Blank (1985), who examined demographic determinants of workers' choice between employment in the public or private sector. Blank's study differs from this one because it examined and compared *employees* from both the public and the private sectors, while ours examined tendency to work in the public sector among *students*. Yet some similarities between the findings of the two studies

Table 10.1 Basic statistics and correlation matrix[ab]

	Mean	S D	1	2	3	4	5	6	7	8	9	10	11	12	13	14	15	16	17	18	19
1. Gender (female)	0.54	0.48																			
2. Marital status (married)	0.21	0.41	0.06																		
3. Age	25.80	4.10	-0.16***	0.37***																	
4. Ethnicity (Jewish)	0.86	0.34	0.06	0.06	0.20***																
5. Country of origin (Israel)	0.83	0.36	0.03	-0.03	-0.03	-0.09*															
6. Major (humanities)	0.24	0.42	0.09*	0.02	0.10*	-0.20***	0.03														
7. Average grade	82.77	6.14	0.16***	0.06	0.08*	0.29***	0.17***	-0.08*													
8. Perceived employment alternatives	2.77	0.90	0.12**	-0.00	0.02	-0.28***	0.04	0.11**	-0.11**												
9. Employment status (employed)	0.70	0.45	-0.04	0.03	0.13**	0.30***	0.05	-0.08*	0.16***	-0.20***											
10. Income	1611	1481	-0.17***	0.019***	0.35***	0.21***	0.06	-0.03	0.05	-0.20***	0.61***										
11. Experience in the public sector (worked)	0.49	0.50	0.04	0.05	0.12**	-0.02	-0.08*	0.11**	0.03	0.03	0.10**	0.11**									
12. Self-monitoring	3.11	0.46	0.16***	0.01	0.01	-0.04	-0.00	0.01	0.04	0.13***	-0.09*	-0.13***	-0.08*	(0.73)							
13. Locus of control	3.00	0.62	0.00	0.00	-0.07*	-0.09*	0.03	-0.03	-0.10**	0.18***	0.10**	-0.08*	-0.06	0.01	(0.66)						

Table 10.1 (continued)

	Mean	S D	1	2	3	4	5	6	7	8	9	10	11	12	13	14	15	16	17	18	19
14. Need for achievement	3.90	0.55	−0.05	−0.00	0.03	0.04	0.11**	0.00	0.11**	−0.15***	0.06	0.11**	0.03	−0.14***	−0.10**	(0.67)					
15. Need for security	4.50	0.57	0.17***	0.02	−0.08*	0.03	−0.00	0.04	−0.05	0.16***	−0.01	−0.07*	0.00	0.10**	0.13***	0.02	(0.85)				
16. Public sector image (total)	3.61	1.29	0.02	−0.00	0.02	−0.09*	−0.05	0.16***	0.13***	−0.00	−0.03	−0.03	0.09*	−0.00	−0.02	0.00	0.06	(0.97)			
17. Public sector image (employment)	3.47	1.38	0.12**	−0.05	−0.07	−0.23***	−0.10*	0.22**	−0.16***	0.06	−0.08*	−0.08*	0.17***	0.00	0.00	0.00	0.05	0.66***	(0.95)		
18. Public sector image (employee)	3.76	1.45	0.08*	−0.03	−0.02	−0.14***	−0.09*	0.21***	−0.16***	0.03	−0.06	−0.06	0.14***	−0.00	−0.00	0.00	0.06	0.90***	0.91***	(0.96)	
19. Tendency to work in the public sector	3.34	0.79	0.01	0.00	0.00	−0.21***	−0.01	0.21***	−0.08*	0.12**	−0.03	−0.03	0.21***	−0.08*	0.06	0.06	0.22***	−0.37***	−0.44***	−0.45***	(0.93)

Notes

a. N = 615–660

b. Internal reliabilities are shown on the diagonals in parentheses

*p ≤0.05 **p ≤0.01 ***p ≤0.01

Table 10.2 *Regression analysis (standardized coefficients) predicting three forms of public sector image and tendency to work in the public sector from the independent variables[a]*

Independent variables	Public sector image			Tendency to work in the public sector
	Employment	Employee	Total	
1. Gender (female)	0.02	0.12**	0.08	−0.04
2. Marital status (married)	−0.01	−0.05	−0.03	0.01
3. Age	0.05	−0.02	0.02	0.02
4. Ethnicity (Jewish)	−0.08	−0.20***	−0.15**	−0.19***
5. Country of origin (Israel)	−0.03	−0.10*	−0.07	−0.02
6. Major (humanities)	0.12**	0.14***	0.14***	0.13**
7. Average grade	−0.12**	−0.10*	−0.12**	0.01
8. Perceived employment alternatives	−0.09	−0.04	−0.07	0.04
9. Employment status (employed)	0.01	−0.01	0.00	0.04
10. Income	−0.04	0.00	−0.02	−0.03
11. Experience in the public sector (worked)	0.08	0.16***	0.13**	0.16***

Table 10.2 *(continued)*

Independent variables	Public sector image			Tendency to work in the public sector
	Employment	Employee	Total	
12. Self-monitor	−0.01	−0.00	−0.01	−0.10*
13. Locus of control	−0.02	0.01	−0.00	0.05
14. Need for achievement	0.01	0.02	0.02	0.03
15. Need for security	0.04	0.02	0.03	0.21***
R^2 (adjusted)	0.06(0.03)	0.14(0.12)	0.11(0.08)	0.16(0.14)
F	2.39**	6.27***	4.59***	7.38***

Notes
a. N = 615–660
* p ≤0.05 ** p ≤0.01 *** p ≤0.001

253

Table 10.3 *Hierarchical regression analysis (standardized coefficients) predicting tendency to work in the public sector by the independent variables controlling for public sector image[a]*

Variables	Tendency to work in the public sector as a multi-dimensional construct		Tendency to work in the public sector as one construct	
	Step 1	Step 2	Step 1	Step 2
1. Public sector image (employment)	−0.12*	−0.13**		
2. Public sector image (employee)	−0.34***	−0.28***		
3. Public sector image (total)			−0.43***	−0.38***
4. Gender (female)		−0.08*		−0.07
5. Marital status (married)		0.02		0.02
6. Age		0.02		0.02
7. Ethnicity (Jewish)		−0.13**		−0.14**
8. Country of origin (Israel)		0.01		0.01
9. Major (humanities)		0.08*		0.08*
10. Average grade		0.05		0.06
11. Perceived employment alternatives		0.06		0.07
12. Employment status (employed)		0.04		0.04

Table 10.3 (continued)

Variables	Tendency to work in the public sector as a multi-dimensional construct		Tendency to work in the public sector as one construct	
	Step 1	Step 2	Step 1	Step 2
13. Income		-0.02		-0.02
14. Experience in the public sector (worked)		0.11^{**}		0.11^{**}
15. Self-monitoring		-0.10^{**}		-0.10^{**}
16. Locus of control		0.05		0.05
17. Need for achievement		0.02		0.02
18. Need for security		0.20^{***}		0.20^{***}
R^2 (Adjusted)	0.19(0.19)	0.29(0.27)	0.18(0.18)	0.29(0.27)
F	67.57^{***}	13.55^{***}	130.73^{***}	14.43^{***}
ΔR^2		0.10		0.11
F for ΔR^2		5.33^{***}		5.63^{***}

Notes
a. N = 615–660
$*$ p ≤ 0.05 $**$ p ≤ 0.01 $***$ p ≤ 0.001

exist. First, Blank's main findings showed that non-whites and veterans, groups protected by federal employment laws, preferred the public sector but women had no statistically distinguishable preference between the sectors. Blank's (1985) finding was supported in general by the findings here. Arab students, a relatively deprived minority in Israel, preferred employment in the Jewish students. It may be concluded that minorities prefer employment in the public sector because they feel more protected by the laws and regulations in it, regardless of culture and country. Another interesting finding is that in both studies gender had no significant effect on employees' working in the public sector in Blank's study, or on students' tendency to work in the public sector here. This finding showed that, regarding employment in the public sector, gender becomes less important in the process of making a sectorial choice. Other characteristics affect females' decisions in both cultures whether or not to work in the public sector, not the anticipation that they will be more protected in the public sector. This conclusion needs to be tested in future research.

Another finding by Blank (1985) was that employees with lower education preferred the public sector, while those with higher education or more experience seemed to prefer the private sector. The logic of Blank's finding was in a way supported here. Education represents human capital, and those with more of this resource felt more confident to compete in the private sector. In this study, grades and major subject represent human capital for students. It is not surprising that students whose major was in social sciences and who won higher grades thought that by having more human capital they had more options in the job market and could compete successfully in the private sector. This was demonstrated here in the negative image that students with higher grades had of the public sector and in the stronger tendency of students whose major was in humanities to work in the public sector. The findings here provide support for human-capital theory in the sense that prospective employees with more human capital do not perceive work in the public sector as employment that will enable them to capitalize on their resources. This study's contribution is to show that what Blank found for employees can be predicted prior to their joining the workforce. Our findings in the Israeli setting accord with those of Jasper (1961) for engineering graduates and novice engineers noted above. The findings here, almost 40 years later and in another culture, seem to support those of Jasper (1961). Note, however, that many differences exist between the above studies, particularly between Blank's work and this one. A major difference is the inclusion in our model of public sector image, which was strongly supported by the data.

Another notable finding is the relatively weak effect of the psychological variables. These had no effect on any of the public sector image forms. This finding emphasizes the role of socialization and not personality in shaping one's attitudes to employment in the public sector. But one cannot ignore the strong effect of personality on tendency to work in the public sector. This was demonstrated in the significant effect of self-monitoring and more especially need for security, on this tendency. This finding shows that certain personalities tend to look for employment in the public sector. The strong effect of need for security shows that not only is the public sector a better environment for protected groups such as minorities, but this pattern is also relevant for those who *feel* unprotected whether or not they are in a protected group. This finding needs to be replicated in future research before definite conclusions can be made.

The findings here strongly support the conceptual framework of person–organization fit (Chatman, 1991; Bowen, Ledford and Nathan, 1991) as appropriate to understanding of the determinants of tendency to work in the public sector. This theory postulates that what determines one's choice is the fit between one's personality, values and beliefs and the strategic needs, norms, and values of the organization. The findings here emphasize the fit from the individuals' point of view. Prospective employees who are from a minority group (Arabs), who are not especially trained (major in humanities and not social sciences), who have some work experience in the public sector, whose personality leans toward a more conformist formalized and dependency environment, and above all who have a strong need for security, prefer to work in the public sector. Support for the person–organizational fit framework is reinforced by the significant effect of two psychological variables on tendency to work in the public sector. This effect supports the approach emphasizing the fit between the individuals' personality and the perceived organizational image or personality (Bowen, Ledford and Nathan, 1991). The effect of the psychological variables was not evident in the relationship between the psychological variables and image of the public sector.

This study offers some practical implications particularly for policy makers. While all will agree on the need to increase the quality of the workforce in the public sector, this study offers new insights into how to do it. Image was found here as a key concept affecting students' tendency to work in the public sector. Some prospective employees will not choose the public sector because of its negative image. But this image can be shaped and influenced. For example, providing students with some experience in the public sector is one practical way to improve the image of the public sector and increase the tendency to work there. Providing social sciences graduates with information on the advantages of working in the public sector is another way to attract them to the public sector. Improving the image of the public sector will probably attract more excellent students.

Person–organization fit theory postulates that the fit can be created by the organization in the selection or the socialization process. The effect of the variable experience in the public sector emphasizes the ability of public organizations to use the socialization process to attract qualified employees to the public sector. The effect of the two psychological variables suggests that the selection process can be used to detect these psychological characteristics. But first a strategic decision has to be made by organizations: do they want employees with high self-monitoring and high need for security? If not, applicants possessing these two characteristics might be rejected. Image is one of the reasons why people who feel less confident about themselves choose to work in the public sector. Improving the public-sector image will probably result in more quality applicants wishing to work in the public sector. This study showed some ways by which the image of the public sector can be enhanced, but much more work is needed to explore other factors that shape it.

Finally, several limitations of this study must be considered. First, because this research examined students, there may be limits to the generalizability of the findings to other populations, especially employees. Second, the study relied on self-report data, allowing for the possibility of same-source bias, a common problem with cross-sectional, non-behavioral measurement. Because the multivariate analysis considered the simultaneous effects of all variables, the extent of this problem was reduced. Third, much of the work on public sector employment has concentrated on American employees, which limits ability to generalize findings across other cultures and settings. While the American data are very important, there must be more diversity in the cultures and nations that are tested. This chapter has attempted to show the usefulness of such research in another culture, the Israeli one, and also to propose some directions for future study.

Despite the limitations, this study has some important contributions. The findings here demonstrate the importance of public sector image and tendency to work in the public sector as important considerations for understanding sectorial choice of prospective employees. The proposed model has some important conceptual and practical implications that can direct future research. More research on this issue seems warranted in light of the findings and before solid conclusions can be made on the findings here. The contribution of this study is its proposing some promising directions for research on an interesting and important issue.

NOTE

1. Based on Cohen, Zalmanovitch and Davidesko, H. 'The role of public sector image and personal characteristics in determining tendency to work in the public sector', *Public Administration Quarterly*, Forthcoming. Copyright with permission.

REFERENCES

Ajzen, I. and Fishbein, M. (1977), 'Attitude–behavior relations: A theoretical analysis and review of empirical research', *Psychological Bulletin, 84*, 888–918.

Baron, R.M. and Kenny, D.A. (1986), 'The moderator–mediator variable distinction in social psychological research: Conceptual, strategic, and statistical considerations', *Journal of Personality and Social Psychology, 51*, 1173–82.

Blank, M. R. (1985), 'An analysis of workers' choice between employment in the public and private sectors', *Industrial And Labor Relations Review, 38*, 211–24.

Blau, G. (1994), 'Testing a two-dimensional measure of job search behavior', *Organizational Behavior and Human Decision Processes, 59*, 288–312.

Bowen, D.E., Ledford, G.E., and Nathan, B.R. (1991), 'Hiring for the organization, not the job', *Academy of Management Executive, 4*, 35–51 .

Burke, R.J. and Deszca, E. (1982), 'Preferred organizational climates of type A individuals', *Journal of Vocational Behavior, 21*, 50–9.

Caldwell, D.F. and O'Reilly, C.A. (1990), 'Measuring person–job fit with a profile-comparison process, *Journal of Applied Psychology, 75*, 648–57.

Chatman, J. A. (1989), 'Improving interactional research: A model of person-organization fit', *Academy of Management Review, 14*, 333–49.

Chatman, J. A. (1991), 'Matching people and organization: Selection and socialization in public accounting firms', *Administrative Science Quarterly, 36*, 459–84.

Dolton, P.J. , Makepeace, G.H. and Inchley, G.D. (1990), 'The early careers of 1980 graduates', *Research Paper, 78*, 1–90.

Ferris, G.R., Frink, D.D., Bhawuk, D.P.S., and Zhou, J. (1996), 'Reactions of diverse groups to politics in the workplace', *Journal of Management, 22*, 23–44.

Fombrun, C. and Shanley, M. (1990), 'What's in a name? Reputation and corporate strategy', *Academy of Management Journal, 33*, 233–58.

Gatewood, R., Gowan, M., and Lautenschlager, G. (1993), 'Corporate image, recruitment image, and initial job choice decisions, *Academy of Management Journal, 36*, 414–27.

Greene, M. and Rogers, J. (1994), 'Education and the earnings disparities between black and white: A comparison of professionals in the public and private sectors', *Journal of Socio-Economics, 23*, 113–30.

James, L. R. and Brett, J. M. (1984), 'Mediators, moderators and tests for mediation', *Journal of Applied Psychology, 69*, 307–21.

Janowitz, M., Wright, D. and Delany, W. (1958), *Public Administration and the Public Perspectives Toward Government in a Metropolitan Community*, Ann Arbor: University of Michigan.

Jasper, W. (1961), *Attitudes toward federal employment as measured by group interview and questionnaire techniques*, Paper presented at the 69th Annual Convention of the American Psychological Association, September.

Kilduff, M. (1992), 'The friendship network as a decision making resource: Dispositional moderators of social influences on organizational choice', *Journal of Personality and Social Psychology, 62*, 168–80.

Kilpatrick, F., Cummings, M. and Jennings, K. (1964), *Source Book of a Study of Occupational Values and the Image of the Federal Service*, Washington, DC: The Brookings Institution.

Krau, E. and Ziv, L. (1990), 'The hidden selection of the occupational appeal: The paradigm of nurses', *International Journal of Sociology and Social Policy, 10*, 1–28.

Leary, M., Wheeler, D. and Jenkins, B. (1986), 'Aspects of identity and behavioral preference: Studies of occupational and recreational choice', *Social Psychology Quarterly, 49*, 11–8.

Lewin-Epstein, N. and Semyonov, M. (1994), 'Sheltered labor markets, public sector employment, and socioeconomic returns to education of Arabs in Israel', *American Journal of Sociology, 100*, 622–51.

Lord, R.G. and Kerman, M.C. (1987), 'Scripts as determinants of purposeful behavior in organizations', *Academy of Management Review, 12*, 265–77.

Maehr, M.L. and Braskamp, L.A. (1986), *The Motivation Factor*, Toronto: Lexington Books.

Moos, M. and Frieze, H.I. (1993), 'Job preferences in the anticipatory socialization phase: A comparison of two matching models', *Journal of Vocational Behavior, 42*, 282–97.

Moos, R.H. (1987), 'Person–environment congruence in work, school and health care settings', *Journal of Vocational Behavior, 31*, 231–47.

Osborn, D.P. (1990), 'A reexamination of the organizational choice process', *Journal of Vocational Behavior, 36*, 45–60.

Perry, J.L. and Wise, L.R. (1990), 'The motivational bases of public service', *Public Administration Review, 50*, 367–73.

Ryan, A, T. (1970), *Intentional Behavior*, New York: The Ronald Press Company.

Rynes, S.L.(1991), 'Recruitment, job choice and post hire consequences: A call for new research directions', in Dunnette, M.D. and Hough, L.M. (eds), *Handbook of Industrial and Organizational Psychology* (pp. 129–66), Greenwich, CT: JAI Press.

Rynes, S.L., Bretz, D.R. and Gerhart, B. (1991), 'The importance of recruitment in job choice: A different way of looking', *Personnel Psychology, 44*, 487–520.

Schneider, B. (1987), 'The people make the place', *Personnel Psychology, 40*, 437–53.

Treadwell, D.F. and Harrison, T.M. (1994), 'Conceptualizing and assessing organizational image: Model, images, commitment, and communication', *Communication Monographs, 61*, 63–83.

11. Administrative Agents of Democracy? An Empirical Examination of the Relationship Between Public Sector Performance and Citizenship Involvement[1]

Eran Vigoda-Gadot

INTRODUCTION

The need continuously to foster democratic values of citizenship participation and involvement is a prominent issue in contemporary political science literature (for example, Box, 1998; 1999; Frederickson, 1982; 1997; King, Feltey, and Susel, 1998; King and Stivers, 1998). Barner and Rosenwein (1985) argued that 'democratic values are in essence participatory values. At the heart of democratic theory is the notion that people should get involved in the process of governing themselves' (p.59). Furthermore, Guyton (1988) suggested that those who do not participate politically are likely to have a highly undemocratic view of the world. To date, studies have been preoccupied with important questions on the nature of these values, their construct and meaning, as well as their existence and change over time and across cultures (Almond and Verba, 1963; Verba, Nie and Kim, 1978; Verba, Schlozman and Brady, 1995). A consensus has also existed among scholars on the centrality of citizenship involvement in the democratic process, and it was argued that theory should further suggest better explanations on how democratic values such as high participation and widespread involvement emerge, develop and transform in an ultra-dynamic and highly-demanding modern society.

Here precisely lies the potential merit of our study, which tries to expand on the responsibility of public administration as another agent of citizenship involvement in modern states. We elaborate on several questions: do public administration outcomes contribute to the expansion of better citizenship involvement and good democratic values among individuals? What is the nature of this relationship, if it exists? Which aspects, if any, of public sector operation are more important for the improvement of performance that supports democratic values of higher citizenship involvement? Answers to these questions may enlarge our knowledge on the role of public administration in democratic cultures. Participatory democratic theory as suggested by Pateman (1970) and by more recent works (for example, Peterson, 1990; Putnam, 1993) highlights the ways in which institutional arrangements and activities leave their imprint on citizens. If better performance of administrative authorities can lead to more political participation, higher community involvement, wider trust in citizenship action, and increased political efficacy, specific lessons must be learned on the required operative and moral course of public systems. Such lessons may prove relevant beyond the simple managerial and financial cost–benefit purposes that are so prevalent in contemporary public management literature. They may justify deeper and farther-reaching demands for effectiveness, efficiency, responsiveness and morality in the public sector, and strengthen the theoretical as well as practical linkage between outcomes of governmental institutions and a redesign of valuable social norms.

To address these questions our study applies original data collected among Israeli citizens. We empirically tested a hypothesis that public administration's outcomes have a generally positive effect on citizenship orientations and on individuals' democratic values. Several theoretical models were posited and examined to elicit not only general 'support' or 'reject' conclusion but also to explore the *nature* of relationship between public administration's performance, faith in citizenship involvement and actual citizenship behaviors as represented by political and communal participation.

CITIZENSHIP INVOLVEMENT IN MODERN DEMOCRACIES: THIS TIME FROM A PUBLIC ADMINISTRATION VIEWPOINT

While recent decades have witnessed some important explorations of the meaning and nature of citizenship involvement in democracies (for example, Almond and Verba, 1963; Brady, Verba and Schlozman, 1995; Milbrath and Goel, 1977; Verba, Schlozman and Brady, 1995) much work remains to be done. One example is the uncertain knowledge of conceivable relationships between public sector performance and the emergence of democratic values among citizens. To date, only sparse empirical evidence exists on how public sector outcomes affect citizens' confidence and trust in government, willingness to participate in political or communal behaviors, and most importantly tangible involvement in the active democratic process. On the one hand, traditional political science literature frequently concentrates on personal, psychological or sociological antecedents of citizenship behavior, involvement and participation (for example, Krampen, 1991; Milbrath and Goel, 1977; Peterson, 1990; Sabucedo and Cramer, 1991). Nevertheless, this group of studies usually pays much less attention to outcomes and performances of public organizations that may serve as additional agents of citizenship involvement. On the other hand, studies in public administration frequently emphasize managerial tools for improving performance in these bodies (Lynn, 1996; 1998; Pollitt, 1988; Rainey, 1990). These studies, like many others, look for better ways of setting, implementing and evaluating public policy, and moreover recognize the valuable contribution of citizenship involvement to these processes. Yet this cluster of studies usually treats public sector performance and outcomes as dependent variables. Hence, much effort has been devoted so far to better explaining public sector operation and performance by means of citizens' participation, involvement, feelings of efficacy, and cooperation with government (Box, 1998; 1999).

Surveying these two research lines, we identify a significant scholarly gap asking to be bridged. Both groups of studies outlined above seem to have overlooked another possible connection between public administration performance and citizenship involvement. According to this idea, public sector operation and performance should be regarded as an additional catalyst for (or alternatively obstruction to) citizens' participation and involvement. In keeping with this argument, Berman (1997) suggested that the literature offered little on the role of public administration in shaping public attitudes. Most studies focus on citizens' roles and better management of citizenship involvement in the administrative process (for example, Box, 1998; 1999; Rimmerman, 1997). However, as with schools, families, peer-groups, media and academia, the special role and responsibility of public sector organizations in the process of democratic socialization has to be elaborated. Indeed, some studies employed theories of skill and resource transaction between social institutions to argue that citizenship involvement is acquired through a process of political learning (for example, Pateman, 1970; Putnam, 1993; Peterson, 1990; Sobel, 1993; Verba, Schlozman and Brady, 1995). Yet while these studies related institutional actions or culture to individual political participation none of them considered the prospect that public administration *performance* may have an impact on various dimensions of citizen participation. Following this, we suggest that more attention should be given the possibility that the administrative system has a meaningful independent effect on framing and shaping citizenship involvement by its very basic function of providing goods and services to the people. Hence, performance by public sector agencies may be part of a socialization process that advances democracy among citizens of modern states.

Public Administration and a Strong Democratic Heritage

A well-performing public administration and strong democracies are tightly bound together since they both rely on productive and widespread citizenship involvement. According to this ethos Woller (1998) indicated that no bureaucracy, nor any democracy, can function properly without a minimal input of citizenship activity. Moreover, modern public administration is deeply rooted in a strong democratic heritage. It is democracy that renders legitimacy to the decisions and actions of the public service, and it is democracy again that must check and balance the tyrannical nature of bureaucracies. Yet both bureaucracy and democracy are also highly important conditions that make possible the proper running of modern states. No prosperous free society can long exist without a continuous improvement of its administrative bodies, bureaucracy, and public managerial process. This improvement is required to meet new needs and demands by citizens that place heavier pressures on government as well as on the public service. Neither can modern societies flourish when democratic values of good citizenship are threatened or spoiled (Verba, Schlozman and Brady, 1995) or when citizens are apathetic, alienated or emotionally discouraged from being involved in the process of ruling and being ruled in return.

Therefore, studies in public administration have recognized the advantages of productive reciprocal relationships between citizens and rulers (Box, 1998). Ideas first mentioned by Hobbes, Locke and Rousseau suggested that a hidden agreement or 'social contract' exists between rulers and citizens. It was argued that such a contract prevails over the natural state of chaos in human lives. In a subtle manner this unwritten social agreement also fostered the emergence of modern democracies. As suggested by Hampton (1986), 'by electing a government, people lend, alienate, or give up their power to political rulers on condition that it be used to satisfy certain of their most important needs' (p.256). Governmental authorities win a mandate to use their executive power (through bureaucracies and public administration bodies) and to make citizens' lives as safe, sheltered, comfortable and pleasant as possible.

A social agreement between citizens, state rulers and executives, as formed in modern democracies, constitutes a powerful mechanism with precious collective advantages for societies and individuals. At the same time, it is beset by many difficulties and hindrances that should not be ignored. For example, what happens when governments and public sector organizations fail to meet citizens' demands? What impact can such a failure have on the legitimacy of governments and their image and prestige in the eyes of citizens–clients? Can poor public sector performance lead to distrust and growing doubt about the democratic process in general? If it can, then how, and how much? These questions are important to all who seek better explanations for the life cycle, stability and survival of modern democracies. Such explanations will also add to our knowledge of the various impacts of public administration actions in terms of citizenship involvement and orientation toward democracy. Still, to provide reliable answers to these questions we must first furnish clear definitions of public sector performance and operation as well as a lucid understanding of the essence of citizenship involvement.

Public Sector Performance and Actions: Several Approaches

Theory has provided many alternatives for the understanding and measurement of public sector performance. Studies have focused on the distinction between public sector outcomes, outputs and productivity as well as the three big E's of performance: effectiveness, efficiency and economy (Carter, Klein and Day, 1992; Halachmi and Bouckaert, 1995). All indicators have gained macro and micro level recognition, yet such trends have been magnified lately with the upsurge of the new public management (NPM) approach. Despite some serious criticism (for example, Golembiewski, Vigoda and Sun, 2000; Hood, 1991) the NPM perspective has become highly influential and dominant in the current apparatus of public administration. A considerable effort was dedicated to recognizing and defining new criteria that may help in determining the extent to which public agencies succeed in keeping pace with the growing needs of the public. As a result, NPM has amplified interest in specific Performance Indicators (PIs) used in private organizations (Pollitt, 1988). It has recommended that they be applied in the public sector as well (for example, Carter, 1989; Smith, 1993). Studies further argued that PIs could function as milestones on the way to better efficiency, effectiveness and performance of bureaucracies. However, it has also become clear that a transference of purely private managerial strategies into the public sector is not simple. Contrary to the private sector, public service performance must take into consideration extra criteria such as social welfare, equity and equality, fair distribution of opportunities, and impartial redistribution of 'public goods' to all citizens. Rhodes (1987) and Palfrey et al. (1992) suggested these criteria among the values that are additional to efficiency, effectiveness and economy that characterize market-driven arenas. In practice, one way of testing performance of governmental actions is going back to the citizens–clients for their personal evaluations of all the aspects mentioned so far. This approach examines how citizens feel when consuming public goods in terms of absolute service, its quality, availability, fairness in distribution, and full orientation to individuals' needs. A well accepted method (for example, Vigoda, 2000) is to apply satisfaction measures to manifold outcomes of public agencies such as productivity, quality of service, quality of operation, equity and equality in distributing goods or services, and general responsiveness to public necessities.

Beyond the significant, yet relatively simple and limited evaluation of public administration outcomes by citizens' satisfaction, it is also useful to examine additional aspects of public administration actions. Based on a previous framework by Vigoda (2000) we propose several dimensions of public agencies' operation that need to be considered to define better the quality and intensity of delivery of goods and services to citizens as clients. These facets constitute (1) a personal dimension of *human quality*, (2) an entrepreneurial dimension of *innovation and creativity*, and (3) a normative aspect of *morality and ethics*.

Quality of public personnel is perhaps the most influential and momentous resource of public serving agencies. For example, Parsons (1995:554) suggests that contemporary literature in public policy 'is for the most part concerned with the evaluation of programmes and policies. However, in a managerial framework it also encompasses the evaluation of people *qua Human Resources*'. No doubt that it is important to gain more knowledge on the evaluation of people as opposed to programs and policy. By so doing we improve methods and strategies through which people are better managed. We encourage them to become more committed, competent, cost-effective, and in sympathy with the aims of the organization, that is to discharge better services to the citizens (Thompson, 1990:307).

Another key aspect of public administration operation in modern times is innovation and creativity of individuals, as well as bureaucracies. Since the late 1960s and early 1970s public administration has been urged to become more effective, efficient and business oriented. To achieve these goals scholars promoted ideas of better flexibility, entrepreneurship, and willingness to adopt creative new opinions. Many historical examples exist today in management legacy for such endeavors. For example, Management by Objectives (MBO), Total Quality Management (TQM), and International Organization for Standardization (ISO) have postulated novel ideas, which over the years have become more applicable in public agencies. Other examples are the philosophy of privatization which was implemented under the Thatcher administration in Britain, innovatory concepts of rebuilding public sector budgets (for example, Zero Based Budgeting), reinventing government initiatives, outsourcing processes, and re-engineering reforms of public administration which were suggested in America (for example,

Bozeman, 1993; Farnham and Horton, 1993; Osborne and Gaebler, 1992). Most importantly, the technological and social environment entered an era of continuous change, which necessitated (1) establishing new standards of operation in the public services of western societies and (2) transformation of orientations and perceptions of public servants. It was argued that these alterations may be the right way to relax the tightening strain between democracy and market forces. Theory was thus urged to pursue better macro- and micro-level techniques that make for enduring improvement and adaptability to a rapidly transforming environment. Scholars agreed that a well performing public sector must rely heavily on creativity and innovation to overcome many of its serious problems and maladies.

In the last decades interest has also risen in issues of administrative morality, ethics and fairness (DeLeon, 1996; Lui and Cooper, 1997; Gortner, 1991; Manzel, 1999). Generally, citizens are sensitive to and critical of sharing resources in society despite having almost no opportunity to use their collective opinion in order to influence decision makers. While the media, the auditing system, the state comptroller, ombudsman, and even the judicial authorities in western societies are those which should play an important part in criticizing public policy and administrative culture, citizens themselves are rarely questioned about their feelings and attitudes on such topics (Vigoda, 2000). Still, citizens seem to have their personal attitudes and impressions of fairness in public bureaucracies (for example, do they work to high standards of morality and ethics? Do they treat all citizens fairly?). It is also expected that citizens as clients increasingly develop independent perspectives on issues such as what kind of moral culture public administration encourages, and how this culture corresponds with general morality in the wider society. We argue in this study that the morality and ethics of public administration agencies and of public personnel may have a momentous effect on perceptions of performance, and in the long run these views may also influence orientations toward democracy, citizenship involvement and active participation. This argument draws substance mainly from the cognitive approach and the expectancy theory. People interpret reality in many ways; one of them is having an exchange relationship with others (Blau, 1964). When an exchange system is unfair or yields no benefits for one side (usually the less powerful) it is only a matter of time until reaction appears. A most serious reaction by citizens to low-performing governments and public agencies may be loss of faith in the democratic process and turning passive or apathetic (Krampen, 1991). When policy agrees with public demands, citizens are more willing to accept administrative actions as responding to their needs and to show more support in the entire democratic process (Vigoda, 2000). Accordingly, we decided to include morality and ethics as additional predictors of public sector performance as well as orientations toward democracy.

Citizenship Involvement: Attitudes Toward Participation and Active Participation

So far we have discussed citizenship involvement as one construct comprising both attitudes and active participation. Practically, positive attitudes of citizens to the democratic process as well as active political participation are essential for building strong liberal states and progressive cultures that last. However, in their extensive work on *Voice and Equality: Civic Voluntarism in American Politics* Verba, Schlozman and Brady (1995) argue that 'citizen participation is at the heart of democracy' and that 'democracy is unthinkable without the ability of citizens to participate freely in the governing process' (p.1). Recently, King and Stivers (1998) and Kramer (1999) further argued that only by becoming active participants in civic life, rather than remaining passive spectators on the sidelines, can citizens regain trust in democratic ideas of involvement, collective responsibility, self-empowerment, and a reconstruction of individuals' creativity and innovation. In light of this, our study distinguished the two types of citizenship involvement: (1) attitudes to participation or *faith in citizenship involvement*, and (2) participation per se or *active citizenship involvement*. As suggested by Verba, Schlozman and Brady (1995) these are separate aspects of the same phenomenon and in our design each of them was built upon two other factors. Citizens' attitudes to participation comprised faith in citizen involvement and perceptions of political efficacy. Active citizenship involvement consisted of a measure of active political participation and a measure of community involvement.

Faith in citizen involvement is an important construct of attitudes toward democracy. It is defined as the extent to which people believe that the average citizen can effect changes in the political system and that by being involved they can influence the political system (Schussler, 1982). By this definition, this variable is a good representation of loyalty and trust in the political system. It also reflects an orientation toward politics and an important aspect of citizenship because it helps to shape individuals' understanding of the political world and their place in it (Peterson, 1990). Theiss-Morse (1993) argued that most people are apparently involved in the political sphere in ways consistent with their citizenship perspective. Her study showed that greater predictive power is gained by measuring people's perspectives on good citizenship, thereby providing better specified models to explain behavior. Hence, people who believe that they can have some say in the political system and are capable of influencing it are also expected to show more active participation under appropriate circumstances. The second facet of faith in citizenship involvement is political efficacy. It reflects an individual's perception of her/his ability to influence political officials and the political system using personal resources and effort (Barner and Rosenwein, 1985; Verba, Schlozman and Brady, 1995). Milbrath and Goel (1977) argued that political efficacy is part of the sense of mastery a child acquires during socialization. Moreover, it is possible that political efficacy is later transformed with further events and experiences one witnesses during adolescence (Verba, Schlozman and Brady, 1995). Like faith in citizen involvement, political efficacy is also expected to lead to political participation. A person with high political efficacy will be highly motivated to participate in the political system, be it in the national or communal arenas.

In line with this, active citizenship involvement is represented here by political participation and community involvement. Participation in political activities is classic and one of the most researched constructs in political science (for example, Almond and Verba, 1963; Barber, 1984; Brady, Verba and Schlozman, 1995; Peterson, 1990; Verba, Schlozman and Brady, 1995). It deals with people's engagement in such political activities as voting, sending support/protest messages to politicians, political demonstrations, or signing petitions on political issues. The second dimension tested was participation in community activities. Barber (1984) argued that 'political participation in common action is more easily achieved at the neighborhood level, where there is a variety of opportunities for engagement' (p 303). Recent political science and sociological literature has strongly developed the concept of communitarianism as a separate and important dimension of political participation (Etzioni, 1995; 1994). Community activity is considered more informal participation than national activities (Sobel, 1993). Certain individual characteristics serve to promote both national and local participation, but other personal and local community characteristics primarily stimulate participation in local politics (Pettersen and Rose, 1996). Some people may avoid political activities because they dislike or are indifferent to politics. They may prefer a closer knit, perhaps more personal domain such as the community, which offers membership of a tenants' committee or of a school parents' committee (Cohen and Vigoda, 2000). All in all, both political participation and community involvement evince some of the most elementary constructs of active citizenship involvement.

THE RELATIONSHIP BETWEEN PUBLIC SECTOR PERFORMANCE AND CITIZENSHIP INVOLVEMENT: ALTERNATIVE MODELS

Five alternative models were posited for the relationship between performance in the public sector and perceptual and actual democratic values of citizenship involvement. Each model was subsequently evaluated against all the others for conclusions as to its fit, quality, predictability power, and adherence with the theory. This way it was possible to obtain some insight into the presumable role of public administration as another agent of democracy, in addition to family, work, media, religious institution, or the educational system (Peterson, 1990). Furthermore, it could provide better understanding of *how* bureaucracies and administrative bodies take part, overtly or covertly, in forming democratic culture and values of participation. While recent studies have discussed some theoretical aspects of this relationship (for example, Schneider and Ingram, 1995; 1997; Soss, 1999) empirical evidence in the field is scarce. The five models as presented here elaborate on several substantially distinguished approaches to these questions.

Model 1: A Simple Direct Effect

This model suggests a direct relationship between several constructs of public administration operation and active citizenship involvement. In line with current knowledge (Milbrath and Goel, 1977; Verba, Schlozman and Brady, 1995) a direct effect is suggested between faith in citizenship involvement and active citizenship involvement. This relationship is also included in most of the other models on the assumption that attitudes toward politics and active participation in politics should be treated as separate but related constructs of citizenship involvement (Verba, Schlozman and Brady, 1995). The simple direct model thus implies that public administration performance, as reported by citizens' satisfaction, has no effect on patterns of active citizenship involvement. By this rationale, citizens' satisfaction has only a minor relationship with active engagement in citizenship behavior, if any. Quality of public personnel, innovation and creativity, and morality and ethics are proposed as having a direct effect on active participation. Note also that this model portrays the null hypothesis of our study. Support for this model will be in the direction of rejecting the 'new' knowledge (or suggested idea) on the role of public sector performance and citizens' satisfaction as another agent of citizenship involvement.

Model 2: A Simple Indirect Effect

This model offers a first alternative to the basic simple direct model, where public administration performance is a mediator between agencies' operation and the two democratic values (faith in citizenship involvement and active citizenship involvement) as examined here. The model further suggests no relationship between faith in citizenship involvement and active participation, and treats both constructs as separate dependent variables. By this model we try to challenge the plausible possibility that attitudes to citizenship involvement and active participation are totally distinguished constructs, each having an autonomous relationship with public sector performance. Here, for comparative reasons, we take to its extreme the notion of Verba, Schlozman and Brady (1995) that political participation and attitudes toward participation should be treated separately and that one should be 'concerned with doing politics, rather than with being attentive to politics' (p.39). According to this model, public administration operation determines performance in the eyes of citizens-as-clients, which in return affects the two types of citizenship involvement.

Model 3: A Complex Indirect Effect

Contrary to the previous model, the complex indirect model redraws a path between faith in citizenship involvement and active citizenship involvement. It relies on the common assumption that political attitudes, beliefs and confidence lead to political behavior and that one's active participation must be predominated by faith in the value and advantages of involvement. In their extensive study Verba, Schlozman and Brady (1995) advised considering active involvement and attitudes to involvement as separate constructs, but they also agreed that a relationship exists between the two. In fact, this is the more common approach to the nature of political participation and involvement, supported in other studies. For example, Orum (1989) mentioned several studies that found psychological political involvement positively related to active participation. Feldman and Kawakami (1991) found that those who were more exposed and interested in political information in the media were more politically active. Other studies by Milbrath and Goel (1977) and Milbrath (1981) also supported this notion. Similar to model 2 however, this model implies that all other paths remain unchanged, arguing for a mediating effect of public administration performance in the attitude–action relationship.

Model 4: Faith in Citizenship Involvement Mediates Between Performance and Active Involvement

This model goes a step farther and elaborates on a specific mediating role of faith in citizenship involvement in the relationship between (1) public administration operation and performance and (2) active political and communal involvement. For the first time, this model offers that faith in citizenship involvement buffers public administration performance and actual participatory behaviors. This idea is in line with the conception of Brady, Verba and Schlozman (1995) on the mediating role of attitudes to politics (for example, political interest and citizenship) in creating a productive voice and political acts.

However, in addition we specify a more imperative role of attitudes and faith in citizenship involvement. In this model, performance of the public sector is described as another antecedent of citizens' faith that in itself may affect political activity. Support for this model may imply that public administration performance can affect active political and communal participation but only through the formation of attitudes and perceptions, and perhaps through the re-creation of civic skills and personal resources that are essential for an active role in politics (Brady, Verba and Schlozman, 1995). According to this model public administration performance has no direct effect on political activity of individuals.

Model 5: A Simultaneous Effect of Faith and Performance on Active Involvement

As in the previous three alternatives (models 2, 3 and 4) this model also suggests performance as a mediator between public administration operation and the formation of democratic values. However, instead of faith playing a separate dependent role (model 2) or a mediating function (models 3 and 4) this model proposes that: (1) faith in citizenship involvement and public administration performance have a separate/parallel direct effect on active citizenship involvement, (2) faith in citizenship involvement and public administration performance are both affected by the independent variables, and (3) public administration performance has no effect on faith in citizenship involvement. Hence, this model offers a simultaneous effect of both faith in citizenship involvement and public administration performance on active political and communal participation. The advantage of this model is that it points to active participation as determined by both faith in citizenship involvement and public administration performance. In fact, both variables are described as mediators between public administration operation and active involvement in politics. Thus the model allows a fair comparison between the consequences of these two variables in terms of citizens' behavior or political activity.

METHODS

Sample, Tools and Procedure

A survey was conducted among 330 residents from six major neighborhoods of a large Israeli city. Data were collected during 1998 using a random sample method. A relatively high return rate was achieved (86.2%) yet only 260 usable questionnaires (final return rate of 78.78%) were appropriate for our needs in this study and used in the final analysis. Interviewers asked participants to provide information about their attitudes to local municipalities' activities and services. Questions probed various opinions and perceptions of citizens as to quality of public personnel (managers and employees), ethical image and morality of public servants, and innovation and creativity in the public service process. An extended separate section of the questionnaires was dedicated to the measurement of public administration performance by citizens' satisfaction. Participation was voluntary and citizens were assured of full confidentiality of all information provided. A breakdown by neighborhood showed that 25.0% lived in low-class areas, 33.0% in average areas, and 42.0% in high-class areas; 54% of the sample were female, 45% married, and 66% had an income which was equal to or less than the average salary in Israel. Average age was 35.5 years (s.d.= 14.0); average time of residence in the city was 24 years (s.d.=16). An academic degree was held by 58% of the respondents; 9% more had partly academic or higher education. Note that the demographic characteristics of the sample were quite similar to those of the total population in the city as reported by the city's research and statistics department: Average age 35.6; 52% female; 46% married; 63.1% with 13+ school years or some academic degree.

Data Analysis

Confirmatory Factor Analysis (CFA)
Prior to the specific evaluation of the five models we performed confirmatory factor analysis (CFA) to assure that all the variables included in the models are best represented by the latent constructs as we framed them. This procedure is recommended in the literature to confirm that the tested models include highly coherent constructs that are clearly defined and measured

(Joreskog and Sorbom, 1994). We compared a large number of models (1- to 12-factor models) that consisted of all latent variables as well as on the sub-scales of employee quality (EQ), leadership quality (LQ), faith in citizen involvement, political efficacy, political participation, and community involvement. For simplicity these results are not included here but they imply that a 6-factor model, which we finally applied, was the most appropriate one in terms of fit and coherence with the data.

Path analysis and evaluation of the models

Path analysis with LISREL VIII was used to examine the five models and compare among them. We used a covariance matrix as input for the path analysis and examined the variations of relationships in the 6-factor model as arising from the CFA. Note that while the usual approach is to estimate structural relationships among variables that are free of measurement errors we employed another technique that was more appropriate for our case. Bollen (1989) showed that the ratio of the number of observed variables to the sample size should be at least 1:5 in order to allow the common estimation approach. When this ratio is close to or lower than 5 (53:260 or 1:4.9 in our case) or when the ratio between latent and observed variables is higher than 1:5 (6:53 or 1:8.6 in our case), it is not recommended to implement the common approach of examination. A better alternative is to treat the multi-item scales as single indicators of each construct. Accordingly, we also corrected for measurement errors in the models by the following procedure. The random error variance associated with each construct was equated to the value of its variance multiplied by the quantity one minus its estimated reliability (Bollen, 1989). Other studies have successfully implemented this approach in the field of public administration (Cohen and Vigoda, 2000). Results of this procedure, however, diverged substantially from the uncorrected single-indicator analysis.

Fit indices

Ten indices were used to assess the fit of the models. The first was the chi-square test, which is the most basic and essential for the nested model comparison. A low and non-significant value of chi-square represents good fit to the data. The chi-square test is sensitive to sample size, so the ratio of the model chi-square to degrees of freedom was used as another fit index. In this study a ratio up to 2 was considered a satisfactory value. Moreover, the use of chi-square is based on the assumption that the model holds exactly in the population. As noted elsewhere this may be an unreasonable assumption in most empirical research since it means that models which hold approximately in the population will be rejected in large samples (Joreskog and Sorbom, 1994). Therefore we used the Root Mean Square Error of

Approximation (RMSEA) as suggested by Browne and Cudeck (1989) and Steiger (1990). A value of 0.05 indicates a close fit, and values up to 0.08 represent reasonable errors of approximation in the population.

In addition, some other fit indices are also reported as less sensitive to sample size differences and to the number of indicators per latent variable increase (Medsker, Williams and Holahan, 1994). Six of these indices were used in our study: the Relative Fit Index (RFI), the Comparative Fit Index (CFI), the Normed Fit Index (NFI), the Non-Normed Fit Index (NNFI), the Goodness of Fit Index (GFI), and the Adjusted Goodness of Fit Index (AGFI). The RFI and the CFI were developed to facilitate the choice of the best fit among competing models that may differ in degree of parameterization and specification of relations among latent variables (Bentler, 1990; Bollen, 1989). They are recommended as being the best approximation of the population value for a single model. The closer their value to 1 the better the fit. NFI was proposed in earlier studies and is additive for the nested-model comparison (Bentler and Bonett, 1980). Its value should be close to 1 to indicate a good fit. However, it has the disadvantage of being affected by sample size, and on some occasions it may not reach 1.0 even when the model is correct (especially in small samples). This difficulty was resolved with the modified index called NNFI, which has the major advantage of reflecting model fit very well at all sample sizes. As with NFI, a value closer to 1 reflects better fit. The last two indices (GFI and AGFI) do not depend on sample size explicitly and measure how much *better* the model fits than no model at all. Both these measures should be between zero and 1, and a value higher than 0.90 is considered very good. Another recommended index for the selection of one of several a priori specified models is the Expected (single sample) Cross-Validation Index (ECVI) (Browne and Cudeck, 1989). This index is a measure of the discrepancy between the fitted covariance matrix in the analysed sample and the expected covariance matrix that would be obtained in another sample of the same size (Joreskog and Sorbom, 1994); thus, its value should be close to zero to indicate a good fit.

Path coefficients
An attempt to compare several alternative models by structural equation modeling (SEM) must first rely on information provided by a variety of fit indices, as described above. However, to determine the superiority or domination of one model one must also consider path coefficients that indicate the quality of the chosen alternative as a 'correct causal model'. Joreskog and Sorbom (1994) defined this as the 'plausibility criterion'. This criterion means that the path coefficients in the plausible better-fit model adhere well to the general theoretical conception and to the hypotheses. This

Model 1:　A simple direct effect

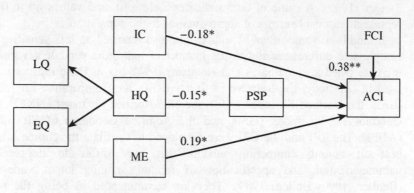

Model 2:　A simple indirect effect

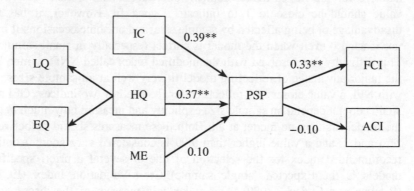

Model 3:　A dual pattern effect

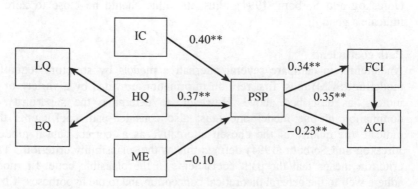

Model 4:   FCI mediates between PSP and ACI

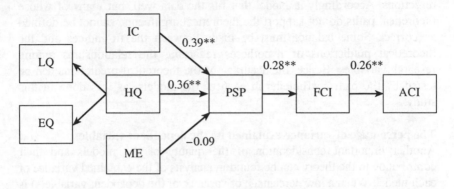

Model 5:   A simultaneous effect of FCI and PSP on ACI

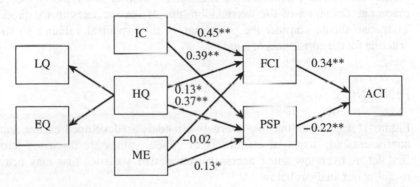

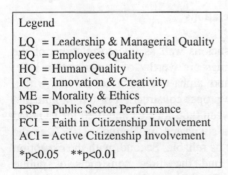

Legend

LQ   = Leadership & Managerial Quality
EQ   = Employees Quality
HQ   = Human Quality
IC   = Innovation & Creativity
ME   = Morality & Ethics
PSP = Public Sector Performance
FCI = Faith in Citizenship Involvement
ACI = Active Citizenship Involvement

*p<0.05   **p<0.01

Figure 11.1   Five alternative models of the relationship between PA performance and citizenship involvement

adherence should hold in terms of magnitude as well as in the expected directions. Accordingly, a model that fits the data well, but many of whose theoretical paths do not support the theoretical arguments, cannot be defined as correct. Some balance must be made between the fit indices and the theoretical predictions or hypotheses regarding the relationships among research variables. Hence, the accuracy of the theoretical predictions can be tested by the path coefficients in each of the models, as was done in this study.

The percentage of variance explained by the dependent variables
Another important consideration of the quality of the models and their contribution to the theory can be found in analysis of the explained variance of each model. When a low percentage of variance of the dependent variable(s) is explained by a given model, this indicates that the model is not a correct one (Saris and Stronkhorst, 1984). Low explained variance can be a result of measurement errors, omission of important variables from the model, or inaccurate definition of the interrelationships of the variables in the model. Thus, one should consider the percentage of the explained variance another criterion for the correctness of a model.

FINDINGS

Figure 11.1 presents the five alternative models as developed earlier. Path coefficients are displayed on this figure. These values are discussed later; first let us overview some necessary descriptive statistics that may prove useful in our analysis below.

Descriptive Statistics and Intercorrelations

Table 11.1 presents descriptive statistics as well as intercorrelations of the study variables. Two important findings are worthy of consideration here. First, means, standard deviations, and alpha-Cronbach levels are within reasonable limits, which attests to the proper construction of our sample and measures. Alpha Cronbach range between 0.66 for FCI and 0.86 for HQ, and are all above the 0.60 level that was suggested by Nunnaly (1967) as the minimum required for treating a scale as reliable. Second, with the exception of the relationships between ACI and the three constructs of public administration operation (HQ, IC, ME) all correlations among research variables are significant, positive, and in the predicted directions. PSP is strongly related to HQ and IC (r=0.60; p<0.001) and to ME (r=0.40; p<0.001). FCI is constantly and positively related to all the other variables in

Table 11. 1 Descriptive statistics and intercorrelations for the study variables (reliabilities in parentheses)

Variable	Mean	S.D.	1	2	3	4	5	6
1. Human Quality (HQ)	2.61	0.73	(0.86)					
2. Innovation and Creativity (IC)	2.71	0.71	0.60***	(0.80)				
3. Morality and Ethics (ME)	2.79	0.77	0.57***	0.47***	(0.75)			
4. Public Sector Performance (PSP)	2.72	0.57	0.60***	0.60***	0.40***	(0.85)		
5. Faith in Citizenship Involvement (FCI)	2.87	0.59	0.17**	0.30***	0.12*	0.22***	(0.66)	
6. Active Citizenship Involvement (ACI)	1.78	0.35	-0.10	-0.04	0.02	-0.15**	0.33***	(0.77)

Notes
N = 260
*P ≤0.05   **P ≤0.01   ***P ≤0.001

279

the models, most importantly to PSP (r=0.22; p<0.001). FCI is positively correlated with ACI (r=0.33; p<0.001) as also evinced in previous studies (Brady, Verba and Schlozman, 1995; Milbrath and Goel, 1977; Verba, Schlozman and Brady, 1995). The only exception here is the negative relationship between ACI and PSP (r=-0.15; p<0.01). This relationship somewhat challenges our hypothesis and indicates that better performance by public sector agencies may cause a decline in active citizenship involvement. In sum, the correlations among the independent variables are quite high but none of them exceeds 0.70, which indicates the absence of multicollinearity in this study.

Evaluation of Models

Evaluation of the research models relies on several parameters: (1) the path coefficients, which were presented earlier in Table 11.1, (2) a goodness-of-fit summary for each model as shown in Table 11.2 and, (3) the explained variance parameters displayed in Table 11.3. Together they provide some essential tools for a proper evaluation of the correctness and theoretical adaptability of the five models.

Although the path coefficients of models 2 and 4, as shown in Figure 11.1, were in the predicted directions these models had a very low fit with the data and had to be rejected. Table 11.2 provides detailed information on the models' fit. The chi-square test produced significant values, indicating that the models did not cohere with the data; chi-square to df ratio (X^2/df) was close to 5 and 8, which exceeds the recommended 2 value. RFI, NFI, NNFI, as well as GFI and AGFI were lower than in all the other models. In addition, RMSEA was much higher than the 0.08 value which is recommended for reasonable models, and ECVI was far higher than the recommended 0 level. Furthermore, the explained variance of the dependent variables in models 2 and 4 as presented in Table 11.3 was lower than in most of the other models. The explained variance of FCI was only 0.10 in model 2 and 0.07 in model 4, compared with a value of 0.18 in model 5. The explained variance of ACI was 0.02 in model 2 and 0.18 in model 4, compared with 0.33 in models 3 and 5 and 0.37 in model 1. Consequently, model 2 (the simple indirect effect model) and model 4 (FCI mediates between PSP and ACI) were rejected.

While model 1 (the simple direct effect model) showed better fit indices than the remaining models (model 3 – the dual pattern effect, and model 5 – the simultaneous effect of FCI and PSP on ACI) we had to conclude that it must also be rejected for several reasons. First, some of the central fit indices such as X^2/df, RFI, NNFI, AGFI and RMSEA were inferior in this model to those in models 3 and 5. Second, the df value was almost minimal (df=1), which indicates that this model is close to a saturated ineffective model. Nor did model 1 include most of the necessary theoretical relationships between PSP and citizenship involvement, as presented earlier. All these arguments resulted in the rejection of model 1, which also represented the null hypothesis of no relationship between public sector performance and citizenship involvement in this study.

A comparison between the remaining models (3 and 5) produced more complex findings. Although model 5 appears highly superior in terms of fit indices (non-significant chi-square value and better fit in all other indices as well) this model was also less parsimonious than model 3. It had only 4 degrees of freedom, compared with 6 degrees of freedom in model 3, which made the latter more efficient and competent. However, the parsimony criterion is not sufficient for concluding that a model is the correct one; other figures should also be considered. For example, the ratio between number of significant path coefficients to the total number of paths in model 3 was 5/6. The same ratio in model 5 was 7/8, which makes this one better in terms of correct path coefficients. In addition, while both models had only one non-significant path (ME to PSP in model 3 and ME to FCI in model 5) the accumulative explained variance of the dependent variables in model 5, as presented in Table 11.3, was higher than in model 3. This was mainly due to increase in the explained variance in FCI from 0.10 (model 3) to 0.18 (model 5), while the explained variance of PSP and ACI remained stable (0.65 and 0.33 respectively).

Hence, despite some weaknesses of model 5, especially its parsimony problem, we concluded that this was the best model among all those examined here. This model, which represents a simultaneous effect of FCI and PSP on ACI, proved to have a very good fit with the data, a good magnitude of path coefficients in most of the expected directions, and sound theoretical adaptability to our conceptual framework. However none of this means that model 5 is the only possible correct model or the best conceivable one. A major obstacle to our concluding that model 5 is the only correct one was the unexpected negative relationship found between PSP and ACI. As shown in model 5, this relationship was moderate, at a value of -0.22. This should be noted especially in light of the expected positive relationship found between PSP and FCI, ranging from 0.28 in model 4 to 0.34 in models 3 and 5.

Beyond these findings one should also note several other relationships in model 5. According to Figure 11.1, innovation and creativity (IC) as well as human quality (HQ) in the public sector were positively related with FCI (0.45 and 0.13 respectively) and with PSP (0.39 and 0.37 respectively). Morality and ethics (ME) was positively related with PSP (0.13) but had no relationship with FCI. Thus, it may be concluded that faith in citizenship involvement was more strongly affected by creativity and innovative

Table 11.2 Goodness-of-fit summary for the research models

Model/Description	df	X²	P	X²/df	RFI	NFI	NNFI	CFI	GFI	AGFI	ECVI	RMSEA
1. A simple direct effect	1	3.27	0.071	3.27	0.90	0.99	0.92	0.99	1.00	0.91	0.17	0.094
2. A simple indirect effect	7	55.60*	0.000	7.94	0.75	0.88	0.77	0.89	0.94	0.81	0.32	0.160
3. A dual pattern effect	6	13.62*	0.034	2.27	0.93	0.97	0.96	0.98	0.98	0.94	0.17	0.070
4. FCI mediates between PSP and ACI	7	34.52*	0.000	4.93	0.84	0.93	0.87	0.94	0.96	0.88	0.24	0.120
5. A simultaneous effect of FCI and PSP on ACI	4	3.76	0.440	0.94	0.97	0.99	1.00	1.00	1.00	0.97	0.15	0.000

Notes
N = 260
*P ≤0.05

Table 11.3 *Explained variance (R²) for the dependent variables in the research models*

Model/Description	Public Sector Performance (PSP)	Faith in Citizenship Involvement (FCI)	Active Citizenship Involvement (ACI)
1. A simple direct effect	–	–	0.37
2. A simple indirect effect	0.65	0.10	0.02
3. A dual pattern effect	0.65	0.10	0.33
4. FCI mediates between PSP and ACI	0.65	0.07	0.18
5. A simultaneous effect of FCI and PSP on ACI	0.65	0.18	0.33

orientations of public administration than by other variables such as human quality or morality and ethics. However, these facets were more strongly related with PSP, which serves as a mediator to active involvement. In other words, while both FCI and PSP are independent mediators among IC, HQ, ME and ACI, the nature of this mediating relationship differed across variants of public sector operation. In addition, the relationship of FCI and ACI was positive and stronger (0.34) than the relationship of PSP and ACI (-0.22). These findings may indicate that ACI is simultaneously affected by various antecedents where faith in citizenship involvement plays a central and strong role but not a unique one. Our model shows that performance of public sector agencies may contribute to the explanation of active involvement and improve its predictive power beyond explanations of resources, psychological engagement and recruitment networks (Brady, Verba and Schlozman, 1995).

DISCUSSION

In recent years a considerable number of studies have elaborated on the ample promise of higher citizenship involvement for the reconstruction of healthy public bureaucracies. Scholars have also pointed to the potential advantages that this collaboration carries for communities and individuals as well as for the goal of bringing the public closer to the administrative process (Box, 1998; 1999; Putnam, 1993; Rimmerman, 1997). However, we believe that a comprehensive analysis of this collaboration must also embody an opposite flow of influences, which is the effect of public sector performance on democratic values, particularly on passive and active citizenship involvement. The impact of public administration actions and performance on citizens' perceptions, attitudes and behaviors in terms of democratic beliefs and values should thus be considered more seriously. As recently argued by Nalbandian (1999), city managers and professionals are frequently seen as community builders and enablers of democracy. Their actions are continuously translated by ordinary citizens to reconstruct an image of the public service that is tightly related to democratic culture. Our goal in this study was to portray some of the possible relationships between administrative outcomes in local government and democratic premises of citizenship involvement. In general, findings from one Israeli city revealed that this relationship may exist, yet its nature is more complex and enigmatic than we might expect.

First and most importantly, the findings quite consistently rejected the null hypothesis on the absence of a relationship between performance of the public sector and citizenship involvement, as represented in model 1. The alternative model 5 (and to a lesser extent model 3) fitted the data quite well and provided the most rational inter-relationships among the study variables. Model 5 further supported our elementary argument on the effect of public sector operation and performance on different dimensions of citizens' involvement. The implications that can be drawn from this model are threefold: (1) public sector performance and faith in citizenship involvement are both separately affected by innovation and creativity (IC), by human quality (HQ), and to a considerably lesser extent by morality and ethics (ME) of the public service; (2) public sector performance is related to democratic values of citizenship involvement, yet this relationship is complex; (3) as we expected, faith in citizenship involvement is positively affected by public sector performance, while contrary to our initial expectation, active citizenship involvement was found to be negatively affected by public sector performance.

Public Sector Performance and Citizenship Involvement: Paradoxical Relationship

Our findings on the relationship between public administration performance and democratic values needs further elaboration. It can be defined as a consistent but paradoxical relationship. Public administration is expected to work effectively, efficiently and economically for the sake of the public interest. It is designed to bring the best and highest possible outcome to all citizens, thereby nurturing and safeguarding democracy. However, challenging this idea, Thompson (1983) argued that actually 'democracy does not suffer bureaucracy gladly. Many of the values we associate with democracy – quality, participation, and individuality – stand sharply opposed to hierarchy, specialization, and impersonality we ascribe to modern bureaucracy' (p.235).

Mae Kelly (1998) argued that public administration scholars are divided over whether the public bureaucracy or the democratic polity ought to be the starting point of public administration scholarship. A utopian perspective will suggest that the two must go together to create a highly efficient liberal culture that provides maximum welfare to all citizens. In some respects our findings may offer another look into the odd couple of bureaucracy and democracy. On the one hand we suggest that performance of the public sector contributes to a healthy development of attitudes and opinions that uphold democracy. Individuals better satisfied with city services and operation are also stronger believers in the democratic process and in their own abilities to play a constructive part in these dynamics. If needed, they express high motivation to be involved in politics and in citizenry actions. Furthermore, they have a sense of being able to make a significant contribution to the manifold expressions of community life. However, quite surprisingly the same people admit that feeling satisfied and well treated by official authorities causes them to be less engaged in *active* political participation and in active community involvement.

How can these paradoxical relationships be resolved? One explanation is that people feel they have a say over politics and administrative agencies, yet at the same time they do not have to use their voice when bureaucracy operates properly and efficiently (and vice versa). This argument relies heavily on the passivity explanation (Soss, 1999) that suggests that government assistance and services make recipients appreciative and even dependent, hence, politically passive. As suggested by Brady, Verba and Schlozman (1995), people do not take part in politics because they can't, because they don't want to, or because nobody asked. Our analysis seems to accord with the second of these causes: people don't want to take part in politics when there is no pressing need to do so. But we take issue with Brady and his co-authors' argument that "'they don't want to" focuses on the absence of psychological engagement with politics – a lack of interest in politics, minimal concern with public issues, a sense that activity makes no difference, and no consciousness of membership in a group with shared political interests'. As also proposed in numerous studies (Milbrath and Goel, 1977; Verba, Schlozman and Brady 1995) the sense of being able to influence is not equivalent to making a decision to become active, or actually engaging in action. Citizens may become engaged only when some of their essential needs are not satisfied by public authorities. Despite feelings of high citizenry influence, motivation to take an active part in state-level politics or in community activities diminishes when there is no obvious need for action. Accordingly, 'don't want to' rather means 'don't need to' which is also substantially different from 'can't' or 'not being asked' to be involved, as proposed by Brady, Verba and Schlozman (1995). In other words, high performance of the public sector may carry great merit in people's minds but not necessarily lead people to act. In the long run this may constitute a dangerous threat to democratic action and participation. A calm, stable and relatively satisfying public arena increases citizens' feeling of welfare and influence but silently and inexorably can eliminate their motivation to seek active involvement and control over bureaucracies.

The Effect of Public Sector Innovation and Creativity, Human Quality, and Morality and Ethics on Citizenship Involvement

Model 5 shows that different aspects of public sector operation were positively related to faith in citizenship involvement, a relationship that carries several implications. First, our study highlighted the possible effect of innovative public administration on the healthy development of citizens' faith in governance, and, through this construct, on the encouragement of active citizenship involvement. Second, this study suggested that innovation and creativity, as well as the human quality of public personnel, may have another indirect positive effect on active involvement, this time through the enhancement of PSP as represented here by citizens' satisfaction. Morality and ethics of public servants may also work in this direction, albeit at a lower magnitude. Thus, a major implication may be that public sector operation yields competing influences on active citizenship involvement. Some of these influences are positive and some negative, but they all work simultaneously through FCI and PSP.

Concluding Remarks

Consensus seems to exist that unless the ancient hidden 'social agreement' is mutually respected by both rulers and citizens no bureaucracy can fully justify its existence and citizens may have the right to ask for better alternatives to democratic regimes. Hence, fair transactions between rulers (who hold power and authority) and citizens (who agree to be ruled and governed) constitute the most important condition for governments to conduct, public administration to manage, and citizens to support democracy. Governments are committed to provide all citizens with the best services and quality outcomes, which not only maintain their safety in unstable environments but also improve their quality of life, safeguard their liberal rights, and allow them to organize their communities as they see fit. Citizens, on the other hand, are obliged to support this system as being genuinely sympathetic and supportive of their needs. According to our findings however, a paradoxical negative relationship exists between the performance of public administration and the active involvement of citizens. This problem deserves much more elaboration and discussion in future scientific works as well as public debates.

Nonetheless, for positive relationships to grow and flourish there is a need to develop quality public services and renew professional bureaucracies (Woller, 1998). High performances of the public sector affect citizens' satisfaction and willingness to play their part in the social agreement. It is also possible that performance may encourage citizenship involvement and participation in communal and national public lives in ways other than what we are used to today. This contribution to democracy by routine administrative actions is a covert purpose of public sector systems. In western democracies public administration bodies have momentous power. It stems from their major role in society, which is equally to serve large populations with heterogeneous needs and to sustain a high level of performance over large areas and lengthy periods. Such functions make for the sound development and healthy progress of democracy. Public organizations should be committed to serve the people to the best of their ability and at the same time encourage authentic citizenship involvement that implies less passivity among individuals. It is further suggested that in return, citizens are expected to respond by active involvement in the administrative process to share ideas, knowledge and experience with civil servants and with state leaders. Therefore, citizens and public administrators join in mutual responsibilities and roles aimed at the development of prosperous modern democracies. This study argued that a most important role of public administrators is to develop a sense of partnership between rulers and citizens. This partnership must rely on simultaneous improvement of institutional performance as well as citizenship involvement by different means. Furthermore, the local community level can be a most appropriate habitat for good democratic values to grow and prosper.

Beyond the advantages of our study it is not free of limitations, which should be considered and overcome in future research. First, this study was based mainly on self-report data, which are subject to measurement biases such as common method error. While this approach is not uncommon in public sector analysis it has weaknesses as well as advantages. Future research on the relationship between public administration performance and citizenship involvement would benefit from more objective measures such as examining public spending, cost–benefit indicators, or additional measures of innovation, creativity and quality of public personnel. Second, this study examined citizens' perceptions at one point in time; it should be replicated to reveal trends and developments in both public performance and citizenship involvement. Third, the data were collected in an Israeli setting, which is quite different from the North American or the European. The results might have been affected by cultural and structural factors unique to Israel. For example, the Israeli public sector is more conservative and centralized, and for many years faced problems typical of relatively new democracies. Hence, our conceptual framework should be replicated in other settings before firm conclusions can be made.

Despite its limitations, this study provided another look at the relationship of public sector performance with patterns of citizenship involvement. Up to now, most of the studies were interested in the opposite flow of influences, which is the contribution of citizenship involvement to the managerial process in bureaucracies. This study also expanded on the advantages of using an advanced statistical method (SEM) for better understanding of these relationships. However, more work is needed to better explore this arena. Hence, the contribution of the study lies in its attempt to suggest a more specific linkage between public administration performance and the cultivation of democratic values in modern societies.

NOTE

1. Based on Vigoda (2002), 'Administrative agents of democracy? A Structural Equation Modeling (SEM) of the relationship between public sector performance and citizenship involvement', *Journal of Public Administration Research and Theory*, **12** (2), 241–72. Copyright with permission from the Public Management Research Association.

REFERENCES

Almond, G.A. and Verba, S. (1963), *The Civic Culture: Political Attitudes and Democracy in Five Nations: An Analytic Study*, Boston: Little Brown.

Barber, B. (1984), *Strong Democracy: Participatory Politics for a New Age*, Berkeley: University of California Press.

Barner, C. and Rosenwein, F. E. (1985), *Psychological Perspectives on Politics*, Englewood, NJ: Prentice Hall.

Bentler, P.M. (1990), 'Comparative fit indexes in structural models', *Psychological Bulletin*, *107*, 238–46.

Bentler, P.M. and Bonett, D.G. (1980), 'Significance tests and goodness-of-fit in the analysis of covariance structures', *Psychological Bulletin*, *88*, 588–606.

Berman, F. V (1997), 'Dealing with cynical citizens', *Public Administration Review*, *57*, 105 12.

Blau, P.M. (1964), *Power and Exchange in Social Life*, New York: Wiley.

Bollen, K.A. (1989), *Structural Equation with Latent Variables*, New York: Wiley.

Box, R.C., (1998), *Citizen Governance: Leading American Communities into the 21st Century*, Thousand Oaks, CA: Sage.

Box, R.C. (1999), 'Running governments like a business: Implications for public administration theory and practice', *American Review of Public Administration*, *29*, 19–43.

Bozeman, B. (1993), *Public Management*, San Francisco: Jossey Bass.

Brady, H.E., Verba, S., and Schlozman, K.L. (1995), 'Beyond SES: A resource model of political participation, *American Political Science Review*, *89*, 271–94.

Browne, M.W. and Cudeck, R. (1989), 'Single sample cross-validation indices for covariance structures', *Multivariate Behavioral Research*, *24*, 445–55.

Carter, N. (1989), 'Performance indicators: 'Backseat driving' or 'hands off' control?' *Policy and Politics*, *17*, 131–8.

Carter, N., Klein, R., and Day, P. (1992), *How Organizations Measure Success: The Use of Performance Indicators in Government*, London: Routledge.

Cohen, A. and Vigoda, E. (2000), 'Do good citizens make good organizational citizens? An empirical examination of the relationship between general citizenship and organizational citizenship behavior in Israel', *Administration and Society*, *32*, 5, 596–624.

DeLeon, L. (1996), 'Ethics and entrepreneurship', *Policy Studies Journal, 24*, 495–510.

Etzioni, A. (1994), *The Spirit of Community,* New York: Touchstone.

Etzioni, A. (1995), *New Communitarian Thinking: Persons, Virtues, Institutions, and Communities,* Charlottesville: Virginia University Press.

Farnham, D. and Horton, S. (eds) (1993), *Managing the New Public Services,* Basingstoke: Macmillan.

Feldman, O. and Kawakami, K. (1991), 'Media use as predictors of political behavior: The case of Japan', *Political Psychology, 12,* 65–80.

Frederickson, H.G. (1982), 'The recovery of civism in public administration', *Public Administration Review, 42,* 501–9.

Fredrickson, H.G. (1997), *The Spirit of Public Administration,* San Francisco: Jossey-Bass.

Golembiewski, R.T., Vigoda, E., and Sun, B.C. (2000), 'Cacophonies in the contemporary chorus about change at the public worksites, as contrasted with some straight-talk from a planned change perspective', *International Journal of Public Administration.* Forthcoming.

Gortner, H.F. (1991), *Ethics for Public Managers,* New York: Praeger.

Guyton, E.M. (1988), 'Critical thinking and political participation: Development and assessment of a causal model', *Theory and Research in Social Education, 16,* 23–49.

Halachmi, A. and Bouckaert, G. (eds) (1995), *Public Productivity through Quality and Strategic Management,* Amsterdam: IOS Press.

Hampton, J. (1986), *Hobbes and the Social Contract Tradition,* Cambridge: Cambridge University Press.

Hood, C. (1991), 'A public management for all seasons?', *Public Administration, 69,* 3–19.

Joreskog, K. and Sorbom, D. (1994), *Structural Equation Modeling with the SIMPLIS Command Language,* Chicago: Scientific Software International.

King, C.M. and Stivers, C. (1998), *Government Is Us: Public Administration in an Anti-Government Era,* Thousand Oaks, CA: Sage.

King, C.S., Feltey, K.M., and Susel, B.O. (1998), 'The question of participation: Toward authentic public participation in public administration', *Public Administration Review, 58,* 317–26.

Kramer, R. (1999), 'Weaving the public into public administration', *Public Administration Review , 59,* 89–92.

Krampen, G. (1991), 'Political participation in an action-theory model of personality: Theory and empirical evidence', *Political Psychology, 12,* 1–25.

Lui, T.T. and Cooper, T.L. (1997), 'Values in flux: Administrative ethics and the Hong Kong public servant', *Administration and Society, 29,* 301–24.

Lynn, L.E. (1996), *Public Management,* Chatham, New Jersey: Chatham House Publishers.

Lynn, L.E. (1998), 'The new public management: How to transform a theme into a legacy', *Public Administration Review, 58,* 231–7.

Mae Kelly, R. (1998), 'An inclusive democratic polity, representative bureaucracies, and the new public management', *Public Administration Review, 58,* 201–8.

Manzel, D.C. (1999), 'Rediscovering the lost world of public service ethics: Do we need new ethics for public administration?' *Public Administration Review, 59,* 443–7.

Medsker, G.J., Williams, L.J., and Holahan, P.J. (1994), 'A review of current practices for evaluating causal models in organizational behavior and human resources management research', *Journal of Management, 20*, 239–64.

Milbrath, L.W. (1981), 'Political participation', in S.L. Long (ed.), *The Handbook of Political Behavior,* (Vol. 4, pp. 197–237), New York: Plenum.

Milbrath, L.W. and Goel, M.L. (1977), *Political Participation* (2nd edn), Chicago: Rand McNally and Company.

Nalbandian, J. (1999), 'Facilitating community, enabling democracy: New roles for local government managers', *Public Administration Review, 59*, 187–97.

Nunnaly, J.C. (1967), *Psychometric Theory,* New York: McGraw Hill.

Orum, A.M. (1989), *Introduction to Political Sociology,* Englewood, NJ: Prentice Hall.

Osborne, D. and Gaebler, T. (1992), *Reinventing Government,* New York: Plume.

Palfrey, C., Phillips, C., Thomas, P., and Edward, D. (1992), *Policy Evaluation in the Public Sector,* Hants: Avenbury.

Parsons, D.W. (1995), *Public Policy,* Aldershot, UK and Brookfield, US: Edward Elgar.

Pateman, C. (1970), *Participation and Democratic Theory,* London: Cambridge University Press.

Peterson, S.A. (1990), *Political Behavior,* Newbury Park, CA: Sage.

Pettersen, P.A. and Rose, L.E. (1996), 'Participation in local politics in Norway: Some do, some don't, some will, some won't', *Political Behavior, 18*, 51–97.

Pollitt, C. (1988), 'Bringing consumers into performance measurement', *Policy and Politics, 16*, 77–87.

Putnam, R. (1993), *Making Democracy Work: Civic Traditions in Modern Italy,* Princeton, NJ: Princeton University Press.

Rainey, H. (1990), 'Public management: Recent development and current prospects', in N.B. Lynn and A. Wildavsky (eds), *Public Administration: The State of the Discipline* (pp. 157–84), Chatham, New Jersey: Chatham House.

Rhodes, R.A.W. (1987), 'Developing the public service orientation, or let's add a soupçon of political theory', *Local Government Studies, May-June,* 63–73.

Rimmerman, C.A. (1997), *The New Citizenship: Unconventional Politics, Activism, and Service,* Boulder, CO: Westview Press.

Sabucedo, J.M. and Cramer, D. (1991), 'Sociological and psychological predictors of voting in Great Britain', *Journal of Social Psychology, 131*, 647–54.

Saris, W. and Stronkhorst, H. (1984), *Causal Modeling in Non Experimental Research: An Introduction to the LISREL Approach,* Amsterdam: Sociometric Research Foundation.

Schneider, A. and Ingram, H. (1995), 'Response', *American Political Science Review, 89*, 441–6.

Schneider, A. and Ingram, H. (1997), *Policy Design for Democracy,* Lawrence: University of Kansas Press.

Schussler, K.F. (1982), *Measuring Social Life Feelings,* San Francisco: Jossey Bass.

Smith, P. (1993), 'Outcome-related performance indicators and organizational control in the public sector', *British Journal of Management, 4*, 135–51.

Sobel, R. (1993), 'From occupational involvement to political participation: An exploratory analysis', *Political Behavior, 15*, 339–53.

Soss, J. (1999), 'Lessons of welfare: Policy design, political learning, and political action', *American Political Science Review, 93*, 363–80.

Steiger, J.H. (1990), 'Structural models evaluation and modification: An interval estimation approach', *Multivariate Behavioral Research, 25*, 173–80.

Theiss-Morse, E. (1993), 'Conceptualizations of good citizenship and political participation', *Political Behavior, 15*, 355–80.

Thompson, D. (1983), 'Bureaucracy and democracy', in G. Duncan (ed.), *Democratic Theory and Practice* (pp. 230-50), Cambridge: Cambridge University Press.

Thompson, J.L. (1990), *Strategic Management: Awareness and Change,* London: Chapman and Hall.

Verba, S., Nie, N.H. and Kim, J. (1978), *Participation and Political Equality: A Seven-Nation Comparison,* Cambridge: Cambridge University Press.

Verba, S., Schlozman, K.L., and Brady, H. (1995), *Voice and Equality: Civic Voluntarism in American Politics,* London: Harvard University Press.

Vigoda, E. (2000), 'Are you being served? The responsiveness of public administration to citizens' demands: An empirical examination in Israel', *Public Administration, 78*, 165–91.

Woller, G.M. (1998), 'Toward a reconciliation of the bureaucratic and democratic ethos', *Administration and Society, 30*, 85–109.

Conclusions

The chapters presented in this book should be viewed as an initial step in the effort to increase our understanding of the relationship between citizenship involvement and bureaucracy. Very little research has been published on this issue, and many of the existing studies are obsolete. This book represents an attempt to renew interest in this important topic by presenting some current studies on it. Much more research is needed on this topic before solid conclusions can be drawn regarding this relationship.

The chapters presented here provide a promising starting point for the continuation of research regarding the interaction between citizenship involvement and bureaucracy. The contributions of the works presented here provide interesting ideas for future research in this area as well as a preliminary direction for developing a theory about the relationship between citizenship and bureaucracy. The main contributions, suggestions, and recommendations as well as some practical implications that resulted from these studies will be presented in the following sections.

Eran Vigoda-Gadot and Robert T. Golembiewski in their chapter 'Citizenship behavior and the new managerialism: A theoretical framework and challenge for governance', presented in the first part of this book, developed a multi-dimensional perspective of citizenship behavior that dovetails nicely with the principles underlying New Public Management (NPM). Their approach elaborated on (1) settings of citizenship (national, communal and organizational); (2) levels of analysis (individual and collective), and; (3) integration of these dimensions with NPM ideas to create a 'spirit of new managerialism'. This spirit asks that governments take strategic steps to promote citizenship values at all levels and that citizens actively participate in spontaneous initiatives and in the process of building their society. The authors argued that the public administrative structure and culture must become more flexible and responsive to citizens' needs. To achieve this goal it should become pro-active and entrepreneurial in the initiation of partnerships between public servants and citizens. The focus of NPM should adjust more vigorously to include the transformation of 'good will' into 'effective operations'. In contrast with 'old' managerialism, the new spirit of public management must call for multivariate citizenry action. Public administration, through its professional cadre, should initiate this process and improve through the lessons learned. Investment in spontaneous behavior is far less costly than other reform efforts, so it should receive a higher priority on the NPM agenda that calls for the improved performance of public agencies.

Vigoda-Gadot and Golembiewski concluded that for a truly democratic government, administrators and citizens must engage each other directly on a regular basis in honest, uninhibited public dialogue. This is an important conclusion with implications for all of the studies presented in this book. Democratic public administration involves active participation by citizens and active administration that uses discretionary authority to foster collaborative work with citizens. In sum, Vigoda-Gadot and Golembiewski argued that NPM is unique compared with other managerial practices in its insistence on the need to incorporate citizenship behavior. Thus, the challenge for governments and the new managerialism is a more comprehensive application of this valuable knowledge in public administration strategies. Accordingly, they suggested the need to broaden the concept of *citizenship* in the study of new managerialism.

In Chapter 2 Eran Vigoda-Gadot suggested that the notions of collaboration and partnership play a key role in defining and improving the relationship between public administration and its citizens. Vigoda-Gadot filled a conceptual gap between perceptions of responsiveness and the quest by citizens, state administrators, politicians and other social players such as the media and academia for a productive partnership with public services. He portrayed a possible normative interaction among these players in an evolving marketplace arena that will become even more turbulent in the future. The administrative–democratic turmoil will lead to growing and serious risks of citizens' alienation, disaffection, skepticism and increased cynicism toward governments. Only a high level of cooperation among all parties in society will safeguard against these negative forces. Vigoda-Gadot concluded that the new generation of public administrators will need a different spirit, perhaps a combination of communitarianism, institutionalism, and energism – but in any case, one that successfully fosters mutual effort. This movement from a 'they' spirit to a 'we' spirit is perhaps the most important mission of public administration in our era.

The second part of the book presents three studies, all of them by Aaron Cohen and Eran Vigoda-Gadot, which concentrate on the relationship between citizenship involvement in terms of political participation and work attitudes and behaviors. The first chapter in this section makes a valuable contribution to the testing of important organizational outcomes by using concepts not frequently studied in organizational behavior. Very little research exists on the effects of general citizenship on work outcomes examined from the perspective of political theory. Graham (1991) and Van Dyne, Graham and Dienesch (1994) proposed preliminary conceptual arguments for testing such relationships, suggesting that some forms of citizenship behaviors can be demonstrated in the organizational setting.

The first study in this part adopted their argument about the need to look at work outcomes from a political theory perspective. The findings show in general that good citizens can be good organizational citizens. Indeed, some forms of general citizenship such as political participation and general altruism have a direct effect on work outcomes. The results support the notion that participation in the civic setting furnishes the individual with positive attitudes and valuable skills that are transferred to the work setting. In sum, the findings of this research show the usefulness of applying concepts from one discipline, political science, to another, organizational behavior.

The second paper in this part also examined the effects of political behaviors and orientations on work outcomes. Preliminary conceptual arguments for testing such relationships were proposed by Graham (1991), who suggested that some forms of citizenship behaviors can be demonstrated in the organizational setting. The findings in this study showing that variables representing political behavior were useful in predicting important work outcomes are in line with those of Kirchmeyer (1992), who found that resources made available for work by participation in community activities positively affected organizational commitment, and time commitment to community activities positively affected job satisfaction. Kirchmeyer's findings, together with the results of this research, support the expansion or the spillover hypothesis, according to which individuals tend to cope with increasing organizational and extra-organizational role demands by responding positively to those demands (Randall, 1988). Adding new roles energizes people, and rather than having their vigor sapped by extensive social involvements, individuals may come away from new involvements more enriched and vitalized. The positive relationships between political behavior variables and work outcomes indicate that more political involvement increases perceived performance and organizational commitment and reduces turnover intentions. Once again the findings of this research demonstrate the usefulness of applying concepts from one discipline, political science, to another, organizational behavior.

However, the study also showed that the relationship between political behavior and work outcomes seems to be complex, as demonstrated by two important findings. The first concerns the interaction effects. This study demonstrated that while most of the relationships between civic behavior and work outcomes are direct, some of them are more complex, in particular the national civic outcomes. The fact that only the national civic behavior variables had a more complex effect on outcomes is interesting and deserves attention in future research. A possible explanation for this finding is that issues in the community have a more immediate effect on one's life, and therefore one will be more motivated to become involved in the local setting. These constructs exert a stronger main effect because more people are involved in civic activity on a local level. However, fewer people participate in, are involved with, or even care about issues on the national level. Therefore, the effect of national civic behavior will vary depending on factors that determine higher or lower levels of participation on the national level such as age, gender and education. This explanation should be tested in future research.

The third study moved beyond the two previous works. In addition to work attitudes it examined the relationship between citizenship involvement and actual performance on the job, a behavioral outcome. Actual performance is one of the most studied outcomes in management and administration literature. This study showed that the relationship between political behavior and performance is not a direct one, but a complex interaction. Performance was affected by the interaction of gender with faith in citizenship involvement and by a main effect of political participation. The moderator effect of gender was quite obvious in light of the strong theories and findings demonstrating that political behavior differs for males and females. However, the direction of this effect was unpredictable. While the expectation was that the relationship between political behavior and work outcomes would be stronger for males, it was found to be stronger for females, and the weak slope for males indicates that this relationship was consistent for males. This finding shows that the spillover effect operated more strongly for females. The skills, confidence and experiences females acquire in the political setting are more helpful for them in the work setting than they are for males. Future research should attempt to replicate this interesting finding and to develop and test theories that consider other possible moderators that might interact with political behavior in their effect on work outcomes.

In short, the findings of the three studies showed that a strong relationship exists between citizenship involvement and work outcomes, but the nature of that relationship seems to be quite complex. Both positive and negative spillovers appear to play roles here. For example while the positive relationship between civility, community involvement and faith in citizenship involvement with all work outcomes except performance represents positive spillover, the negative relationship of political participation with performance represents a negative one. This negative effect shows that citizenship involvement alone seems to have negative consequences for behaviors and attitudes at work. It would be interesting to explore possible explanations for this finding. What is so different about political involvement compared with community involvement and faith in citizenship involvement that it results in opposite effects on work attitudes and behaviors? Is it that people are involved in politics because they are looking for an entirely new role, one that will compensate them for what they perceive as negative experiences at work? In such a case, is involvement in politics so different from community involvement? How? Future research should deal with these questions conceptually and empirically.

The third part of this book covers one of the more current and up-to-date concepts regarding the interaction between citizenship and bureaucracy, namely Organizational Citizenship Behavior (OCB). Apart from Graham (1986, 1991) and Van Dyne, Graham and Dienesch (1994), no study has tried to explain OCB from a more general perspective of the global concept of *citizenship*. The chapters in this part conceptualize, define and measure OCB by applying political theory to the organizational setting. OCB is conceptually a good representation of work behavior that can be related to general citizenship. Participation in civic activities is basically a voluntary behavior. People may choose or not choose to participate in civic activities such as voting or community activities. OCB is also a voluntary behavior because it is not formally required by employees. Involvement in voluntary behavior in the civic sphere may be expected to encourage similar behavior in the work setting, namely OCB.

The first chapter in this part by Cohen and Vigoda-Gadot is an excellent demonstration of the above arguments. The findings of this study showed that good citizens can be good organizational citizens, but forms of general citizenship do not have a direct effect on OCB. The data demonstrated that work experiences strongly filter the effects of citizenship behaviors on OCB. The results support the idea that participation in the civic setting furnishes the individual with positive attitudes and valuable skills that can be transferred to the work setting. However, the individual's perception of his or her work setting as equitable and agreeable will determine whether these civic skills will be transferred to it. The findings supported the notion that the three contextual work attitudes mediate the effect of civic behavior on OCB. The organization thus plays an important role in determining whether external skills and attitudes acquired elsewhere will be applied in the work setting. The practical implication of this finding is that participation in non-work activities in general and in citizenship activities in particular can contribute to organizations by increasing their employees' OCB. Therefore, organizations should encourage such activities by their current employees and consider evidence of such activities on the résumés of prospective employees as an advantage during the selection process.

The second chapter in this part by Vigoda-Gadot examines a different aspect of the correlates of OCB. While Chapter 6 examined general citizenship as a determinant of OCB, this chapter concentrates on internal politics as a potential determinant of both in-role and extra-role (OCB) behavior. During the last two decades the concept of Organizational Politics (OP) has received increased attention in management literature. This attention relied partly on the expectation of finding new answers to some old questions, such as what motivates individuals at work and how we can better explain variations in employees' behavior and productivity. As a result, studies focused on the potential relationship between workplace politics and individuals' performances. The primary goal of these studies was to examine whether internal politics plays a significant role in setting organizational outcomes, and if so, what the nature and characteristics of this relationship are.

The common perception was that politics in the workplace was a necessary evil that no individual or society could avoid, but an evil nonetheless. Therefore, management literature consistently considered politics, power and influence relations among stakeholders as illegitimate, informal and dysfunctional. Such political machinations were seen as working against authority and the formal organizational design, both of which were described as apolitical and functional. OP was presumed to describe a deviant and seedy aspect of workplace activity. With growing interest in workplace politics, some studies have suggested utilizing a more empirical approach to the examination of its outcomes. However, only recently a few scholars have responded positively to this challenge, and most of them have focused on employees' attitudes as the prime outcome of OP. As a result, scant empirical evidence exists today that can support the (possibly negative) effect of internal workplace politics on employees' outcomes, and especially on objective performance evaluations. The main contribution of Vigoda-Gadot's study was to extend the theoretical thinking about OP, and more specifically to demonstrate the relationship between job congruence, perception of organizational politics, and two constructs of employees' reactions: in-role performances and organizational citizenship behavior (OCB).

The thesis developed by Vigoda-Gadot was that employees respond to the political climate of their work environment both formally and informally. Job congruence was expected to affect individuals' perception of politics, and both politics and congruence with the work sphere were presumed to have an influence on employee performance as represented by in-role duties and by citizenship behaviors. Vigoda-Gadot's findings supported the notion that the perception of organizational politics is a good mediator between constructs of job congruence and these work outcomes. These results affirm the complex relationship between politics and performance that was noted in other studies. The present findings reveal that politics contributes to our understanding of organizational dynamics and outcomes. The most profound finding of this study is that internal politics is pervasive and does make a difference in public administration systems. The results imply that politics may function as the silent enemy within organizations and can be even more destructive for public administration systems than for private organizations. Thus, internal politics works against modern approaches to the management of public agencies (for example, the quality movement of the 1980s and 1990s and the new public management approach (NPM)). In addition to discouraging the service orientation of public personnel, internal politics may have a negative effect on entrepreneurial activities and the generation of spontaneous and creative ideas (that is, citizenship behaviors) that are vital for the prosperity of modern society and a healthy public administration. Vigoda-Gadot concluded that practitioners and managers in the public sector must not ignore internal politics and should be aware of its hazardous consequences on both public personnel and citizens. Naturally, these implications deserve further examination in future studies, especially studies that compare the current results with findings from the private arena.

The third chapter in this part by Vigoda-Gadot and Cohen elaborates on the notion of work congruence by exploring its meaning and its relationship with employees' performance in the non-profit sector. Cohen and Vigoda-Gadot proposed work congruence as a certain measure of person-organization fit (POF) and met expectations (ME), and the study examined the effects of this construct on various aspects of performance. In general, the findings of this study showed a positive relationship between one or both of the two constructs and several work outcomes such as job satisfaction, organizational commitment, turnover intentions and organizational citizenship behavior. An important conceptual contribution of this study is the finding implying that POF affects ME, which in turn affects performance. The mediation effect of ME should be examined in future research.

Vigoda-Gadot and Cohen argued that a good fit between individuals and organizations is especially important for non-profit organizations. Recruiting and training employees who are a good match with their jobs and maintaining a satisfactory level of met expectations is without a doubt beneficial for organizations of all sectors. While this is a recommended strategy for for-profit companies, it is an imperative for non-profit agencies whose culture is more heterogeneous and loosely defined and whose structure, work tradition, values, position and role in society are more complex. Promoting congruence in the non-profit sector is, according to Vigoda-Gadot and Cohen, an ambitious challenge that has practical ramifications beyond simple budgetary efficiency.

Vigoda-Gadot and Cohen concluded that the importance of work congruence for public and third sector organizations has communal, ecological, educational and civic–cultural implications that are relevant to all citizens and to society in general. Their study hints at the importance of such congruence, but future research should be dedicated to comparing these findings with similar data in the private sector. Vigoda-Gadot and Cohen suggested that based on their findings, person–organizational fit and met expectations should be taken more seriously by human resource managers in the non-profit sector because of their influential and important role in determining multiple aspects of organizational performance.

The third and last part of this book makes several suggestions and recommendations for future research about the interface between citizenship and bureaucracy. The first chapter in this part by Vigoda-Gadot argues that public organizations tend to have goals that are difficult to quantify, meaning that it is difficult to measure their outcomes. If this is true, then having citizens measure public sector responsiveness to their needs is not just another yardstick for measuring performance in public administration. Rather, it is a vital tool through which the public sector can achieve its goal of 'getting closer to the public'. Drawing on a document from the Local Government Training Board (LGTB) in Britain, Palfrey et al. (1992, p. 132) suggested that responsiveness and the idea of 'getting closer to the public' must involve a profound examination of the public's views on a range of issues. For example, it is necessary to find out the public's preferences and priorities, the kind of services they want, expect and need, their views on the quality of service and their experience as customers, the image they have of the local authority and the things they would like to be done better or differently. This information, when used appropriately, is valuable for every public agency. It can assist in improving future policy and administrative actions while providing citizens with better 'value for money'. Therefore, Vigoda-Gadot concluded, it is important that administrators and scholars alike remain ever mindful of changes in the public will. Questions as to what affects citizens' perceptions of public administration's responsiveness and how citizens' satisfaction rises and falls during policy determination and implementation may assist in: (1) initiating a more effective and service oriented public bureaucracy, (2) improving decision making processes and the management styles of administrators, and (3) establishing some well grounded criteria for better responsiveness in the public sector.

The second paper by Aaron Cohen, Yair Zalmanovitch and Hani Davidesko focused on a neglected issue in the public administration literature, namely the propensity to choose to work in the public sector. The findings of their study strongly supported the notion that public sector image mediates the relationship between determinants and the inclination to work in the public sector. The findings also showed that individuals choose the sector in which they want to work based on information evaluation. Individuals collect information that assists them in deciding whether or not to work in the public sector.

This study has some practical implications, particularly for policy makers. While all will agree on the need to increase the quality of the workforce in the public sector, this study offers new insights into how to accomplish that task. Image was identified as a key concept affecting students' inclination to work in the public sector. Some prospective employees will not choose the public sector because of its negative image. The study suggests a number of ways in which this image can be burnished and improved. For example, providing students with some experience in the public sector is one practical way to improve the image of the public sector and increase the possibility that they will later seek jobs there. Providing social sciences graduates with information on the advantages of working in the public sector is another way to attract them to the public sector. Improving the image of the public sector will probably attract a higher caliber of student.

Person–organization fit theory postulates that the fit can be created by the organization in the selection or the socialization process. The effect of the variable of experience in the public sector emphasizes the ability of public organizations to use the socialization process to attract qualified employees to the public sector. The effect of the two psychological variables suggests that the selection process can be used to detect these psychological characteristics. But first a strategic decision has to be made by organizations: do they want employees who are self-assured and have a strong need for job security? If not, applicants possessing these two characteristics might be rejected. Image is one of the reasons that people who feel less confident about themselves choose to work in the public sector. Improving the public sector image will probably result in more quality applicants seeking work in the public sector. This study demonstrated some ways by which the image of the public sector can be enhanced, but much more work is needed to explore other factors that shape this image.

In short the findings of Cohen et al.'s research demonstrate the importance that public sector image plays in a young person's decision about whether or not to seek employment in the public realm. The proposed model has some important conceptual and practical implications that can direct future research. Naturally, more research on this issue seems warranted in light of the findings and before solid conclusions can be made regarding the findings here.

The last chapter in this book by Eran Vigoda-Gadot provided another look at the relationship between public sector performance and patterns of citizenship involvement. Most of the book's other studies have focused on the opposite issue, namely the contribution of citizenship involvement to the managerial process in bureaucracies. The findings portray some of the possible relationships between administrative outcomes in local government and democratic premises about citizenship involvement. In general, the findings revealed that this relationship might exist, yet its nature is more complex and enigmatic than we might expect.

The implications that can be drawn from the findings are threefold: (1) public sector performance and faith in citizenship involvement are both separately affected by innovation and creativity (IC), by human quality (HQ), and to a considerably lesser extent by the morality and ethics (ME) of the public service; (2) public sector performance is related to the democratic values of citizenship involvement, yet this relationship is complex; (3) as we expected, faith in citizenship involvement is positively affected by public sector performance, while contrary to our initial expectation, active citizenship involvement was found to be negatively affected by public sector performance.

Vigoda-Gadot's study argued that the most important role of public administrators is to develop a sense of partnership between rulers and citizens. This partnership must rely on simultaneous improvement of both institutional performance and citizenship involvement. Furthermore, the local community level can be a most appropriate habitat for good democratic values to grow and prosper. While more work is needed to better explore this area, the study suggests a link between the performance of public administration and the cultivation of democratic values in modern societies.

SUMMARY

The above studies have increased our understanding and provided some suggestions for future research on a broad range of interesting and provocative issues. However, the collection of research projects presented here is only a preliminary work, and many more studies are needed before solid conclusions can be drawn about the relationship between citizenship and bureaucracy. What is needed in particular is a longitudinal research design that will enable us to examine issues of cause and effect. More cross-cultural and/or cross-national research is also needed to examine whether culture moderates the relationship between citizenship involvement and bureaucracy. Thus, this book is a starting point for what will hopefully be the continuation of research in this very compelling field.

REFERENCES

Graham, J.W. (1986), *Organizational citizenship informed by political theory*, Paper presented at the meeting of the Academy of Management Journal.

Graham, J.W. (1991), 'An essay on organizational citizenship behavior', *Employee Responsibilities and Rights Journal, 4,* 4, 249–70.

Kirchmeyer, C. (1992), 'Nonwork participation and work attitudes: A test of scarcity vs. expansion models of personal resources', *Human Relations, 45,* 775–95.

Palfrey, C., Phillips, C., Thomas, P., and Edward, D. (1992), *Policy Evaluation in the Public Sector,* Hants: Avebury.

Randall, D.M. (1988), 'Multiple roles and organizational commitment', *Journal of Organizational Behavior, 9,* 309–17.

Van Dyne, L., Graham, J.W., and Dienesch, R.M. (1994), 'Organizational Citizenship Behavior: Construct redefinition, measurement, and validation', *Academy of Management Journal, 37,* 765–802.

Index

academia 47–8
accountability 209–11
accuracy 30, 209
achievement, need for 242, 243, 247
ACI (active citizenship involvement)
    278, 280, 281, 284
active citizenship syndrome 127
active participation 268–9
activists 10
adjusted goodness-of-fit index 164, 275,
    280
age 86–7, 88, 108, 109, 154, 196, 296
agency theory 40
Aiken, L.S. 96
Ajzen, I. 336
Allen, R.W. 152, 153
Almond, G.A. 14, 61, 87, 105, 173
    good citizenship and organizational
        citizenship behavior 128, 144
    public sector performance and
        citizenship involvement 261, 262,
        269
    responsiveness and collaboration 45,
        47
alternative employment opportunities
    241
alternative model 161
altruism 8, 65, 74, 295
    civic behavior and work outcomes 84,
        88, 89, 98
    good citizenship and organizational
        citizenship behavior 137, 145,
        146
    job congruence, organizational
        citizenship behavior and in-role
        performance 163, 164, 169
analysis, levels of 16
Anderson, S.E. 133, 159
ANOVA 245
Anthony, R.N. 210
Aristotle 3, 104, 127

Armstrong, M. 182, 185
Ashforth, B.E. 184, 189
Aucoin, P. 39
Australia 44
authorization–criticism, knowledge and
    economic-goods transaction 42

Bacharach, S.B. 153
background variables 239, 240–42, 249
Balk, W.K. 225
Barber, B. 8, 14, 64–5, 83, 129, 144, 269
Barner, C. 85, 261, 269
Baron, R.M. 163, 196, 244, 245–7, 248
Bateman, T.S. 97, 107, 114, 121
Ben-Eliezer, U. 144
Bentler, P.M. 72, 275
Berman, E.M. 15, 32
Berman, E.V. 263
Beutell, N.J. 64, 146
Birnbaum, D. 69
Blank, M.R. 204, 235–6, 240, 243, 249,
    256
Blau, G. 235
Blau, P.M. 180, 181, 197, 267
Block, P. 152
Bollen, K.A. 71, 72, 74, 136, 145,
    162–3, 164
    public sector performance and
        citizenship involvement 274, 275
Bonett, D.G. 72, 275
Bouckaert, G. 265
Bourgeois, L.J. 157
Bowen, D.E. 237, 238, 257
Box, R.C. 44, 261, 263, 264, 284
    citizenship behavior and new
        managerialism 7, 8, 10, 16, 21
Bozeman, B. 7, 11, 267
Bozeman, D.P. 152, 154, 157, 160, 213,
    226
Bradford, L. 141
Brady, H.E. 37, 45, 47, 57, 85, 87

citizenship and work outcomes 61, 62,
    63, 64, 69, 70, 77
good citizenship and organizational
    citizenship behavior 126, 128,
    129, 132, 133, 134, 141, 145
public sector performance and
    citizenship involvement 261, 262,
    263, 264, 268, 269, 270–71, 272,
    280, 284, 286
Braskamp, L.A. 241
Brass, D.J. 153
Breckler, S.J. 74, 145
Brett, J.M. 163, 196, 244
Bretz, R.D. 155, 156, 180, 184, 197, 238
Brief, A.P. 8
Brinton, M.H. 18, 45
Broadfield, A. 157
Brower, H.H. 182, 185
Browne, M. 72, 275
Brudney, J. 8, 13, 17, 44, 45, 126, 130,
    144
bureaucracy 3, 4, 5, 31–2, 264
Burke, R.J. 242
Burns, T. 153
Burton, S. 71, 136, 163
business orientation 218, 219, 224,
    225

Caldwell, D.F. 181, 184, 189, 238
Callahan, K. 28
Carlson, D.S. 154
Carter, N. 210, 265
Cary, C.D. 104, 127
Cascio, W.F. 69
CFA (confirmatory factor analysis) 171,
    274
Charng, H.W. 17
Chatman, J. 87, 107, 181, 184, 189, 237,
    238, 257
Chess, W.A. 217
chi-square test 72, 73, 136, 164, 274,
    280, 281
children, number of 88
citizens
    as clients/customers 37
    committees 20
    conferences 20
    conventions 33
    demands *see* responsiveness to
        citizens' demands in Israel

as subjects 36
as voters 36
citizenship behavior and new
    managerialism 7–22
    critique 9–13
    see also dimensionality
citizenship involvement *see* public
    sector performance and citizenship
    involvement
civic behavior 295–6
    see also civic behavior and work
        outcomes
civic behavior and work outcomes
    83–100
    contribution of study 97–9
    findings 88–96
    interaction effects 96–7
    limitations of study 99
    local 84
    method 88
    moderator effect of gender, age and
        eduation 86–7
    national 84–6
    work outcomes, examination of 87–8
civility 105, 108, 115, 129, 130–31, 137,
    146, 296
Clark, C. 85
clients 40–43
Coble, R. 18, 45
coerciveness 36
Cohen, A. 8, 17, 269, 294–5, 297–8,
    299–300, 300–301
Cohen, J. 219
Cohen, P. 219
Cohen, S. 225–6
collaboration *see* responsiveness and
    collaboration
collectivism 16, 17–18
Collin, S.O. 32
commitment 145
common method error 288
communal arena 13–14
communitarianism approach 49
community commitment 84, 88, 89
community involvement 64–5, 296
    civic behavior and work outcomes 84,
        88, 89, 98
    good citizenship and organizational
        citizenship behavior 129–30, 131,
        137, 146

political behavior and work outcomes 105, 108, 109, 110, 115
public sector performance and citizenship involvement 268, 269, 270, 271, 274
comparative fit index 72, 73, 136, 164, 271, 275
compliance 137, 145, 163, 164, 169
confirmatory factor analysis 163–4, 273–4
congruence *see* job congruence; work congruence
Conover, P.J. 17
consumerism 211
contribution of study 97–9
control variables 108, 109
Cooper, M.L. 62, 64, 71, 136, 163
Cooper, T.L. 214, 267
Cotton, J.L. 8, 66
country of origin 108, 109, 246, 249
covenantal relationships 69
Craig, S.C. 85
Cramer, D. 263
Crank, J. 216
creativity 286–7
Crewe, I. 17
Cronbach alpha 79, 187, 278
Cropanzano, R. 152, 154, 155, 157, 160, 171
Cudeck, R. 72, 275
culture 213–15, 219, 225, 228
Cummings, M. 204, 235, 236, 238, 241, 243, 248–9
customer-oriented behavior 126, 144
cynicism 85

Dalton, D.R. 66
data analysis 108, 218, 244–5, 273–8
Davidesko, H. 235–59, 300–301
Day, D. 179
Day, P. 265
debureaucratization 38
decentralization 38
DeCottis, T.A. 133
Delany, W. 238
delegation 36–7
DeLeon, L. 182, 214, 226, 267
democracy 31–2
democratic heritage, strong 264–5

demographic variables 239, 240, 243, 246, 247, 249
Denmark 20, 33
dependent variables 278
descriptive statistics 73–4, 163, 278–80
Deszca, E. 242
Dienesch, R.M. 12, 85, 125, 128, 195, 207, 295
dimensionality 13–21
  analysis, levels of 16
  collective level 17–18
  foundations and settings 13
  individual level 16–17
  micro-citizenship 19–21
  multi-dimensional model 18–19
  national and communal arenas 13–14
  organizational arena 14–16
Dipboye, R.L. 160
direct model 66–9, 73, 74, 136, 161, 164
direct relationship model 64–7, 131, 132, 134, 137, 145
disillusionment with government 65–6, 86, 89, 96
Dolton, P.J. 240
downsizing 38
Drory, A. 169, 226
Du-Gay, P. 226
dual pattern effect model 280
DuBrin, A.J. 153
Dulebohn, J.H. 152, 155, 170, 171, 172
Duncombe, W.D. 13, 17, 45

economy 265
education 20, 44, 86–7, 88, 108, 109, 296
  civic behavior and work outcomes 96
  image and personal characteristics 256
  work congruence and excellence 196
Edwards, D.J. 157
effective operations 21, 45
effectiveness 265
efficiency 265
Eimicke, W.B. 225–6
Eisenhardt, K.M. 157
Eisinger, R.M. 32, 37
El-Bassel, N. 217
Elchanan, M. 154–5
Elden, M.J. 62, 70, 78, 79
emotional motives 236
employee quality 274

employees' performances 158–60
entrepreneurship 218, 219, 224, 226,
    228
Erez, M. 153
Esformes, Y. 154–5
ethics 214–15, 218–19, 224–6, 228,
    266–7, 286–7
    see also morality and ethics
ethnicity 246, 249
Etzioni, A. 12, 14, 33, 65, 83, 130, 144,
    269
Europe 4, 11, 37, 38, 288
    responsiveness to citizens' demands
        207, 213, 214, 229
evaluation of models 274
evolutionary continuum 34–6
excellence *see* work congruence and
    excellence in human resource
    management
exit 40, 185, 188, 189, 196, 211
expectancy theory 156
expected (single sample) cross-validation
    index 164, 275, 280
experience variables 239, 240–42, 247,
    249
external efficacy 85
external indicators 210
extra-role behavior 158–9, 297

fairness 214–15, 267
faith in citizen involvement 296, 302
    good citizenship and organizational
        citizenship behavior 129, 131,
        137, 146
    political behavior and work outcomes
        105–6, 108, 109, 110, 115
    public sector performance and
        citizenship involvement 268–72,
        273, 274, 278, 280, 281, 284–6,
        287
Fandt, P.M. 154
Farh, J.L. 70, 133, 159
Farkas, A.J. 71, 136, 163
Farnham, D. 39, 213, 226, 267
Federal Service 235
Fedor, D.B. 154, 169
Feldman, O. 271
Feltey, K.M. 11, 18, 43, 46, 261
Ferris, G.R. 71, 97, 152, 154, 195, 226,
    247

internal politics, job congruence,
    organizational behavior and
    in-role performance 152, 153,
    154, 155, 157, 159, 160, 170,
    171, 172, 173
Fishbein, M. 336
fit indices 72, 274–5
    see also goodness of fit; non-normed
    fit; normed fit; person–
    organization fit; relative fit
Fombrun, C. 238
foundations 13
Fox, C.J. 47, 49–50
France 4
Frederickson, G.H. 7, 8, 12, 21, 28, 36,
    37, 42, 261
freeriders 10
Friedland, N. 154–5
Friesen, D. 216
Frieze, H.I. 235, 237, 242, 249
Frone, M.R. 62, 64, 71, 136, 163
future research 229–30

Gaebler, T. 38, 213, 226, 267
Gandz, J. 153, 157
Garson, D.G. 11, 39
Gatewood, R. 235, 237, 238, 240, 249
Gawthrop, L.C. 214
gender 86–8, 96, 106, 108–10, 115, 154,
    249, 256, 296
general citizenship 145–7
    see also general citizenship and work
    outcomes
general citizenship and work outcomes
    61–79
    direct model 66–9
    direct relationship 64–6
    findings 73–4
    limitations of study 79
    mediated model 69–71
    method 71–3
    work outcomes 66
Gerhart, B. 238
Germany 44
Gerstner, R.C. 179
Ghadially, R. 157
Gibson, J.L. 145
Gidron, B. 18, 32, 45, 183
Gladstone, D. 213, 214
Glaister, S. 32

Goel, M.L. 85, 262, 263, 269, 270, 271, 280, 286
Goldman, D.D. 40
Golembiewski, R.T. 22, 32, 39, 40, 43, 46, 179, 182, 265, 293–4
  citizenship and work outcomes 61, 63, 70, 78
  work congruence and excellence 179, 182
good citizenship and organizational citizenship behavior in Israel 125–47
  dimensions 129–31
  general citizenship and work setting 145–7
  models, examination of 136–7
  relationship 131–4
  socio-political heritage 127–9
  study 134
goodness-of-fit indices 73, 136, 164, 275, 280
Goodsell, C.T. 4
goodwill 21, 45
Gortner, H.F. 267
governance and public administration agencies xviii–xix
Gowan, M. 235, 237, 238, 240, 249
grades 241, 246, 247, 256
Graham, J.W. 104, 114, 195, 207, 295, 297
  citizenship behavior and new managerialism 12, 14, 17
  civic behavior and work outcomes 85, 97
  general citizenship and work outcomes 66, 74
  good citizenship and organizational citizenship behavior 125, 127, 128, 132
Grant, N.K. 215
Greece 3, 42
Green, S.A. 70, 97, 159
Greene, M. 240
Greenhaus, J.H. 64, 146
Griffin, R.W. 97, 107, 114
Grubbs, J.W. 32
Gunn, L. 212
Guthrie, J.P. 179
Guyton, E.M. 261

Halachmi, A. 265
Hampton, J. 207, 264
Hardy, C. 152
Harrell-Cook, G. 152, 155, 170, 171, 172
Harrison, T.M. 241
Hart, D. 28, 215
Hays, S.W. 38
Hazer, J.T. 136
Heater, D. 4
Hendricks, J.S. 87–8, 107
Herman, R.D. 181
hidden agreement 264, 287
Hirschman, A.O. 40, 157, 171, 210, 227
Histadrut 141
Hobbes, T. 4, 9–10, 207, 264
Holahan, P.J. 72, 136, 275
Hollensbe, E.C. 179
Holzer, M. 28, 215–16
Hom, P.W. 185
Hood, C. 264
Horton, S. 39, 213, 226, 267
Hughes, O.E. 33
Hulin, C.L. 155
human capital 256
human quality 266, 278, 281, 284, 285, 286–7, 302
human resource management 212, 215–17, 300
  see also work congruence and excellence in human resource management
human resource variables 219, 224, 225, 226, 228
Hunt, R.G. 99, 103, 115
Hurd, D. 14

image and personal characteristics role in tendency to work in public sector 235–59, 300–301
  conceptual framework 236–9
  findings 245–8
  method 244–5
  research model and hypotheses 239–43
    background and experience variables 240–42
    demographic variables 240
    image, mediating role of 243

personal psychological variables
242–3
in-role performance 185, 187, 188, 189,
297
see also organizational politics, job
congruence, organizational
citizenship behavior and in-role
performance
Inchley, G.D. 240
indirect model 161, 164, 171
indirect relationships 131, 132–4
individualism 16–17, 43
Ingrahm, P.W. 40
Ingram, H. 270
Inkeles, A. 61, 127, 128
innovation 286–7
and creativity 266, 278, 281, 284, 285,
302
institutionalist/constitutionalist approach
49
interacting with citizens: evolutionary
continuum 34–6
interaction effects 96–7
intercorrelation 278–80
internal efficacy 85
internal indicators 210
International Organization of
Standardization 213, 266
interpersonal politics 26, 218, 219, 224,
225
intra-role behavior 159
Israel xx–xxii, 58, 204
civic behavior and work outcomes 86,
99
general citizenship and work
outcomes 71, 78, 79
image and personal characteristics
236, 240, 244, 256, 258
job congruence, organizational
citizenship behavior and in-role
performance 155, 161
political behavior and work outcomes
106, 108
public sector performance and
citizenship involvement 262, 273,
284, 288
work congruence and excellence 187,
197
see also good citizenship and
organizational citizenship

behavior; responsiveness to
citizens' demands in Israel; work
congruence and excellence in
human resource management:
non-profit sector in Israel
Israel, B. 216
Iverson, R.D. 146, 184, 189
Izraeli, D. 153

Jackson, S.L. 160
James, L.R. 163, 196, 244
Janoski, T. 17
Janowitz, M. 104, 238
Jasper, W. 238, 239, 256
Jayaratne, S. 217
Jenkins, B. 242
Jennings, K. 204, 235, 236, 238, 241,
243, 248–9
Jo, D.G. 184, 189
job choice 237, 238, 249
job congruence 128, 298
see also organizational politics, job
congruence, organizational
citizenship behavior and in-role
performance
job satisfaction 107, 109, 110, 114, 157,
160, 299
good citizenship and organizational
citizenship behavior 131–2, 133,
134, 137, 145, 146, 147
work congruence and excellence 184,
185, 187, 188, 189, 196
job search 235, 237, 238, 241, 249
job stress 157
job–work environment influences 154
John, D. 28, 34, 42
Johnston, M.W. 71, 136, 163
Jonsson, E. 227
Joreskog, K. 71, 136, 161, 274, 275
Judge, T.A. 155, 156, 180, 184, 197

Kacmar, K.M. 152, 153, 154, 155, 160,
195
Kahn, R.L. 12, 15, 121, 125, 158, 171
Kanter, R.M. 69, 212
Katz, D. 12, 15, 121, 125, 158, 171
Kaufman, H. 227
Kavanagh, D. 173
Kawakami, K. 271
Kearney, R.C. 38

Keller, R.T. 15
Kenny, D.A. 163, 196, 244, 245–7, 248
Keon, C.S. 28
Kerman, M.C. 237, 249
Kettl, D.F. 33
Kewin, K. 154
Kilduff, M. 237, 242
Kilpatrick, F. 204, 235, 236, 238, 241, 243, 248–9
Kim, J. 261
King, C.M. 14, 16, 22, 261, 268
King, C.S. 11, 18, 43, 46, 261
King, T.R. 152, 154, 157, 226
Kipnis, D. 153
Kirchmeyer, C. 62, 98, 99, 114, 115, 146, 295
Kirkman, L. 141
Kisil, M. 28, 34
Klein, R. 265
Konovsky, M. 17, 70, 121, 123, 125, 132, 158, 159
Kraemer, K. 7, 225
Kramer, R. 18, 22, 32, 45, 183, 268
Krampen, G. 263, 267
Krau, E. 243
Kumar, P. 157

Lane, J.E. 216, 227
Latham, G.L. 70, 132, 133
Lautenschlager, G. 235, 237, 238, 240, 249
Lawler, E.J. 153
leadership quality 274
Leary, M. 242
Ledford, G.E. 237, 238, 257
legitimacy–services transaction 42
Lewin-Epstien, N. 240
limitations of studies 79, 99, 172–3, 229–30
Lipsky, M. 18, 45
LISREL VIII xix, xx–xxi, xxiii, 58, 204
    general citizenship and work outcomes 71
    good citizenship and organizational citizenship behavior 136
    job congruence, organizational citizenship behavior and in-role performance 162, 163

public sector performance and citizenship involvement 274
work congruence and excellence 185
Local Government Training Board 229, 300
Locke, E.A. 107
Locke, J. 207, 264
locus of control 242, 243, 247
loop democracy 47
Lord, R.G. 237, 249
loyalty 104, 128
Lui, T.T. 214, 267
Lum, L. 15
Lynn, L.E. 7, 10, 40, 183, 263

Mcdonald, R.P. 72
McEvoy, G.M. 69
Machiavelli, N. 3–4
MacKenzie, S.B. 8, 17, 22, 126, 144, 145, 195
McKevitt, D. 16
McPherson, J. 17, 85
macro-citizenship xviii, 18, 19, 21
Mae Kelly, R. 285
Maehr, M.L. 241
major subject studied by students 241, 246, 247, 256
Makepeace, G.H. 240
Management by Objectives 213, 266
management theory 156
managerialism 38, 39–40, 294–5
MANOVA 245
Manzel, D.C. 267
marital status 196
Marsh, H.W. 72
Marshall, D. 21
Marshall, T.H. 13, 36
Maslyn, J.M. 169
Mattei, F. 85
Mayes, B.T. 152, 153
media 47–8
mediated model 69–71, 73–4, 134, 136, 137, 145, 164
mediated variable 78
mediating relationship 244–5
mediation 245, 246, 247
    analysis strategy 196
Medsker, G.J. 72, 136, 275
Meier, K. 179

met expectations xxi, 299, 300
  job congruence, organizational
     citizenship behavior and in-role
     performance 155, 156, 163, 164,
     169, 170
  work congruence and excellence
     180–82, 184–5, 187, 188, 189,
     195, 196, 197
meta-citizenship xviii, 18, 19, 21, 22
Meyer, J.P. 136
Michael, H. 17
micro-citizenship xviii, 18, 19–21, 22
midi-citizenship xviii, 18, 19, 21, 22
Milbrath, L.W. 14, 70, 85, 86–7, 106,
     133
  public sector performance and
     citizenship involvement 262, 263,
     269, 270, 271, 280, 286
Miller, H.T. 47, 49–50
Milward, B.H. 33
Mintzberg, H. 152, 153, 157
Mitra, A. 66
Mobley, W.H. 66
models 134, 135, 161
  evaluation 72–3, 162–3, 164–9,
     280–84
  examination 136–7
Molm, L.D. 156
Monroe, K.R. 17
Montesquieu, C. 4, 13
Moorman, R.H. 70, 132, 159
Moos, M. 235, 237, 242, 249
Moos, R.H. 238
morality 266, 267, 286–7
morality and ethics 278, 281, 284, 285,
     302
Morrison, E.W. 8, 20
Morrison, W.E. 159
Motowidlo, S.J. 8
Mowday, R.T. 66, 87, 97, 107, 114,
     134
Mueller, C.W. 184, 189
multi-dimensional partnership 18–19,
     40–48, 245, 248, 249
  between clients and partners 40–43
  citizens, role of 45–7
  government and public administration,
     role of 43–5
  media and academia, role of 47–8
Murray, V.V. 153, 157

Nalbandian, J. 28, 34, 284
Nathan, B.R. 237, 238, 257
national arena 13–14
Near, J.P. xv, 8, 99, 103, 115, 121–2
neglect 185, 188, 189, 195
neo-managerialism 39–40
Netemeyer, R.G. 71, 136, 163
new managerialism 40
new public management xviii, 7, 8–9,
     16, 18, 21–2, 172, 293–4, 299
  good citizenship and organizational
     citizenship behavior 126, 144
  governance and collaboration 28, 30,
     31, 33, 37, 38, 39, 40
  public sector performance and
     citizenship involvement 265
  responsiveness to citizens' demands
     212, 213, 230
Nie, N.H. 14, 261
Niehoff, B.P. 70, 159
Niemi, R.G. 85
Nigro, L.G. 214
NNFI (non-normed fit index) 72, 136,
     164, 275, 280
  see also TLI
normative motives 236
normed fit index 72, 73, 136, 275,
     280
North America 79, 87, 99, 106, 141,
     144, 229, 288
  see also United States
not-for-profit sector (third sector) 15, 16,
     18, 32, 43, 45–6, 299–300
  see also work congruence and
     excellence in human resource
     management: non-profit sector
     in Israel
Nunnaly, J.C. 187, 278

obedience 104, 127–8
O'Connell, B. 18, 45, 46, 183
Oliver, D. 4
Olsen, J.P. 227
Olshafski, D.O. 63, 103
O'Reilly, C.A. 87, 107, 181, 184, 189,
     238
Organ, D.W. 5, 70, 121–2, 133, 158,
     159, 195
  citizenship behavior and new
     managerialism 8, 12, 15, 17, 19

good citizenship and organizational
    citizenship behavior 125, 127,
    132, 133
organizational arena 14–16
organizational behavior 184, 189
    see also organizational citizenship
        behavior
organizational citizenship behavior 8, 12,
    17, 19, 297–8, 299
    work congruence and excellence 185,
        187, 188, 189, 195
    see also good citizenship and
        organizational citizenship
        behavior; organizational politics,
        job congruence, organizational
        citizenship behavior and in-role
        performance
organizational commitment 157, 160,
    299
    civic behavior and work outcomes 87,
        89, 96, 97, 98
    good citizenship and organizational
        citizenship behavior 131–2, 133,
        134, 137, 146, 147
    political behavior and work outcomes
        107, 109, 110, 114, 116
    work congruence and excellence 184,
        185, 188, 189, 196
organizational culture profile 184
organizational development 212
organizational politics 185, 298
    see also organizational politics,
        job congruence, organizational
        citizenship behavior and in-role
        performance; Perception of
        Organizational Politics Scale
organizational politics, job congruence,
    organizational citizenship behavior
    and in-role performance 151–73
    findings 163–9
        confirmatory factor analysis 163–4
        descriptive statistics 163
        summary of model's evaluation
            164–9
    limitations of study 172–3
    method 161–3
    theory, hypotheses and models
        153–61
        consequence of organizational
            politics 157–8

employees' performances 158–60
job congruence and organizational
    politics 155–6
models 161
perception of organizational
    politics 153–5
organized citizenry actions 43
orientations 104–6
Orum, A.M. 271
Osborne, D. 38, 213, 226, 237, 267
O'Toole, L.J. 179
Ott, S. 48
Overman, E.S. 11, 39

PA (public administration) 32, 40
Palfrey, C. 30, 209, 210, 211, 229, 265,
    300
Parker, C.P. 160
parsimony criterion 281
Parsons, D.W. 212, 228, 266
Parsons, T. 5
participation 13, 268–9
    active 268–9
    in community activities *see*
        community involvement
    in decision-making 107, 109,
        110, 131–2, 133, 137, 145,
        146, 147
    good citizenship and organizational
        citizenship behavior 128
    in political activities *see* political
        participation
    political behavior and work outcomes
        104
    variables 89
participative leader 70
partners 40–43
Pateman, C. 8, 15, 104, 262, 263
    citizenship and work outcomes 61, 62,
        63, 70
    good citizenship and organizational
        citizenship behavior 126, 127,
        131, 132, 133
path
    analysis 71–2, 162–3, 185, 274
    coefficients 72–3, 275–8
Pearson's correlations 187
perceived performance 87, 89, 96, 97, 98
Perception of Organizational Politics
    Scale 154, 163, 185, 188, 195

performance 109, 110, 209–12, 225, 296
    general citizenship and work
        outcomes 66
    political behavior and work outcomes
        115
    see also perceived performance
Perry, J.L. 7, 225, 236
person–organization fit 299, 300, 301
    image and personal characteristics
        237–8, 242, 243, 257, 258
    job congruence, organizational
        citizenship behavior and in-role
        performance 155, 156, 163, 164,
        169, 170
    work congruence and excellence
        180–82, 184, 185, 187, 188, 189,
        195, 196, 197
personal characteristics *see* image and
    personal characteristics role
personal influences 154
personal–psychological variables 239,
    242–3, 246, 247
personality 257
Peters, G.B. 38, 40, 43
Peterson, S.A. 8, 57, 84, 85, 86, 103,
    105, 106–7
    citizenship and work outcomes 61, 62,
        63, 64, 65, 70
    good citizenship and organizational
        citizenship behavior 128, 129,
        131, 132, 133
    public sector performance and
        citizenship involvement 262, 263,
        268, 269, 270
Pettersen, P.A. 65, 83, 130, 269
Pfeffer, J. 152, 153
Piliavin, J.A. 17
Plato 104, 127
plausibility criterion 275
pluralism 37
Podsakoff, P.M. 8, 17, 22, 70, 126, 133,
    144, 145, 159, 195
policy 219, 225, 228
political behavior 12, 31, 97, 98, 99,
    209, 265
    variables 108, 109
    and work outcomes 103–16
        findings 108–14
        literature review and hypotheses
            104–7

method 108
political efficacy 85, 96, 268, 269, 274
political participation 64, 74, 96, 98,
    104–6, 295, 296
    good citizenship and organizational
        citizenship behavior 129–30, 131,
        146
    political behavior and work outcomes
        104–5, 108, 109, 110, 115
    public sector performance and
        citizenship involvement 268, 269,
        271, 274
politics 211–12
    see also interpersonal politics;
        political
Pollitt, C. 31, 39, 40, 126, 144, 209, 212,
    263, 265
    citizenship behavior and new
        managerialsm 7, 10, 12
Porter, L.M. 66, 87, 97, 107, 114, 134
Posner, B.Z. 196
Powell, W.W. 126
Priem, R.L. 179
private sector 32
privatization 38, 266
prosocial behavior 8
psychological variables 256, 257, 258
    see also personal–psychological
        variables
public policy 213–15
public sector performance and
    citizenship involvement xxiii,
    261–89
    alternative models 270–73
    citizenship involvement: participation
        and active participation 268–9
    findings 278–84
        descriptive statistics and
            intercorrelation 278–80
        models evaluation 280–84
    innovation, creativity, human quality,
        morality and ethics 286–7
    methods 273–8
    modern democracies 262–9
        democratic heritage, strong 264–5
        performance and actions 265–8
    paradoxical relationship 285–6
Pugh, S.D. 70, 123, 132, 159
Punch, K. 217
Putnam, L.L. 158

Putnam, R. 8, 14, 78, 262, 263, 284

quality 215–17
of employees 218, 219, 224, 225, 226, 228
of leadership and management 218, 219, 224, 226, 227
of operation 227
of services 227

Rabin, J. 215–16
Rainey, H. 11, 37, 185, 263
Randall, D.M. 98, 114, 295
Ranson, R. 126, 144, 183, 208, 209, 210
Ranson, S. 29
rational choice theory 40
rational motives 236
regression analysis 245, 247, 248
relative fit index 72, 136, 164, 275, 280
Renz, D.O. 181
research model 161, 171
responsiveness 300
    see also responsiveness and collaboration; responsiveness to citizens' demands in Israel
responsiveness and collaboration 27–50
    coerciveness 36
    collaboration with citizens as partners 31–3
    delegation 36–7
    hats and ladies metaphor 33–4
    interacting with citizens: evolutionary continuum 34–6
    next generation 48–50
    responsiveness 37–40
    responsiveness to citizens as clients 29–31
    see also multi-dimensional partnership
responsiveness to citizens' demands in Israel 207–30
    findings 218–24
    human resources and quality of public servants 215–17
    limitations of study and future research recommendations 229–30
    method 217–18
    theoretical overview 208–17
        politics and performance 211–12

public management and responsiveness 212–13
public policy and culture 213–15
responsiveness, accountability and performance 209–11
Rhodes, R.A.W. 30, 209, 265
Rice, R.W. 99, 103, 115
Richardson, W.D. 5, 214
Rim, Y. 153
Rimmerman, C.A. 8, 15, 44, 263, 284
RNI (relative non-centrality index) 136
Rogers, J. 240
Rollinson, D. 157
Romzek, B.S. 87–8, 107
Root Mean Square Error of Approximation 72, 136, 164, 274–5, 280
Rose, L.E. 65, 130, 269
Rosenbloom, D.H. 40
Rosenwein, F.E. 85, 261, 269
Rotolo, T. 17
Rourke, F.E. 28, 29, 34, 184, 208
Rousseau, J.-J. 4, 13–14, 207, 264
Roy, P. 146
Russ, G.R. 154
Russell, M. 62, 64, 71, 136, 163
Ryan, A.T. 236
Ryan, K. 133
Ryan, M. 157
Rynes, S.L. 238, 243

Sabucedo, J.M. 263
Saks, A.M. 184, 189
Salamon, L.M. 32
Saris, W. 278
Sarros, J.C. 216
satisfaction 228, 266, 300
    from operation 218, 224, 225, 226, 227
    from service 218, 219, 224, 225, 226, 227
Savas, E.S. 39
Schein, E.H. 155, 160
Schlozman, K.L. 37, 45, 47, 85, 87
    citizenship and work outcomes 61, 62, 63, 64, 69, 70, 77
    good citizenship and organizational citizenship behavior 126, 128, 129, 132, 133, 134, 141, 145

public sector performance and
    citizenship involvement 261, 262,
    263, 264, 268, 269, 270–71, 272,
    280, 284, 286
Schmidt, S.M. 153
Schnake, M. 70, 122, 159
Schneider, A. 32, 270
Schneider, B. 237
Schussler, K.F. 86, 106, 131, 268
Schwab, D.P. 69
Searing, D.D. 17
security, need for 242–3, 247, 257, 258
self-efficacy 157
self-monitoring 154, 242, 243, 247, 257,
    258
Semyonov, M. 240
settings 13
Shanley, M. 238
Shrader, C.B. 182, 185
Sieber, S.D. 63–4, 65, 77, 83–4, 85, 105
    good citizenship and organizational
        citizenship behavior 129, 130,
        132, 145
simple direct effect model 270, 280
simple indirect effect model 271, 280
simultaneous effect model 280
Skarlicki, D.P. 70, 132, 133
skill-acts 62
Smith, C.A. 8, 121–2
Smith, P. 31, 209, 210, 265
Smith, S.R. 18, 45
Sobel, R. 8, 14, 57, 83, 85, 103, 105,
    106–7, 263, 269
    citizenship and work outcomes 61, 62,
        63, 64, 65, 66, 70, 79
    good citizenship and organizational
        citizenship behavior 126, 128,
        130, 132, 133
social agreement 287
social contract 207, 264
socialization 237, 257, 258
    –information and human-resources
        transaction 42
socio-economic status 129
Somers, J.M. 69
Sommers, T.P. 133
Sorbom, D. 71, 136, 161, 274, 275
Soss, J. 270, 286
speed 30, 209
spillover 98, 132, 146, 295, 296

general citizenship and work
    outcomes 63–4, 69, 77
political behavior and work outcomes
    103, 114, 115
Staats, E.B. 215
Steers, R.M. 66, 87, 97, 107, 114, 134
Steiger, J.H. 275
Stewart, J. 29, 126, 144, 183, 208, 209,
    210
Stivers, C. 14, 16, 22, 28, 29, 34, 39,
    208, 261, 268
stress 218, 224, 226, 227, 228
Strickland, R.A. 63, 103
Stronkhorst, H. 278
Structural Equation Modeling 58, 196,
    204, 275, 288
Summers, D.V. 212
Sun, B.C. 265
Susel, B.O. 11, 18, 43, 46, 261
Suzuki, P.T. 214
Szilagyi, A. 153

t-tests 110
Tancredi, F.B. 28, 34
Tansky, J.W. 159
tendency to work in public sector *see*
    image and personal characteristics
    role in tendency to work in public
    sector
Terry, L.D. 38
Tetrick, L.E. 71, 136, 163
Tett, R.P. 136
Theiss-Morse, E. 65, 84, 85, 131, 268
third sector *see* not-for-profit sector
Thomas, J.C. 11
Thomas, P. 30, 209, 210
Thompson, A.A. 28, 32, 34
Thompson, D. 31–2, 285
Thompson, J.L. 213, 266
TLI (Tucker Lewis index) 72, 73, 136
    see also NNFI
Tocqueville, A. de 141
Todor, W.D. 66
Total Quality Management 213, 266
Tracey, J.B. 153
Treadwell, D.F. 241
Tuetteman, E. 217
turnover intentions 66, 87, 157, 299
Tuttle, J.M. 66
Tziner, A. 157

uni-dimensional construct 11, 245, 248, 249
United Kingdom 39, 44, 213, 266
United States 4, 11, 16, 18, 99, 103, 213, 266
    Culver City (California) 20, 33
    governance and collaboration 37, 38, 39
    image and personal characteristics 239, 258
    responsiveness and collaboration 44, 46, 48, 49

Van Dyne, L. 12, 14, 85, 195, 207, 295
    citizenship and work outcomes 65, 69, 74
    good citizenship and organizational citizenship behavior 125, 128
Vandenberghe, C. 184, 189
Vardi, Y. 19
variance percentage 278
Verba, S. 14, 85, 87, 105, 173
    citizenship and work outcomes 61, 62, 63, 64, 69, 70, 77
    good citizenship and organizational citizenship behavior 126, 128, 129, 132, 133, 134, 141, 144, 145
    public sector performance and citizenship involvement 261, 262, 263, 264, 268, 269, 270–71, 272, 280, 284, 286
    responsiveness and collaboration 37, 45, 47
Vigoda-Gadot, E. 8, 17, 19, 21, 28, 29, 30, 32, 39, 40, 46, 179, 182, 185, 195, 265, 266, 267, 269, 293–4, 294–5, 297–8, 298–302
voice 40, 185, 188, 189, 210–11
voluntary organizations *see* nonprofit organizations
volunteer programs 20, 44
Vroom, V.H. 156, 170, 180, 181, 197

Waldo, D. 37
Wallace, M. 153
Walzer, M. 104, 127
Wanous, J.P. 155, 156, 180, 184, 197
watchdogs 10
Wayne, S.J. 70, 71, 97, 122, 159

Weber, M. 5, 31
Weikart, L.A. 36, 38
Welch, S. 85
West, S.G. 96
Wheeler, D. 242
Whicker, M.L. 63, 103
Wiener, Y. 19
Wildawski, A. 229
Wilenski, P. 214
Wilkinson, I. 153
Williams, L.J. 72, 133, 136, 159, 275
Wilson, J. 17
Wilson, P.A. 104
Wilson, W. 37, 225, 251
Winkler, F. 30, 209, 211
Wise, L.R. 236
Witt, L.A. 169
Woehr, D.J. 15
Woller, G.M. 264, 287
Worchel, S. 15
work congruence 299–300
work congruence and excellence in human resource management: non-profit sector in Israel 179–98
    findings 187–9
    method 187
    work congruence, essence of and meaning 180–83
    work congruence and performance 184–7
work experience 241, 243, 247, 249, 257
work outcomes 296, 298
    see also civic behavior and work outcomes; general citizenship and work outcomes; political behavior and work outcomes
work setting 145–7
Wright, D. 238

Young, B.S. 15
Young, D.W. 210
Yukl, G. 153

Zalmanovitch, Y. 235, 300–301
Zeffane, R. 133
Zero Based Budgeting 266
Zhou, J. 152
Ziv, L. 243

DATE DUE